MEDICAL ASSISTANT

Law and Ethics, Psychology, and
Therapeutic Procedures
Module G

MEDICAL ASSISTANT
Law and Ethics, Psychology, and Therapeutic Procedures
Module G

Material Selected from:

Mastering Healthcare Terminology
Second Edition
by
Betsy J. Shiland, MS, RHIA, CPHQ, CTR

Saunders Textbook of Medical Assisting
(textbook and workbook)
by
Diane M. Klieger, RN, MBA, CMA

Kinn's The Medical Assistant
Tenth Edition
(textbook and study guide)
by
Alexandra Patricia Young, BBA, RMA, CMA
and
Deborah B. Proctor, EdD, RN, CMA

SAUNDERS

ELSEVIER

3251 Riverport Ln
Maryland Heights, MO 63143

LAW AND ETHICS, PSYCHOLOGY, AND THERAPEUTIC   ISBN: 978-1-4377-0346-7
PROCEDURES—MODULE G

Copyright © 2010 by Saunders, an imprint of Elsevier Inc.

Chapters 1 and 7 from Young AP, Proctor DB: *Kinn's the medical assistant: an applied learning
approach,* St Louis.
Copyright © 2007, Saunders

Chapters 2, 3, 4, 5, 6, 9, and 10 from Klieger DM: *Saunders textbook of medical assisting,*
St Louis.
Copyright © 2005, Elsevier

Chapter 8 from Shiland BJ: *Mastering healthcare terminology,* ed 2, St Louis.
Copyright © 2006, Mosby

Appendixes A and B from Klieger DM: *Workbook to accompany Saunders textbook of medical
assisting,* St Louis.
Copyright © 2005, Elsevier

Portions of Appendixes A and B copyright © 2010 by Corinthian Colleges, Inc.

ISBN: 978-1-4377-0346-7

Printed in the United States of America

Last digit is the print number: 9 8 7 6 5 4 3

ACKNOWLEDGMENTS

Thank you to our advisory board members and the CCi Medical Assisting Program community for your dedication, teamwork, and support over the years.

This textbook has been designed for your success. Each feature has been chosen to help you learn medical assisting quickly and effectively. Colorful boxes, tables, and illustrations will visually spark your interest, add to your knowledge, and aid in your retention of the material. Most chapters end with a review that asks you to apply the terms and concepts you have learned.

USE ALL THE FEATURES IN THE CHAPTER

Key Terms

The key terms list provides you with a quick overview of the terms you will encounter as you work your way through the chapter. You can also use this page to help you review for tests.

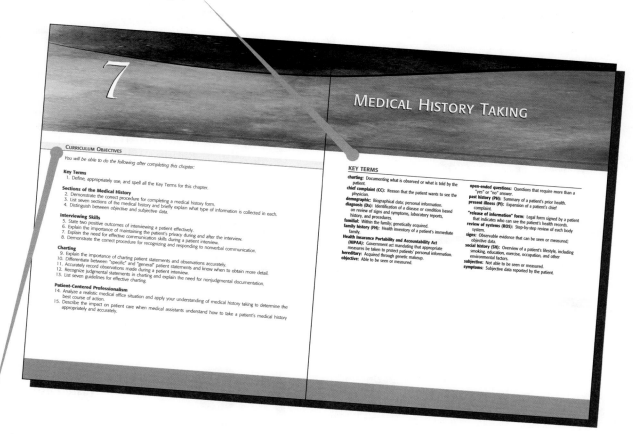

Objectives

Each objective is a goal for you. You should refer to these objectives before you study the chapter to see what your goals are and then again at the end of the chapter to see if you have accomplished them.

Exercises

Some chapters have exercises located after passages of information. Make sure you do these exercises to help you retain your new knowledge. Your instructor can check your work.

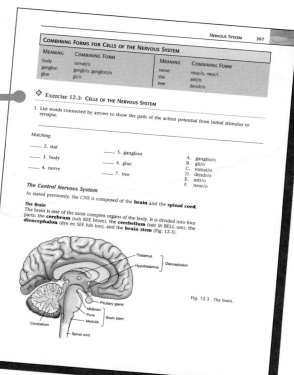

Procedures

Many chapters will contain illustrated step-by-step procedures showing you how to perform administrative and clinical procedures. Rationales for most steps explain why the step is important, and icons let you know which standard precautions to follow:

 Handwashing

 Gloving

 Personal Protective Equipment

 Biohazardous Waste Disposal

 Sharps Disposal

Plus, sample documentation shows you how to chart clinical procedures.

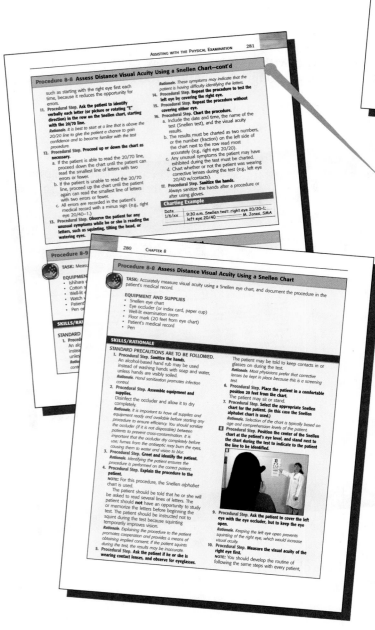

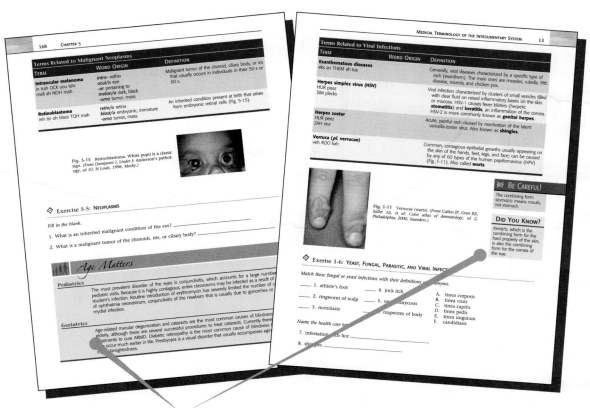

Special Information Boxes

Special information boxes that offer interesting facts or cautions are scattered throughout each chapter.
- *Did You Know?* boxes highlight the fascinating, sometimes strange history that underlies the origins of health care terms.
- *Be Careful!* boxes point out common pitfalls that you might experience when health care terms and word parts are spelled similarly but have different meanings.
- *Age Matters* boxes highlight important concepts and terminology for both pediatric and geriatric patients.

- *Careers* boxes are intended to give you more information about the job outlook, tasks, and educational requirements for the other members of the health care team.

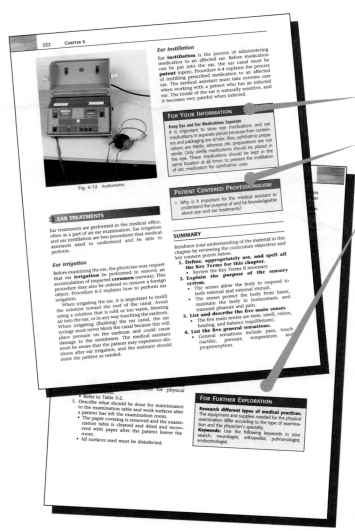

222   CHAPTER 6

Fig. 6-12 Audiometer.

EAR TREATMENTS

Ear treatments are performed in the medical office, often as a part of an ear examination. Ear irrigation and ear instillation are two procedures that medical assistants need to understand and be able to perform.

Ear Irrigation

Before examining the ear, the physician may request that ear **irrigation** be performed to remove an accumulation of impacted **cerumen** (earwax). This procedure may also be ordered to remove a foreign object. Procedure 6-3 explains how to perform ear irrigation.

When irrigating the ear, it is important to instill the solution toward the roof of the canal. Avoid using a solution that is cold or too warm, blowing air into the ear, or in any way touching the eardrum. When irrigating (flushing) the ear canal, the ear syringe must never block the canal because this will place pressure on the eardrum and could cause damage to the membrane. The medical assistant must be aware that the patient may experience dizziness after ear irrigation, and the assistant should assist the patient as needed.

Ear Instillation

Ear **instillation** is the process of administering medication to an affected ear. Before medication can be put into the ear, the ear canal must be **patent** (open). Procedure 6-4 explains the process of instilling prescribed medication to an affected ear. The medical assistant must take extreme care when working with a patient who has an infected ear. The inside of the ear is naturally sensitive, and it becomes very painful when infected.

FOR YOUR INFORMATION

Keep Eye and Ear Medications Separate
It is important to store eye medications and ear medications in separate places because their containers and packaging are similar. Also, ophthalmic preparations are not sterile, whereas otic preparations should be placed in the eye. These sterile medications should be kept in the same location at all times to prevent the instillation of otic medication for ophthalmic uses.

PATIENT CENTERED PROFESSIONALISM

• Why is it important for the medical assistant to understand the purpose of and be knowledgeable about eye and ear treatments?

SUMMARY

Reinforce your understanding of the material in this chapter by reviewing the curriculum objectives and key content points below.
1. **Define, appropriately use, and spell all the Key Terms for this chapter.**
   • Review the Key Terms if necessary.
2. **Explain the purpose of the sensory system.**
   • The senses allow the body to respond to both internal and external stimuli.
   • The senses protect the body from harm, maintain the body in homeostasis, and transmit pleasure and pain.
3. **List and describe the five main senses.**
   • The five main senses are taste, smell, vision, hearing, and balance (equilibrium).
4. **List the five general sensations.**
   • General sensations include pain, touch (tactile), pressure, temperature, and proprioception.

• Refer to Table 3-2.
5. Describe what should be done for maintenance to the examination table and work surfaces after a patient has left the examination room.
   • The paper covering is removed and the examination table is cleaned and dried and recovered with paper after the patient leaves the room.
   • All surfaces used must be disinfected.

FOR FURTHER EXPLORATION

Research different types of medical practices. The equipment and supplies needed for the physical examination differ according to the type of examination and the physician's specialty.
Keywords: Use the following keywords in your search: neurologist, orthopedist, pulmonologist, endocrinologist.

• *For Your Information* boxes provide interesting informational "tid-bits" on topics related to the subject at hand.
• *Patient-Centered Professionalism* boxes prompt you to think about the patient's perspective and encourage empathy.
• *For Further Exploration* boxes suggest topics for further Internet research to expand your comprehension of concepts and inspire you to "learn beyond the text."

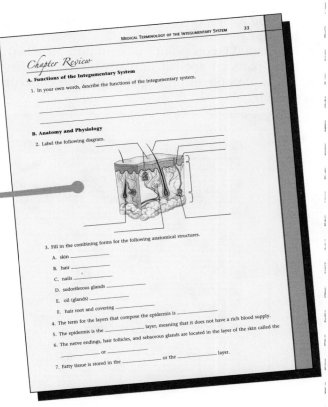

MEDICAL TERMINOLOGY OF THE INTEGUMENTARY SYSTEM   33

Chapter Review

A. Functions of the Integumentary System
1. In your own words, describe the functions of the integumentary system.

B. Anatomy and Physiology
2. Label the following diagram.

3. Fill in the combining forms for the following anatomical structures.
   A. skin
   B. hair
   C. nails
   D. sudoriferous glands
   E. oil (glands)
   F. hair root and covering
4. The term for the layers that compose the epidermis is
5. The epidermis is the _____ layer, meaning that it does not have a rich blood supply.
6. The nerve endings, hair follicles, and sebaceous glands are located in the layer of the skin called the _____ or _____
7. Fatty tissue is stored in the _____ or the _____ layer.

Chapter Review

A variety of exercises, including reviews of chapter terminology, theory, and critical-thinking, are included at the end of each chapter to help you test your knowledge. Most chapter reviews also include case studies to give you the opportunity to apply your recently gained knowledge to real-life situations. Your instructor can check your work on the chapter review section.

514   APPENDIX A

Date _____

Student Name _____

CHECKLIST: PERFORM PROPER HANDWASHING FOR MEDICAL ASEPSIS

TASK: Prevent the spread of pathogens by aseptically washing hands, following Standard Precautions.

CONDITIONS: Given the proper equipment and supplies, the student will be required to demonstrate the proper method of performing handwashing for medical asepsis.

EQUIPMENT AND SUPPLIES
- Liquid antibacterial soap
- Nailbrush or orange stick
- Paper towels
- Warm running water
- Regular waste container

STANDARDS: Complete the procedure within _____ minutes and achieve a minimum score of _____%.

Time began _____ Time ended _____

Steps	Possible Points	First Attempt	Second Attempt
1. Assemble all supplies and equipment.	5		
2. Remove rings and watch or push the watch up on the forearm.	5		
3. Stand close to the sink, without allowing clothing to touch the sink.	5		
4. Turn on the faucets, using a paper towel.	5		
5. Adjust the water temperature to warm—not hot or cold. Explain why proper water temperature is important.	10		
6. Discard the paper towel in the proper waste container.	5		
7. Wet hands and wrists under running water, and apply liquid antibacterial soap. Hands must be held lower than the elbows at all times. Hands must not touch the inside of the sink.	10		
8. Work soap into a lather by rubbing the palms together using a circular motion.	10		
9. Clean the fingernails with a nailbrush or an orange stick.	5		
10. Rinse hands thoroughly under running water, holding them in a downward position and allowing soap and water to run off the fingertips.	10		
11. Repeat the procedure if hands are grossly contaminated.	10		
12. Dry the hands gently and thoroughly using a clean paper towel. Discard the paper towel in proper waste container.	10		
13. Using a dry paper towel, turn the faucets off, clean the area around the sink, and discard the towel in regular waste container.	10		
Total Points Possible	100		

Comments: Total Points Earned _____   Instructor's Signature _____

Appendixes

Appendixes include competency checklists. They are organized into two groups. There are Core Competency Checklists for core skills, such as taking vital signs, giving injections, and assigning insurance codes, that you will be practicing in every module. The Core Competency Checklists are followed by the Procedure Competency Checklists, which are unique to the topics you are learning in this module. Each group of checklists has a Grade Sheet to summarize your performance scores when demonstrating your competencies to your instructor.

CONTENTS

1

OBJECTIVES

1. Define, spell, and pronounce the terms listed in the vocabulary.
2. Identify the ancient cultures that contributed a major portion of our medical terminology.
3. Explain the history of medicine and how it has affected today's medical industry.
4. Distinguish between and describe the two medical symbols in general use today.
5. Explain why a medical education at Johns Hopkins was considered superior, even in its early years.
6. List several medical pioneers, and discuss the importance of their contributions to the medical profession.

THE HISTORY OF MEDICINE

KEY TERMS

accreditation (u-kre-duh-ta′-shun) The process through which an organization is recognized for adherence to a group of standards that meet or exceed expectations of the accrediting agency.

cited Quoted by way of example, authority, or proof or mentioned formally in commendation or praise.

contamination (kun-ta-mu-na′-shun) A process by which something is made impure, unclean, or unfit for use by the introduction of unwholesome or undesirable elements.

dissection (di-sek′-shun) Separation into pieces and exposure of parts for scientific examination.

fermentation (fur-men-ta′-shun) An enzymatically controlled transformation of an organic compound.

indicted (in-di′-ted) Charged with a crime by the finding or presentment of a jury according to due process of law.

innocuous (i′-nuh-kyu-wus) Having no effect, adverse or otherwise; harmless.

mysticism The experience of seeming to have direct communication with God or ultimate reality.

pandemic (pan-de′-mik) A condition in which the majority of the people in a country, a number of countries, or a geographic area are affected.

philanthropist (fu-lan′-thruh-pist) An individual who makes an active effort to promote human welfare.

putrefaction (pyu-truh-fak′-shun) Decomposition of animal matter that results in a foul smell.

robotics Technology dealing with the design, construction, and operation of robots in automation.

telemedicine The use of telecommunications in the practice of medicine, in which great distances can exist among health care professionals, colleagues, patients, and students.

teleradiology The use of telecommunications devices to enhance and improve the results of radiological procedures.

treatises (truh-te′-ses) Systematic expositions or arguments in writing including a methodical discussion of the facts and principles involved and the conclusions reached.

What Would You Do?

Read the following scenario and keep it in mind as you learn about the history of medicine and medical assisting in this chapter.

Carlos Santos, CMA (AAMA), is a medical assisting instructor with 10 years' experience in the clinical area. He worked for a group of family practitioners and for an allergist during his career as a medical assistant before becoming an instructor. Mr. Santos believes that it is very important to give his students an overview of the health care industry early in their training. He knows that it is exciting to show them the history and progress of medicine and introduce them to the current types of facilities available for patient care on both a national and a local level. This helps the student to understand where he or she fits into the whole picture as a medical assistant. Often Mr. Santos assigns the students a short report on one person who contributed to the progress of medicine. He finds that this is a good way to encourage the students to use the Internet and conduct research right from the start of their training; in addition, the students get a chance to grow more comfortable speaking in front of a group. The knowledge that the students will gain about the different areas of patient care will be useful once they graduate and begin working in a health care facility. All of these skills will make Mr. Santos's students more versatile and valuable to their eventual employers.

The growth of today's health care industry seems unstoppable. Thanks to modern technological advances, medicine speeds forward faster than ever in its quest to improve the health of humankind. Modern advances, such as **telemedicine,** are experiencing significant growth, and the images produced with **teleradiology** have vastly improved in their resolution. **Robotics** is assisting health care professionals in surgery and even delivers drugs to hospital floors using laser sensors. Education in medicine has grown exponentially: computers, the Internet, and video have enabled an instructor in New York to communicate with a student in Los Angeles. The key to this technology lies within the development and widespread use of elaborate information systems that have revolutionized the way that medicine is practiced today. Technology is advancing at an astounding rate of speed; the health care environment of the future is barely imaginable. This chapter looks back at the history of medicine, gazes at its present, and glances toward its future.

THE HISTORY OF MEDICINE

Medical Language and Mythology

Today's medical professional uses words with origins stemming from the romance and fantasy of classical and ancient languages. The study of anatomy reaches back to the dawn of recorded history. Today's modern terms are often similar to their original versions. Some terms are inaccurate when translated literally, because the ancients did not fully understand body functions. The word *artery,* for example, which comes from the Greek word *arteria,* literally means "a windpipe." The early Greeks believed that the arteries carried air, not blood. Greek and Roman mythology have contributed a major portion of our medical terminology, but we have also borrowed liberally from Arabic, Anglo-Saxon, and Germanic sources. Several terms originate from the Bible.

The human head rests on the first cervical vertebra, which is called the *atlas.* Atlas was the famous Greek Titan who was condemned by Zeus to bear the heavens on his shoulders. Achilles was held by the heel as his mother dipped him into the river Styx, so that he would become invulnerable. However, his heel was not immersed, and he later died from a wound in that area. "Achilles heel" is a common expression used today to show a point of weakness. Aphrodite, the Greek goddess of love and beauty, is the source of the name for drugs used to enhance sexual arousal, called *aphrodisiacs.* The equivalent Roman goddess of love, Venus, is associated with lustful desires. A portion of the female anatomy, the mons *veneris* (mons pubis), and *venereal* diseases were named after her.

Aesculapius, the son of Apollo, was revered as the god of medicine. The early Greeks worshiped the healing powers of Aesculapius and built temples in his honor where patients were treated by trained priests. His daughters were Hygeia, goddess of health, and Panacea, goddess of all healing and restorer of health. Our modern word "hygiene" has its origin in Hygeia, and the modern meaning for panacea is "a remedy for all ills and difficulties." The staff of Aesculapius is a common medical icon. It depicts a serpent encircling a staff and signifies the art of healing. The staff of Aesculapius has been adopted by the American Medical Association as the symbol of medicine. The mythological staff belonging to Hermes, the messenger of the gods, is the

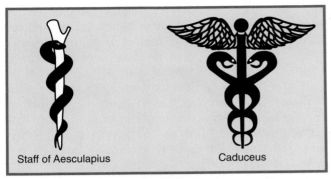

Fig. 1-1 Staff of Aesculapius and the caduceus.

caduceus, which was thought to have magical powers. The caduceus is a staff encircled by two serpents with wings at the top. This icon is the medical insignia of the U.S. Army Medical Corps and is often misused as a symbol of the medical profession (Fig. 1-1).

Medicine in Ancient Times

Although religious and mythological beliefs were the basis of care for the sick in ancient times, evidence suggests the use of drugs, surgery, and other treatments based on theories about the body from as early as 5000 BC. In the well-developed societies of the Egyptians, Babylonians, and Assyrians, certain men acted as physicians and used the little knowledge they had to try to treat illness and injury.

Moses presented rules of health to the Hebrews at approximately 1205 BC. He was the first advocate of preventive medicine and is considered the first public health officer. Moses knew that some animal diseases could be passed to humans and that **contamination** existed, so a religious law was developed forbidding humans to eat or drink from dirty dishes. The people of that era believed that doing so would defile their bodies and they would lose their souls.

Hippocrates, known as the Father of Medicine, is the most famous of the ancient Greek physicians (Fig. 1-2). He was born in 450 BC on the island of Cos in Greece. He is best remembered for the Hippocratic Oath, which has been administered to physicians for more than 2000 years. Hippocrates is credited with taking **mysticism** out of medicine and giving it a scientific basis. During this period of history, most believed that illness was caused by demon possession; for the illness to be cured, the demon had to be removed from the body. Hippocrates' clinical descriptions of diseases and his volumes on epidemics, fevers, epilepsy, fractures, and instruments were studied for centuries. He believed that the body had the capacity to heal itself and that the physician's role was to help nature.

Fig. 1-2 Hippocrates is known as the Father of Medicine. *(Courtesy National Library of Medicine.)*

Very little was known about anatomy, physiology, and pathology, and there was no knowledge of chemistry. Despite these limitations, many of the classifications of diseases and descriptions of symptoms that Hippocrates developed are still in use today.

Galen was a Greek physician who migrated to Rome in 162 AD and became known as the Prince of Physicians. He is said to have written more than 500 **treatises** on medicine. He wrote an excellent summary on anatomy as it was known at the time, but his work was faulty and inaccurate because it was largely based on the **dissection** of apes and swine. He is considered the Father of Experimental Physiology and the first experimental neurologist. He was the first to describe the cranial nerves and the sympathetic nervous system, and he performed the first experimental section of the spinal cord, producing hemiplegia. Galen also produced aphonia by cutting the recurrent laryngeal nerve, and he gave the first valid explanation of the mechanism of respiration. Galen was also a champion of medical ethics: he felt that physicians "must learn to despise money," and that if a physician was interested in profit, he was not serious in his devotion to the art of medicine. Galen's beliefs about monetary profit from medicine parallel the views of many modern health care professionals, who understand the nature of the health care crisis the world faces today. Although much of what he believed about the body was incorrect, Galen's teachings remained intact until human dissections began and physicians were able to visualize exactly what was inside the human body.

Because both Hippocrates and Galen were highly respected, the authority of their observations went unquestioned. This had a negative effect on the progress of science throughout the Dark Ages and well into the 16th century. Their theories and descriptions were considered immutable principles, so few physicians were innovative and curious enough to challenge them. Those who did experiment in medicine were scorned by their colleagues, and physicians continued to use methods that were at best ineffectual or **innocuous** and at worst harmful to the patient. However, the establishment of universities led to a study of theories of disease rather than observation of the sick.

Early Development of Medical Education

Medical knowledge developed slowly, and distribution of such knowledge was poor. Before the printing press was invented in the mid-15th century, very little exchange of scientific knowledge and ideas occurred; scientists were not well informed about the investigations of other scientists. The printing press allowed books to be distributed faster and over a widespread area. Another development important to science occurred in the 17th century, when European academies or societies were established, consisting of small groups of men who met to discuss subjects of mutual interest. The academies provided freedom of expression that, with the stimulus of exchanging ideas, contributed significantly to the development of scientific thought. One of the earliest of the academies was the Royal Society of London, formed in 1662. The development of communications during this era was important, and these societies contributed to the exchange of information.

Our world became more complex over the centuries, which prompted a greater need for regulation. The passage of the Medical Act of 1858 in Great Britain was considered one of the most important events in British medicine. The act established a statutory body, the General Medical Council, which controlled admission to the medical register and had regulatory power over medical education and examinations.

In the United States, medical education was greatly influenced by the Johns Hopkins University Medical School in Baltimore, Maryland, established in the early 1890s. The school admitted only college graduates with a year's training in the natural sciences. The clinical education at Johns Hopkins was superior because the school partnered with Johns Hopkins Hospital, which had been created expressly for teaching and research by members of the medical faculty. The first four professors at Johns Hopkins were Sir William Osler (Professor of Medicine), William H. Welch (Chief of Pathology), Howard A. Kelley (Chief of Gynecology and Obstetrics), and William D. Halsted (Chief of Surgery). Together these four men transformed the organization and curriculum of clinical teaching and made Johns Hopkins the most famous medical school in the world at that time.

The earliest medical school **accreditation** resulted from a report published by Abraham Flexner. He received a grant from the Carnegie Foundation Commission to study the quality of medical colleges in the United States and Canada. His report, called the Flexner Report, resulted in the closure of many low-ranking schools and the upgrading of others. These events legitimized medical education and opened new doors for many individuals to the world of medicine.

STOP AND THINK?

- Mr. Santos asks his class to identify which of the individuals involved in early medicine have had the most impact on modern health care. Whom would you choose, and why?
- The students point out that early research was often viewed in a negative manner. How does research affect us now, and how is it viewed by the public?

Early Medical Pioneers

Andreas Vesalius (1514-1564) was a Belgian anatomist known as the Father of Modern Anatomy (Fig. 1-3). At the age of 29 he published his great *De Corporis Humani Fabrica*, in which he described the structure of the human body. This work marked a turning point by breaking with past traditional beliefs in Galen's theories. Vesalius introduced many new anatomic terms, but because of his radical approach, he was subjected to persecution from his colleagues, teachers, and pupils. Despite his great contributions to the science of anatomy, his name is not used to identify any significant anatomic structures.

Other important advances and discoveries took place throughout the world. Gabriele Fallopius (1523-1562), an Italian student of Vesalius, was also an accurate dissector. He described and named many parts of the human anatomy. He named the fallopian tubes after himself and also named the vagina and placenta. In 1628 William Harvey

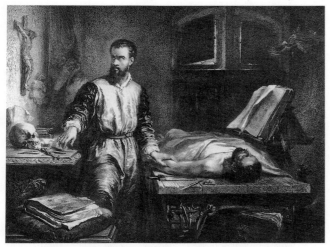

Fig. 1-3 Andreas Vesalius is known as the Father of Modern Anatomy. *(Courtesy National Library of Medicine.)*

(1578-1657) announced his discovery that the heart acts as a muscular pump, forcing and propelling the blood throughout the body. He revealed that the blood's motion is a continuous cycle, basing his conclusion on his experimental vivisection, ligation, and perfusion as well as brilliant reasoning. Harvey's writings were recognized in Germany before the English permitted their publication at home. Modern England now considers Harvey to be its medical Shakespeare.

The unseen world of microorganisms was first revealed by Anton van Leeuwenhoek (1632-1723), a Dutch linen draper and haberdasher. Haberdashers made their living dealing in men's clothing and accessories, but it was Leeuwenhoek's hobby of grinding lenses that eventually led to his amazing discovery of the magnification process. He ground more than 400 lenses during his lifetime, some of which were no larger than a pinhead. In the grinding process, Leeuwenhoek learned how to use a simple biconvex lens to magnify the minute world of organisms and structures, never before seen. Leeuwenhoek was the first to ever observe bacteria and protozoa through a lens, and his accurate interpretations of what he saw led to the sciences of bacteriology and protozoology.

Marcello Malpighi (1628-1694) was born near Bologna, Italy, and attended the University of Bologna, where he earned a doctorate in both medicine and philosophy. He pioneered the use of the microscope in the study of plants and animals. Microscopic anatomy became a prerequisite for advances in physiology, embryology, and practical medicine. In 1661 he described the pulmonary and capillary network connecting the smallest arteries with the smallest veins. This was one of the most important discoveries in the history of science, and

it validated Harvey's work. Malpighi is commonly regarded as the first histologist.

Medical Advances in the 18th and 19th Centuries

English scientist John Hunter (1728-1793) is known as the Founder of Scientific Surgery. An army surgeon, he became an expert on gunshot wounds and experimented with tissue transfer. His surgical procedures were soundly based on pathological evidence. He was the first to classify teeth in a scientific manner and introduced artificial feeding by means of a flexible tube passed into the stomach. He provided a classic description of the syphilitic chancre, which is sometimes called a Hunterian chancre. During his studies of venereal diseases, he inoculated himself with what he thought was gonorrhea, but instead he acquired syphilis. His results in this study actually caused confusion in the medical community because he mistakenly thought that gonorrhea was a symptom of syphilis. This misconception was not corrected until the beginning of the 20th century. His collection of anatomical and animal specimens formed the basis for the museum of the Royal College of Surgeons. After Hunter's death he was buried in St. Martin. His remains were later moved, however, to Westminster Abbey as a gesture of honor. A tablet was placed over his grave by the Royal College of Surgeons to "record their admiration of his genius as a gifted interpreter of the Divine Power and Wisdom at work in the laws of Organic Life and their grateful veneration for his services to mankind as the Founder of Scientific Surgery." Today in Australia the John Hunter Hospital serves more than 600 inpatients and 1000 outpatients per day.

Edward Jenner (1749-1823) was a student of John Hunter and a country physician from Dorsetshire, England. He is considered one of the immortals of preventive medicine for his development of the smallpox vaccine. While Jenner was serving as an apprentice, he assisted in treating a dairymaid. Smallpox was mentioned, and she commented, "I cannot take that disease, for I have had cowpox." Smallpox at that time was a deadly **pandemic.** Jenner observed that those who had contracted cowpox never contracted smallpox. Later, as a practicing physician, Jenner continued investigating the relationship between cowpox and smallpox almost obsessively, but the medical society members grew bored with his obsession and threatened to expel him from their ranks. On May 14, 1796, Dr. Jenner took purulent matter from a pustule on the hand of Sarah Nelmes, a dairymaid, and inserted it through two small superficial incisions into the arm of James Phipps, a healthy 8-year-old boy. This was the first vaccination. On July 1 a virulent dose of smallpox matter was given to the boy in the same arm. Phipps' vaccination kept him safe from the dreaded disease, and Jenner's method of vaccination spread throughout the world. The results of his experiments were published in 1798. He called this method of protection *vaccination,* from the Latin word *vacca,* which means "cow," and at that time, cowpox was called *vaccinia.* Today smallpox has been eradicated throughout the world as a result of a planned program of global vaccination.

Austrian physician Leopold Auenbrugger (1722-1809) developed the use of percussion in diagnosis. He became physician-in-chief to the Hospital of the Holy Trinity at Vienna in 1751, where he tested his discovery. Although scorned and ignored by his contemporaries, his techniques later made him famous and are still used today during physical examinations. René Laennec (1781-1826) was a French physician who developed the stethoscope in 1819. At first he used only a cylinder of rolled paper in his hands; later he used a wooden device because of its sound-conducting properties. With today's sophisticated stethoscopes physicians are able to hear sounds in the body, including a fetus inside the mother. Laennec's book, *Treatise on Mediate Auscultation and Diseases of the Chest,* was readily accepted and translated into many languages. It is said to be the most important treatise on diseases of the thoracic organs ever written.

Several men of the early 1800s are remembered for their fight against puerperal fever and their concern for women's health. Puerperal fever, an infectious disease that can be contracted during childbirth, was also called *puerperal sepsis* or *childbed fever.* The term *puerperal,* denoting a woman in childbed, originates from the Latin *puer,* "a child," and *pario,* "to bring forth." The word *puerperium* now designates the period from delivery to the time the uterus returns to normal size (approximately 42 days after childbirth).

The best known of these men was the Hungarian physician Ignaz Philipp Semmelweis (1818-1865); history has called him the Savior of Mothers. His fight against puerperal fever is a sad story of hardships. His theories were resisted by many professionals, including his instructors. Semmelweis noted that the fever often attacked women who were delivered by medical students coming straight from the autopsy or dissecting rooms. Semmelweis directed that in his wards the students were to wash and disinfect their hands before going to examine the women and deliver the children. This process brought about a marked reduction of cases of puerperal fever on his ward, but he still faced unrelenting opposition. As his theories were proved correct, Semmelweis felt an incredible guilt that the doctors

Fig. 1-4 Louis Pasteur was a brilliant chemist who made numerous contributions to medicine. *(Courtesy National Library of Medicine.)*

themselves had caused so many deaths. He died at the age of 47—ironically, from the very disease he had fought. He was infected with puerperal fever from a cut on his finger during an autopsy. His grave had hardly been closed when scientists began to understand the causes of this disease, largely as a result of the investigations of two great scientists, Louis Pasteur and Joseph Lister.

Pasteur (1822-1895) was a Frenchman who did brilliant work as a chemist, but it was his studies in bacteriology that made him one of the most famous men in medical history (Fig. 1-4). He was bestowed the title of Father of Bacteriology and has also been honored as the Father of Preventive Medicine. He gave unselfishly of his time outside his profession to help others solve problems. Pasteur's adventures included studying the difficulties in the **fermentation** of wine. He averted disaster in France's critical winemaking industry by a process he developed, now called *pasteurization.* This achievement alone would have made him an immortal among the French. Through a process of supplying enough heat to destroy microorganisms, wine was prevented from turning to vinegar. The French people called on Pasteur again to help the ailing silkworm industry. He devoted years to the conquest of diseases that infected the silkworm. His efforts were impeded when he was stricken with hemiplegia, but after a long, difficult recovery, he was able to continue with a stiff hand and a limp.

Convinced that the infinite world of bacteria held the key to the secrets of contagious diseases,

Pasteur left chemistry again to continue studying his theory. Many renowned scientists denied the germ theory of disease and devoted themselves to degrading Pasteur's theories and experiments. In the midst of this controversy he became involved in the prevention of anthrax, which threatened the health of cattle and sheep. Pasteur was eventually honored for his work with many other diseases, such as rabies, chicken cholera, and swine erysipelas. He devoted the last 7 years of his life to the Pasteur Institute, which was founded as a clinic for rabies treatment, a research center for infectious disease, and a teaching center. The Pasteur Institute still exists today. He died in 1895, with his family at his bedside. It is said that his last words were, "There is still a great deal to do."

Joseph Lister (1827-1912) revolutionized surgery through the application of Pasteur's discoveries. He understood the similarity between infections in postsurgical wounds and the processes of **putrefaction.** Pasteur proved that these processes were caused by microorganisms. Before this time, surgeons accepted that infections in surgical wounds were inevitable. Lister reasoned that microorganisms must be the cause of infection and should be kept out of wounds. His colleagues were indifferent to his theories, because most believed infections were God-given and natural. Lister disagreed, and he developed antiseptic methods by using carbolic acid for sterilization. By spraying the rooms with a fine mist of the acid, soaking the instruments in carbolic solutions, and washing his hands in a similar solution, he was able to prove his theories. He is honored as the Father of Sterile Surgery. Pasteur and Lister met after years of great mutual admiration. The meeting was filled with emotion, and it was written in *Pathfinders in Medicine* that "a new star should have appeared in the heavens to commemorate the event." Medicine truly owes a deep gratitude to these two pioneers for the knowledge they imparted to the art.

Robert Koch (1843-1910) is a familiar name to all bacteriologists because of his famous Koch's Postulates—his theory of rules that must be followed before an organism can be accepted as the causative agent in a given disease. Koch was a German physician who earned great honors in bacteriology and public health. He introduced many of the tools used in the laboratory, such as the culture-plate method for isolation of bacteria. He discovered the cause of cholera and demonstrated its transmission by food and water. This discovery completely transformed health departments and proved the importance of bacteriology in everyday life. Koch's greatest disappointment was his failure to find a cure for tuberculosis, but in his attempt he isolated tuberculin, the substance produced by tubercle bacteria. Its use as a diagnostic aid was of immense value to medicine. In 1885 the University of Berlin created the Chair of Hygiene and Bacteriology in honor of Robert Koch. He became a Nobel Laureate in 1905.

One of Koch's students was a German physician named Paul Ehrlich (1854-1915). He pioneered the fields of bacteriology, immunology, and especially chemotherapy. Chemotherapy is the process of treating diseases by injecting chemicals into the body to destroy microorganisms, and this was a new science in Koch's day. Ehrlich was only 28 when he wrote his first paper on typhoid, but his greatest gift to humanity was called his "magic bullet," or formula 606, which was designed to fight syphilis. With the organism identified by scientists Bordet and Wasserman, Ehrlich set out to find a chemical that would destroy the organism but not harm the host, specifically, the human body. The 606th drug that Ehrlich tried finally brought about healing. He called it *salvarsan* because he believed that it offered mankind salvation from the disease. This endeavor also marked the beginning of the practice of injecting chemicals into the body to destroy a specific organism. In 1908 Ehrlich shared the Nobel Prize with Eli Metchnikoff, who is remembered for his theory of phagocytosis and immunology.

Crawford Williamson Long (1815-1878) was the first to employ ether as an anesthetic agent. Early in 1842 a group of students would have a social gathering after chemistry lectures and inhale ether, a chemical commonly found in chemistry labs, as a form of amusement. Ether, an intoxicant similar to nitrous oxide, functions as a soporific or sleep-inducing agent. However, at one of these "ether frolics," as they were called, Dr. Long also observed that people under the influence of ether did not seem to feel pain. After considerable thought, he decided to use ether for a surgical operation. In March 1842 he removed a tumor from the neck of James M. Venable after placing him under the influence of ether. Dr. Horace Wells was a dentist who reported using nitrous oxide as an anesthetic in 1844. Another dentist, Dr. William T.G. Morton, reported using ether in 1846 when he extracted a tooth from a patient, and he also used the gas at Massachusetts General Hospital for a surgical procedure.

Surgeons are grateful to Wilhelm Konrad Roentgen (1845-1923), a professor of physics at the University of Wurzburg, Germany. Roentgen discovered the x-ray in 1895 while experimenting with electrical currents passed through sealed glass tubes. He was awarded the Nobel Prize in Physics in 1901. Although he called it an *x-ray,* history has honored him by calling it the *roentgen ray.* Marie and Pierre Curie discovered radium in 1898, and they were

Fig. 1-5 Considered the founder of nursing, Florence Nightingale is also known as the Lady with the Lamp. *(Courtesy National Library of Medicine.)*

Fig. 1-6 Elizabeth Blackwell was the first woman to receive a degree as a medical doctor in the United States. *(Courtesy National Library of Medicine.)*

awarded the 1902 Nobel Prize in Physics for their work on radioactivity. Unfortunately, Pierre was killed 3 years later while crossing a street in a rainstorm. Marie was awarded his teaching position at the Sorbonne, a medical university in France; no woman had taught at the school in its 650-year history. In 1911 she was awarded the Nobel Prize for her discoveries of radium and polonium, the first person to receive the award twice. She died in 1934 from pernicious anemia, which was believed to have been caused by her over-exposure to radiation and years of overwork.

Nineteenth Century Women in Medicine

Many other women made great contributions to medicine in the early 19th century. Florence Nightingale (1820-1910) is known as the founder of nursing and is fondly called the Lady with the Lamp (Fig. 1-5). She was of noble birth, and somewhat late in life she sought nursing training in both England and Europe. By the dawn of the Crimean War in 1854, she had established a fine reputation for her work in hospital organization. She was invited by the British Secretary of War to visit the Crimea to help correct the terrible conditions that existed in caring for the wounded. She created the Women's Nursing Service in Scutari and Balaklava. The physicians treated her and the other 38 nurses poorly until a crisis brought thousands of wounded and sick soldiers to the army hospitals. The bravery and competence of the nurses helped the doctors realize their value to the medical profession. In 1860 she founded the Nightingale School and Home for Nurses in London, which marked the beginning of professional nursing education.

started record keeping

Clara Barton (1821-1912), an American, began her nursing career early in life. When she was 11 years of age her brother fell from the roof of their barn, and Clara nursed him back to health over a 2-year period. She later was a battlefield nurse and **philanthropist** whose work during the Civil War led her to recognize that very poor records were kept in Washington to aid in the search for missing men who were wounded or killed in combat. Her efforts to remedy this led to the formation of the Bureau of Records. Her organization and recruitment of supplies for the wounded led to her eventual involvement with the Red Cross in the Franco-Prussian War. In 1881 she organized a Red Cross Committee in Washington, the original formation of the American Red Cross. She served as its first president from 1881 to 1904. Her retirement came at the age of 82, just after personally leading dangerous expeditions to help victims of fires, hurricanes, and floods. The American Red Cross remains a vital organization to this day.

Elizabeth Blackwell (1821-1910) was the first woman in the United States to receive the Doctor of Medicine degree from a medical school (Fig. 1-6). Blackwell's family immigrated to New York from England in 1832. She began her medical education by reading medical books and later obtained private instruction. Medical schools in New York and Pennsylvania initially refused her applications for formal study, but finally in 1847 she was accepted at the Geneva Medical College in New York. Ten years later, she established the New York Infirmary for

world's 1st public school nursing system

Indigent Women and Children, the first hospital staffed entirely by women. In 1869 Blackwell returned to her native England and became a professor of gynecology at the London School of Medicine for Women, of which she was a founder.

Lillian Wald (1867-1940), a social worker and nurse, made great contributions to medical care when she founded the Henry Street Settlement in New York City. Wald operated a visiting nurse service from this establishment. When one of her nurses was assigned to the city's public schools in 1902, the New York City Municipal Board of Health established the world's first public school nursing system.

Margaret Sanger (1883-1966) was born in Corning, New York, and trained as a nurse at the White Plains Hospital. She became the American leader of the birth control movement. While working among the poor in New York City, she came to understand the public's need for information about contraception. She left nursing to devote herself to that objective. In 1873 the federal Comstock law declared it illegal to import or distribute any device, medicine, or information designed to prevent conception or induce abortion, or to mention in print the names of sexually transmitted diseases. Nurses and physicians were legally prohibited from providing this information to their patients. In 1914 Sanger was **indicted** for circulating the magazine *The Woman Rebel*, in which she attacked the legislative restrictions of the Comstock law. The case was dismissed 2 years later. In the same year she established the first American birth control clinic; this led to her arrest, conviction, and time in the county jail. She continued her work, and after World War II, she successfully advocated research into hormonal contraception, because of the newfound concern about population growth. This research ultimately led to development of the birth control pill. When the Planned Parenthood Federation of America was formed in 1941, she was named honorary chairperson.

STOP AND THINK?

Mr. Santos asks his students to tell him which of these early pioneers they would most like to have worked with. Whom would you choose, and why? What difficulties did they face as they worked?

≋ MEDICAL MILESTONES

In recognition of the achievements of scientists of the past, Sir Isaac Newton spoke of our ability to discover and innovate in the medical field. He humbly said, "If I have seen a little further than others, it is because I have stood on the shoulders of giants." Great strides in medicine accompanied the 20th century, and technology began to advance rapidly. Medical leaders continued their contributions, and knowledge, treatment, and research grew by leaps and bounds.

Walter Reed was a U.S. Army pathologist and bacteriologist who proved that yellow fever was transmitted by the bite of a mosquito. Persons with diabetes should be grateful to Sir Frederick Grant Banting, a Canadian physician who isolated insulin for treatment, along with Charles Herbert Best, a Canadian physiologist. In 1928 Sir Alexander Fleming discovered penicillin accidentally while researching influenza and working with staphylococcal bacteria. He found a substance in mold that prevented growth of bacteria even when the substance was diluted 800 times.

Cardiologist Helen Taussig and surgeon Alfred Blalock explored the health issues of children born with cyanosis resulting from a malformed heart. Dr. Taussig collaborated with Dr. Blalock to develop a lifesaving operation for these children, called "blue babies." History often omits the contributions of Vivien Thomas, an African-American who was Dr. Blalock's surgical research technician at Johns Hopkins Hospital. Thomas was a former carpenter who constructed several of the medical instruments used in the Blalock-Taussig procedure. Thomas actually created the blue-baby condition in dogs, on which he regularly practiced the surgical procedure. When Dr. Blalock and Dr. Taussig performed the first blue-baby operation at Johns Hopkins University, Thomas stood over Blalock's shoulder and advised him during the procedure, since Thomas had done the surgery several more times than Blalock. This happened at a time when African-Americans were not allowed on the main floors of the hospital, much less in the surgical suite. This surgery became known as the Blalock-Taussig procedure, and although the first blue-baby operation prolonged the patient's life by only 2 months, subsequent operations were successful and children were able to leave the hospital with hope of a healthy life.

Jonas Edward Salk and Albert Sabin almost eradicated poliomyelitis, once the killer and crippler of thousands in the United States. Salk's injectable vaccine was developed in 1952, and after wide-scale testing in 1954 it was distributed nationally, greatly reducing the incidence of the disease. Sabin's live-virus vaccine, in a form that could be swallowed, became available less than a decade later. Werner Forssmann, a German surgeon, originated a cardiac technique called *catheterization* that is used in the diagnosis and treatment of heart disease. Christiaan

Barnard, a South African surgeon, performed the first human-heart transplant in 1967. Dr. Elisabeth Kübler-Ross, a Swiss-born psychiatrist who died in 2004, was shocked at the treatment of terminally ill patients at her hospital in New York. She wrote the best-selling book *On Death and Dying,* which helped professionals and laypersons alike to understand the stages of grief.

STOP AND THINK?

- During class discussion Mr. Santos points out that the leaders in the health care industry had specific goals for their careers and achieved worldwide recognition for their contributions. What individuals have made contributions to medicine in recent years?
- How can the individual medical assistant make a contribution to medicine?

MODERN MEDICINE

Many modern physicians are making important discoveries and contributions to the field of medicine. Dr. David Ho is considered by many to be one of the most brilliant minds today helping to piece together the puzzle of the human immunodeficiency virus (HIV). Ho is the scientific director and chief executive officer (CEO) of the Aaron Diamond AIDS Research Center in New York City and is also a professor at Rockefeller University. He was born in Taiwan in 1952, and his family immigrated to the United States when he was 12 years of age. He eventually entered college to study physics—medicine was actually his second choice—but once he discovered molecular biology and the concept of gene splicing, he decided to become a researcher. He still does calculations in Chinese. Ho was named *Time* magazine's "Man of the Year" in 1996 for his work in the battle against HIV and acquired immunodeficiency syndrome (AIDS).

Dr. Eve Slater served as the Assistant Secretary for Health at the U.S. Department of Health and Human Services (DHHS). Dr. Slater was former Secretary Tommy G. Thompson's primary advisor on matters regarding issues concerning the nation's public health and oversaw DHHS's U.S. Public Health Service (PHS). Before she joined DHHS, Dr. Slater served as a senior vice president of Merck Research Laboratories' external policy, and also as Vice President of Corporate Public Affairs. Dr. Slater was the first woman to hold this rank. During her time with Merck, she spearheaded the approval of major med-

icines used to treat the HIV infection, osteoporosis, cardiovascular disease, arthritis, chickenpox, and many others. In 1976, Dr. Slater became the first woman appointed chief resident in medicine at Massachusetts General Hospital. She served as an assistant professor at Harvard Medical School and directed laboratory research funded by the National Institutes of Health (NIH) and the American Heart Association. Currently, Dr. Slater is a board member of several prestigious medical organizations, including Theravance, Inc. and VaxGen, the company co-founded by Dr. Don Francis, who led the fight against AIDS when the disease was first discovered.

Dr. C. Everett Koop [*former Surgeon General*] was graduated from Cornell University as a medical doctor in 1941 and spent most of his career as a pediatric surgeon. During his terms as the U.S. Surgeon General, he became a proponent of tobacco awareness, insisting that tobacco advertisements must be less attractive to the youth of today. Dr. Koop is a professor at Dartmouth Medical School. He founded the Koop Institute, an organization whose mission is to "promote the health and well-being of all people." Dr. Koop has been honored with many awards, including 41 honorary doctorates.

Dr. Marcia Angell is the former editor-in-chief of [*teach harvard*] the *New England Journal of Medicine* (NEJM), one of the most prestigious medical publications in the United States. Her career with NEJM began in 1979, and her excellent articles spanned a variety of subjects, from the pharmaceutical companies' profit margins to the effects of socioeconomic status on Americans seeking health care services. Angell was named one of the 25 most influential Americans in 1997 by *Time* magazine. She has written and contributed to several books, including *Science on Trial: The Clash of Medical Evidence and the Law in the Breast Implant Case.* Angell is a board-certified pathologist and currently serves as senior lecturer in the Department of Social Medicine at Harvard Medical School.

As the director of the National Institute of Allergy and Infectious Diseases at the NIH, Dr. Anthony Fauci leads research efforts on immune-mediated disorders. His scientific leadership has resulted in major advances in several diseases, such as polyarteritis nodosa and Wegener's granulomatosis. Many of his studies now relate to HIV and the body's response to the AIDS virus, and ways to improve HIV treatment and prevention, including HIV vaccine development. Out of more than 1 million scientists who published during the period between 1981 and 1994, Dr. Fauci was the fifth most **cited.** He received his MD from Cornell University Medical College, and his career with the NIH has spanned more than 30 years.

Dr. Antonia Novello was the first woman, and the first Hispanic, to be honored with the post of Surgeon General. She served at the NIH and was the honorary chairperson of the National Youth Summit for Mothers Against Drunk Driving (MADD). Novello played a key role in writing the warning labels on cigarette packages. She supported and promoted the National Organ Transplant Act of 1984 and has contributed to the efforts of the United Nations Children's Fund (UNICEF). Novello was a clinical professor at Georgetown University Hospital and in 1994 was inducted into the National Women's Hall of Fame. She currently serves as New York State's health commissioner.

THE HISTORY OF MEDICAL ASSISTING

According to the U.S. Department of Labor's *Occupational Outlook Handbook,* medical assisting is projected to be one of the fastest-growing occupations in the United States over the 2004 to 2014 period. Much of this growth is a result of the increase in the number of group practices, clinics, and other facilities that need a high number of support personnel. This makes the flexible medical assistant who can handle both clinical and administrative duties particularly valuable to the physician.

A career as a medical assistant is challenging and offers job satisfaction, opportunities for service, financial reward, and possibilities for advancement. Men and women can be equally successful as medical assistants. Individuals considering the medical assisting discipline must be dedicated and committed and must have a strong desire to become caregivers. Caregivers are people who have the ability to put the needs of the patient first and have a sincere concern for those who are not at their best. A caregiver must feel an obligation to assist the patient in whatever way possible and have patience with those who, at times, are more difficult. This strong inner desire is one of the most important qualities of the successful professional medical assistant. Through development of this "caregiving" mentality, many personal rewards will follow, as will a long and beneficial career.

The first medical assistant was probably a neighbor of a physician who was called on to help when an extra pair of hands was needed. As time passed and the practice of medicine became more organized and more complicated, some physicians hired nurses to help in their office practices. Gradually, record keeping, data reporting, and an increasing number of business details became important to physicians, and they realized a need for an assistant with both administrative and clinical training. Nurses were likely to have training only in clinical skills, so many physicians began training them or other individuals to assist with all of the office duties. Community and junior colleges began offering training programs that focused on both administrative and clinical skills in the late 1940s. Medical assistant organizations at the local and state level began developing around 1950, and soon after, certifying examinations became available. Today medical assisting is one of the most respected allied health fields in the industry, and training is readily available through community colleges, junior colleges, and private educational institutions throughout the United States.

Allergy & infection

Chapter Review

Vocabulary Review

Fill in the blanks with the correct vocabulary terms from this chapter.

1. A physician who has been _____ has been charged with a crime but has not yet been tried in a court of law.

2. Physicians who conduct a great amount of research are often _____ in medical journals and articles within their field of study.

3. A new hospital contacts The Joint Commission to begin the _____ process, which will verify that the facility meets or exceeds standards.

Skills and Concepts

Part I: Pioneers in Medicine

Fill in the blanks.

4. The surgical research technician who contributed to the success of the Blalock-Taussig procedure was _____.

5. _____ presented rules of health to the Jews around 1205 BC, making him the first advocate of preventive medicine and the first public health officer.

6. _____ known as the father of medicine, was the most famous of the ancient Greek physicians, best remembered for an oath that has been taken by many physicians for more than 2000 years.

7. _____ was a Greek physician who migrated to Rome in 162 AD and became known as the "Prince of Physicians."

8. _____ was a Belgian anatomist who is known as the "Father of Modern Anatomy."

9. In 1628 _____ announced his discovery that the heart acts as a muscular pump, forcing and propelling the blood throughout the body.

10. _____ was the first to observe bacteria and protozoa through a lens.

11. The famous English scientist _____ is known as the "Founder of Scientific Surgery."

12. _____ observed that those who had contracted cowpox never contracted smallpox.

13. _____ directed that in his wards the students were to wash and disinfect their hands before going to examine women in labor and deliver infants.

14. _____ saved the dairy industry of France during the 19th century from disaster by developing a process now called *pasteurization*.

15. _____ reasoned that microorganisms must be the cause of infection and should be kept out of wounds.

16. _____ was the first to use ether as an anesthetic agent.

17. Marie and Pierre _____ discovered radium in 1898, and they were awarded the 1902 Nobel Prize in Physics for their work on radioactivity.

18. _____ is known as the founder of nursing and fondly called "The Lady With the Lamp."

19. In 1881 _____ organized a committee in Washington that became the American Red Cross.

20. _____ became the American leader of the birth control movement.

21. _____ _____ wrote about death and dying.

22. Salk and _____ almost eradicated polio, which was once a killer and crippler of thousands in the United States.

23. David _____, MD, is considered by many to be one of the most brilliant minds today helping to piece together the puzzle of the human immunodeficiency virus (HIV).

24. During his terms as the Surgeon General of the United States, _____ became a proponent of tobacco awareness, insisting that tobacco advertisements must be made less attractive to the youth of today.

Part II: Word Find

Use the answers from the previous section, and find the names of past and present leaders in the health care industry.

S	K	H	U	N	T	E	R	Q	T	W	L
E	E	O	S	S	G	R	E	N	N	E	J
M	O	L	O	H	M	E	I	B	C	V	M
M	H	I	P	P	O	C	R	A	T	E	S
E	N	S	C	Y	S	X	U	R	C	S	A
L	E	T	K	E	E	P	C	T	E	A	N
W	W	E	H	V	S	D	K	O	G	L	G
E	U	R	I	R	T	C	V	N	X	I	E
I	E	J	G	A	L	E	N	O	Z	U	R
S	E	E	K	H	W	B	P	B	X	S	K
S	L	O	N	G	V	S	A	B	I	N	M
E	L	A	G	N	I	T	H	G	I	N	Y
P	A	S	T	E	U	R	Z	F	M	G	E
F	Y	Z	S	A	M	O	H	T	X	M	O
K	U	B	L	E	R	R	O	S	S	C	T
O	B	T	S	K	O	O	P	L	D	N	C

Part III: Short Essay Questions

Answer the following questions using complete sentences.

25. Why was the education offered by Johns Hopkins University Medical School so effective in training physicians?

_____

_____

_____

26. Explain the differences between the two medical symbol icons discussed in the chapter and what each icon represents.

_____

_____

_____

27. Why is the history of medicine important to us today?

_____

_____

_____

28. Which ancient cultures contributed to the medical terminology we use today?

_____

_____

_____

29. Which medical pioneer do you feel contributed the most to medicine?

_____

_____

_____

Internet Activities

1. Choose one of the early medical pioneers discussed in this chapter, and research him or her using the Internet. After conducting the research, write a report and present the person to the class. Be creative with the presentation, using PowerPoint or some type of audiovisual equipment.

What Would You Do?

Carlos Santos, CMA (AAMA), is a medical assisting instructor with 10 years' experience in the clinical area. He worked for a group of family practitioners and for an allergist during his career as a medical assistant before becoming an instructor. Mr. Santos believes that it is very important to give his students an overview of the health care industry early in their training. He knows that it is exciting to show them the history and progress of medicine and introduce them to the current types of facilities available for patient care on both a national and a local level. This helps the student to understand where he or she fits into the whole picture as a medical assistant. Often Mr. Santos assigns the students a short report on one person who contributed to the progress of medicine. He finds that this is a good way to encourage the students to use the Internet and conduct research right from the start of their training; in addition, the students get a chance to grow more comfortable speaking in front of a group. The knowledge that the students will gain about the different areas of patient care will be useful once they graduate and begin working in a health care facility. All of these skills will make Mr. Santos's students more versatile and valuable to their eventual employers.

1. Why is continuing medical research so important to the health care industry?

_____

_____

_____

2. How can the individual medical assistant contribute to the progress of medicine in today's world?

_____

_____

_____

3. What is the value in gaining an overview of the entire health care industry as one begins a career in medical assisting?

_____

_____

_____

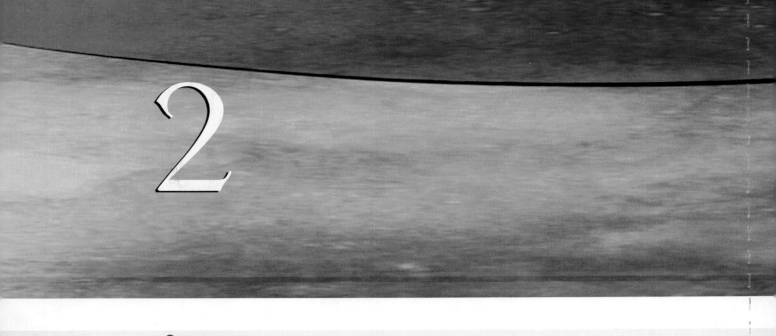

OBJECTIVES

You will be able to do the following after completing this chapter:

Key Terms
1. Define, appropriately use, and spell all the Key Terms for this chapter.

Medical Practice Settings
2. List four different types of medical practice settings.

Medical Specialties
3. Explain the difference between a family practitioner and a specialist.
4. Explain what it means to be "board certified."

The Professional Health Care Team
5. List the members of the professional health care team and explain their training and duties.
6. List five types of medical organizations in which a medical assistant can find employment.

Health Care Delivery Settings
7. Explain the importance of being knowledgeable about the various health care delivery settings in your community.
8. List seven health care delivery settings other than the medical office.

Patient-Centered Professionalism
9. Analyze a realistic medical office situation and apply your understanding of the diversity in health care delivery to determine the best course of action.
10. Describe the impact on patient care when medical assistants have a solid understanding of the various settings in which health care is provided and the various roles of health care professionals.

DIVERSITY IN HEALTH CARE DELIVERY

KEY TERMS

corporation Large business entity that has incorporated to avoid personal liability from the company's debts and taxes.

diversity Having a variety of skills or types.

entity A particular type of business.

group practice Practice owned by three or more people who are held legally responsible for the debts and taxes of the business.

management service organization (MSO) Organization (e.g., hospital) that handles patient services for a medical practice (e.g., billing and payment services).

partnership Business owned by two people who are held legally responsible for the debts and taxes of the business.

sole proprietorship Business owned by one person who is legally responsible for the debts and taxes of the business; also known as *private practice*.

specialization Focus on a particular work specialty that occurs when additional training and educational requirements have been met.

What Would You Do?

Diversity means "having variety." People are diverse in many ways. There is variety in people's size, shape, gender, age, race, and culture. Because people are so diverse, health care must be diverse as well. Health care must meet the needs of both the people seeking health care and the people delivering health care services. Examples of the diversity of health care delivery include the different types of medical practice settings, medical specialties, health care professionals, and even the settings in which health care is provided. It is important for you to learn about the various ways health care is delivered so that you can understand how the whole system works.

PATIENT-CENTERED PROFESSIONALISM

Take a moment to consider the impact of different events on various medical practice settings.

- How are the physicians in a corporate practice setting affected by a lawsuit as compared with a physician in a private practice setting?
- Why do you think most practices today are group and corporate practices?
- How might a patient's experience differ in each of the four types of medical practice settings?
- How might your experience as a medical assistant differ in each of the four types of medical practice settings? Which setting do you think you would prefer?

MEDICAL PRACTICE SETTINGS

A medical practice is a business **entity.** A business entity is basically a particular type of business, such as a medical practice. There are three major types of medical practices: private practice **(sole proprietorship), partnership** practice, and **group practice** (Table 2-1). A solo practice, or sole proprietorship, and a group practice may be a practice that has "incorporated," or become a **corporation.** Often, group and corporate practices have their patient billing and payment services handled by a **management service organization (MSO).** In this situation the physician is considered an employee of the MSO. Fees that a physician can charge are limited by the agreement signed by the MSO and the practice.

MEDICAL SPECIALTIES

Advances in technology have required physicians to seek additional training to keep their skills up to date. More and more physicians have decided to specialize in order to focus on the advances in one area. It is important for you to know about the various specialties so that you can make decisions about the type of practice in which you want to work. This knowledge will also help you when dealing with patients who are referred to different types of specialists for treatment.

TABLE 2-1 Differences among Medical Practice Settings			
	Private Practice (Sole Proprietorship)	**Partnership Practice**	**Group Practice**
Ownership	One owner May be incorporated	Two owners sharing the same specialty or different specialties	Three or more owners sharing the same specialty or multiple specialties
Life of the business	Ends when owner dies or closes practice	Ends when one partner dies or leaves, or when the practice closes	Ends when a predetermined number of owners die or leave, or when the practice closes, or shareholders vote to close; the physician can be replaced and the group continues
Liability	Owner is responsible for all debt of the practice	Each partner is responsible for debt of the practice and is liable for the other partner's actions; personal assets can be used for liabilities	The practice is responsible for the debt incurred (owners have "incorporated," or formed a corporation)
Advantages	Owner is sole decision-maker	More potential for profit; shared decision making	More potential for profit; shared decision making; shared facilities, equipment, and employees; many tax advantages
Disadvantages	Sole physician is responsible for patient care 24 hours a day	Partners may not have similar values; each partner is held responsible for the other's actions	Owners may not have similar values; each owner is held responsible for the actions of the other owners; individuals have less control over business decisions

Specialty Fields

Many physicians are family or general practitioners. *Family practitioners* are medical doctors that treat all ages from the newborn to the elderly. They diagnose and treat a variety of diseases and disorders, and they are patients' long-term health care providers or primary care physicians. When patients need more specialized care for specific conditions, they are referred to specialists. A *specialist* is a physician who has completed additional training and educational requirements to become more knowledgeable about specific conditions or medical areas. Table 2-2 provides an overview of some of the areas of **specialization** available. Table 2-3 lists other specialists not recognized as medical physicians who treat patients for certain disorders.

Specialty Boards and Certification

The additional training a physician can complete to become a specialist often involves a 3- to 7-year residency in the specialty area and a national board examination. There are many individual boards,

each governed by the American Board of Medical Specialists (ABMS) (Fig. 2-1). Continued training and education is an ongoing requirement even after board certification. The following three organizations offer recognition for additional training:

American College of Surgeons: Fellow of the American College of Surgeons (FACS)
American College of Physicians: Fellow of the American College of Physicians (FACP)
American College of Family Physicians: Fellow of the American College of Family Physicians (FACFP)

PATIENT-CENTERED PROFESSIONALISM

Take a moment to consider the advantages of specialization.
- How does the existence of medical specialties improve the care provided to all patients?
- How does specialization improve the care that a single physician can provide to patients?
- How does specialization improve the entire health care system?

TABLE 2-2 Medical Practice Specialties

Specialty	Specialist	Scope of Practice
Aerospace medicine	Aerospace medical specialist	Researches the effect of space environment on people
Allergy & immunology	Allergist-immunologist	Treats allergies and the immune system's response to contagious disease, transplantation, and immunizations
Anesthesiology	Anesthesiologist	Administers and maintains anesthesia during surgery; oversees pain management
Cardiology	Cardiologist	Provides noninvasive treatment for heart and vascular disease
Dermatology	Dermatologist	Treats diseases of the skin
Emergency medicine	Emergency physician, trauma physician	Treats acutely ill patients and trauma victims in emergency departments
Endocrinology	Endocrinologist	Treats diseases of the endocrine system
Gastroenterology	Gastroenterologist	Treats diseases of the digestive system
Gerontology	Gerontologist	Treats diseases of elderly persons
Gynecology	Gynecologist	Treats disorders of the female reproductive system
Hematology	Hematologist	Treats disorders of the blood
Infertility	Infertility specialist	Treats problems of conception and maintaining pregnancy
Internal medicine	Internist	Provides nonsurgical treatment of internal organs
Nephrology	Nephrologist	Treats diseases of the kidneys
Neurology	Neurologist	Provides nonsurgical treatment of the nervous system
Nuclear medicine	Nuclear medicine physician	Treats diseases with radionuclides
Obstetrics	Obstetrician-gynecologist	Provides care during pregnancy, delivery, and aftercare of women
Oncology	Oncologist	Treats all forms of cancer
Ophthalmology	Ophthalmologist	Treats disorders of the eye
Orthopedics	Orthopedist	Treats disorders of the musculoskeletal system
Otorhinolaryngology	✳ENT specialist, otorhinolaryngologist	Treats disorders of the ear, nose, and throat (ENT) _Allergy & cold_
Pathology	Pathologist	Examines tissue samples for signs of disease
Pediatrics	Pediatrician	Treats both well and sick children
Plastic surgery	Surgeon	Performs restorative (e.g., cancer, burns) and cosmetic (e.g., "facelift") surgery
Psychiatry	Psychiatrist	Treats mental, behavioral, and emotional disorders
Radiology	Radiologist	Uses x-ray films to diagnose and treat disease
Surgery	Surgeon	Treats disease and trauma by surgical procedures
Urology	Urologist	Treats the male and female urologic and reproductive systems

TABLE 2-3 Additional Medical Specialties

Specialty	Specialist	Degree	Scope of Practice
Chiropractic medicine	Chiropractor	DC	Treats the patient by manipulation of the spine to relieve musculoskeletal disorders
Dentistry	Dentist	DDS	Treats diseases and disorders of the teeth and gums
Naprapathy	Naprapath	DN	Specialist in treatment of myofascial disorders
Naturopathy	Naturopath	ND	Holistic treatment focusing on disease prevention and treatments using physical methods
Optometry	Optometrist	OD	Tests vision and prepares lenses to correct refractive problems
Oral surgery	Oral surgeon	DMD	Treats dental disorders requiring surgery
Podiatry	Podiatrist	DPM	Treats disorders of the feet
Psychology	Psychologist	MA and/or PhD	Counsels patients with stress or emotion-related disorders

American Board of Allergy and Immunology
American Board of Anesthesiology
American Board of Colon and Rectal Surgery
American Board of Dermatology
American Board of Emergency Medicine
American Board of Family Practice
American Board of Internal Medicine
American Board of Medical Genetics
American Board of Neurological Surgery
American Board of Nuclear Medicine
American Board of Obstetrics and Gynecology
American Board of Ophthalmology
American Board of Otolaryngology
American Board of Pathology
American Board of Pediatrics
American Board of Physical Medicine and Rehabilitation
American Board of Plastic Surgery
American Board of Preventive Medicine
American Board of Psychiatry and Neurology
American Board of Radiology
American Board of Surgery
American Board of Thoracic Surgery
American Board of Urology

Fig. 2-1 American medical boards.

THE PROFESSIONAL HEALTH CARE TEAM

The physician and all the other allied professionals in a medical setting make up a team. The team works together to provide health care services to a community. From the time the patient schedules an appointment, many members of the health care team are involved in providing quality care (Fig. 2-2). As a medical assistant, you need to know about the role of each member of the team so that you can help the team in caring for patients.

Physician

Hippocrates, known as the "Father of Medicine," was the first to document the disease process. Today, the physician is the health care team member solely responsible for diagnosing and treating patients. Each state establishes licensing requirements through its medical board. Two often-confused types of licensed physicians are the Doctor of Medicine (MD) and the Doctor of Osteopathy (DO) (Table 2-4).

TABLE 2-4	Doctor of Medicine (MD) Compared with Doctor of Osteopathy (DO)			
	Type of Doctor	**Emphasis**	**Training**	**Licensing**
MD	Medical	Treats specific symptoms of disease and injury Family practitioner, internist, or specialty area	Graduation from 4-year college with emphasis on scientific courses Completion of 4 years of medical school Completion of a residency (intensive hospital-based training) Option to practice in a specialty area with additional 2 to 6 years of training (e.g., surgery, psychiatry)	Must pass series of examinations in the state where MD will practice Must meet the established criteria set by the medical board in that state
DO	Medical	Uses the "whole person" approach to medicine. Assesses overall health of patient to include home and work environment, focusing on the musculoskeletal system. Primary care physicians	Same as for MD	Same as for MD

Fig. 2-2 Patients depend on many professionals to assist with their health care treatment. **A,** Medical assistant makes an appointment for a patient. **B,** Medical assistant greets a patient arriving for her appointment. **C,** Medical technologist processes a patient's laboratory specimen to assist the physician with a diagnosis. **D,** Physician interacts with a patient. **E,** Medical assistant discusses the office visit charges with the patient.

Physician Assistant

The physician assistant (PA) can perform certain procedures under the physician's supervision. As a member of the health care team, the PA can perform the following duties:

1. Take medical histories.
2. Examine and treat patients.
3. Order and interpret laboratory tests and x-rays.
4. Make diagnoses.
5. Prescribe medications.

In some rural areas and inner-city clinics, PAs may function as the principal provider and confer with other medical professionals as needed or as required by law. The PA should not be confused with the medical assistant. PA training requires completing a formalized program of college credit and clinical experience.

Nurse

Nursing is a profession in health care that provides for a patient's well-being. Nurses have a wide range of responsibilities depending on their educational background and skills. At one time they worked solely in the hospital and nursing home settings, but they now work in many settings, including medical clinics, home health care, hospices, and schools. All nurses are licensed by their state after passing an examination.

Nurse Practitioner

The nurse practitioner (NP) is schooled in the typical duties of a nurse but has additional training and education for diagnosis and treatment in a specialized field (e.g., family nurse practitioner [FNP], American registered nurse practitioner [ARNP]). The NP receives a Master's of Science in Nursing (MSN). Often this is the first professional seen by a patient for common illnesses and injuries (Fig. 2-3). In some states the NP can prescribe medications.

Registered Nurse

The registered nurse (RN) has the typical bedside care duties but can also perform administrative and supervisory responsibilities. RNs must have 2 to 4 years of college and pass the National Council Licensure Examination (NCLEX-RN).

Licensed Practical Nurse and Licensed Vocational Nurse

The licensed practical nurse (LPN) or licensed vocational nurse (LVN) is trained in basic nursing duties and works under the supervision of the RN or physician. The LPN has passed the NCLEX-PN. LPN and

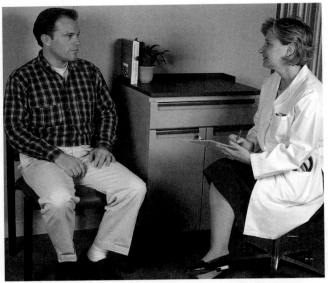

Fig. 2-3 A nurse practitioner can diagnose and treat common acute illnesses. *(From Jarvis C:* Physical examination and health assessment, *ed 4, Philadelphia, 2004, Saunders.)*

LVN duties are usually limited under state law. This credential can be upgraded to RN with additional educational credits and clinical training.

Certified Nursing Assistant

The certified nursing assistant (CNA) completes a state-approved course that includes a skills examination. The CNA provides basic patient care in a variety of settings, including hospitals, long-term care facilities, and home health care. The CNA's duties include personal care (e.g., bathing, hygiene), assisting with food service, and taking vital signs.

Medical Assistant

A certified medical assistant (certified by the American Association of Medical Assistants) (CMA [AAMA]) or registered medical assistant (RMA) has completed an accredited medical assistant program and passed a national examination. The MA works under the direct supervision of a licensed physician. Many skills are needed to perform a wide variety of duties. MAs perform clinical duties such as drawing blood, performing basic laboratory tests, and assisting with examinations and procedures. They also perform administrative (office-related) duties, including scheduling appointments and billing. In addition, the MA provides valuable patient education and a communication pathway between the physician and the patient (Fig. 2-4). MAs work not only in medical offices and clinics, but also in hospitals, research centers, insurance companies, and correctional institutions.

Other Allied Health Professionals

In addition to physicians, physician assistants, nurses, and medical assistants, other allied health professionals are involved with patient care. Fig. 2-5 lists some of the many health care professionals you may encounter on a day-to-day basis.

PATIENT-CENTERED PROFESSIONALISM

Take a moment to consider the importance of clarifying your role as medical assistant to patients.

- What would you do if a patient referred to you as a nurse?
- Does it really matter if a medical assistant is thought of as a nurse or if a nurse or physician assistant is thought of as a physician?
- Why is it important for all health care professionals to practice within their scope of training?
- How might a patient feel if she finds out later that the health professional she thought was a nurse was actually a medical assistant? What are some actions the patient might take?

Fig. 2-4 A medical assistant provides valuable education and information to the patient.

HEALTH CARE DELIVERY SETTINGS

The medical office is one type of health care delivery setting. As a medical assistant, one of your responsibilities will be to assist in referring patients to a variety of other health care delivery settings. For example, the primary care physician may want patients to go to an outside laboratory for blood work, a diagnostic center for x-ray films, or to a specialist such as an endocrinologist for further evaluation. In addition, patients may require assistance at home after a hospital stay or long-term illness. This may require the intervention of a home health care agency or hospice. You need to know about not only the various health-related services patients need, but also the types of services offered in your community. Being knowledgeable about other health care delivery settings benefits patients. It allows you to interact efficiently with the health care professionals in other settings to coordinate the services patients need. The health care delivery settings most often used by patients and their families are as follows:

- **Hospital:** Provides inpatient care and treatment for acute (serious) conditions.
- **Ambulatory surgery center:** Provides outpatient services for surgery, with patients admitted and discharged on the same day.
- **Short-term care facility:** Provides a place for patients who cannot function on their own after being discharged from the hospital. Restorative care is provided so that the patient can return home.
- **Long-term care facility (skilled nursing home):** Provides 24-hour-a-day nursing services to those who are unable to function on their own on a long-term basis.
- **Assisted living facility:** Provides services and assistance to people who require minimal help, such as with cooking, laundry, and medications.

Medical Technologist
Clinical Laboratory Technician
Histologist
Cytotechnologist
Phlebotomist

Registered Dietitian
EKG Technician
Health Information Technologist
Respiratory Therapist
Physical Therapist
Occupational Therapist
Unit Secretary
Radiology Technologist
Medical Secretary
Medical Transcriptionist
Registered EMT
Medical Assistant

Pharmacist
Pharmacy Technician

Surgical Technologist

Fig. 2-5 Allied health professionals.

- **Home health care agency:** A contracted service that provides for the social and medical needs of patients in their homes.
- **Hospice care:** Assists and meets the needs of terminally ill patients and their families.

PATIENT-CENTERED PROFESSIONALISM

Take a moment to consider the importance of being knowledgeable about the various types of health care delivery settings.

- Are medical office staff qualified and prepared to deliver any type of care a patient might need?
- How might a terminally ill patient and his family be affected by a medical assistant who is not aware of the types of services such as hospice care? What is the difference a knowledgeable medical assistant could make to the patient and family in this situation?
- How can a medical assistant who knows about the health care delivery services in the community influence the entire community's opinion of the medical clinic?

CONCLUSION

All health care professionals must perform only the duties listed under their scope of practice. If they take on the duties of professionals without the proper training, education, and licensure, they can be found guilty of practicing without a license. Physicians who allow their employees to perform duties for which they are not qualified can be found guilty for permitting this to happen. Medical boards and state legislators have established consequences for these unethical and illegal choices. Understanding your duties and training and the duties and training of other members of the health care team helps you make the right choices.

SUMMARY

Reinforce your understanding of the material in this chapter by reviewing the curriculum objectives and key content points below.

1. Define, appropriately use, and spell all the Key Terms for this chapter.
   - Review the Key Terms if necessary.
2. List three different types of medical practice settings.
   - A private practice (sole proprietorship) is a practice owned by one person who is legally responsible for the debts and taxes of the business.
   - A partnership is a practice owned by two people who are held legally responsible for the debts and taxes of the business and whose personal assets may be used for liabilities of the practice.
   - A group practice is a practice owned by three or more people who are held legally responsible for the debts and taxes of the business. Group practices can be corporate practices or professional associations.
3. Explain the difference between a family practitioner and a specialist.
   - Family practitioners treat patients of all ages, from newborns to elderly persons.
   - Physicians in specialty fields provide patients with current procedures and up-to-date information in their specialty.
   - Specialty fields are based on a specific condition (e.g., asthma) or medical area (e.g., orthopedics).
4. Explain what it means to be "board certified."
   - Physicians can take additional training to gain proficiency in a specialty.
   - Physicians are considered board certified once they have completed the additional training and examination required by the national board of their specialty.
5. List the members of the professional health care team and explain their training and duties.
   - A medical physician can be an MD or a DO.
   - A nurse requires a license to work and may work in one of several categories (i.e., nurse practitioner, registered nurse, licensed practical nurse, or licensed vocational nurse).
   - A physician assistant performs routine diagnostic procedures and works under the physician's supervision.
   - A medical assistant is a multiskilled professional who is knowledgeable about both administrative and clinical procedures.
   - Other allied health care professionals work with various members of the team daily.
6. List five types of medical organizations in which a medical assistant can find employment.
   - Medical assistants work in medical offices and clinics, hospitals, research centers, insurance companies, and correctional institutions.
7. Explain the importance of being knowledgeable about the various health care delivery settings in your community.
   - Medical assistants interact with health care professionals in other delivery settings to coordinate services needed by patients and their families.

- Being aware of the various health care delivery settings in your community helps you provide better care to patients.

8. List seven health care delivery settings other than the medical office.
   - Hospitals, ambulatory surgery centers, short-term care facilities, long-term care facilities, assisted living facilities, home health care agencies, and hospice care are the most common types of health care delivery settings outside of the medical office.

9. Analyze a realistic medical office situation and apply your understanding of the diversity in health care delivery to determine the best course of action.
   - Understanding the setting in which you work allows you to operate effectively within that setting.
   - Always stay within the scope of your practice.

10. Describe the impact on patient care when medical assistants have a solid understanding of the various settings in which health care is provided and the various roles of health care professionals.

- Medical assistants must understand their role, as well as the role of the other health care professionals with whom they work.
- When health care professionals work together as a team, patients benefit.

FOR FURTHER EXPLORATION

1. **Research osteopathic medicine to learn more about the practices and beliefs of DOs.** The difference between an MD and a DO can be confusing. Although both are medical doctors, their training is based on different beliefs about how treatment should be provided.
   Keywords: Use the following keyword in your search: Doctor of Osteopathic Medicine.

2. **Research allopathic physicians to discover what they do.** Although you learned about some of the different medical specialties in this chapter, many more exist. It is helpful for medical assistants to know about the various medical specialties.
   Keywords: Use the following keyword in your search: allopathic physician.

THERAPEUTIC PROCEDURES

Casts
18. Explain the purpose of a cast.
19. Demonstrate the correct procedure for providing supplies and assistance during plaster-of-Paris or fiberglass cast application and instructing the patient in cast care and nutritional requirements for healing.
20. Describe the process of cast removal, and explain patient instructions that medical assistants may need to provide during the procedure.

Range-of-Motion Exercises
21. Demonstrate correct technique for performing range-of-motion exercises

Patient-Centered Professionalism
22. Analyze a realistic medical office situation and apply your understanding of therapeutic procedures to determine the best course of action.
23. Describe the impact on patient care when medical assistants understand the purpose and use of therapeutic procedures in the medical office.

KEY TERMS

air cast Device that is inflated with air to immobilize an injured area.

ambulation device Any device that assists a patient to walk.

axillary crutches Devices that aid in walking and fit under the armpit.

cane Hand-held mobility device that provides minimal support for walking.

cast Plaster or fiberglass mold applied to immobilize a body part.

cast cutter Instrument used to divide a cast for removal.

cast padding Cotton material applied over a stockinette to protect the skin and to prevent pressure sores over bony areas.

cast spreader Instrument used to open the cast after it has been cut for removal.

chemical hot/cold pack Device that uses a chemical action to produce heat or cold.

cold therapy Therapy using ice or cold application to reduce or prevent swelling by decreasing circulatory flow to the injured body part.

compress Folded pad of soft absorbent material used for hot or cold therapy.

coupling agent Water-soluble lotion or gel used to transmit energy provided by an ultrasound wand.

crutches Devices that assist in walking when full weight cannot be placed on an injured lower extremity.

fiberglass cast Cast made of fiberglass or plastic resin tapes.

forearm (Lofstrand) crutches Devices that provide contact with the hand and forearm.

gait patterns Patterns of walking used with crutches.

goniometer Instrument used to measure angles.

heat therapy Therapy that uses application of heat to increase blood flow to a body area.

heating pad Electrical device that delivers a set temperature of heat for heat therapy.

hot water bag Device that holds water warm enough to increase blood flow for heat therapy.

ice bag Device that holds ice for cold therapy.

orthopedist Physician whose specialty is to correct musculoskeletal disorders.

plaster cast Mold that is made by wetting bandages that contain plaster that hardens when it dries to immobilize a body part.

platform crutches Devices used for walking that provide a shelflike device to support the forearms and a handgrip.

pressure ulcer Ulcer created when the skin over a bony area has contact and pressure with an irritating source for long periods causing ulceration or breakdown of the skin.

soak Procedure that requires a body part to be immersed in water warm enough to increase blood flow to an area or cold enough to slow blood flow to an area.

stockinette Knitted cotton material used over extremities to cover an area before application of cast material.

synthetic cast Limb immobilizer made of fiberglass used for simple fractures and sprains.

therapeutic procedures Procedures done to enhance the body's healing processes and assist in patient mobility.

ultrasound therapy Therapy that uses high-frequency sound waves to produce heat and vibrations to aid in the healing of inflammation in soft tissue.

walker Lightweight mobility device providing a stable platform that is used when a patient needs optimal stability and support.

What Would You Do?

Read the following scenario and keep it in mind as you learn about taking patients' medical history in the office.

Lynn is a medical assistant in a family practice setting. She is responsible for assisting Dr. James, performing prescribed procedures, and communicating instructions for home care. Judy Crissip, a 73-year-old patient of Dr. James, comes to the office complaining of joint stiffness, swelling, and discomfort that are decreasing her ability to continue with her social and recreational activities.

Dr. James completes his examination and tells Ms. Crissip that he did not observe any redness or feel warmth in her joints and is therefore ordering x-rays of her affected joints to confirm his initial diagnosis of a degenerative joint disease called osteoporosis. He prescribes 800 mg of ibuprofen, t.i.d., and heat and cold applications several times a day. Dr. James asks Lynn to provide Ms. Crissip with instructions for self-administering heat and cold therapy at home.

Therapeutic procedures are performed to enhance the body's healing processes. These procedures also can assist patients in their mobility. Physicians prescribe various therapeutic treatments and order therapeutic devices based on a patient's condition and the desired outcome. The medical assistant must understand and be able to use the proper techniques for heat and cold therapy, ultrasound therapy, and measurement of patients for ambulatory devices. In addition, the assistant must provide instructions to patients on the use of these procedures. The medical assistant may also be asked to assist the physician with the application and removal of casts. Box 3-1 reviews charting requirements when documenting therapeutic procedures.

By performing these techniques effectively, the medical assistant can provide comfort and support to the patient while aiding in the healing process.

BOX 3-1 **Documentation when Charting Therapeutic Procedures**

1. Date
2. Time
3. Name or explanation of therapeutic procedure performed stating exact location on body
4. Results
5. Patient reaction, if any. If no reaction, can state, "Pt. tolerated procedure well."
6. Proper signature and credential

≋ COLD AND HEAT THERAPY

Hot and cold packs are effective tools for pain control. When applied alone or in combination, heat and cold therapy often provide relief not only from the pain itself, but also from accompanying swelling or infection. Each therapy causes physiological changes within the tissue.

Overuse of either hot or cold therapy may cause the opposite of the desired therapeutic effect. Heat normally causes blood vessels to dilate, thus increasing blood supply to the surrounding tissues. Prolonged heat could cause the opposite: constriction and reduced blood supply. Cold normally causes blood vessels to constrict and decreases the blood supply to the surrounding tissues. Prolonged cold could cause the opposite: dilation and increased blood supply. Timing of either therapy is essential to produce the desired effect.

Cold Therapy

Cold therapy is used to reduce or prevent swelling by temporarily decreasing circulatory flow to the injured body part. The use of cold applications causes the blood vessels to constrict, decreasing the blood supply to an area. The decrease in blood supply slows cellular growth and reduces bleeding.

Cold therapy is often prescribed after excessive muscle use, such as physical therapy, as a temporary anesthetic for burns, or it may be the initial treatment for an eye injury (e.g., black eye). Physicians may prescribe cold therapy to be followed by heat therapy 24 to 48 hours later or after swelling is brought under control. Methods of cold application include the ice bag, cold compress, and chemical cold pack.

Ice Bag
An **ice bag** is a device that holds ice cubes or ice chips so they can be applied to an area of the body to reduce swelling. Small cubes or ice chips are preferred because they allow the ice bag to mold easily. A protective covering must be applied to protect the patient's skin. Procedure 3-1 explains how to apply an ice bag to a swollen area.

Procedure 3-1 Apply an Ice Bag

TASK: Properly apply an ice bag to a swollen area.

EQUIPMENT AND SUPPLIES
- Ice bag with protective covering
- Small pieces of ice (ice chips or crushed ice)
- Patient's medical record

SKILLS/RATIONALE

STANDARD PRECAUTIONS ARE TO BE FOLLOWED.

1. **Procedural Step. Sanitize the hands.**
   An alcohol-based hand rub may be used instead of washing hands with soap and water, unless hands are visibly soiled.
   Rationale. Hand sanitization promotes infection control.

2. **Procedural Step. Assemble equipment and supplies.**
   Check the ice bag for leaks.
   Rationale. It is important to have all supplies and equipment ready and available before starting any procedure to ensure efficiency. A leaking bag will get the patient wet and cause chilling.

3. **Procedural Step. Obtain the patient's medical record.**

4. **Procedural Step. Escort the patient to the examination room, and greet and identify the patient.**
   Rationale. Identifying the patient ensures the procedure is performed on the correct patient.

5. **Procedural Step. Explain the procedure to the patient.**
   Rationale. Explaining the procedure to the patient promotes cooperation and provides a means of obtaining implied consent.

6. **Procedural Step. Fill the bag one-half to two-thirds full with crushed or chipped ice.**
   Rationale. Small pieces of ice work better than larger pieces because they reduce the amount of air space in the bag, resulting in better conduction of cold. In addition, small pieces of ice allow the bag to mold better to the body area.

7. **Procedural Step. Compress the empty top half of the bag to remove the air, and replace the cap.**
   Rationale. The ice bag will mold to the affected area of the body more readily if the air has been removed from the bag, and removing the air keeps the bag colder for a longer period.

8. **Procedural Step. Dry the outside of the bag, and place the bag inside a protective covering.**
   The protective covering may be a disposable premade covering or simply a terrycloth towel.
   Rationale. The protective covering absorbs moisture that may be caused by condensation on the outside of the bag and provides more comfort for the patient.

9. **Procedural Step. Apply the ice bag to the affected area, and ask the patient if the temperature is tolerable.**
   Rationale. Application of cold is typically uncomfortable, but the patient will have more tolerance if you have explained the procedure and the patient understands the principle or reasoning behind the application.

10. **Procedural Step. Leave the ice bag in place for the time prescribed by the physician.**
    The duration is typically 20 to 30 minutes. Check the patient's skin every few minutes for any signs of increased redness or swelling, a mottled blue appearance, or extreme paleness. Ask the patient whether the area being treated is painful. If so, or if any of the conditions listed is apparent, remove the bag and notify the physician.

11. **Procedural Step. Refill the bag with ice and change the protective covering as needed.**

12. **Procedural Step. Provide verbal and written follow-up instructions to the patient.**

Procedure 3-1 Apply an Ice Bag—cont'd

13. **Procedural Step. Sanitize the hands.**
    Always sanitize the hands after every procedure or after using gloves.
14. **Procedural Step. Document the procedure.**
    Include the date and time, method of cold application (ice bag), location and duration of the application, appearance of the application site, and the patient's reaction.
15. **Procedural Step. Properly care for the ice bag and covering, and return them to storage.**
    Drain the contents from the ice bag, and dispose of or launder the protective covering as required. Clean the bag with detergent and warm water, rinse, and allow the bag to air-dry by hanging it upside down with the cap off.

Allow the bag to fill with air, and replace the cap before returning the bag to storage.
Rationale. *Allowing air to remain inside the bag with the cap on during storage prevents the sides from sticking together and the fabric from deteriorating.*

Charting Example

Date	
12/30/xx	9:30 a.m. Ice bag applied to ® wrist × 15 min. No complaints of discomfort, area is pink. Verbal & written instructions for home use provided. Pt. verbalized understanding of instructions.————————— S. Jones, CMA (AAMA)

Photo from Zakus SM: *Mosby's clinical skills for medical assistants,* ed 4, St Louis, 2001, Mosby.

*15-20 min
    cold compress

Cold Compress

A **compress** is made of a soft, absorbent material (e.g., gauze squares, washcloth) and is moistened before being applied to a body part in order to penetrate the tissues more deeply. Cold compresses reduce pain caused by swelling, headaches, and injuries to an area. Procedure 3-2 describes the process of applying a cold compress to an affected area.

Chemical Hot/Cold Pack

A **chemical hot/cold pack** can also be used to relieve swelling in an area. A pack is activated when pressure is applied on the inner bag and it ruptures. Water is released into a larger bag, and the chemical reaction between the water and chemical crystals produces a warmth or coldness that lasts for 30 to 60 minutes. These bags are disposable and must be discarded when the effectiveness has worn off. Procedure 3-3 explains the process of applying a chemical cold pack.

Heat Therapy

Heat therapy, or the application of heat on the skin, is used to treat an infectious condition or a traumatized body area. Heat treatments are used to relieve discomfort from deep muscle tissue and muscle strains and spasms. Once swelling from an injury has been reduced (e.g., by cold therapy or 24 to 48 hours after injury), heat also provides comfort and aids the healing process by increasing blood flow to an area.

When heat is applied to a body surface, the blood vessels dilate. This results in an increased blood supply to the area, promoting growth of new cells and tissues by removing wastes faster and increasing nutrients to the site. The physician will specify the type of treatment, frequency, and duration.

To prevent injury to a patient, the medical assistant must carefully observe temperature and skin condition when applying any heat therapy to avoid burning or overheating. Heat therapy must *not* be applied if the following conditions exist:

- Major circulatory problems
- Pregnancy (heat could prematurely start uterine contractions)
- Damaged skin areas (e.g., blisters, burns, or scar tissue caused by poor circulation in the area or on existing reddened skin)

Methods of heat application include the hot water bag, heating pad, hot compress, and hot soak.

Hot Water Bag

A **hot water bag** is a device used to hold water warm enough to increase the blood supply to an area. The bag is filled one-third to one-half full of water, and the excess air is expelled from the bag (as air is a poor conductor of temperature). This allows the bag to mold more easily to the affected part. A protective covering placed over the bag helps absorb perspiration and reduces the risk of burns to the patient. Procedure 3-4 describes the process of applying a hot water bag.

Heating Pad

Although such pads are not frequently used in the medical office, the physician may recommend the patient use a **heating pad** at home. The medical assistant must be able to instruct the patient in its proper application.

The heating pad consists of a group of wires that take electrical energy and convert it to heat. The wires must never be bent because this would damage the pad and could result in overheating and a possible fire. No pins or wet dressings are used because they could result in an electrical shock to the patient. A heating pad should not be in place for longer than

30 minutes and should never be placed on the high setting to avoid the potential for burns. The patient should be instructed not to use the pad when sleeping. Also, after 30 minutes, the therapeutic effect greatly diminishes and may even have the reverse effect. Procedure 3-5 explains the process of applying a heating pad.

Hot Compress

As with cold compresses, hot compresses are made of soft, absorbent materials and are moist when applied to penetrate the tissues more deeply. Hot compresses are used to increase circulation to an area for healing purposes. Procedure 3-6 explains how to apply a hot compress to increase circulation.

Text continued on p. 47

Procedure 3-2 **Apply a Cold Compress**

TASK: Properly apply a cold compress to an affected area.

EQUIPMENT AND SUPPLIES
- Ice cubes
- Washcloths or gauze squares (compress)
- Basin
- Towel
- Ice bag
- Patient's medical record

SKILLS/RATIONALE

STANDARD PRECAUTIONS ARE TO BE FOLLOWED.

1. **Procedural Step. Sanitize the hands.**
   An alcohol-based hand rub may be used instead of washing hands with soap and water, unless hands are visibly soiled.
   Rationale. Hand sanitization promotes infection control.

2. **Procedural Step. Assemble equipment and supplies.**
   Rationale. It is important to have all supplies and equipment ready and available before starting any procedure to ensure efficiency.

3. **Procedural Step. Prepare the water by placing a small amount of cold water in a basin and adding large ice cubes.**
   Rationale. Small ice cubes, ice chips, or crushed ice will stick to the compress. Using larger ice cubes also slows the rate at which the ice melts, keeping the water colder for a longer period.

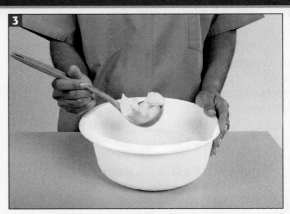

4. **Procedural Step. Prepare an ice bag following the steps in Procedure 3-1.**
5. **Procedural Step. Obtain the patient's medical record.**
6. **Procedural Step. Escort the patient to the examination room, and greet and identify the patient.**

Procedure 3-2 Apply a Cold Compress—cont'd

Rationale. Identifying the patient ensures the procedure is performed on the correct patient.

7. Procedural Step. Explain the procedure to the patient.
Rationale. Explaining the procedure to the patient promotes cooperation and provides a means of obtaining implied consent.

8. Procedural Step. Immerse the compress into the cold water, and wring the compress until it is moist but not dripping wet.

9. Procedural Step. Apply the compress gradually and gently to the affected area, allowing the patient to adjust progressively to the cold. Cover the compress with an ice bag.
Rationale. Application of cold is typically uncomfortable, but the patient will have more tolerance if it is applied gradually and gently to the affected area. Covering the compress with an ice bag helps to keep the compress colder for a longer time, reducing how frequently the compress needs to be changed.

10. Procedural Step. Ask the patient how the temperature feels.

11. Procedural Step. Place additional compresses in the cold water to be ready for use as needed.

12. Procedural Step. Repeat the application of the compress every 2 to 3 minutes for the duration specified by the physician.
The duration is usually 15 to 20 minutes.
NOTE: If an ice bag is used on top of the compress, the compress will not need to be replaced as frequently.

13. Procedural Step. Check the patient's skin periodically for signs of blueness or numbness, and ask the patient whether the site is painful.
If any of these conditions is apparent, remove the bag and notify the physician.

14. Procedural Step. Add ice if needed to keep the water cold.

15. Procedural Step. Thoroughly dry the affected area with a dry towel.

16. Procedural Step. Provide verbal and written follow-up instructions to the patient.

17. Procedural Step. Sanitize the hands.
Always sanitize the hands after every procedure or after using gloves.

18. Procedural Step. Document the procedure.
Include the date and time, method of cold application (cold compress), location and duration of the application, appearance of the application site, and the patient's reaction.

19. Procedural Step. Properly care for the equipment and return it to storage.
Launder or dispose of compresses and towels. If an ice bag is used, refer to Procedure 3-1 for proper storage of the ice bag.

Charting Example

Date	
11/10/xx	1:45 p.m. Cold compresses applied to ® cheek × 15 min. Area appears less swollen, and pt. states pain has lessened. Verbal and written instructions provided for patient follow-up care. —J. Wittenburg, CMA (AAMA)

Photo from Bonewit-West K: *Clinical procedures for medical assistants,* ed 6, Philadelphia, 2004, Saunders.

Procedure 3-3 Apply a Chemical Cold Pack

TASK: Properly activate and apply a chemical cold pack.

EQUIPMENT AND SUPPLIES
- Chemical cold pack
- Protective covering
- Patient's medical record

SKILLS/RATIONALE

STANDARD PRECAUTIONS ARE TO BE FOLLOWED.
1. Procedural Step. Sanitize the hands.

An alcohol-based hand rub may be used instead of washing hands with soap and water, unless hands are visibly soiled.
Rationale. Hand sanitization promotes infection control.

Continued

Procedure 3-3 Apply a Chemical Cold Pack—cont'd

2 **Procedural Step. Assemble equipment and supplies.**
Rationale. It is important to have all supplies and equipment ready and available before starting any procedure to ensure efficiency.

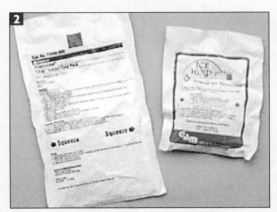

3. **Procedural Step. Obtain the patient's medical record.**
4. **Procedural Step. Escort the patient to the examination room, and greet and identify the patient.**
Rationale. Identifying the patient ensures the procedure is performed on the correct patient.
5. **Procedural Step. Explain the procedure to the patient.**
Rationale. Explaining the procedure to the patient promotes cooperation and provides a means of obtaining implied consent.
6. **Procedural Step. Follow the manufacturer's instructions to activate the chemical reaction creating the cold pack.**
The following steps are typical for most chemical cold packs:

a. Shake the chemical crystals to the bottom of the bag.
b. Apply firm pressure to the center of the bag to break the inner water bag.
c. Shake the bag vigorously to mix the contents.

7. **Procedural Step. Apply a cover to the bag and apply to the affected area.**
Rationale. Cold packs must never be placed directly on the patient's skin. A cover also protects the patient's skin from chemical burns if the bag leaks.
8. **Procedural Step. Administer the treatment for the proper length of time, as ordered by the physician.**
Most chemical cold packs will remain cold for up to 60 minutes.
9. **Procedural Step. Discard the bag in an appropriate receptacle.**
10. **Procedural Step. Provide necessary verbal and written follow-up instructions to the patient.**
Rationale. The physician may provide a patient with a chemical ice pack to take home and use, so it is important that you provide the patient with thorough instructions.
11. **Procedural Step. Sanitize the hands.**
Always sanitize the hands after every procedure or after using gloves.
12 **Procedural Step. Document the procedure as you would for any cold application.**

Charting Example

Date	
10/20/xx	3:30 p.m. Cold pack applied to Ⓡ forearm × 15 min. No complaints of discomfort, area is pink. Verbal & written instructions for home use provided. Pt. verbalized understanding of instructions. ———C. Martin, CMA (AAMA)

Photo from Zakus SM: *Mosby's clinical skills for medical assistants*, ed 4, St Louis, 2001, Mosby.

Procedure 3-4 Apply a Hot Water Bag

TASK: Properly fill and apply a hot water bag to an affected area.

EQUIPMENT AND SUPPLIES
- Hot water bag with protective covering
- Pitcher to hold water
- Bath thermometer
- Patient's medical record

Procedure 3-4 Apply a Hot Water Bag—cont'd

SKILLS/RATIONALE

STANDARD PRECAUTIONS ARE TO BE FOLLOWED.

1. **Procedural Step. Sanitize the hands.**
   An alcohol-based hand rub may be used instead of washing hands with soap and water, unless hands are visibly soiled.
   Rationale. Hand sanitization promotes infection control.

2. **Procedural Step. Assemble equipment and supplies.**
   Rationale. It is important to have all supplies and equipment ready and available before starting any procedure to ensure efficiency.

3. **Procedural Step. Obtain the patient's medical record.**

4. **Procedural Step. Escort the patient to the examination room, greet and identify the patient, and ask the patient to have a seat on the end of the examination table.**
   Rationale. Identifying the patient ensures the procedure is performed on the correct patient.

5. **Procedural Step. Explain the procedure to the patient.**
   Rationale. Explaining the procedure to the patient promotes cooperation and provides a means of obtaining implied consent.

6. **Procedural Step. Prepare the water to be used in the hot water bag.**
   Fill a pitcher with hot tap water. Test the temperature of the water with a bath thermometer. It should range between 115° and 125° F (46° and 52° C) for adults and older children and between 105° and 115° F (41° and 46° C) for infants, children under 2 years of age, and elderly patients.
   NOTE: If the water temperature cannot be measured, the temperature should be adjusted to body comfort.
   Rationale. The temperature should never exceed 125° F (52° C) to avoid burning the patient.

7. **Procedural Step. Fill the hot water bag one-third to one-half full of water.**
   A hot water bag that is not completely full is lighter and easier to mold to the body area.

8. **Procedural Step. Expel the excess air from the bag.**
   Rest the bag on the table and flatten it while holding the neck upright until the water reaches the neck. Air can also be expelled by holding the bag upright and squeezing the unfilled part until the water reaches the neck screw in the

stopper, or fastening the top with special closure tabs.
Rationale. Air is a poor conductor of heat and also makes it difficult to mold the hot water bag to the body area.

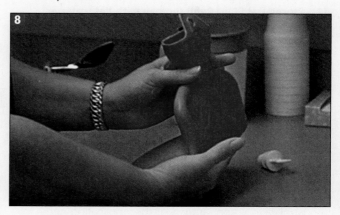

9. **Procedural Step. Dry the outside of the bag and test for leakage by holding the bag upside down.**
   Rationale. Leaking water will get the patient wet and may burn the patient.

10. **Procedural Step. Place the bag in the protective covering.**
    Rationale. The cover helps absorb perspiration and lessens the danger of burning the patient.

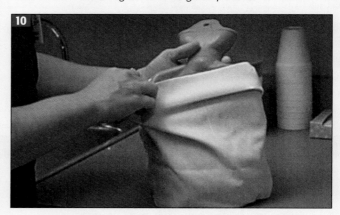

11. **Procedural Step. Place the patient in a position of comfort, and place the bag on the patient's affected body area.**
    Ask the patient how the temperature feels. The hot water bag should feel warm but not uncomfortable.
    Rationale. Individuals vary in their ability to tolerate heat.

Continued

Procedure 3-4 Apply a Hot Water Bag—cont'd

12. **Procedural Step. Administer the treatment for the proper length of time, as designated by the physician.**
    The duration is typically 10 to 20 minutes. Check the patient's skin periodically for signs of an increase or decrease in redness or swelling, and ask the patient whether the site is painful.

13. **Procedural Step. Refill the bag with hot water as needed to maintain the proper temperature, making sure to remove an equal amount of the cooler water with each addition.**

14. **Procedural Step. Provide written follow-up instructions to the patient.**

15. **Procedural Step. Sanitize the hands.**
    Always sanitize the hands after every procedure or after using gloves.

16. **Procedural Step. Document the procedure.**
    Include the date and time, method of heat application (hot water bag), temperature of the hot water, location and duration of the application, appearance of the application site, and the patient's reaction.

17. **Procedural Step. Properly care for the hot water bag.**
    Dispose of or launder the protective covering. Cleanse the hot water bag with a warm detergent solution, rinse thoroughly, and dry by hanging the bag upside down with the top removed. Store the bag by screwing on the stopper, leaving air inside to prevent the sides from sticking together.

Charting Example

Date	
12/9/xx	10:00 a.m. Applied hot water bag, water temp @ 115° F, to Ⓛ shoulder area for 20 minutes. Pt. states pain is relieved and skin is dry and intact. Provided verbal and written instructions for home use. Pt. verbalized understanding of instructions. ———————— P. Thomas, CMA (AMMA)

Photos from Zakus SM: *Mosby's clinical skills for medical assistants,* ed 4, St Louis, 2001, Mosby.

Procedure 3-5 Apply a Heating Pad

TASK: Properly apply a heating pad to an affected area.

EQUIPMENT AND SUPPLIES
- Heating pad
- Protective cover
- Patient's medical record

SKILLS/RATIONALE

STANDARD PRECAUTIONS ARE TO BE FOLLOWED.

1. **Procedural Step. Sanitize the hands.**
   An alcohol-based hand rub may be used instead of washing hands with soap and water, unless hands are visibly soiled.
   Rationale. Hand sanitization promotes infection control.

2. **Procedural Step. Assemble equipment and supplies.**
   Rationale. It is important to have all supplies and equipment ready and available before starting any procedure to ensure efficiency.

3. **Procedural Step. Obtain the patient's medical record.**

4. **Procedural Step. Escort the patient to the examination room, greet and identify the patient, and ask the patient to have a seat on the end of the examination table.**
   Rationale. Identifying the patient ensures the procedure is performed on the correct patient.

5. **Procedural Step. Explain the procedure to the patient.**
   Instruct the patient not to lie directly on the heating pad.
   Rationale. Explaining the procedure to the patient promotes cooperation and provides a means of obtaining implied consent. Lying on the pad causes heat to accumulate and can burn the patient.

Procedure 3-5 Apply a Heating Pad—cont'd

6. **Procedural Step. Inspect the heating pad's electrical wires before each use to make sure they are intact.**
   Rationale. Frayed or damaged wires can cause an electrical burn to the patient.

7 **Procedural Step. Place the heating pad in the protective covering.**
   Rationale. Covering the heating pad provides more comfort for the patient, functions to absorb perspiration, and also reduces the risk of a burn.

8. **Procedural Step. Connect the plug to an electrical outlet, and set the selector switch at the proper setting, as designated by the physician (low or medium).**

9. **Procedural Step. Place the patient in a position of comfort, and place the heating pad on the patient's affected body area.**
   Ask the patient if the temperature is comfortable. The heating pad should feel warm but not hot. The patient should be cautioned not to turn the heating pad to a higher setting if it no longer feels hot enough after a time.
   Rationale. The patient's heat receptors eventually become adjusted to the temperature change, resulting in a decreased heat sensation, and the patient may be tempted to increase the temperature.

10. **Procedural Step. Administer the treatment for the proper length of time, as ordered by the physician (usually 15 to 20 minutes).**
    Periodically check on the patient. Examine the site for signs of an increase or decrease in redness or swelling, and ask the patient if the site is painful.
    Rationale. Administering heat to an area of the body for a specified time increases circulation and promotes healing. After the specified period, typically 20 minutes, the treatment has the opposite effect. Leaving the heating pad on for longer than the specified time may also cause burns, redness, and swelling. If the site is painful, the treatment should be stopped and the physician notified.

11. **Procedural Step. Provide verbal and written follow-up instructions to the patient.**

12. **Procedural Step. Sanitize the hands.**
    Always sanitize the hands after every procedure or after using gloves.

13. **Procedural Step. Document the procedure.**
    Include the date and time, method of heat application (heating pad), temperature setting of the pad, location and duration of the application, appearance of the application site, and the patient's reaction.

14. **Procedural Step. Replace the equipment to its appropriate storage area.**

Charting Example

Date	
12/20/xx	10:00 a.m. Heating pad temp set to low and applied to lower back area × 15 min. Pt. states relief. Area is dry and intact. Verbal & written instructions for home use provided. Pt. verbalized understanding of instructions.
	—D. Goodwin, CMA (AAMA)

Photo from Bonewit-West K: *Clinical procedures for medical assistants,* ed 6, Philadelphia, 2004, Saunders.

Hot Soak

A hot **soak** requires a body part to be submerged in a water bath with or without medication. Generally, a soak is applied to an extremity. A hot soak is used to clean an open wound and to increase blood supply to an area to aid in healing or reduce swelling. To use a hot soak on an open wound, sterile techniques must be used. Procedure 3-7 explains how to apply a hot soak to an affected area.

PATIENT-CENTERED PROFESSIONALISM

- Why must the medical assistant understand the proper uses of heat and cold?

⚌ ULTRASOUND THERAPY

Ultrasound therapy uses high-frequency sound waves. When used therapeutically, these sound waves produce heat and vibrations to affect soft tissues in the body. Low-intensity ultrasound is used for therapeutic purposes, including pain relief for muscle spasms, inflammation (e.g., tennis elbow), and arthritis. The therapeutic dose prescribed by the physician will produce the appropriate heat to facilitate the healing process.

Procedure 3-6 Apply a Hot Compress

TASK: Properly apply a hot compress to an affected area to increase circulation.

EQUIPMENT AND SUPPLIES
- Solution ordered by physician
- Bath thermometer
- Washcloths or gauze squares
- Basin

- Towel
- Patient's medical record

Alternative: Commercially prepared hot moist heat packs

SKILLS/RATIONALE

STANDARD PRECAUTIONS ARE TO BE FOLLOWED.

1. **Procedural Step. Sanitize the hands.**
   An alcohol-based hand rub may be used instead of washing hands with soap and water, unless hands are visibly soiled.
   Rationale. Hand sanitization promotes infection control.

2. **Procedural Step. Assemble equipment and supplies.**
   Rationale. It is important to have all supplies and equipment ready and available before starting any procedure to ensure efficiency.

3. **Procedural Step. Obtain the patient's medical record.**

4. **Procedural Step. Escort the patient to the examination room, greet and identify the patient, and ask the patient to have a seat on the end of the examination table, or help the patient into the proper position depending on the site of application.**
   Rationale. Identifying the patient ensures the procedure is performed on the correct patient.

5. **Procedural Step. Explain the procedure to the patient and the reason for applying the compress.**
   Rationale. Explaining the procedure to the patient promotes cooperation and provides a means of obtaining implied consent. Moist heat improves vascular circulation, promotes relaxation, and increases mobility. Moist heat penetrates the tissues better than dry heat.

6. **Procedural Step. Ask the patient to remove all jewelry in the area to be treated.**
   Rationale. Applying any heat therapy, including a hot moist compress, over metal jewelry may burn the patient.

7. **Procedural Step. Fill the basin one-half to three-fourths full of the solution ordered by the physician, and check the temperature with a bath thermometer.**
   The temperature for an adult should range between 105° and 115° F (41° and 44° C).

8. **Procedural Step. Apply the compress.**
   a. Place the patient in a position of comfort.
   b. Place the compress material (washcloth or gauze squares) into the hot water. Wring the compress so that it is wet but not dripping.
   c. Cover the compress with a waterproof cover to help hold in the heat.
   d. Gradually apply the compress to the affected site, allowing the patient to become accustomed to the heat.
   e. Ask the patient if the temperature is comfortable. The compress should be applied as hot as the patient can comfortably tolerate within the acceptable temperature range.
   Rationale. Covering the compress with a waterproof cover slows down the cooling process of the compress and reduces the number of times the compress will need to be rewarmed and reapplied.

Procedure 3-6 Apply a Hot Compress—cont'd

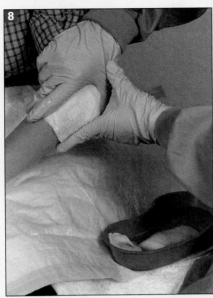

9. **Procedural Step. Prepare additional compresses if needed during the application of the current compress so that they are ready for use when the current compress begins to cool.**

10. **Procedural Step. Reapply the compress as needed, and periodically check the patient's progress.**
Repeat the application of the compress every 2 to 3 minutes for the duration specified by the physician (usually 15 to 20 minutes).
Periodically examine the site for signs of an increase or decrease in redness or swelling, and ask the patient if the site is painful. Remove the compress immediately if either condition occurs, and alert the physician.

11. **Procedural Step. Periodically check the temperature of the water in the basin with the bath thermometer, and replace the cooled water with hot water as needed.**

12. **Procedural Step. After the prescribed treatment time has elapsed, thoroughly and gently dry the affected part with a clean dry towel.**

13. **Procedural Step. Provide verbal and written follow-up instructions for the patient.**

14. **Procedural Step. Sanitize the hands.**
Always sanitize the hands after every procedure or after using gloves.

15. **Procedural Step. Document the procedure.**
Include the date and time, method of heat application (hot compress), name and strength of the solution, temperature of the solution, location and duration of the application, appearance of the application site, and the patient's reaction.

16. **Procedural Step. Properly care for the equipment and return it to its appropriate storage place.**

Charting Example

Date	
12/16/xx	1:30 p.m. Normal saline hot compresses at 110° F to Ⓛ forearm × 15 min. Site slightly reddened, warm to touch. No discomfort noted by the patient. Verbal and written instructions provided to pt. for home care. Pt. verbalized understanding of instructions. ————————B. Clappe, CMA (AAMA)

Procedure 3-7 Apply a Hot Soak

TASK: Properly apply a hot soak to an affected area for relief of pain or swelling.

EQUIPMENT AND SUPPLIES
- Soaking solution ordered by physician
- Bath thermometer
- Basin
- Bath towels
- Patient's medical record

Continued

Procedure 3-7 Apply a Hot Soak—cont'd

SKILLS/RATIONALE

STANDARD PRECAUTIONS ARE TO BE FOLLOWED.

1. **Procedural Step. Sanitize the hands.**
   An alcohol-based hand rub may be used instead of washing hands with soap and water, unless hands are visibly soiled.
   Rationale. Hand sanitization promotes infection control.

2. **Procedural Step. Assemble equipment and supplies.**
   Rationale. It is important to have all supplies and equipment ready and available before starting any procedure to ensure efficiency.

3. **Procedural Step. Obtain the patient's medical record.**

4. **Procedural Step. Escort the patient to the examination room, greet and identify the patient, and ask the patient to have a seat on the end of the examination table.**
   Rationale. Identifying the patient ensures the procedure is performed on the correct patient.

5. **Procedural Step. Explain the procedure to the patient.**
   Rationale. Explaining the procedure to the patient promotes cooperation and provides a means of obtaining implied consent.

6. **Procedural Step. Fill the basin one-half to three-fourths full of the solution ordered by the physician, and check the temperature with a bath thermometer.**
   The temperature for an adult should range between 105° and 115° F (41° and 44° C).

7. **Procedural Step. Place the patient in a position of comfort.**
   Pad the side of the basin with a towel, if needed.
   Rationale. The patient will be soaking for approximately 20 minutes and must be in a comfortable position to avoid fatigue and strain of the muscles. Padding the side of the basin may be done to provide comfort to the patient, if necessary.

8. **Procedural Step. Gently and slowly immerse the patient's affected body part into the solution.**
   Ask the patient if the temperature is comfortable.
   Rationale. The patient's affected body part should become accustomed to the change in temperature gradually.

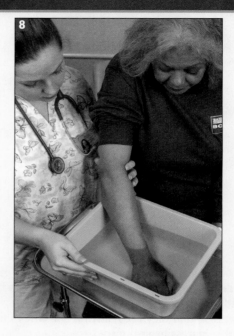

9. **Procedural Step. Periodically check the temperature of the water in the basin with the bath thermometer, and replace the cooled water with hot water as needed to keep the temperature constant.**
   Be very careful not to pour hot water directly onto the patient's skin. Add the water at the edge of the basin by pouring the hot water over your hand first, then stirring the hot water into the cooled water as you pour.
   Rationale. Water should be added away from the patient's body part to prevent splashing hot water on the patient. Stirring the water helps distribute the heat and keep the temperature constant.

10. **Procedural Step. Apply the hot soak, and periodically check on the patient.**
    Continue applying the hot soak for the proper length of time, as ordered by the physician (usually 15 to 20 minutes). Periodically examine the site for signs of an increase or decrease in redness or swelling, and ask the patient if the site is painful. Remove the patient from the hot soak immediately if either condition occurs, and alert the physician.

11. **Procedural Step. After the prescribed treatment time has elapsed, thoroughly and gently dry the affected part with a clean, dry towel.**

12. **Procedural Step. Provide verbal and written follow-up instructions for the patient.**

Procedure 3-7 Apply a Hot Soak—cont'd

13. **Procedural Step. Sanitize the hands.**
    Always sanitize the hands after every procedure or after using gloves.
14. **Procedural Step. Document the procedure.**
    Include the date and time, method of heat application (hot soak), name and strength of the solution, temperature of the soak, location and duration of the application, appearance of the application site, and the patient's reaction.
15. **Procedural Step. Properly care for the equipment and return it to its appropriate storage place.**

Charting Example

Date	
12/23/xx	3:00 p.m. Hot water soak @ 105° F applied to Ⓡ wrist × 15 min. Area pink and no discomfort noted by the patient. Verbal & written instructions provided to pt. for home care. Pt. verbalized understanding of instructions. ——M. Kohen, CMA (AAMA)

As the sound waves are absorbed into body tissues, heat is produced. Also, because ultrasound therapy vibrates the soft tissues, a massage-like action takes place. A **coupling agent** must be used to make certain the energy given off by the ultrasound head (on the wand) is taken to the body tissues. This agent is a water-soluble lotion or gel that is spread over the area to be treated. The head of the wand must be in contact with the coupling agent to produce the desired effect. Never use ultrasound therapy over eyes or burn tissue.

The dosage is prescribed in watts (power) and in a time frame. The order will vary according to the site and severity of the condition. Areas of pain may respond better to low to moderate doses because less nerve activity is involved. The medical assistant must always ask how the patient is tolerating the treatment and must monitor the patient's condition throughout the ultrasound treatment. Procedure 3-8 explains how to administer ultrasound therapy.

AMBULATORY DEVICES

Many patients require assistance with walking after an injury (e.g., sprain, fracture), after surgery (e.g., joint replacement), and because of disease (e.g., gout, osteoarthritis, polio) or congenital deformity. The type of **ambulation device** used depends on the patient's injury or condition.

The medical assistant must learn how to fit and adjust these assistive devices properly. Whether the ambulatory device is crutches, cane, or walker, improper fitting will likely cause decreased stability, increased use of the patient's energy, and decreased function, with the patient's safety at risk. Improper fit also may cause the patient to develop bad gait habits or unsafe gait patterns and may result in painful tissue trauma (e.g., under armpit if crutches are too high or low).

4-6 inches crutches

PATIENT-CENTERED PROFESSIONALISM

- Why must the medical assistant be knowledgeable about basic principles and proper procedure when performing ultrasound?

Procedure 3-8 Administer an Ultrasound Treatment

TASK: Properly administer an ultrasound treatment.

EQUIPMENT AND SUPPLIES
- Ultrasound machine
- Coupling agent
- Paper towels or tissues
- Patient's medical record

Continued

Procedure 3-8 Administer an Ultrasound Treatment—cont'd

SKILLS/RATIONALE

STANDARD PRECAUTIONS ARE TO BE FOLLOWED.

1. **Procedural Step. Sanitize the hands.**
   An alcohol-based hand rub may be used instead of washing hands with soap and water, unless hands are visibly soiled.
   Rationale. Hand sanitization promotes infection control.

2. **Procedural Step. Assemble equipment and supplies.**
   The coupling agent must be at room temperature.
   Rationale. It is important to have all supplies and equipment ready and available before starting any procedure to ensure efficiency. If the coupling agent is too cold or too warm, it will cause the patient discomfort. Some offices keep the coupling agent slightly warmed, as in a baby bottle warmer.

3. **Procedural Step. Obtain the patient's medical record.**

4. **Procedural Step. Escort the patient to the examination or treatment room, and greet and identify the patient.**
   Rationale. Identifying the patient ensures the procedure is performed on the correct patient.

5. **Procedural Step. Explain the procedure to the patient.**
   Assure the patient that there should be minimal or no discomfort. If the patient experiences any discomfort or pain, the patient should tell you immediately, and the intensity of the treatment dosage should be decreased (per the physician's order) until the patient is comfortable.
   Rationale. Explaining the procedure to the patient promotes cooperation and provides a means of obtaining implied consent.

6. **Procedural Step. Prepare the patient and treatment area.**
   a. Place the patient in a position of comfort. Ask the patient to remove the appropriate clothing to expose the treatment area. Tell the patient that the coupling agent may feel cold.
   b. Liberally apply the coupling agent to cover the treatment area completely. Never apply the coupling agent to the ultrasound machine wand.
   c. Use the ultrasound applicator head to spread the coupling agent evenly over the treatment area before turning on the machine.
   Rationale. The treatment area should be adequately covered with the coupling agent, but not to excess. The coupling agent is used to

provide a better transmission of the ultrasound waves to the patient's tissues.

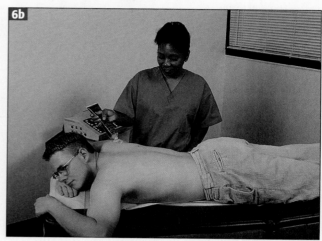

7. **Procedural Step. Set the ultrasound machine.**
   Turn the ultrasound machine "on," and place the intensity control knob at the minimum position. Set the timer to the required time ordered by the physician.
   Rationale. The timer activates the ultrasound machine, and the intensity must be at zero watts.

8. **Procedural Step. Increase the intensity level (measured in watts) to the degree ordered by the physician.**

9. **Procedural Step. Place the applicator head at a right angle into the coupling agent on the patient's skin using firm pressure.**
   Inform the patient that the applicator head may feel cold.

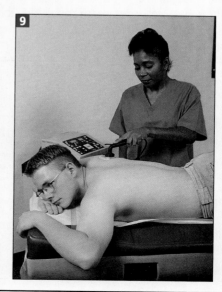

Procedure 3-8 Administer an Ultrasound Treatment—cont'd

10. **Procedural Step. Depending on the area of the body being treated, move the applicator in either a continuous back-and-forth sweeping motion or a circular motion.**
    The back-and-forth sweeping motion is used for larger areas of the body (e.g., back, thigh). The circular motion is used for smaller areas and over bony prominences (e.g., wrist, ankle).
    Use short strokes, approximately 1 inch in length or diameter, continuously moving the applicator head at a rate of 1 to 2 inches per second. Gradually move the applicator head so that each stroke overlaps the previous stroke by ½ inch. Do not remove the applicator head from the patient's skin.
    Rationale. The applicator head must be in constant motion to prevent the tissues from overheating and creating a hot spot or burn. Removing the applicator head from the patient's skin and holding it in the air may cause the applicator head to overheat and may burn the patient when reapplied to the treatment area. The excessive heat may also damage the crystal in the applicator head.

11. **Procedural Step. If the patient complains of any pain or discomfort, stop the treatment immediately and notify the physician.**

12. **Procedural Step. Continue the ultrasound treatment until the prescribed time has expired.**
    The timer automatically shuts off the machine at the end of the prescribed time.

13. **Procedural Step. Remove the applicator head from the patient's skin, and turn the intensity control to the minimum position.**

14. **Procedural Step. Wipe the excess coupling agent from the patient's skin and applicator head with a paper towel or tissues.**

15. **Procedural Step. Instruct the patient to dress; assist as needed.**

16. **Procedural Step. Sanitize the hands.**
    Always sanitize the hands after every procedure or after using gloves.

17. **Procedural Step. Document the procedure.**
    Include the date and time, location of the treatment, duration (in minutes), intensity used (in watts), and the patient's reaction.

Charting Example

Date	
11/10/xx	10:45 a.m. Ultrasound treatment applied to Ⓡ lower back @ 2 watts for 15 min. Pt. states relief of discomfort.
	— C. Rabney, RMA

Photos from Bonewit-West K: *Clinical procedures for medical assistants,* ed 6, Philadelphia, 2004, Saunders.

Crutches

Crutches allow a foot, ankle, leg, knee, or other area of the leg or hip to heal after an injury, surgery, or metabolic disease (e.g., gout). Crutches must be properly fitted and a crutch-walking gait taught to promote ambulation. In addition, various gait (walking) patterns are used for stability, support, and mobility.

Types of Crutches

There are several types of crutches, including axillary, forearm, and platform crutches.

Axillary crutches are used when a patient needs less stability than provided by a walker or the patient cannot bear weight on an affected lower extremity. This type of crutch requires the patient to have good strength in the upper extremities and trunk muscles. Axillary crutches are usually made of wood or aluminum and most are easily adjustable for a proper fit. If improper gait patterns are used, damage to blood vessels and nerves in the axillary area may result.

When being measured for axillary crutches, the patient stands erect with the crutch tips about 6 inches away from the toes (using a **goniometer** at 45-degree angle). Two fingers should fit between the axilla (armpit) and the top of the crutch pads. The handgrip is adjusted to the wrist crease with a 30-degree bend at the elbow. The weight is placed on the handgrips, not the crutch pads. Procedure 3-9 explains the process of measuring a patient for axillary crutches.

Forearm (Lofstrand) crutches are used when more stability and support are needed than a cane can provide. Using the forearm crutch requires the patient to have superior standing balance and upper body strength (Fig. 3-1).

Platform crutches are used by patients with poor arm strength. A shelflike device with arm straps for supporting the forearm and a handgrip for grasping provides the patient with the needed stability (Fig. 3-2).

Fig. 3-1 Medical assistant teaching a patient to use forearm crutches.

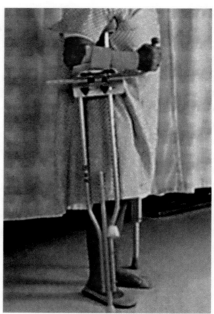

Fig. 3-2 Patient with platform crutches. Patient uses forearms to lean on crutches. *(From Zakus SM: Mosby's clinical skills for medical assistants, ed 4, St Louis, 2001, Mosby.)*

Procedure 3-9 Measure for Axillary Crutches

TASK: Properly measure a patient for crutches.

EQUIPMENT AND SUPPLIES
- Crutches
- Goniometer
- Patient's medical record

SKILLS/RATIONALE

STANDARD PRECAUTIONS ARE TO BE FOLLOWED.

1. **Procedural Step. Sanitize the hands.**
   An alcohol-based hand rub may be used instead of washing hands with soap and water, unless hands are visibly soiled.
   Rationale. Hand sanitization promotes infection control.

2. **Procedural Step. Assemble equipment and supplies.**
   Rationale. It is important to have all supplies and equipment ready and available before starting any procedure to ensure efficiency.

3. **Procedural Step. Obtain the patient's medical record.**

4. **Procedural Step. Greet and identify the patient.**
   The patient will most likely be in the examination room.

   Rationale. Identifying the patient ensures the procedure is performed on the correct patient.

5. **Procedural Step. Explain the procedure to the patient.**
   Rationale. Explaining the procedure to the patient promotes cooperation and provides a means of obtaining implied consent.

Determining Crutch Length

6. **Procedural Step. Position the patient.**
   Assist the patient as needed into a standing position. The measurement must be taken with the patient wearing at least one good walking shoe on the foot of the uninjured leg.
   Rationale. Measurement will not be accurate if the patient is sitting or is not wearing a shoe on the unaffected foot.

Procedure 3-9 Measure for Axillary Crutches—cont'd

7 **Procedural Step. Position the crutch tips approximately 2 inches anterior and 4 to 6 inches lateral to the foot, creating a triangle.**
The large dots in the accompanying figure represent the crutch tips.

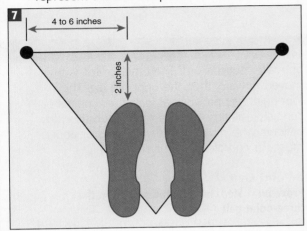

8 **Procedural Step. Adjust the crutches.**
Remove the bolt and wing nut on the side of the crutch, and slide the central strut of the crutch either upward or downward to adjust the length of the crutch. The height of the crutch should be about 2 to 3 finger-widths below the patient's armpits. Replace the bolt and wing nut, and tighten to secure the strut.
Rationale. Height adjustment is critical; without the gap of 2 or 3 finger-widths between the top of the crutch and the patient's armpit, nerve damage in the axillary region may result from the patient supporting body weight on the top of the crutch instead of on the handgrips.

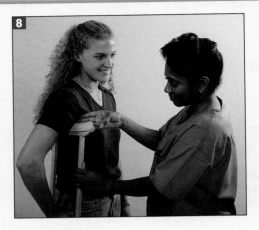

Handgrip Positions
9. **Procedural Step. Once the height has been correctly adjusted, ask the patient to stand erect with a crutch beneath each axilla and to support his or her weight on the handgrips.**
10. **Procedural Step. Adjust the handgrips.**
The handgrip level is adjusted in the same manner as the height was adjusted. Remove the bolt and wing nut and slide the handgrip upward or downward, as required. Secure the handgrip by replacing the bolt and tightening the wing nut. The handgrips should be adjusted so that the patient's elbows are flexed at an angle of 20 to 30 degrees. Verify the angle of the elbow using a goniometer.
11. **Procedural Step. Perform a final check of the fit of the crutches.**

Figures from Bonewit-West K: *Clinical procedures for medical assistants,* ed 6, Philadelphia, 2004, Saunders.

Axillary Crutches fingers

Gait Patterns
The selection of the **gait pattern** depends on the patient's balance, coordination, strength, ability to bear weight, and energy level. Procedure 3-10 describes the process for providing instructions to a patient for the appropriate crutch gait depending on the patient's injury or condition. The tripod position is the beginning position (Fig. 3-3). Crutches can be used in four different gait patterns: four-point, two-point, three-point, and swing-through gaits.

FOUR-POINT GAIT
The four-point gait pattern requires the use of two ambulation aids (e.g., two crutches, two canes). The gait begins with the patient first placing one crutch or cane forward, followed by placing the *opposite* lower extremity forward (i.e., right crutch, left foot; left crutch, right foot). This gait is stable and slow but is the safest approach in crowded areas. The patient does not exert much energy because the patient must walk slowly to maintain balance (Fig. 3-4, *D*).

Procedure 3-10 Instruct the Patient in Crutch Gaits

TASK: Provide proper instructions to the patient for the appropriate crutch gait, depending on the injury or condition.

EQUIPMENT AND SUPPLIES
- Properly adjusted crutches
- Patient's medical record

SKILLS/RATIONALE

STANDARD PRECAUTIONS ARE TO BE FOLLOWED.

NOTE: This procedure will most likely be performed immediately after adjusting the height and handgrip position of the crutches (see Procedure 3-9).

1. **Procedural Step. Sanitize the hands.**
   An alcohol-based hand rub may be used instead of washing hands with soap and water, unless hands are visibly soiled.
   Rationale. Hand sanitization promotes infection control.

2. **Procedural Step. Assemble equipment and supplies.**
   Obtain the appropriate crutches previously fitted to the patient.
   Rationale. It is important to have all supplies and equipment ready and available before starting any procedure to ensure efficiency.

3. **Procedural Step. Obtain the patient's medical record.**

4. **Procedural Step. Greet and identify the patient.**
   Rationale. Identifying the patient ensures the procedure is performed on the correct patient.

5. **Procedural Step. Explain the procedure to the patient.**
   Rationale. Explaining the procedure to the patient promotes cooperation and provides a means of obtaining implied consent.

6. **Procedural Step. Ask the patient to stand erect and face straight ahead.**

7. **Procedural Step. Position the crutches.**
   Place the tips of the crutches 4 to 6 inches anterior and 4 to 6 inches lateral to the side of each foot. This is referred to as the *tripod* position (see Fig. 3-3).
   Rationale. The tripod position provides the patient with a wide base of support and is the basic crutch stance used before crutch walking.

Four-Point Gait

8. **Procedural Step. Instruct the patient in the four-point gait.**
   The four-point gait is a slower gait used for patients who are able to move each leg independently and bear weight on both legs. The patient moves one crutch forward, then the opposite foot forward. The other crutch is then moved forward, then the opposite leg. The four-point gait provides at least three points of contact at all times and is most often used for patients who have muscle weakness or poor muscular coordination. (See Fig. 3-4, *D*.)

Three-Point Gait

9. **Procedural Step. Instruct the patient in the three-point gait.**
   The three-point gait is used for the patient who can support full body weight on one leg and can touch the foot of the affected leg to the ground, but not bear weight on it. The patient moves forward by moving the crutches forward at the same time as the affected leg. The crutches bear the weight, and the affected foot touches the ground only for balance. The unaffected leg is then moved forward, and body weight is transferred to the unaffected leg. Patients who use this gait most often have musculoskeletal or soft tissue trauma to a lower extremity (e.g., fracture, sprain). This gait requires the patient to have good upper body strength and coordination. (See Fig. 3-4, *C*.)

Two-Point Gait

10. **Procedural Step. Instruct the patient in the two-point gait.**
    The two-point gait is used when a patient is capable of bearing partial weight on each leg. It is similar to the four-point gait but requires the patient to have greater coordination and balance. Two-point gait is an advanced gait and is typically used only after the four-point gait is mastered. The patient moves one crutch and the opposite leg forward while bearing partial weight on the opposite leg and crutch. The opposite crutch and opposite leg are then moved forward in the same manner. (See Fig. 3-4, *B*.)

Swing Gaits

11. **Procedural Step. Instruct the patient in swing gaits.**
    The swing gaits include the *swing-to* gait and the *swing-through* gait. The gait is accomplished

Procedure 3-10 Instruct the Patient in Crutch Gaits—cont'd

by moving both crutches forward and then swinging the legs up to meet the crutches (swing-to) or to stop slightly in front of the crutches (swing-through). Patients who use these gaits include those with severe lower extremity disabilities (e.g., paralysis) and those wearing supportive braces or prosthetic legs (See Fig. 3-4, *A*.)

12. **Procedural Step. Sanitize the hands.**
Always sanitize the hands after every procedure or after using gloves.

13. **Procedural Step. Document the instruction.**
Document in the patient's medical record that the patient was provided with verbal and written instructions as well as a demonstration of the

proper crutch use and gait, and that the patient understood the procedure and could return demonstrate the crutch gait to be used.

Charting Example

Date	
8/16/xx	10:00 a.m. Patient instructed in basic 4-point gait after crutches adjusted appropriate for height. After several min of assisted gait, pt. demonstrated 4-point gait independently and appropriately. Questions answered and pt. discharged with crutches and telephone # to call for problem. Will rtn in 1 week for f/u. —————— W. Campbell, CMA (AAMA)

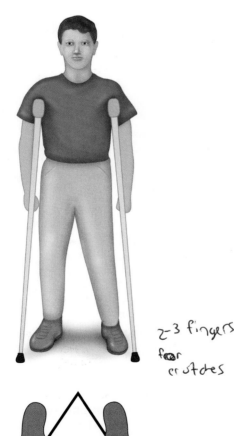

2-3 fingers for crutces

Fig. 3-3 Basic crutch stance is the tripod position. *(Modified from Zakus SM: Mosby's clinical skills for medical assistants, ed 4, St Louis, 2001, Mosby.)*

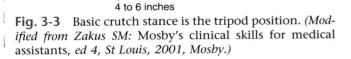

2 inches

4 to 6 inches

TWO-POINT GAIT

As with the four-point gait, the two-point gait requires two ambulation aids. Instead of using an alternating pattern, however, the crutch or cane is placed forward *at the same time* as the opposite lower extremity (Fig. 3-4, *B*). This gait is quicker than the four-point gait and is closest to a person's normal gait. It requires more coordination because the upper extremity and the opposite lower extremity are moving at the same time. There is less stability with the two-point gait.

THREE-POINT GAIT

The three-point gait, or *tripod* position, requires two crutches. The patient basically "steps through" the crutches. This gait is typically used when the patient can bear weight on one lower extremity but not the other (e.g., foot sprain). The non–weight-bearing extremity (leg not able to support weight) and crutches are moved forward, and the patient steps through the crutches (Fig. 3-4, *C*). The three-point gait pattern is less stable than four-point gait but is quicker for the patient. The patient's upper body strength must be strong. The three-point gait also requires more energy from the patient.

SWING-THROUGH GAIT

In the swing-through gait the patient moves both crutches forward. Both legs are swung through to a position ahead of the crutches. This gait is used with amputees, patients who have paralysis, or in cases where full weight-bearing is a problem (Fig. 3-4, *A*).

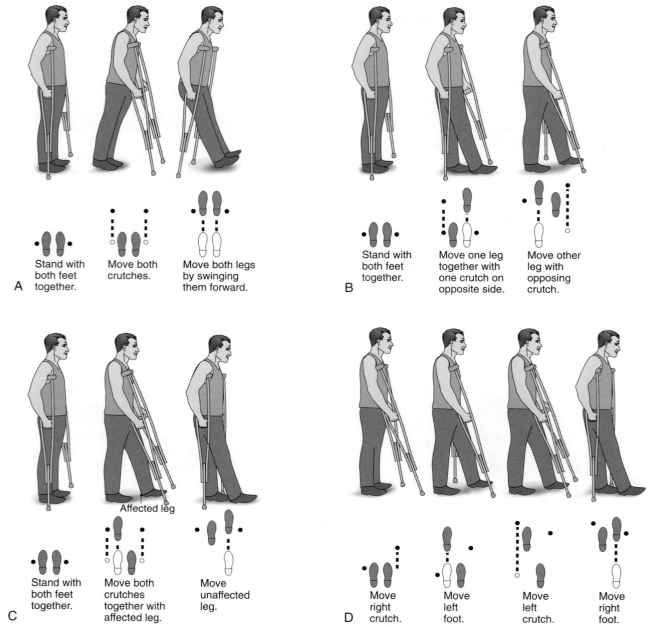

Fig. 3-4   Crutch gait patterns. **A,** Swing-through gait. **B,** Two-point gait. **C,** Three-point gait. **D,** Four-point crutch gait. *(Modified from Young AP, Kennedy DB: Kinn's the medical assistant, ed 9, Philadelphia, 2003, Saunders.)*

Walkers

The physician prescribes a **walker** when the patient needs optimal stability, support, and a way to be mobile. It may be prescribed even when there is no apparent leg injury. There are various styles of walkers, and all are adjustable for proper fit. Walkers with wheels in front allow the patient to move more quickly but are less stable. Most walkers can be folded.

Measurement for proper height is done with the patient standing in the walker with the crossbar in front, as follows:

- The top of the handgrip should be level with the crease in the patient's wrist when the arms are relaxed at the sides.
- The feet of the walker should be resting flat on the floor.
- When the patient grasps the handgrip, the shoulders should be level and the elbows flexed 15 to 25 degrees.

The patient should move the walker forward 6 inches and then step into the walker. After the patient becomes stronger and more skilled at using the walker, the forward space may need to be adjusted. The medical assistant must observe the patient walking to determine if the fit is adequate. Procedure 3-11 explains how to measure a patient for a walker and provides instructions for its use.

Canes

A **cane** provides the least amount of support for the patient of all the ambulatory devices. Several styles of standard canes are available. A cane is used primarily to relieve weight bearing and is placed on the "good" side, or the side opposite the weaker lower extremity. Having the base of support on the strong side allows the patient's weight to be shifted toward this side and away from the weaker side. Be aware, however, that patients have a tendency to want to use the cane on their weak side.

Proper fitting can be established with the patient in an upright position and the top of the cane at the wrist crease. The elbow should be flexed 15 to 25 degrees, and the force of the cane should be directed downward. The cane should be alongside the patient's toes. When a *quad cane* (four-legged cane) is used, it is positioned away from the patient, reducing the risk of catching the foot on the leg of the cane and falling. Procedure 3-12 describes the process of properly measuring the patient for a cane and providing instructions for its use.

Procedure 3-11 Instruct the Patient in the Use of a Walker

TASK: Accurately measure and provide patient instructions for proper use of a walker.

EQUIPMENT AND SUPPLIES
- Walker
- Patient's medical record

SKILLS/RATIONALE

STANDARD PRECAUTIONS ARE TO BE FOLLOWED.

1. **Procedural Step. Sanitize the hands.**
   An alcohol-based hand rub may be used instead of washing hands with soap and water, unless hands are visibly soiled.
   Rationale. Hand sanitization promotes infection control.

2. **Procedural Step. Assemble equipment and supplies.**
   Rationale. It is important to have all supplies and equipment ready and available before starting any procedure to ensure efficiency.

3. **Procedural Step. Obtain the patient's medical record.**

4. **Procedural Step. Greet and identify the patient.**
   Rationale. Identifying the patient ensures the procedure is performed on the correct patient.

5. **Procedural Step. Explain the procedure to the patient.**
   Rationale. Explaining the procedure to the patient promotes cooperation and provides a means of obtaining implied consent.

6. Procedural Step. Adjust the height of the walker.
   The top of the walker should be just below the patient's waist at the same height as the top of the hipbone. When properly adjusted, the

patient's elbows will bend at approximately a 30-degree angle.

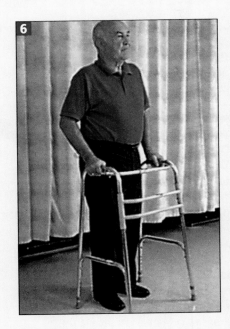

7. **Procedural Step. Instruct the patient to pick up the walker and move it forward approximately 6 inches.**

Continued

Procedure 3-11 Instruct the Patient in the Use of a Walker—cont'd

8. **Procedural Step. Have the patient move the dominant foot and then the nondominant foot into the "cage" of the walker.**

9. **Procedural Step. Caution the patient to be sure he or she has good balance before moving the walker ahead again.**
   NOTE: If the patient does not have enough strength to pick up the walker, obtain a walker that has wheels in the front.
   Rationale. Moving the walker forward requires that the patient have good balance before moving it. If not, the patient may fall and be injured.

10. **Procedural Step. Repeat Steps 7 and 8 through the distance to be covered.**

11. **Procedural Step. Observe the patient for several repetitions to make sure the patient understands the process and can manage the walker.**

12. **Procedural Step. If the walker folds for storage or transport, provide the patient with instructions, demonstrate the process, and observe the patient performing this function. It may be necessary and** desirable to involve a family member or other caregiver in this task as well.

13. **Procedural Step. Sanitize the hands.**
    Always sanitize the hands after every procedure or after using gloves.

14. **Procedural Step. Document the instruction.**
    Document in the patient's medical record that the patient was provided with verbal and written instructions as well as a demonstration of the proper use of the walker, and that the patient understood the procedure.

Charting Example

Date	
9/12/xx	10:40 a.m. After properly adjusting the walker to patient, pt. demonstrated proper use of walker for stability. Wife present and both pt. and wife were shown how to fold walker for storage. Questions answered and pt. discharged with walker; rtn in 1 week for follow-up.
	— L. Nagle, RMA

Photo from Zakus SM: *Mosby's clinical skills for medical assistants,* ed 4, St Louis, 2001, Mosby.

Procedure 3-12 Instruct the Patient in the Use of a Cane

TASK: Accurately measure and provide patient instructions for proper use of a cane.

EQUIPMENT AND SUPPLIES
- Cane
- Patient's medical record

SKILLS/RATIONALE

STANDARD PRECAUTIONS ARE TO BE FOLLOWED.

1. **Procedural Step. Sanitize the hands.**
   An alcohol-based hand rub may be used instead of washing hands with soap and water, unless hands are visibly soiled.
   Rationale. Hand sanitization promotes infection control.

2. **Procedural Step. Assemble equipment and supplies.**
   Obtain the appropriate cane for the patient. Several styles of canes are available.
   Rationale. It is important to have all supplies and equipment ready and available before starting any procedure to ensure efficiency.

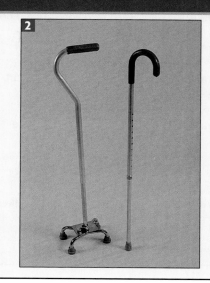

Procedure 3-12 Instruct the Patient in the Use of a Cane—cont'd

3. **Procedural Step. Obtain the patient's medical record.**

4. **Procedural Step. Greet and identify the patient.**
   Rationale. Identifying the patient ensures the procedure is performed on the correct patient.

5. **Procedural Step. Explain the procedure to the patient.**
   Rationale. Explaining the procedure to the patient promotes cooperation and provides a means of obtaining implied consent.

6. **Procedural Step. Measure for the correct height of the cane.**
   For the cane to fit properly, the patient should stand straight. Measure from the crease at the patient's wrist to the floor. You may increase this measurement by 2 inches if it is more comfortable for the patient. The patient's elbow should bend at a 30-degree angle when the cane is adjusted correctly for the patient.

7. **Procedural Step. Position the cane.**
   Place the cane on the strong side of the patient's body (in the hand opposite the affected extremity) 4 to 6 inches to the side of the foot. The top of the cane should be placed level with the greater trochanter of the hip, and the elbow should be flexed 30 degrees.

8. **Procedural Step. Instruct the patient to move the cane and affected leg forward at the same time.**

9. **Procedural Step. Instruct the patient to move the unaffected leg forward just past the cane.**

10. **Procedural Step. Repeat Steps 8 and 9 through the distance to be covered.**

11. **Procedural Step. Document the instruction.**
    Document in the patient's medical record that the patient was provided with verbal and written instructions as well as a demonstration of the proper use of the cane, and that the patient understood the procedure.

12. **Procedural Step. Sanitize the hands.**
    Always sanitize the hands after every procedure or after using gloves.

Charting Example

Date	
9/11/xx	11:50 a.m. Cane adjusted for patient use on left side for assisting c̄ weakness in right ankle. Pt. was instructed and assisted in cane walking until comfortable, then demonstrated same independently. Questions answered; pt. discharged with cane and written instructions. Rtn in 1 wk for f/u. ————S. Abrahms, CMA (AAMA)

Step 2 photo courtesy 3M Health Care, St Paul, Minn.

TRANSFERRING A PATIENT

Frequently patients need assistance to move from a chair to the examination table or back again. There are multiple ways to transfer patients, but all should focus on correct body mechanics. If the patient is in a wheelchair, move the chair close to the examination table, lock the wheels, and lift the foot rests of the wheelchair out of the way (Figure 3-5). Explain the procedure to the patient, and ask for his or her assistance.

If one side of the patient is stronger than the other, always provide support on the strong side. Place a step stool in front of the wheelchair next to the side of the examination table. Support the patient close to your body on the strong side, with one hand under the axillary region and the other either grasping the patient's hand or holding the forearm. When bending, always bend at the knees

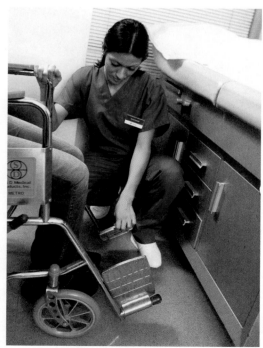

Fig. 3-5 Wheels locked and foot rests elevated.

and maintain the back's three natural curves, allowing the leg muscles to help in lifting. Give the patient a signal and lift as the patient assists. Anchor the step stool with one foot, and help the patient step up onto the stool with the strong leg, then pivot (Figure 3-6). Ease the patient down onto the table, bending your knees while keeping your back aligned. Make sure the patient is comfortable and safely positioned on the table (Figure 3-7). It may be necessary to remain with the patient until the examination is completed to ensure patient safety. If the physician prefers that the patient be in a supine position, place one arm across the patient's shoulders and the other under the knees and smoothly lower the patient's upper body to the table while raising the legs. Use the same pivoting techniques with proper body mechanics to help transfer the patient from the examination table back to the locked wheelchair. If the patient must hold onto you, have him or her hold your waist or shoulders, not your neck.

CASTS

The purpose of a **cast** is to immobilize a body part (e.g., arm, leg). The immobilization of the fractured bone allows for alignment until the bone has healed. Think of a cast as a rigid dressing. Casts are most often applied to bones that have been fractured. Casts are also used to promote postoperative healing and in areas that have been severely sprained or dislocated (Box 3-2). With proper care, a cast facilitates healing and speeds the patient's recovery.

Normally, an **orthopedist,** a physician whose specialty is to correct musculoskeletal disorders, applies casts. The medical assistant is responsible for the following:

- Assembling the needed supplies and equipment.
- Preparing the patient.
- Assisting the physician in cast application.
- Providing the patient with guidelines for cast care (Box 3-3).
- Cleaning the examination room after the patient leaves.

Cast Materials

Casts can be of several types: plaster-of-Paris, synthetic, fiberglass, and air. The type of material selected depends on the type of injury and its severity. Casts are applied to immobilize both the joint above and the joint below the fracture or injury.

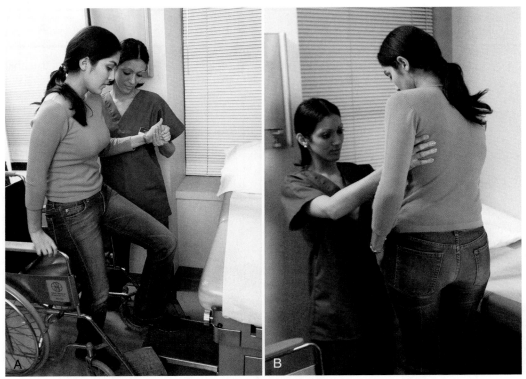

Fig. 3-6 A, Strong side support. **B,** Pivot with support.

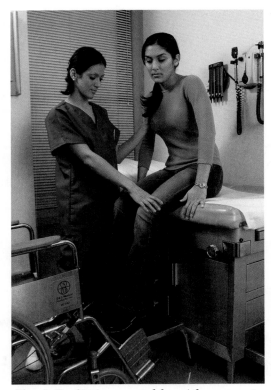

Fig. 3-7 Sitting on table with support.

- An **air cast** is a plastic cover filled with air that is used in emergency situations for stabilization.
- A **synthetic cast** is more of an *immobilizer* that can be removed when the limb is not being used; it is preferred for simple breaks (fractures) or sprains (Fig. 3-8).
- Plaster and fiberglass casts are normally used for more complicated fractures.

Plaster Casts

Plaster casts are formed by wetting bandage rolls that contain calcium sulfate crystals and then molding the rolls to the injured body part. When the bandage roll comes in contact with water and is applied to the affected body part, the patient experiences a sense of warmth as the plaster hardens. As the bandage is being applied, it molds to the site. The medical assistant needs to instruct the patient not to lay a cast against anything until it dries; a dent in the cast will cause pressure on the underlying skin, which may result in pain and a **pressure ulcer** later. As the cast dries, usually within 72 hours, it forms a rigid protective dressing.

BOX 3-2   Types of Casts

Short arm cast is used for a fracture or dislocation of the wrist. It extends from about mid-palm to just below the elbow.

Long arm cast is used for a fracture of the forearm or upper arm (humerus). It extends from the axilla to mid-palm, with a 90-degree bend at the elbow.

Short leg cast is used for fracture of the ankle. It extends from just below the knee to the toes. The foot extends naturally.

Long leg cast is used for fractures of the tibia, fibula, or femur. It extends from the upper thigh to the toes. The knee is slightly bent and the foot extends naturally.

Walking cast is a cast with a walking heel.

Illustrations modified from Bonewit-West K: *Clinical procedures for medical assistants*, ed 6, Philadelphia, 2004, Saunders.

BOX 3-3   Patient Guidelines for Cast Care

1. A wet cast may be dried with a small fan. This allows air to circulate and assists in drying the cast.
2. Do not apply pressure to a wet or damp cast. This could create a pressure area under the cast and cause tissue damage.
3. Maintain elevation of the extremity with pillows to reduce swelling and discomfort.
4. Keep the cast uncovered until completely dry.
5. Frequently assess the fingers and toes for color, feeling, or temperature change (e.g., pain, bluish discoloration, tingling, or coldness to fingers or toes may be an indication that a cast is too tight because of swelling). The physician should be notified immediately if changes occur.
6. Do not insert any item between the cast and body part (e.g., coat hanger to scratch irritated skin). This prevents injury to and infection of the skin tissues.
7. Avoid getting the cast wet. Cover it with a protective covering when bathing. (A plastic bag that protects a newspaper works well.) The skin and tissue may break down if the cast becomes and remains wet.
8. Only use water-soluble marking pens to write on the cast. This allows the cast to "breathe."
9. Clean the cast with a damp cloth.

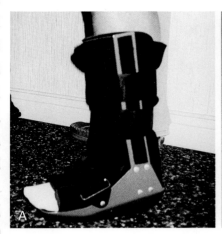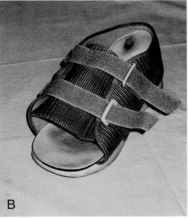

Fig. 3-8   A, Synthetic boot cast. **B,** Synthetic foot immobilizer. *(From Kinn MA, Woods ME: The medical assistant, ed 8, Philadelphia, 1999, Saunders.)*

Fiberglass Casts

Using tapes in combination with a fiberglass or a plastic resin forms a **fiberglass cast.** The advantages of a fiberglass cast are that it is lighter, dries more quickly, and resists water better than a plaster cast (but cannot get soaking wet because the skin underneath may break down). Fiberglass also comes in various colors, which may appeal to adults (for stylistic reasons) as well as children.

Cast Application

When the physician applies the cast, adequate space for blood circulation is needed for possible swelling, and to allow healing. The medical assistant must check for capillary refill in fingers or toes (pressing the fingernails or toenails and watching the blood return). Application of the casting material involves the following stages:

1. *Inspecting the skin.* The area to be cast needs to be clean and dry. The location of all bruises, reddened areas, and skin breaks needs to be recorded in the patient's medical record.
2. *Applying the stockinette.* A **stockinette** is a knitted cotton material in tubular form. The diameter of the material stretches to accommodate a body part. A stockinette is used to protect the patient's skin at the edges of the cast. It is folded back over the casting material as it is molded. This keeps the hard casting material from rubbing the skin after the cast has been applied.
3. *Applying the cast padding.* The **cast padding** is a soft cotton material that comes in a roll of varying widths. The cast padding is applied over the stockinette. Its purpose is to protect the patient's skin when the cast is removed and to protect bony areas under the cast. Extra padding is applied to bony areas to prevent pressure ulcers and it is easily torn so the irregular bony areas can be padded more smoothly with fewer bumps.
4. *Applying cast bandage or tape.* Whichever type of cast is being applied, the material is applied over the cast padding. The number of layers of casting material used will depend on the desired strength needed. Gloves are required when applying the plaster or fiberglass material. Some physicians use a hand cream on their gloves to keep the fiberglass from sticking to the gloves.
5. *Allowing for drying time.* A cast must be allowed to dry adequately before weight bearing. To reduce strain on the body part and minimize swelling, the physician may prescribe an arm sling or crutches. The medical assistant must instruct the patient not to lean against anything with the cast until it is fully dry so the cast does not become damaged.

The patient needs to be reminded not to insert anything in the cast or use anything inside the cast to eliminate an itch (e.g., pen, pencil, wire hanger). The object could injure the tissue and result in an infection.

Procedure 3-13 explains the process of providing supplies and assistance during the application of a plaster-of-Paris or fiberglass cast, as well as instructing the patient in cast care and nutritional requirements.

Procedure 3-13 Assist in Plaster-of-Paris or Fiberglass Cast Application

TASK: Provide supplies and assistance during cast application, and instruct the patient in cast care and nutritional requirements.

EQUIPMENT AND SUPPLIES
- Cast material to be used (plaster or fiberglass)
- Stockinette to fit extremity
- Sheet wadding (cast padding)
- Basin or bucket to hold warm water
- Scissors
- Disposable gloves
- Hand cream
- Patient's medical record

SKILLS/RATIONALE

STANDARD PRECAUTIONS ARE TO BE FOLLOWED.

1. **Procedural Step. Sanitize the hands.**
   An alcohol-based hand rub may be used instead of washing hands with soap and water, unless hands are visibly soiled.
   Rationale. Hand sanitization promotes infection control.

2. **Procedural Step. Assemble equipment and supplies.**
   Rationale. It is important to have all supplies and equipment ready and available before starting any procedure to ensure efficiency.

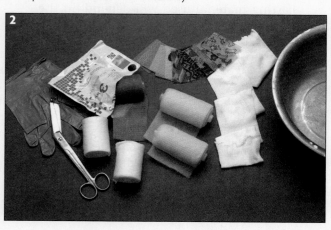

3. **Procedural Step. Obtain the patient's medical record.**

4. **Procedural Step. Greet and identify the patient.**
   Rationale. Identifying the patient ensures the procedure is performed on the correct patient.

5. **Procedural Step. Explain the procedure to the patient.**
   Rationale. Explaining the procedure to the patient promotes cooperation and provides a means of obtaining implied consent.

6. **Procedural Step. Place the patient in a position of comfort (sitting, lying down, or standing) for the type of cast to be applied.**
   Body parts to be cast must be supported and must be in alignment for cast application.

7. **Procedural Step. Clean and dry the area to be cast as directed by the physician, and observe for areas of broken skin, redness, and bruising.**
   Note observations in the patient's medical record.
   Rationale. Determining the condition of the skin before cast application provides information for later evaluation.

8. **Procedural Step. Prepare the stockinette.**
   Cut the appropriate size (width and length) of stockinette with 1 to 2 inches above and below the area being cast. The physician will apply and remove any creases. The physician will leave 1 to 2 inches of excess stockinette above and below the area to be cast.
   Rationale. Using stockinette that is too large could cause creases to form, thus causing tissue damage. Excess stockinette will be used later to finish the edges of the cast.

Procedure 3-13 Assist in Plaster-of-Paris or Fiberglass Cast Application—cont'd

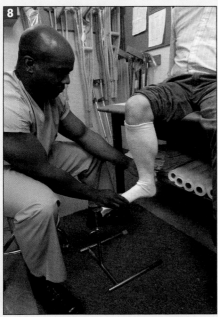

9 **Procedural Step. Prepare the cast padding.**
Choose the appropriate size (width and length) of cast padding for the area being cast. The physician will apply the padding using a spiral bandage turn application. Extra padding will be added to areas of bony prominence (e.g., wrist, anklebone).
Rationale. Using cast padding that is too large could cause creases to form, resulting in pressure on skin tissue.

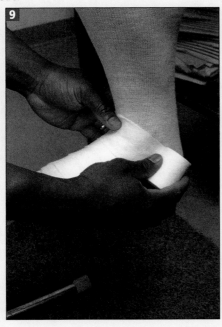

10. **Procedural Step. When the physician is ready to apply the cast, put on disposable gloves.**
11 **Procedural Step. Prepare the plaster or fiberglass roll.**
Depending on the type of cast material used, do one of the following:
a. Hold the plaster roll in the container of water until the bubbles stop (about 5 seconds). Remove it from the water and gently squeeze the excess water from the roll, and hand it to the physician.
b. Hold the fiberglass roll under warm water for 10 to 15 seconds. Gently squeeze to remove excess water.

12. **Procedural Step. Assist as needed by holding the body part in the position requested by the physician.**
13. **Procedural Step. Repeat Step 11 (a or b) until the cast is completed.**
14. **Procedural Step. Reassure the patient as needed.**
15 **Procedural Step. Assist with folding the stockinette or padding down over the outer edge of the cast to form a smooth edge.**

Continued

Procedure 3-13 Assist in Plaster-of-Paris or Fiberglass Cast Application—cont'd

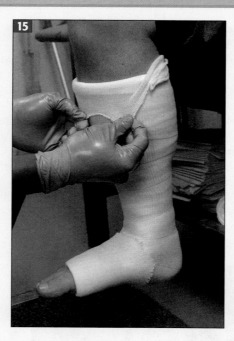

16. **Procedural Step. Provide scissors or a plastic knife to the physician to trim areas around thumb, fingers, or toes as necessary.**
    NOTE: Handle the casted extremity with palms only, since fingers can cause indentations that could create pressure areas.

17. **Procedural Step. Provide verbal and written cast instructions and isometric exercise instructions if prescribed by the physician.**

18. **Procedural Step. Clean the equipment and room.** Discard water and excess materials.

19. **Procedural Step. Remove gloves and sanitize the hands.**
    Always sanitize the hands after every procedure or after using gloves.

20. **Procedural Step. Document the procedure.** Include the date and time, location, condition of underlying tissue and type of cast, and the patient's reaction. Document that the patient was provided with verbal and written instructions.

Charting Example

Date	
12/14/xx	10:30 a.m. Ⓡ short leg fiberglass cast applied. Skin under cast is intact and clean, bruising over lateral ankle. Pt. tolerated procedure well. Pt. given verbal and written follow-up instructions and cast care. ———— C. Williams, RMA

Fig. 3-9 A cast cutter makes a separation in the cast without cutting through the wadding underneath.

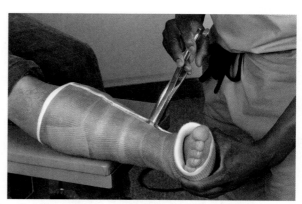

Fig. 3-10 A cast spreader is used to increase the space between the two sections of the cast so that the wadding and stockinette can be cut with scissors.

Cast Removal

To remove a cast, the physician uses a **cast cutter** to divide the cast in two parts (top and bottom). The cast cutter does not truly cut, but instead vibrates back and forth to separate the casting material (Fig. 3-9). A **cast spreader** is then used to open up the cast. Bandage scissors are used to cut through the cast padding and stockinette (Fig. 3-10).

When the cast is removed, the normal appearance of the limb is pale (white to yellowish), and scaly, with old, dried skin and the limb has a foul smell. The muscle tissue appears soft and flabby from lack of use. The medical assistant may need to provide instructions on skin care and exercises the physician has prescribed for regaining use of the limb. The physician will often prescribe physical therapy for the patient to regain the maximum range of motion of the affected limb. Some helpful hints for cast removal are as follows:

1. Prove to the patient (especially children) that the cast saw will not hurt them. This can be done by touching the saw to their hand. This provides reassurance that the patient will not be cut.
2. If the cast is cut so that a top and bottom are available, the body part can be left in the bottom half until the physician checks the patient. This eliminates possible reinjury of the body part.
3. Gently wash the body part with a warm, moist towel after the cast is removed. Avoid scrubbing the delicate skin because it will slough off within a few days, and hard scrubbing could cause the skin to break down.

PATIENT-CENTERED PROFESSIONALISM

- How would the medical assistant explain cast application and removal to a patient?

RANGE-OF-MOTION EXERCISES

No matter what the cause of immobility, the patient will have to receive some type of exercise to prevent muscle atrophy and joint problems. Exercise prevents some complications of immobility and helps prepare the patient for ambulation. Range-of-motion (ROM) exercises help maintain both muscle and joint function.

Typically ROM exercises put each joint through as full a range of motion as possible without causing discomfort. There are basically three types of ROM exercises:

1. *Active*—the patient can perform ROM exercises without assistance
2. *Passive*—the ROM exercises are performed on the patient by the medical assistant
3. *Active-assisted*—the ROM exercises are performed by the patient with assistance from the medical assistant

Both active and active-assisted exercises help to prevent muscular atrophy and maintain joint function. Passive exercises assist in maintaining joint function but do not maintain muscle tone. Procedure 3-14 provides proper techniques for performing range of motion exercises.

Procedure 3-14 Perform Range-of-Motion Exercises

TASK: Utilize the correct technique for performing range-of-motion (ROM) exercises.

EQUIPMENT AND SUPPLIES
- Patient
- Patient's medical record

SKILLS/RATIONALE

STANDARD PRECAUTIONS ARE TO BE FOLLOWED.

1. **Procedural Step. Sanitize the hands.**
   An alcohol-based hand rub may be used instead of washing hands with soap and water, unless hands are visibly soiled.
   Rationale. Hand sanitization promotes infection control.

2. **Procedural Step. Assemble equipment and supplies.**
   Rationale. It is important to have all supplies and equipment ready and available before starting any procedure to ensure efficiency.

3. **Procedural Step. Verify the physician's order.**

4. **Procedural Step. Obtain the patient's medical record.**

5. **Procedural Step. Greet and identify the patient.**
   Rationale. Identifying the patient ensures the procedure is performed on the correct patient.

6. **Procedural Step. Explain the procedure to the patient.**
   Rationale. Explaining the procedure to the patient promotes cooperation and provides a means of obtaining implied consent.

7. **Procedural Step. Assess initial joint function. If resistance is encountered do not continue, notify the physician.**

Continued

Procedure 3-14 Perform Range-of-Motion Exercises—cont'd

Rationale. Assessment is necessary for evaluating ROM capabilities.

8. **Procedural Step. Observe for any signs of redness or feeling of warmth, in skin over joint and tenderness on palpation in or around a joint.**
   Rationale. May indicate inflammatory process that contraindicates ROM exercise.

9. **Procedural Step. Perform ROM exercises slowly and gently.**
   Do not force movement of any joint.
   Rationale. Prevents joint strain.

10. **Procedural Step. Perform flexion and extension of the fingers.**
    Support the patient's wrist and gently curl all of the fingers to form a fist, then straighten them so that the hand is flat. Repeat five times. Repeat motions with each individual finger five times each.
    Rationale. Flexibility of fingers and thumb is necessary to grasp items.

11. **Procedural Step. Perform flexion and extension of the wrist.**
    Support the arm and gently rock the wrist forward and back. Repeat this five times.

12. **Procedural Step. Perform shoulder flexion.**
    Keep the patient's arm straight by the side and hold at the wrist and elbow. Keeping the arm straight, lift the arm up and over the head and bring the arm back down to the side. Repeat this five times.
    Rationale. Shoulder exercising increases deltoid and triceps muscles.

13. **Procedural Step. Perform shoulder abduction and adduction.**
    Keep the patient's arm straight by the side and hold at the wrist and elbow. Keeping the arm straight, bring the arm away from the body to the right then back and across the body. Repeat five times.
    Rationale. Strength of shoulder muscles will help if the patient needs ambulation device (e.g., crutches).

14. **Procedural Step. Perform hip abduction and adduction.**
    Hold the patient's leg at the knee and the ankle. Keeping the patient's leg straight, move the entire leg to the right, away from the body, then move back towards the midline.

15. **Procedural Step. Perform hip and knee flexion and extension.**
    Hold the patient's leg at the knee and the ankle. Bend the patient's knee and raise it towards the chest, then lower and straighten the leg. Repeat five times.
    Rationale. Restriction of joint function can cause unsteady gait or difficult ambulation.

16. **Procedural Step. Assist patient to sitting position.**

17. **Procedural Step. Sanitize the hands.**
    Always sanitize the hands after every procedure.

18. **Procedural Step. Provide the patient with verbal and written follow-up instructions.**

19. **Procedural Step. Document the procedure in the patient's medical record.**

20. **Procedural Step. Clean the equipment and examination room.**

Charting Example

Date	
12/4/xx	1:30 p.m. ROM exercises done on all extremities, head, and neck. No signs of inflammation or joint restriction. Patient mentioned slight discomfort with knee and hip flexion and extension. All other motions done without mention of discomfort by patient. ————L. Johnson, CMA (AAMA)

CONCLUSION

Many types of therapeutic procedures are prescribed by physicians and performed in the medical office. The physician must perform some of these procedures, but medical assistants perform others or assist the physician with others. Therapeutic procedures reduce pain, help the body heal after injury or disease, and assist in patient mobility during recovery or when body parts are weak.

Understanding the correct techniques to perform these procedures is essential for medical assistants. Equally important is the ability to prepare for therapeutic procedures and provide the support and education that patients need before, during, and after the procedure. When these skills are mastered and performed with competence and professionalism, the patient's experience will be positive, and the patient will be more likely to follow the prescribed treatment plan.

SUMMARY

Reinforce your understanding of the material in this chapter by reviewing the curriculum objectives and key content points below.

1. Define, appropriately use, and spell all the Key Terms for this chapter.
   - Review the Key Terms if necessary.
2. Explain the effects of local application of cold therapy on an injured body part.
   - Cold therapy serves to temporarily decrease circulatory blood flow to an injured body part.
   - Decreased blood flow helps reduce or prevent swelling, slows cellular growth, and reduces bleeding.
3. Demonstrate the procedure for properly applying an ice bag.
   - Review Procedure 3-1.
4. Demonstrate the procedure for properly applying cold compresses.
   - Review Procedure 3-2.
5. Demonstrate the procedure for properly activating and applying a chemical cold pack.
   - Review Procedure 3-3.
6. Explain the effects of local application of heat therapy on an injured body part.
   - Heat therapy serves to increase blood flow to a traumatized body area.
   - Heat reduces pain and speeds up the inflammatory process, promoting cell and tissue growth by removing wastes faster and increasing nutrients to the area.
7. Demonstrate the procedure for properly applying a hot water bag.
   - Review Procedure 3-4.
8. Demonstrate the procedure for properly applying a heating pad.
   - Review Procedure 3-5.
9. Demonstrate the procedure for properly applying a hot compress to increase circulation.
   - Review Procedure 3-6.
10. Demonstrate the procedure for properly applying hot soaks for pain or swelling relief.
    - Review Procedure 3-7.
11. List three therapeutic uses of ultrasound therapy.
    - Ultrasound procedures are used for pain relief for muscle spasms, arthritis, and inflammation.
12. Demonstrate the correct procedure for administering an ultrasound treatment.
    - Review Procedure 3-8.
13. Explain the importance of ensuring that an ambulatory device properly fits the patient.
    - An ambulatory device that does not fit prop-

erly can decrease stability, increase use of energy, decrease function, and compromise patient safety.
    - Improper fit also may cause the patient to develop bad gait habits or unsafe gait patterns and may result in tissue trauma (e.g., armpit).
14. Demonstrate the procedure for properly measuring a patient for crutches.
    - Review Procedure 3-9.
15. Demonstrate the correct procedure for providing instructions to the patient for the appropriate crutch gait depending on the patient's injury or condition.
    - Review Procedure 3-10.
16. Demonstrate the procedure for properly measuring and instructing the patient in the use of a walker.
    - Review Procedure 3-11.
17. Demonstrate the procedure for properly measuring and instructing the patient in the use of a cane.
    - Review Procedure 3-12.
18. Explain the purpose of a cast.
    - Casts immobilize body parts to allow for proper alignment until bones or injured areas have healed.
19. Demonstrate the correct procedure for providing supplies and assistance during plaster-of-Paris or fiberglass cast application and instructing the patient in cast care and nutritional requirements for healing.
    - Review Procedure 3-13.
20. Describe the process of cast removal and explain patient instructions that medical assistants may need to provide during the procedure.
    - Patients must be instructed not to lean the cast on anything until it is dry and not to put anything in the cast or use anything inside the cast to scratch an itch.
    - A cast cutter, cast spreader, and bandage scissors are used to remove the cast, padding, and stockinette.
21. Demonstrate correct technique for performing range-of-motion exercises.
    - Review Procedure 3-14.
22. Analyze a realistic medical office situation and apply your understanding of therapeutic procedures to determine the best course of action.
    - When the medical assistant is knowledgeable about each procedure he or she performs, there is less chance for error when performing the procedure.
23. Describe the impact on patient care when medical assistants understand the purpose and use of therapeutic procedures in the medical office.
    - When the medical assistant understands the

purpose and expected outcome of each therapeutic procedure, the patient benefits by having high-quality care.

- Thoroughly understanding each procedure allows the medical assistant to answer all the patient's questions.

FOR FURTHER EXPLORATION

Research legal requirements regarding the performance of therapeutic procedures (e.g., ultrasound treatments) in your state.

Keywords: Use the following keywords in your search: therapeutic procedures, medical procedures.

THE MEDICAL OFFICE

Policy and Procedures Manuals

19. Explain the purpose of policy manuals and procedures manuals.
20. Demonstrate the correct procedure for identifying types of marketing tools that can increase the medical practice's visibility in the community.

Community Resources

21. Explain why it is important for medical assistants to be aware of the community resources available in their area.
22. Demonstrate the correct procedure for gathering community resources.

Patient-Centered Professionalism

23. Analyze a realistic medical office situation and apply your understanding of the medical office to determine the best course of action.
24. Describe the impact on patient care when medical assistants have a solid understanding of all aspects of a well-planned and well-maintained medical office.

KEY TERMS

agenda Document that includes the length of the meeting, topics to be covered, their order of discussion, and the person responsible for each.

Americans with Disabilities Act (ADA) Federal act that provides equal accessibility to services by disabled persons.

back-ordered Out-of-stock items that will be shipped at a later date by a supplier.

breach of confidentiality Break in a right to privacy of personal information.

capital goods Goods that are durable and are expected to last a few years; often expensive.

disposable goods Expendable or consumable supplies that are used and then discarded.

facilities management Maintaining the atmosphere and physical environment of an office.

facsimile Fax.

fax machine Office equipment that scans a document, translates the information to electronic impulses, and transmits an exact copy of the original document from one location to another using a telephone line.

Health Insurance Portability and Accountability Act (HIPAA) Federal act of 1996 that mandates patient rights in health care and provides guidelines for maintaining confidentiality of patient information by health care providers and insurance carriers.

inventory records Documentation of physical assets using information that includes item description, date of purchase, price, and where purchased, as well as equipment serial numbers and service agreements.

invoice Form prepared by the vendor describing the products sold (by item number and quantity) and the price; used for paying vendor for purchased supplies and equipment.

itinerary Travel document that describes the overall trip and indicates what is scheduled to happen each day.

lead time Time it takes to receive an order that has been placed.

noncapital goods Equipment that is reusable but less expensive and less durable than capital equipment.

notebook computer Small, portable computer (size of a notebook).

order quantity Optimal quantity of a supply to be ordered at one time.

packing slip Document received with an order that lists the items ordered and itemizes those sent and those to arrive at a later date.

personal digital assistant (PDA) Pocket-sized computer used for appointments, phone numbers, notes, and other information (e.g., Palm Pilots, Blackberries).

policy manual Manual that explains the policies used in the day-to-day operations of the medical office and provides general information that affects all employees.

postage meter Automated stamp machine.

preventive maintenance Regular servicing to prevent the breakdown of equipment.

procedures manual Manual containing specific instructions on how procedures are to be performed.

purchase order Document used to order supplies; contains the name, address, and telephone number of a vendor and the quantity, price, and description of the items ordered.

reorder point Minimum quantity of a supply to be available before a new order is placed.

safety stock Items kept on hand to avoid running out of supplies until a reorder is obtained (backup supply).

vendor Entity that sells supplies, equipment, and services (e.g., office cleaning, office supplies).

warranty card Card accompanying a purchased item that provides protection for the buyer against defective parts for a certain amount of time.

What Would You Do?

Read the following scenario and keep it in mind as you learn about the planning and maintenance of a medical office in this chapter.

Janine is a new member of the office staff. She has not had any training in the medical assisting field, but she has been working as a receptionist in a loan office. On her first day at work Janine is assigned to work at the front desk with the receptionist. As the patients for the day come in, she asks many personal questions about each patient and then proceeds to tell the receptionist what she knows about each patient. When told to be sure the names of the patients have been obliterated from the sign-in sheet, she uses a yellow highlighter. As she answers the phone, everyone in the office can hear her conversations. Janine immediately rearranges the large plants in the reception area, and now a plant is partially blocking the doorway.

A fax from a surgeon arrives for Dr. Lopez, and Janine places it on the front counter next to the sign-in sheet until she has a chance to give it to Dr. Lopez. When asked to move the fax, Janine replies that it would "definitely be easier" if the fax was just placed next to the front window rather than in the back room so she would not have to walk so far. Also, Janine does not understand why the office needs a dedicated line for the fax machine. Why not just have the fax line connected to the multiline telephone at the front desk?

Janine was asked to leave a week later after she refused to maintain the equipment. As the office personnel looked for the manuals for the new equipment that had been purchased, no manuals could be found; when she was contacted, Janine admitted to discarding them.

What would you tell Janine about why she was asked to leave her job at the medical office?

The success of a medical practice depends on the organization and efficient functioning of the medical office. All staff members have a responsibility for high-quality patient care, whether it is provided directly or indirectly. The medical assistant is directly involved in how smoothly medical office tasks are accomplished. Understanding effective facilities management; office equipment use, purchase, and maintenance; supply inventory control; office management; policy and procedures manuals; and community resources available will help medical assistants keep the medical office running smoothly and provide the best environment for patient care.

FACILITIES MANAGEMENT

The concept of maintaining the atmosphere and physical environment of an office is called **facilities management.** Facilities management in the medical office is the responsibility of all staff members. The atmosphere and environment of the medical facility send a nonverbal message to the patients and even staff; this should be a positive message, not negative. Attention to decor of the reception room, its cleanliness, and a pleasant patient greeting can lift the spirit of patients and make their waiting time more agreeable.

When planning for, improving, or maintaining a medical office, several legal considerations must be taken into account (e.g., HIPAA, ADA), and available guidelines can help create a good reception area environment for patients.

Health Insurance Portability and Accountability Act

The **Health Insurance Portability and Accountability Act (HIPAA)** of 1996 mandates patient rights. It provides guidelines for health care providers and insurance carriers for administrative procedures concerning the following issues:

- Electronic transfer of claims
- Disclosure of patient information
- Privacy and security issues to protect the privacy of a patient's health care information

Protected information includes all demographic or health information that identifies or can potentially identify an individual.

HIPAA puts a new focus on how day-to-day operations are handled. For example, business associates (staff) should sign a confidentiality agreement that states they agree to comply with the medical office's privacy regulations (Box 4-1). The office environment must be arranged in a manner that protects the privacy of the patient and his or her information. For example, computer monitors need to be positioned so that no unauthorized individuals can see the screen containing private patient information. As you explore the administrative aspects of the medical office, you learn how these guidelines

BOX 4-1 Example of a Confidentiality Agreement*

It is the purpose of Sunshine Medical Practice to protect the confidentiality of the medical records and privacy of all its patients, as mandated by the HIPAA legislation.

The patient has a legal right to privacy concerning his or her medical information and medical records. It is the obligation of Sunshine Medical Practice to uphold that right. For this reason, no member of this office to whom patient medical information or medical records is available may in any way violate this confidentiality except with the written consent of the patient and in accordance with the policy of Sunshine Medical Practice and the rules and regulations of the State of Florida.

I have read the above statement and agree to abide by its contents.

SIGNATURES:

Employee: _____ Date _____

Witness: _____ Date _____

*Medical staff must sign a confidentiality agreement that requires them to protect the confidentiality of their patients' medical information.

affect the medical assistant's role in maintaining these patients' rights to confidentiality.

FOR YOUR INFORMATION

Breach of Confidentiality

Breach of confidentiality occurs, for example, when a sign-in sheet that requests the patient to identify the reason for the visit to the medical office is used for unauthorized reasons, breaking the patient's right to privacy.

Americans with Disabilities Act

The **Americans with Disabilities Act (ADA)** also affects the physical structure of the medical office. The architectural standards and alterations portion of the ADA requires that physically accessible routes and fixtures be available to all who enter the facility. People in wheelchairs and those with other types of disabilities must be able to enter, exit, and safely move about the building. This includes having ramps, making sure the size of door openings accommodates wheelchairs, and having lavatory sinks and toilets that are accessible to all. Box 4-2 provides examples of requirements that must be met in order for a medical office to be ADA compliant.

BOX 4-2 Facilities Management Requirements to Meet ADA Requirements

Entrance

Access

1. Width of area leading to the door of the building must be 36 inches wide, slip resistant, and made of a stable material.
2. Ramps longer than 6 feet must have two railings, 34 to 36 inches high. The width of the ramp must not be less than 36 inches.
3. Elevators and ramps must be available to all public areas.

Doors

1. Door must be 32 inches wide and the door handles no higher than 48 inches.
2. Door handles and interior doors must open easily.

Internal

Restrooms

1. Identification of the restroom must include a tactile (braille) sign.
2. Door width must be 32 inches wide.
3. Access for wheelchairs into the stalls requires a width of at least 5 feet by 5 feet.
4. Sinks, soap dispensers, and hand dryers must be easily accessible and able to be operated with a closed fist.

Reception Area

The medical office, including the reception area, must be designed to protect patient privacy as well as allow access to all individuals. It is important to keep in mind the main functions of the reception area when considering its design and maintaining it.

Function

The reception area serves two main functions: providing a place to greet patients on arrival and providing an area for patients to wait until they can see their health care provider.

Design

A patient's first impression of a medical facility and its staff is often influenced by the condition of the reception area. A disorganized, cluttered room may give the impression that the staff and physician are uncaring and may not pay attention to detail. Because of this, the reception area should be well

Fig. 4-1 Waiting area in a medical office.

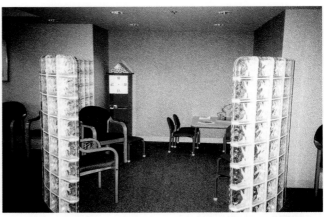

Fig. 4-2 Children's play area in medical office waiting area. *(From Eggers DA, Conway AM:* Front office skills for the medical assistant, *St Louis, 2000, Mosby.)*

maintained for the *aesthetic* (pleasant to look at or experience) comfort as well as the physical comfort of the patient. Every attempt should be made to create a comfortable, welcoming environment (Fig. 4-1). Considerations for making the reception area more pleasant for patients include the following:

- The colors in the area should be calming (e.g., soft colors).
- The lighting should be adequate to allow patients to read.
- Furniture needs to be comfortable, and there should be enough seating to accommodate peak times in office scheduling. Single-seating arrangements are used most often because choosing an empty seat on a sofa next to a stranger may not be comfortable for patients.
- The placement of plants can soften the institutional look of a medical office. They also act as a noise barrier. Keep in mind that any plants or flowers in the medical setting should be artificial because some patients have allergies.
- Updated window treatments and artwork create a professional image for the waiting area.
- The temperature should not be above 73°F, and good air exchange is important.
- Reading materials or other appropriate materials should be provided to occupy patients while they wait.

The selection of reading material available to patients and guests should include current magazines and reading material for children. Pamphlets concerning health maintenance and various organizations (e.g., American Diabetes Association) are also appropriate.

Some offices add a fish tank or have piped-in music to provide a sense of calm to the waiting area.

A TV with special programming channels on health maintenance can occupy the patient's time while waiting. Specialty offices may require additional touches to accommodate their patients. In a pediatrician's office, for example, the furniture must be durable to accommodate active children. There should be a place for controlled activity, including quiet toys (e.g., puzzles), and children's reading materials should be available (Fig. 4-2). A TV and VCR or DVD player with age-appropriate movies also works well in the pediatric setting.

Maintenance

The medical assistant is responsible for keeping the reception area neat and orderly throughout the day. The reception area should be checked for neatness often during the day, but especially before the office opens and again when returning from lunch. The room needs to be straightened again at the end of the day. This lessens the time spent refreshing the area in the morning before opening. A professional cleaning staff is often hired to clean the office completely at least weekly (e.g., floors, dusting, windows).

FOR YOUR INFORMATION

Office Maintenance and HIPAA
The HIPAA Privacy Rule does not consider a cleaning service a "business associate" because the work they perform does not involve the use or disclosure of protected health information. However, if the service was hired to shred documents that contain protected health information, a business associate relationship may exist, and the service would be bound by the HIPAA guidelines.

PATIENT-CENTERED PROFESSIONALISM

- What is the purpose of a confidentiality agreement?
- How can the medical assistant make certain that the medical office is accommodating for all patients?

≋ SAFETY IN THE HEALTHCARE FACILITY

Patient safety

Patient safety is a critical component of the quality of care provided in a healthcare facility. The U.S. Department of Health and Human Services (DHHS) has conducted extensive research on the features of safe patient environments in physicians' offices. The DHHS has found the following factors to be crucial to patient safety:

- Open lines of communication must be established among all employees about possible safety issues, and employees must work together to solve these problems before a patient is injured.
- If an injury occurs (e.g., a medication is administered to the wrong patient), policies and procedures must be in place so that all employees recognize the potential for an error and protocols are established for preventing a similar problem in the future.
- Procedures must be standardized in the facility's policy and procedures manual so that all employees can refer to specific guidelines on how procedures should be performed. For example, in the case of a blood spill, the policy and procedures manual must outline a specific, step-by-step procedure for cleaning up the spill that safeguards both patients and staff members.
- The facility must provide ongoing staff training in patient safety factors.
- Staff members must work as a team to maintain a safe environment for patients. For example, all staff members must follow Standard Precautions to prevent the spread of disease in the facility.

You must constantly be on guard to protect patients from possible injury. For example, studies have shown that healthcare workers frequently confuse drug names, which results in administration of the wrong medication; they also fail to identify a patient correctly before performing a procedure and neglect to perform hand sanitization consistently, thus promoting the spread of infectious diseases. The medical assistant is an important link in the delivery of quality and safe care. Can you think of anything you have learned thus far in your studies that could help keep patients safe in the physician's office?

Employee Safety

The healthcare facility should safeguard patients as well as staff members from the possibility of accidental injury. Data compiled by the Occupational Safety and Health Administration (OSHA) reveal that the leading causes of accidents in an office setting are slips, trips, and falls. You must think and work safely to prevent accidents. The following are some suggestions from OSHA for vigilant accident prevention methods:

1. Use proper body mechanics in all situations. For example, bend your knees and bring a heavy item close to you before lifting rather than bending from your back; push heavy items rather than pulling them; and ask for assistance when transferring patients.
2. Constantly check the floors and hallways for obstructions and possible tripping hazards, such as telephone and computer cables or boxes.
3. Store supplies inside cabinets rather than on top, where they can fall and injure someone; store heavier items on lower shelves so that they do not have to be lifted any higher than necessary.
4. Clean up spills immediately; slippery floors are a danger to everyone.
5. Use a step stool to reach for things, not a chair or a box that could collapse or move.
6. Have handrails available as needed in the facility; use them and encourage patients to use them.
7. Do not overload electrical outlets.
8. Perform a safety check of the facility routinely; look for unsafe or defective equipment, torn carpeting that could catch heels, adequate lighting both inside and outside the facility, and so on.

A primary concern for personnel and patient safety is infection control. The goal is to protect staff members from occupational exposure to blood-borne pathogens while at the same time safeguarding patients in the facility. OSHA's guidelines include management of sharps and providing current safety-engineered sharps devices; providing hepatitis B immunization free of charge to all employees at risk of exposure to blood and body fluids; using latex-free supplies as much as possible to prevent allergic reactions in both staff members and patients; identifying all chemicals in the facility with Material Safety Data Sheets (MSDS) and adequately storing potentially dangerous substances; and performing proper hand hygiene consistently throughout the work day.

Another serious concern that faces all of us today is the prevention of workplace violence. Unfortunately, rarely does a week go by without reports of violence in a public place. Employees in a health-care facility are no exception. Employers should provide training on how to identify potentially violent patients and discuss safe methods for managing difficult patients. Many employers offer training on how to manage assaultive behaviors.

In addition to these concerns, staff members should constantly be on the alert for possible safety hazards in and around the building, such as improper lighting, unlimited access to the facility, and inadequate use of security systems.

Environmental Safety

Personal safety guidelines include numerous work safety practices, such as office security, management of smoke detectors and fire extinguishers, posting of designated fire exit routes, and the importance of securing certain items (e.g., narcotics and dangerous chemicals) in locked storage areas in the facility.

The medical assistant must be prepared to use a fire extinguisher to prevent injury to patients and to protect the medical facility. An ABC fire extinguisher is effective against the most common causes of fire including cloth, paper, plastics, rubber, flammable liquids, and electrical fires. Most small extinguishers empty within 15 seconds, so it is important to call 911 immediately if the facility fire is not small and confined. If the fire is small, no heavy smoke is present, and you have easy access to an exit route, use the closest fire extinguisher. However, do not hesitate to evacuate the facility if you believe any danger exists to yourself or others.

Each facility should have a policy and procedure in place for evacuating the building. According to OSHA, the facility's plan first should identify the situations that might require evacuation, such as a natural disaster or a fire. The following provisions should be included in the facility's evacuation plan:

- An emergency action coordinator must be designated, and all employees must know who this individual is. This person is in charge if an emergency occurs.

- The coordinator is responsible for managing the emergency at the facility and for notifying and working with community emergency services.
- Evacuation routes with clearly marked exits must be posted in multiple locations throughout the facility. Maps of floor diagrams with arrows pointing to the closest exits are an easy means of finding the closest door out, even for individuals unfamiliar with the facility.
- Exit doors must be clearly marked, well lit, and wide enough for everyone to evacuate.
- Any hazardous areas in the facility to avoid during an emergency evacuation must be identified.
- A meeting place must be designated outside the facility for all those evacuating to make sure everyone got out of the facility safely.
- Employees should be trained to assist any co-worker or patient with special needs.
- A designated individual must check the entire facility, including restrooms, before exiting. He or she also must make sure to close all doors when leaving to try to contain the fire or other disaster.

OFFICE EQUIPMENT

Medical assistants handle office equipment daily by using, evaluating, and maintaining it and training others in its use. Because of this, assistants must keep up with technological advances. Office equipment continues to become smaller in size, larger in capacity, and faster in processing speed. These advances and good organizational skills assist the office staff in completing time-consuming tasks more quickly. Equipment manuals provide instructions for use as well as troubleshooting guidelines for when equipment malfunctions.

Typical office equipment includes the fax machine, photocopy machine, telephone system, mailing equipment, and computers. Medical assistants also need to know (1) what information should be kept in the equipment inventory records about each piece of office equipment, (2) the difference between leasing and buying equipment, and (3) how each piece of equipment is maintained to prolong its efficiency.

Types of Equipment

Fax Machine
Using **facsimile** communication (fax transmission) is a fast, reliable, and inexpensive (the cost of a

BOX 4-3 Legal Concerns when Faxing Patient Information

Legal Issues	Resolution
1. Confidentiality	Need "authorization to release records" form signed by patient or legal guardian and dated.
2. Information	Fax only the minimum medical information needed to accomplish the task, and never financial information about the patient.
3. Location	Only fax information to secure areas in a physician's office, nursing station, or pharmacy.

Does the HIPAA Privacy Rule allow patient medical information to be faxed to another physician's office?

Yes; the rule allows physicians to disclose protected health information to another physician's office for treatment purposes as long as reasonable and appropriate administrative, technical, and physical safeguards are in place. For example, the sender must confirm that the fax number to be used is in fact the correct one for the physician's office, and that the fax machine is in a secure location to prevent unauthorized access to the information. Good business practices to follow include making certain the person to whom the fax is addressed is waiting for it and not allowing faxes to sit in the machine, where unauthorized people can view them.

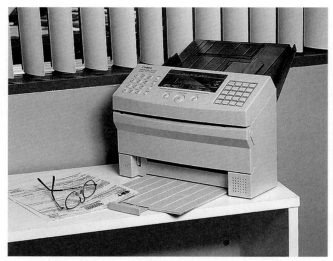

Fig. 4-3 Typical fax machine. *(From Young AP, Kennedy DB: Kinn's the medical assistant: an applied learning approach, ed 9, Philadelphia, 2004, Saunders.)*

phone call) way to send information. A *dedicated phone line* may be used to operate the fax machine, which does not interfere with incoming patient phone lines. This line permits faxes to be sent and received 24 hours a day. Medical records, insurance information, and laboratory and x-ray results can be faxed. A medical assistant should fax information only when necessary and only at the physician's direction.

To protect patient privacy and confidentiality, documents should be faxed only to *secured* areas, where privacy is assured and there is no general patient or visitor traffic. In addition, confirmation should be requested that the documents have been received by the party for whom they were intended. Legal concerns with regard to the HIPAA Privacy Rule for fax use are listed in Box 4-3.

The **fax machine** scans each page, translates the information to electronic impulses, and electronically transmits an exact copy of the original document from one location to another using a telephone line (Fig. 4-3). Some fax machines can

photocopy a single document. Each of the many brands of fax machines works somewhat differently, but the basic process is similar from machine to machine.

A cover sheet should be used because it provides protection (by covering potentially sensitive information) and precedes the document to be faxed (Fig. 4-4). It should include the name of the sender, receiver, number of pages, and the telephone number to call if a problem occurs during the transmission. The cover page and document are inserted into the machine, the telephone number of the receiving machine is dialed, and the "send" button is pressed.

Procedure 4-1 provides general instructions for using a fax machine. Some fax machines operate with "thermal" paper instead of bond paper. When a fax is received on thermal paper, it must be photocopied because the printing on thermal paper will fade over time.

Photocopy Machine

After the telephone, the photocopier is the most frequently used piece of equipment in the medical office. Its purpose is to duplicate a document by taking a picture and transferring it to a piece of paper using a heat process. Copies of medical records, medical reports, insurance claims, correspondence, and other medical documents can be made quickly and easily.

Features available for photocopiers include enlargement and reduction capabilities, sheet feeders, color and black and white options, and two-sided copying. Paper and toner supplies are needed to keep the copier functional. As with fax

---

Facsimile transmittal

To: P.J. Morales, M.D.   **Fax:** 007-555-6655

From: Rosier Park Family Practice   **Date:** 10/21/2004

Re: Referral Information   **Pages (including coversheet):** 2

CC:

☐ **Urgent**   ☒ **For Review**   ☐ **Please Comment**   ☐ **Please Reply**   ☐ **Please Recycle**

Note: Call 555-9876 if any questions

The information contained within this fax transmission contains confidential information. If this transmission has been received in error, notify the sender by calling **555-9876** to arrange for the return of documents.

Fig. 4-4   Example of cover sheet for fax transmittal.

Procedure 4-1 Prepare, Send, and Receive a Fax

TASK: Correctly send and receive information by fax, maintaining confidentiality.

EQUIPMENT AND SUPPLIES
- Cover sheet
- Document(s) to be faxed
- Pen
- Fax machine

SKILLS/RATIONALE

1. **Procedural Step. Gather equipment and supplies.**
   Rationale. This provides for efficient use of time.
2. **Procedural Step. Prepare the fax to send.**
   a. Obtain the document to be faxed. Check the file for a signed and dated "release of information" authorization form.
      When patient information is to be faxed, such as to another physician or to an attorney, a signed and dated "release of information" authorization form must be on file in the patient's medical record. A patient may give permission to release all of his or her information or may limit what information is to be released to a specific visit, time frame, or condition.
   b. Obtain the information of the intended recipient.
      Verify that you have the correct fax number. If the faxed document is to be read only by the intended recipient, a telephone call should be made to the recipient in advance of the document being faxed to ensure that the recipient is available to receive the fax and is waiting at the fax machine for its arrival.
      Rationale. Medical records are highly confidential. Every effort should be made to ensure that the information being faxed is sent to the correct party.
   c. Create a company cover sheet.
      The medical facility may already have a "template" for a fax cover sheet, or a template or cover sheet will need to be created. A fax cover sheet must contain areas for the following information (see Fig. 4-4):
      (1) Sender information: date, company name, company telephone number, name of person sending the fax. Company address and fax number may also be included.
      (2) Receiver information: company name, company fax number, name of person

Continued

Procedure 4-1 Prepare, Send, and Receive a Fax—cont'd

receiving the fax (Attention:). Company address and telephone number may also be included.

(3) Number of pages to be faxed, description of fax contents (Re:), notice of confidentiality. A short message to the receiver may be included.

d. Prepare the cover sheet.

Using either your computer or a black or dark-blue ink pen (never pencil), fill in the required information on the form as illustrated. *Never* send a fax without a cover sheet.

e. Prepare the document.

Documents being faxed should not be on colored paper. If a document is on colored paper, a copy should be made and lightened before faxing. Documents must be free of staples and paper clips.

Rationale. A fax machine will interpret colored paper as having a black background, and when the fax is received, it will be too dark to be read. Also, dark colors slow transmission rate. Staples and paper clips "jam" the machine, causing damage.

3. **Procedural Step. Send the fax.**

a. Place the cover sheet and document into the fax machine according to the manufacturer's instructions.

Read the manufacturer's instructions for the operation of your facility's fax machine.

Rationale. The correct process for fax machines may vary slightly from manufacturer to manufacturer. For example, some fax machines may require that the documents are inserted faceup, whereas others are facedown.

b. Dial the telephone fax number of the recipient.

Before pressing the "start" button to send the fax, check the display window to ensure the correct number has been entered. If the number is incorrect, press the "clear" or "reset" button, then reenter the correct number. Remember to include the area code as needed.

c. Press "start."

d. When the document has completely processed through the machine, press the button to receive a receipt.

If the number rings busy, some fax machines will redial the number at timed intervals. If the fax is not transmitted, the receipt will indicate this. Verify that the number is correct before resending the document. When programmed to do so, machines will automatically print out a receipt, or the receipt may be printed in the top margin of the document. Be familiar with error messages the fax machine may display.

e. Remove the document from the machine, and attach the receipt to the document.

The document and the receipt should be returned to the file where originally obtained. If this is a newly created document, a file should be created.

4. **Procedural Step. Receive the fax.**

a. On receipt of a fax, immediately remove the document from the machine.

Your facility will be the recipient of confidentially faxed documents. All documents should be delivered to the intended recipients, with the cover sheet in place, and should not be read by unauthorized personnel. Authorized personnel such as medical assistants may read the document and determine what actions should be taken.

b. Determine the intended recipient of the document.

A faxed document is considered as equally valid as an original document and should be treated as the original document would be.

c. Deliver the document to its intended recipient or review for action.

Occasionally a fax will be intended for only the physician to view. The fax should be delivered personally to the physician and should not be read by any other party.

d. Perform the action or file the document.

If the fax is a laboratory report, for example, the action taken would be to "pull" the patient's medical record, attach the faxed lab results to the front, and deliver to the physician for review. Once the fax has been reviewed and the physician has indicated reading the report, the fax is inserted in the patient's medical record, and the patient's medical record is filed.

NOTE: Although it is rare, some fax machines may still use "thermal" paper. Documents received on this type of paper must be photocopied because the images fade in approximately 1 year.

machines, many brands of copy machines are available, with each operated according to the individual manufacturer's instructions. To make a photocopy, the original document is correctly placed, usually facedown, on the glass (or fed into the document feeder), and the "start" button is pressed.

Telephone Equipment

As a medical assistant you should be familiar with the various types of telephone equipment that may be used in the office.

Multiple telephone lines are standard in most offices today (Fig. 4-5). A typical multiline telephone has six buttons. Four are for incoming and outgoing calls, one is an intercom button, and the other is to place a caller on hold. When the telephone rings, you need to identify which line is ringing (the incoming call is typically indicated by a flashing light). To answer the call, the button that corresponds to the flashing light is pressed. In larger offices, calls may be handled through a switchboard.

You may be asked to provide input when the office is considering updating the telephone system. Important factors to consider include the following:

- *Ease of expansion.* As a practice grows, the system should be equipped to have telephone lines added easily. A multipractitioner medical practice typically has four lines available initially.
- *Ease of use for the staff.* A complicated system could result in lost calls.
- *Dedicated telephone lines.* Having separate telephone lines for the fax machine and on-line Internet services leaves the telephone lines open for patient calls.

- *Special features:*
  1. *Call forwarding* can be used to forward calls to other departments (e.g., billing, prescription refill, laboratory).
  2. *Conference calling* can be used to have a three-way conversation with consulting physicians and patients' families.
  3. The *privacy button* is for the physician to use when speaking without being interrupted.
  4. The *repeat call* (or *redial*) feature redials the last number called up to 30 minutes previously.
  5. *Caller ID* allows the person answering the phone to see the telephone number of the person who is calling.
  6. *Speaker phone* is a feature that allows the phone to be used without the phone being held next to the face and ear. It enables a small group of people near the phone to hear the conversation and to be heard when they speak. Care must be taken not to use the speaker phone function when patient information may be overheard by unauthorized people.
  7. A *headset* allows you to use both hands while speaking on the phone (Fig. 4-6).

A telephone system can be programmed to have an automated menu (e.g., "If you want to make an appointment, press 1; for a prescription refill, press 2"). The menu should always have an option to press for immediate personal assistance in the event the call is an emergency. Physicians and office managers routinely carry cellular phones and pagers to maintain a link to the medical office.

Fig. 4-6 Telephone headset leaves the hands free and facilitates good body posture.

Fig. 4-5 Multiline telephone systems are a common feature in medical offices. A headset can be attached to the telephone.

Answering Systems

A medical office usually closes for lunch, at the end of the business day, and sometimes for staff meetings. A system must be in place to handle patient calls during these periods. Two methods are routinely used: an answering service and an answering machine or a voice mail system.

ANSWERING SERVICE

An answering service is a business entity that handles patient calls during hours the medical practice is closed. If the physician needs to respond to the caller, the answering service will page the physician. In some cases the call will be forwarded to the physician's location. At other times a message will be taken and given to the medical assistant when the office reopens.

ANSWERING MACHINE

Answering machines are often found in a small medical office setting. When the staff is leaving the office, the machine should be turned "on." The message should identify the name of the office, what to do in case of an emergency, and what information is needed for a nonemergency call. When the office reopens, messages should be retrieved immediately and calls returned as soon as possible.

VOICE MAIL

Voice mail is a computerized answering service that automatically answers a call, plays a prerecorded greeting, and then records a message from the caller. Voice mail is typically part of the telephone system and not a separate piece of equipment. Messages can be retrieved, replied to, saved, deleted, and even forwarded to someone else.

Computers

Computers can organize, store, and process information and are an essential part of the modern medical office. As a medical assistant you need to understand many of the computer's functions and must be able to use it efficiently.

PLACEMENT IN THE OFFICE

Considerations in the placement of a computer in the office include (1) privacy requirements, to ensure screens containing financial and medical information cannot be viewed by others; (2) amount of desk space, allowing adequate space for the monitor, keyboard, and peripheral equipment; and (3) proximity of electrical outlets. Also, the computer must be ergonomically positioned to avoid injury to the user (Fig. 4-7). *Ergonomics* is the science of adjusting the work environment (e.g., workstations,

equipment) to prevent injuries. For example, proper positioning of the computer monitor, keyboard, and chair can reduce the risk of wrist, arm, back, and eye strain.

MOBILE COMPUTERS

Physicians routinely use **notebook computers** to store patient information and the smaller **personal digital assistants (PDAs)** to keep appointments, phone numbers, addresses, to-do lists, notes, and other important information they need to have "on hand."

FOR YOUR INFORMATION

Computers and HIPAA

If a patient can view medical information simply by glancing at a computer screen, the HIPAA regulation has been violated. To avoid this, the computer screen needs to be angled away from a patient's view. Computer screens should never face a reception area or a corridor. Patients should go directly from the reception area to the examination area. This avoids having a patient wandering around a restricted area.

Mailing Equipment

In a large medical practice the fastest way to process mail is by using a **postage meter.** With a postage meter, postage can be printed on adhesive strips for use on large envelopes or packages. For regular-size envelopes the postage can be placed directly onto the envelope.

To use a postage meter, the medical assistant should make certain the correct date is set, weigh the envelope, and select the correct rate according to postal regulations. Next, the envelope is fed through the letter-sealer base of the machine, where postage is automatically applied and the letter is sealed. After this, the letter is ready for mailing.

If a mass mailing is to leave the office (e.g., statements), the postage rate would be the same on all envelopes, so time is saved in processing. The advantage of using a metered mail system is that it does not need to be postmarked by the post office, and therefore moves on to its destination faster. It is important to remember that the letter-sealer portion of the equipment can be purchased, but the meter must be leased. When the meter runs low on postage the meter box can be taken to the local post office for additional postage. Some postage meter companies have toll-free numbers to call so that postage is charged to an office credit card and updated automatically.

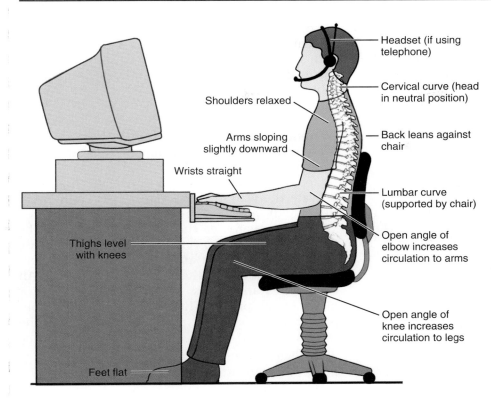

Headset (if using telephone)

Cervical curve (head in neutral position)

Shoulders relaxed

Back leans against chair

Arms sloping slightly downward

Wrists straight

Lumbar curve (supported by chair)

Thighs level with knees

Open angle of elbow increases circulation to arms

Open angle of knee increases circulation to legs

Feet flat

Fig. 4-7 Example of good posture at a computer workstation. *(From Hunt SA:* Fundamentals of medical assisting, *Philadelphia, 2002, Saunders.)*

- Top of monitor at eye level
- Keyboard below elbows, sloped slightly away from user
- Chair supports lower back, height allows feet to rest on floor slightly ahead of knee on footrest if necessary
- Mouse within easy reach
- At least 2 inches from chair seat to back of knee

Equipment Inventory Records

The purpose of maintaining **inventory records** is to document the physical assets of the medical office. Information kept about an item should include the following:

- Description of the item
- Date of purchase (original receipt if possible)
- Purchase price
- Place of purchase
- Serial number
- Service agreement

This information can be used for *depreciation* purposes, an insurance claim in the case of fire or theft, and is useful when deciding possible updates. This information should be placed in a safe location, away from possible damage or loss.

Lease Versus Buy

As a medical assistant, you need to understand how purchasing decisions are made in a medical office. An important decision facing the medical office is whether major office equipment should be purchased or leased. Leasing has definite advantages and disadvantages that should be considered. The practice type and the needs of the practice are major factors in decision making.

Buying a product gives ownership to the practice and allows the owners the freedom to use the equipment as they see fit.

Leasing requires an agreement that outlines conditions for the use of the equipment and requires an initial up-front fee followed by monthly payments. There are different types of lease agreements, and each must be considered carefully.

For example, mailing equipment (letter-sealer) can be bought, but because postage rates are under government control, a postage meter must be leased.

Advantages of Leasing

- Leasing equipment that requires excessive use, needs to be replaced frequently, or requires costly repairs saves the medical practice money in the long run because replacement and repairs are often included in the terms of the lease.

- Leasing technical equipment that needs to be frequently updated will be less expensive for the practice because some lease agreements provide for frequent equipment updating at no additional cost to the office.
- The initial cost to buy an item may be a sizable cash drain on the facility, and since leasing requires less cash up front, it may be a favorable alternative.

Disadvantages of Leasing
- The practice does not own the leased equipment.
- Lower interest rates on purchase agreements may make purchasing the equipment a better choice for the facility.
- Leased equipment cannot be sold because it is not owned by the practice.
- Leasing can be more expensive than buying over a period of time because of overuse fees or higher payments.

Maintaining Equipment

Both administrative and clinical office equipment, whether leased or owned, must be maintained to keep it in working condition. Lawsuits as a result of alleged faulty equipment can be averted if a formal maintenance program is in place. It is also essential to keep records on preventive and corrective measures taken. These records can be kept on a computer or in card files and should include dates of inspection and repair. Procedure 4-2 provides guidelines for establishing a maintenance program for all office equipment. It is best if one person is assigned the responsibility of this task. Preventive maintenance needs to be performed by the medical staff, and warranties may protect against faulty or damaged equipment.

Preventive Maintenance
Preventive maintenance is the action taken by the medical office to identify potential failures and to avoid a breakdown of equipment (similar to having regular vehicle inspections). For example, if a door gasket on an autoclave is replaced at regular intervals before it becomes brittle, the machine will operate at optimum capacity.

Many equipment companies offer preventive maintenance agreements or service agreements on purchased equipment. *Maintenance agreements* are contracts that provide for regular maintenance service at defined intervals or on an as-needed basis. The purpose of a maintenance agreement is to prevent or minimize breakdowns. *Service agreements* provide for labor costs and usually a

discounted price on parts for a set time. These agreements are usually based on 1 year of service, with renewal as an option. As with all contracts, these should be secured in a locked, fireproof cabinet.

Warranties
A **warranty card** accompanies most major equipment purchases. The purpose is to provide protection for the buyer against defective items. To activate the warranty, the card must be filled out (registered) and returned to the manufacturer. Warranties guarantee that the equipment will be free from defect for a certain period after purchase (e.g., 90 days). When an item is misused, vandalized, or mistreated, the warranty is voided. An extended warranty is often offered on major pieces of equipment. This protects the buyer from paying for replacement parts and labor. When the warranty period is over, the warranty card can be discarded.

PATIENT-CENTERED PROFESSIONALISM
- Why must the medical assistant be aware of how to operate all office equipment and have good organizational skills?
- How would you describe the lease versus buy option?
- Once equipment is acquired, what administrative functions should be done in the office?
- How does more efficiency in the medical office translate to better service and care to patients?

SUPPLIES

All medical offices use supplies, the items used in patient care and administrative procedures. Supplies can be identified as being disposable, capital, or noncapital.

- **Disposable** (expendable or consumable) **goods** are used then discarded. For example, tongue blades and other medical supplies, housekeeping items, and office supplies are all disposable goods.
- **Capital** (durable) **goods** are usually expensive and are expected to be permanent or to last several years (e.g., autoclaves, examination tables, office furniture, surgical instruments).

Procedure 4-2 Maintain Office Equipment

TASK: Create a list of office equipment to be used for maintenance of equipment.

EQUIPMENT AND SUPPLIES
- List of office equipment to include all administrative and medical equipment, such as:

Computer(s)	Electrocardiograph machine
Telephone system	Glucometer
Transcription machine	Cholesterol machine
Fax machine	Electronic thermometer(s)
Photocopy machine	Sigmoidoscope
Mail meter	Ultrasound equipment
Printer	X-ray equipment

- Maintenance, service, and warranty agreements
- List of office repair and supply companies
- File folder(s)
- Computer with spreadsheet and word-processing software
- Pen or pencil

SKILLS/RATIONALE

1. **Procedural Step. Create a list of all office equipment used in the facility (classroom).**
Separate the list into administrative and clinical equipment. Identify the vendor for each item.
Rationale. This establishes a "template" that can be used electronically or that can be photocopied and kept on file to be referred to as maintenance is required.

2. **Procedural Step. Create a file folder for each piece or type of equipment (e.g., administrative, clinical).**
Files can be created by vendor, type of equipment, or for each piece of equipment.
Rationale. This provides the facility with a complete list of all office equipment. Depending on the amount and type of equipment, create a folder that best suits the needs of the office.

3. **Procedural Step. File the maintenance, service, or warranty agreement for each piece of equipment.**
Using correct filing procedures, alphabetically file by vendor name, or alphabetically file by type of equipment.
Rationale. This allows for quick access to each piece of equipment's information for accurate and efficient documentation of maintenance or repairs.

4. **Procedural Step. Create a maintenance log for each piece of equipment. Attach each maintenance log on the left inside cover of the file folder.**
Print the name of the piece of equipment in the top right-hand corner. List the manufacturer, identification number, date of purchase, and purchase price directly below the name.
Rationale. This establishes a beginning record of all equipment used by the facility.

5. **Procedural Step. Physically inspect each piece of equipment.**

Ensure that each piece of equipment is in proper working order and is calibrated as mandated by the manufacturer. Look for frayed cords, broken parts, and improper functioning. Note on the maintenance log the date and the status of the equipment (e.g., "works correctly and calibrated to manufacturer's standards," "performs function but LED readout does not register," or "not working and needs repair").
Rationale. This provides the facility with a beginning status report of all equipment. As new equipment is purchased, a file can be established and a maintenance log started.

6. **Procedural Step. Determine the manufacturer's recommended time frame for maintenance.**
Since some pieces of equipment require routine maintenance, a schedule should be established to have a technician "service" the equipment on a regular basis. (You may want to create a "tickler" file to remind you that maintenance is required.) Other office equipment will only require maintenance if the equipment is not working properly. In this case, the service agent can be called and an appointment set for repair.
Rationale. Following this procedure will ensure that all office equipment is in good repair and working whenever it is needed.

7. **Procedural Step. Document all maintenance and repairs on the maintenance log, and keep all receipts of repairs or maintenance in the folder along with the agreements.**
Rationale. Keeping all documentation together in one place for each piece of equipment provides a complete overview of the equipment's history.

- **Noncapital goods** are reusable but are less costly than capital goods (e.g., blood pressure equipment, scales).

An inventory must be kept of all supplies, and care must be taken when ordering, receiving, paying for, and storing them.

Supply Inventory

To avoid running out of needed supplies, one person in the medical office should be designated to handle supplies management. Often a medical assistant is responsible for the inventory and maintenance of supplies and for initiating requests for supplies, or one medical assistant may be responsible for clinical supplies and another for office supplies. A system to handle this responsibility must be chosen to fit the needs of the office.

If the supply cabinet is well organized and a habit is developed to check supplies at least weekly, a shortage of items can be avoided. Dividing items into categories (administrative and clinical) and urgency of need (vital to office operation or incidental use only) makes the process easier. It is also important to know which suppliers require advance notice for orders (e.g., supplier for letterhead that must be custom-printed with information about the practice) and the expected time for delivery. All order information should be documented so ordering can be accomplished if the designated person is not available.

Ordering

A set method for ordering supplies should be established. The following factors should be considered when establishing an inventory control system (Fig. 4-8).

- **Reorder point:** Minimum quantity of a supply to be on hand. When this quantity is reached a supply should be reordered. Establishing a reorder point is based on how much an item is used, the time it takes from ordering an item to receiving the item, how much **safety stock** or how many extra items are on hand, and the time before the next inventory will be done.
- **Order quantity:** Optimal quantity of a supply to be ordered at one time.
- **Lead time:** Amount of time it takes to receive an order once placed.

To be effective, an ordering system must be designed for the needs of the office. One efficient system is using inventory control cards (Fig. 4-9).

If several supplies are needed from a **vendor,** a **purchase order** is usually initiated. A purchase order gives the name, address, and telephone number of both the vendor and the medical office. A preassigned number is stamped on the purchase order. To order items, the medical assistant needs to list the name, product number, quantity, unit of order, unit price, and total price. In some situations either the office manager or the physician will need to authorize the purchase of items. Procedure 4-3 provides general instructions for ordering supplies and maintaining inventory control.

Receiving

When an order is received, a **packing slip** is included. The packing slip lists all items ordered, the items sent, and the number of items **backordered** (out-of-stock items). When the order is received, the packing slip should be dated. The packing slip(s) must be compared to the original purchase order(s). This prevents items being added to an order and the office being charged later for items not received. Each item should be checked against the packing slip for size, style, amount, and condition. When completed, the packing slip is attached to the purchase order, and the inventory

ITEM	MINIMUM QUANTITY ON HAND	AMOUNT ON SHELF	DATE INVENTORY TAKEN
2X2 NS GAUZE SQ	6 BAGS		
2X2 ST GAUZE SQ	6 BOXES		
EXAM TABLE PAPER	12 ROLLS		

Fig. 4-8　Example of inventory control system.

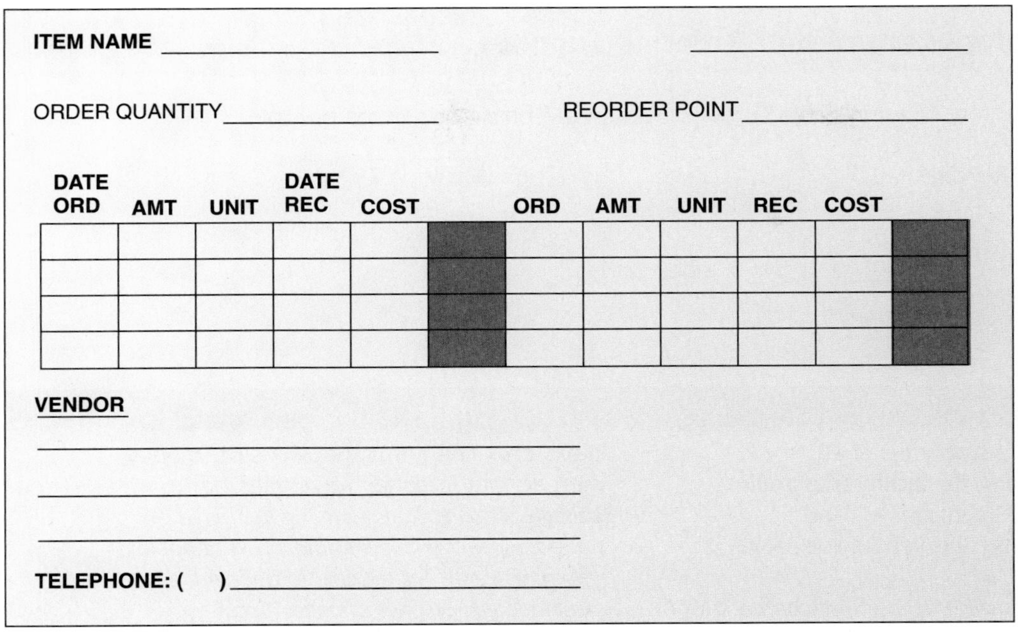

ITEM NAME _____											

ORDER QUANTITY _____   REORDER POINT _____

DATE ORD	AMT	UNIT	DATE REC	COST		ORD	AMT	UNIT	REC	COST	

VENDOR

_____

_____

_____

TELEPHONE: (   ) _____

Fig. 4-9 Example of an inventory control card.

card is updated to reflect the addition of these items in stock. Any errors found must be reported to the vendor immediately.

Payment
The vendor sends an invoice either with the order or separately to let the office know the total charges for the order. The statement shows the summary of the order or account activity.

INVOICE
An **invoice** is a form prepared by the vendor describing the products sold by item number, the quantity, and the price. The invoice is considered a source document and is used for paying the vendor. When received, the invoice should be dated, compared against the packing slip to verify that items were received, and signed, indicating the order is correct and payment should be made. If the order is incorrect and does not agree with the packing slip, it should be noted on the invoice.

STATEMENT
The vendor produces a statement giving the purchase order number, date items sent, and total cost of all items sent to the buyer. The statement should be compared to the invoice to make sure only items received have been billed. The office management should pay only after the invoice has been checked for accuracy and the statement shows the same amount. If the office has only one order from the source, the invoice sent with the order will be used for payment. Statements for a set time may include information from several orders made.

Storage Control
Guidelines for storing supplies include the following:

1. Supplies should be kept in an area that is clean, dry, and well lit. It is best to establish an area for administrative supplies and one for clinical supplies.
2. It is helpful if cabinets are labeled to indicate specific items stored inside.
3. When placing the items on the shelf, newer items should be placed in the back to help with rotation of supplies.
4. Always follow the manufacturer's instructions for storage (e.g., refrigeration, protection from light).
5. Items that have an expiration date can be marked with a highlighter to indicate they need special attention.
6. Shelves should be labeled to identify items on each shelf, which is especially helpful for new employees. An empty space indicates an item is out of stock.
7. Always be sure items have been properly handled in shipment, especially items requiring refrigeration.

PATIENT-CENTERED PROFESSIONALISM

• What steps can be taken to make certain that medical supplies are available in the office?

Procedure 4-3 Inventory Control and Ordering Supplies

TASK: Perform an inventory of expendable supplies used in the physician's office or clinic.

EQUIPMENT AND SUPPLIES
- Supply list
- File box
- Supply inventory order cards: 3 × 5 or 5 × 7 index cards
- Blank divider cards for file box
- Pen or pencil

SKILLS/RATIONALE

1. **Procedural Step. Create a supply list of all disposable supplies used in the facility (classroom).**
   Separate the list into "administrative" and "clinical" supplies. Identify the vendor for each item.
   Rationale. This establishes a "template" that can be used electronically or that can be photocopied and kept on file to be referred to at each inventory period.

2. **Procedural Step. Create a divider card for each vendor.**
   On a file box divider card, neatly print the name of the vendor with the address, telephone number, fax number, and e-mail address. If you have a specific contact person or sales representative, list that name.
   Rationale. This provides the facility with a complete list of all vendor information.

3. **Procedural Step. File the completed vendor divider cards.**
   Using correct filing procedures, alphabetically file by vendor name, or alphabetically file by type of supplies purchased from the vendor.
   Rationale. This allows for quick access to each vendor's information for accurate and efficient ordering of supplies.

4. **Procedural Step. Create an inventory card for each disposable supply item on the supply list.**
   Print the name of one disposable item on each inventory card in the upper left-hand corner of the card. Print the name of the vendor in the lower left-hand corner of the card. Directly below the item's name, print the product identification number. (See Fig. 4-9.)
   Rationale. This establishes a record of all items used by the facility.

5. **Procedural Step. Enter the unit price.**
   The "unit price" is the smallest quantity the vendor accepts as a minimum order and the current price of the item. In pencil, print these numbers directly beneath the vendor name (e.g., $2.50 each, 100 per box, 1 box $76.29, 1 carton $158.00). Also enter the possible price breaks on given items that will save money when bought in certain quantities.
   Rationale. This indicates how the item is to be ordered. By writing this information in pencil, the medical assistant will be able to update the inventory cards as price changes occur.

6. **Procedural Step. Establish or review the reorder point.**
   The "reorder point" is the minimum number of items the facility should keep on hand. Typically, this is half the quantity that is ordered at a time (e.g., 12 units are ordered at a time; when the inventory reaches 6, a new order is placed). Write this number directly beneath the product identification number listed in Step 4.
   Rationale. When supplies on hand fall to or below this number, more of the item must be ordered from the vendor.

7. **Procedural Step. Inventory all items on the inventory list, noting the date the inventory was taken.**
   Count each item on the list the facility currently has available. (See Fig. 4-8.)
   Rationale. Some items require an exact number (e.g., print cartridges for the computer printer), whereas other items will be counted by box (e.g., 7 boxes of small, powder-free latex gloves). Each facility will establish its own guidelines for how often supplies should be inventoried (e.g., once a week, monthly, every 2 months).

8. **Procedural Step. Write the current number on hand (in stock) next to the item on the supply list.**
   Example: Small, powder-free latex gloves—5 boxes.
   Rationale. This establishes a baseline for determining what needs to be ordered.

9. **Procedural Step. Compare the quantity on hand to the reorder point on the inventory control card.**
   Example: The facility has 5 boxes in the cabinet; the reorder point is 7 boxes. Small gloves need to be ordered.
   Items that are below the minimum standards should be highlighted on the supply list.

Procedure 4-3 Inventory Control and Ordering Supplies—cont'd

Rationale. This provides a quick visual reference and establishes which items will need to be ordered.

10. **Procedural Step. Give the supply list to the person assigned to order supplies.**
Monitor how the order is placed (e.g., telephone, fax, or e-mail) to each vendor. When an order has been placed, indicate the date ordered on the inventory card, amount ordered, and unit price.
Rationale. This provides the facility with an ongoing record of how much is being ordered and how often.

11. **Procedural Step. When the order is received, indicate the date and quantity received.**
Note any back-ordered items or price changes.

Rationale. This keeps your inventory control cards current with up-to-date prices and allows for follow-up of the back-ordered items.

12. **Procedural Step. Restock the items.**
Place new items on the shelf behind the currently stocked supplies.
Rationale. Most medical supplies have an expiration date. Placing the new supplies on the shelf behind the supplies already stocked ensures that the oldest supplies will be used first, and that supplies are not being thrown away because they were pushed back on the shelf and expired before they could be used.
NOTE: It is not acceptable to be out of any item that the physician may require to treat a patient.

OFFICE MANAGEMENT

The medical office must be managed effectively to ensure that the staff have the equipment and supplies they need and that they are able to perform their duties. In addition, office records and documents must be stored in such a way that they can be easily retrieved when needed. Meetings and travel should be planned with careful attention to detail. Effective management will eliminate time spent correcting mistakes and save the time of the other office staff involved.

Personnel

Staffing in a medical office requires the office manager to evaluate the needs of each department. Each area is responsible for a variety of duties, and it is important for all personnel to have a good understanding of their responsibilities and those of the other team members. The office manager and the physician should foster an approach that makes employees understand that they play an important part in the quality of patient care. Understanding how your work contributes to the overall success of the practice is important.

A valued employee will develop effective working relationships with other employees so that together they can achieve the goals of the medical practice. The office team is made up of individuals with varied backgrounds and experiences, which influences perception and values. The success of the medical office is built on cooperation and team effort. The health care team must have a common purpose to work together effectively. The goals of the employee and the employer cannot be in conflict; high-quality patient care must be the common goal.

Office conflicts can be kept to a minimum by applying the concepts learned about human relations:

- A team member must be willing to accept others who have a different point of view.
- Good listening can help avoid conflicts that result from a lack of understanding.
- Cooperation with other employees is necessary to attain the goals of the practice.
- Accepting the appropriate share of job responsibility is important in maintaining a pleasant work environment for all personnel.

FOR YOUR INFORMATION

Professionalism
Professionalism includes not only doing what is expected, but also taking the time to see what needs to be done.

Insurance Records

All insurance policies related to the medical practice should be listed, logged, and filed in a fireproof cabinet. Insurance policies may include life insurance, health and accident coverage, vehicle insurance, property insurance, disability insurance, and malpractice insurance. The log should include the policy number, effective date, expiration date, and insurance company name, phone number, and contact person. Policies should be kept in a locked, fireproof cabinet or a bank safety deposit box.

Having the policies protected and accessible makes it easy to file claims if needed. Policies that protect the physician or office against liability should never be discarded, even when they expire. A lawsuit could be filed against the practice, and the policy in effect at the time of the incident is the one that would cover the costs.

Logistical Planning

At some time in any type of medical practice, a medical assistant will be asked to arrange a meeting or travel for employees.

Meetings

Whether the meeting is *external* (outside the office; e.g., a medical association meeting) or *internal* (within the medical office; e.g., a meeting of office employees), attention to detail is necessary. External meetings require that the vital information needed for planning the meeting (e.g., day, time, length, and location) be obtained in advance.

Planning for external and internal meetings includes the following steps:

Step 1: Once the day and time have been selected, a meeting room at the desired location should be secured. If the meeting room is not familiar, a diagram of the room is helpful. This provides room size, room arrangement, proximity to eating places, and available audiovisual aids needed for the meeting.

Step 2: An **agenda** should be prepared that sets the tone for an effective meeting. Agendas include information such as the length of the meeting, topics to be covered, their order, and the individual responsible for each topic.

Step 3: Once the agenda is set and distributed to the attendees, materials required for the meeting need to be assembled (duplicate copies, charts, paper, pencils, audiovisual equipment).

Step 4: At least 5 days before the meeting, all participants should receive a reminder notice or telephone call. At this time questions can be answered as to availability of parking and location of other necessary facilities.

Step 5: The final responsibility is to check the meeting room, including seating arrangements, temperature control, lighting, and a person to handle last-minute problems.

Internal meetings (e.g., office staff only) are less formal and more relaxed, but still need to be conducted in a professional manner. The tone of the meeting should encourage participation by all staff members. Interoffice meetings should be held regularly to improve and maintain office communication and to identify and resolve potential problems.

MINUTES

The "minutes" from a meeting serve as a reminder of what occurred and allow for task follow-up. A medical assistant may be asked to record the events of a meeting. It is important that the minutes always reflect the agenda. The date, place, time, and names of those attending and absent are noted. The items discussed are written in the same order as the agenda, even if discussed out of order. The minutes should be typed and signed by the person transcribing them as soon as possible. The minutes should be filed in a secure place.

Travel

Making travel arrangements for the physician or other staff members can be simplified if it is approached as assembling pieces of a puzzle. Close attention to detail and careful planning cannot eliminate problems, but will minimize them. If arrangements are to be made regularly, an experienced travel agent can be helpful. The Internet has made it easy for individuals to make arrangements on their own. No matter what method is chosen, basic preliminary information must be gathered, as follows:

- The dates of travel
- Means of transportation (i.e., airplane, train)
- Hotel reservations
- Number of people traveling
- Car rental, if required

After all the arrangements have been made, an **itinerary** can be prepared. An itinerary describes the overall trip and indicates what is scheduled to happen each day. The departure point with the exact day and time, the flight and seat number, and hotel accommodations with confirmation and telephone numbers are items also included on an itinerary.

PATIENT-CENTERED PROFESSIONALISM

- Why must office management make the health care team understand that they play an important role in high-quality patient care?
- How should insurance policies be stored?
- What is the difference between an *agenda* and an *itinerary*?

POLICY AND PROCEDURES MANUALS

An office **policy manual** explains the day-to-day operations of the medical office and provides general information that affects all employees. Examples of the need for office policies include employee responsibilities, job descriptions, dress code, office hours, jury duty, vacation time, benefits, and "calling in sick." The policy manual provides a reference for new employees and serves as a guide to clarify expectations of experienced staff members. The expectations of all employees with regard to HIPAA regulations and the Privacy Rule must be explained in the policy manual or a separate manual.

A **procedures manual** contains specific instructions on how procedures are to be performed, including calibration and operation of equipment.

Manuals provide a basis for setting priorities. Box 4-4 provides information on how a policy regarding patient information could be combined with procedural information. Tasks should be identified to clarify what has immediate priority and what may be routine (to determine whether something can be postponed or must be done immediately). Once manuals are created, time should be spent annually updating and using them as a reference. All employees are required to read both the policy manual and the procedures manual, and sign and date that they have done so. If they have questions about any policy or procedure, they need to clarify them with office management at this time. As procedures change or new equipment is purchased, procedure manuals should be revised.

Development

Development of a procedures manual begins with a list of all procedures done in the medical practice. Each step listed for a procedure should be in the order that it is performed, similar to the procedures in this textbook. All instruments and supplies needed for the procedure should be listed. It is helpful to have a photo included with the procedure. Once a procedure is learned, it is not necessary to refer to the procedure manual unless changes occur, but new or temporary employees find the manual useful. All employees should date and initial that they have read the manual and understand what is expected of them.

Maintenance

Maintaining and updating the manuals is important for continuity. All staff members should be involved in keeping procedures current. Updates could come from new regulations passed by the

---

BOX 4-4   Example of Policy and Procedure for HIPAA Regulation

This example shows how a medical office could write a policy for disclosure of protected patient health information* and could include the procedure for carrying out this function.

Policy

It is the policy of Sunshine Medical Practice to protect the privacy of patient health information, as mandated by HIPAA legislation. Therefore, the amount of information accessible in response to a request for information is limited to the minimum amount needed to perform a specific type of work or to complete a function.

Procedure

1. Define why an individual would need patient health information.
   a. Providing patient care
   b. Billing for patient care
   c. Legal issues (addressed in a separate policy and procedure)
2. Requests for patient information are limited solely to individuals who need the information to carry out patient care duties.
   a. Physicians, nurse practitioners, physician's assistants, medical assistants
   b. Ancillary personnel (e.g., pharmacy, laboratory, radiology)
3. Determine the reason for which the information would be needed.
   a. Request of patient
   b. Treatment or billing
   c. Laboratory or pharmacy services needing additional information to provide care
   d. Determining health care compliance and utilization

*Each medical facility will determine its own policies and procedures for release of protected patient health care information.

---

federal government, journals, and even textbooks. If a policy or procedure is revised, the date of the revision should be noted, and all employees should initial that they have reviewed the revision.

Enforcement

A written description of job expectations is important so that all employees understand their responsibilities. By having written guidelines, an employee can be held accountable for job duties.

Normally, employees are first notified verbally that they have violated set policy or procedure. This verbal notification needs to be documented in the employee's personnel file. If the *infraction* occurs again, the second warning is in written form, noting the date, time, and circumstances of the second infraction. At this time the employee should be counseled that continuation of the infraction could lead to dismissal. Documentation of the counseling session must be signed by the office manager and the employee, then placed in the employee's personnel file.

If these documentation steps are taken, when an employee is dismissed for failure to follow policy or procedure, the employee cannot deny knowledge of a set policy or procedure being in place or claim that he or she had no previous warnings that the policy or procedure had been violated.

Marketing

Marketing tools may also be developed using elements of the office's policy and procedures manuals. Marketing tools may include brochures, web pages, press releases, or even seminars and classes for other medical professionals or the community. Any marketing tools should promote the medical office's expertise and skill and can also highlight important policies of the office.

PATIENT-CENTERED PROFESSIONALISM

- If you were a new employee, how would you use the policy manual and the procedure manual?
- What questions could you ask in an interview about the medical office's manuals?

≋ COMMUNITY RESOURCES

A medical practice frequently needs to refer a patient to an agency for assistance. For example, a patient may need counseling, support, or access to social services. Some agencies will provide assistance on a sliding scale based on income and the ability to pay, whereas others may be free of charge. Typical referral agencies are as follows:

- Family and marriage counseling
- Behavioral counseling
- Substance abuse counseling
- Genetic counseling
- Financial and legal counseling
- Easter Seals
- March of Dimes
- Society for the Blind
- American Heart Association
- Homeless shelters
- Child abuse and domestic violence agencies
- Food banks
- Support groups by condition
- Hospice
- Assisted living facilities
- Meals on Wheels
- Medical transport

The names and telephone numbers of these agencies should be kept readily available for a patient's use. Professional organizations can provide additional information to patients about their illness; for example, a patient with hypertension might be interested in information from the American Heart Association, and a patient with nutrition or weight concerns may benefit from contact with the American Dietetic Association.

Each community typically has a network of support groups for various diseases. These groups will provide the patient with encouragement and the emotional support necessary to follow the treatment regimen and will sometimes assist with transportation. Often the local newspaper lists the various support groups available, with meeting days and times. Procedure 4-4 provides criteria for locating a community resource for a patient's specific need.

Patient Advocacy

The patient trusts that you will ensure that they are treated fairly when looking for assistance. Whether you like it or not the patient sees you as their advocate, a trusted voice that looks out for their welfare. What issues are important to you? Is the expansion of the Family and Medical Leave Act to include paid leave an issue that is important to you? Could you become an advocate to expand affordable child care for working parents? How do you plan on promoting or supporting the issues of your patients?

PATIENT-CENTERED PROFESSIONALISM

- Why is it important for the medical assistant to be aware of community resources available for patients?

Procedure 4-4 Gather Community Resources

TASK: Gather information from your local phone book, library, and newspaper, or search the Internet, and create a reference document for community resources.

EQUIPMENT AND SUPPLIES
- Local phone book
- Local or regional newspaper
- Internet access
- Computer with spreadsheet and word-processing software
- Pen or pencil

SKILLS/RATIONALE

1. **Procedural Step. Research the following resources available in your area using the local phone book, local or regional newspaper, local library, or Internet:**
   - Council on Aging
   - Hospice services
   - Civic organizations
   - Social services
   - American Heart Association
   - American Red Cross
   - American Cancer Society
   - Public Health Department
   - Various support groups (e.g., cancer, diabetes, Alzheimer disease, Alcoholics Anonymous)
   - Local agricultural service extension for dietary help

   Rationale. Becoming familiar with the available resources in your area will help you to provide community resource referral information to your patients.

2. **Procedural Step. Create a list of each resource available. Include a telephone number, address, contact person, hours of operation, and what types of services each agency provides.**
   Call each agency or service organization personally. Identify yourself and explain the reason for the call. Group similar services together.
   Rationale. This provides the facility with a comprehensive list of all available resources and provides a patient with choices of organizations.

3. **Procedural Step. Key the information gathered into a document using either a word-processing or spreadsheet software program. Double-check your information for accuracy. Print a hard copy and save an electronic file on the computer.**
   Rationale. By printing a hard copy, you will have a quick reference guide that can be photocopied and given to a patient. A copy can also be kept near the phone to refer to as needed when providing recommendations to patients who call the office for a referral.

4. **Procedural Step. Update the information routinely.** This can be done quarterly, semiannually, or annually. Information should also be updated whenever new information or resources are discovered.
   Rationale. This keeps your resource list current. By keeping this information on the computer, you can retrieve the document easily, correct information quickly, and provide your patients with up-to-date information.

CONCLUSION

The organization of a medical office is the responsibility of all staff members. The reception area is important for the smooth functioning of the medical office and should be designed and maintained with the patient in mind. The office should adhere to HIPAA and ADA guidelines to protect patient confidentiality, regulate how patient information can be disclosed, and to provide physical access to all patients. To create an environment that benefits patients and staff and meets the requirements, all staff must pay close attention to how they perform their duties.

The needs of the patients and the size of the practice will dictate the type and functionality of equipment needed and the amount of supplies to keep on hand. Keeping accurate inventory records for supplies and equipment assists those responsible for updating equipment and ordering supplies to maintain an efficient workflow within the office.

Office management requires that all medical office personnel understand the importance of structure in meetings, accurate travel arrangements, secure insurance records, and being actively aware of policy and procedures in the medical facility. Being part of a medical office team requires that each individual maintain a professional work ethic and attitude.

Patients may require additional assistance from community agencies. It is beneficial if the medical office has the names and phone numbers of organizations in the area to help patients make contact.

Medical offices can be efficient and can provide high-quality patient care only when everyone works together.

SUMMARY

Reinforce your understanding of the material in this chapter by reviewing the curriculum objectives and key content points below.

1. Define, appropriately use, and spell all the Key Terms for this chapter.
   - Review the Key Terms if necessary.
2. Define facilities management and explain its importance to the medical office.
   - Facilities management is the concept of maintaining the physical environment of an office.
   - Maintaining the atmosphere and physical condition of the medical office is the responsibility of the staff.

3. Explain the impact of HIPAA legislation on the management of office facilities.
   - The Health Insurance Portability and Accountability Act (HIPAA) provides mandates for health care providers and insurance carriers about the release of private patient information.
   - Medical offices have confidentiality agreements that all staff must sign.
4. Explain the impact of the Americans with Disabilities Act (ADA) on the physical structure of the medical office.
   - Medical offices must be designed to provide access to all individuals, including those with disabilities.
5. List two functions of the reception area.
   - The reception area is where patients are greeted on arrival and checked in for services.
   - Patients wait in the reception area until their health care provider can see them.
6. Design a plan for a medical office reception area that reflects HIPAA and ADA regulations and incorporates the seven considerations for a reception area.
   - Light, color, furniture, plants, window treatments, and temperature should be considered when planning an effective reception area.
   - Patient confidentiality must be maintained at all times.
   - Refer to Box 4-2.
   - Age-appropriate activities and materials should be provided in the reception area to give patients something to do while they wait.
   - The reception area should be welcoming, clean, and professional.
7. Describe the daily and weekly maintenance of the reception area.
   - The reception area should be straightened several times each day and refreshed before opening each morning.
   - A professional cleaning staff usually does a thorough cleaning at least weekly.
8. List six types of office equipment and explain how each is used in the medical office.
   Medical assistants need to know how to use the following:
   - Fax machines for transmitting and receiving patient information.
   - Photocopy machines for copying patient records and insurance cards.
   - Telephone systems for patient communication.
   - Answering systems for taking messages when the office is not available to patients.
   - Office computers for patient accounts.

- Postage meters for mailing correspondence, claims, and statements.

9. Demonstrate the procedure for preparing, sending, and receiving a fax.
   - Refer to Procedure 4-1.

0. Explain why inventory records are kept.
   - Inventory records are used in maintaining an adequate supply for use in the office, for depreciation purposes, and in case of fire or theft.
   - Inventory records are also useful when purchasing updated equipment.

1. Assess the advantages and disadvantages of leasing versus buying office equipment.
   - Leasing is essentially "renting" equipment for the office; it is not owned.
   - Leasing may be more convenient for maintaining and updating equipment.
   - Buying equipment conveys ownership.
   - Buying equipment may be more costly to cash flow.
   - The best method for each medical office depends on the type and needs of the practice.

2. Demonstrate the correct procedure for maintaining office equipment.
   - Review Procedure 4-2.
   - Equipment that is properly maintained can be used for its lifetime with fewer problems.
   - Service or maintenance agreements can be purchased to help maintain equipment.
   - Warranties protect the buyer against defective items for a period of time after purchase.

. Differentiate between capital and noncapital goods.
   - Capital (durable) goods are expected to be permanent or to last a long time.
   - Noncapital goods are reusable, but not as expensive as capital goods, with a shorter life span than capital goods.

. List three factors to be considered when establishing an inventory control system.
   - Reorder point, order quantity, and lead time must be considered when establishing an inventory control system.

. Demonstrate the correct procedure for creating and maintaining an inventory and ordering system.
   - Refer to Procedure 4-3.

Explain the importance of teamwork in the medical office.
   - The entire office staff must share the common goal of providing quality care to patients.

Describe the five steps in planning for a meeting.
   - Secure a meeting room for the correct time and date.

- Prepare and distribute an agenda to meeting participants.
- Assemble materials needed for the meeting.
- Reminder phone call or e-mail notice should be sent 5 days before the meeting.
- Check the meeting room; assign a detail person for last-minute problems.
- Meetings may be *internal* (inside the office) or *external* (out of the office).
- Meeting minutes need to be typed as soon as the meeting is over and filed in a secure location.

18. Differentiate between an *agenda* and an *itinerary*.
   - An agenda includes information about the length of the meeting, topics to be covered, their order, and the individual(s) responsible for each topic.
   - An itinerary describes an overall trip and what will happen each day. It includes the departure point, flight and hotel information, and ground transportation.

19. Explain the purpose of policy manuals and procedures manuals.
   - A policy manual explains the day-to-day operations of the medical office and provides general information that affects all employees.
   - A procedures manual contains specific instruction on how procedures are to be performed.

20. Explain why it is important for medical assistants to be aware of the community resources available in their area.
   - Patients may need assistance from community agencies for health maintenance.
   - Information from organizations about their illness may benefit patients.

21. Demonstrate the correct procedure for gathering community resources.
   - Review Procedure 4-4.

22. Analyze a realistic medical office situation and apply your understanding of the medical office to determine the best course of action.
   - The medical assistant must protect patient confidentiality at all times.
   - A thorough understanding of the reasons behind the guidelines for effective front office functioning is necessary.

23. Describe the impact on patient care when medical assistants have a solid understanding of all aspects of a well-planned and well-maintained medical office.
   - A good impression of the practice is formed when the medical office is planned, maintained, and running smoothly.

FOR FURTHER EXPLORATION

Research the topic of risk management to better understand the medical assistant's responsibility in preventing accidents in the work environment. Risk management should be approached from a proactive standpoint. To prevent accidents, careful planning, identification, analysis, management, and tracking are necessary. Every employee must take ownership in minimizing the patients' exposure to risk.

Keywords: Use the following keywords in your search: risk management, risk concepts, accident prevention.

Chapter Review

Vocabulary Review

Matching

Match each term with the correct definition.

Americans with Disabilities Act (ADA)

breach of confidentiality

Health Insurance Portability and
Accountability Act (HIPAA) of 1996

agenda

fax machine (facsimile)

itinerary

notebook computer

personal digital assistants (PDAs)

postage meter

preventive maintenance

facilities management

policy manual

procedures manual

backordered

capital goods

disposable goods

inventory records

invoice

lead time

noncapital goods

U. order quantity

V. packing slip

W. purchase order

_____ 1. Document received with an order that lists the items ordered and itemizes those sent and those to arrive at a later date

_____ 2. Status of being out of stock; items that will be shipped at a later date

_____ 3. Office equipment that scans document, translates the information to electronic impulses, and transmits an exact copy of the original document from one location to another through a telephone line

_____ 4. Pocket-sized computer used for appointments, telephone numbers, notes, and other information used on a daily basis

_____ 5. Violation of a patient's right to privacy

_____ 6. Entity that sells supplies, equipment, and services

_____ 7. Expendable or consumable supplies that are used and then discarded

_____ 8. Equipment that is reusable but less expensive and durable than capital equipment

_____ 9. Travel document that describes the overall trip and indicates what is scheduled to happen each day

_____ 10. Form prepared by the vendor describing the products sold by item number, quantity, and the price; used for paying the vendor

_____ 11. Provides for accessible routes and fixtures for use by the disabled

_____ 12. Regular servicing meant to prevent the breakdown of equipment

X.   reorder point

Y.   safety stock

Z.   vendor

AA. warranty card

_____ 13. Card that accompanies a purchased item that provides protection for the buyer against defective parts for 90 days

_____ 14. Time it takes to receive an order once placed

_____ 15. Document used to order supplies; contains the name, address, and telephone number of a vendor and the quantity, price, and description of the items ordered

_____ 16. Document that includes the length of the meeting, topics to be covered, their order, and the person responsible for each

_____ 17. Maintaining the atmosphere and physical environment of an office

_____ 18. Optimal quantity of a supply to be ordered at one time

_____ 19. Manual containing specific instructions on how procedures are to be performed

_____ 20. Small, portable computer that can be carried easily

_____ 21. Documentation of physical assets and information that includes item description, date of purchase, price, and where purchased. Equipment serial numbers and service agreements are also recorded

_____ 22. Extra items on hand to avoid running out of stock (back-up supply)

_____ 23. Automated stamp machine

_____ 24. Mandates patient rights by providing guidelines for health care providers and insurance carriers to maintain confidentiality

_____ 25. Goods that are durable and are expected to last a few years; expensive

_____ 26. Minimum quantity of a supply to be available before a new order is placed

_____ 27. Manual that explains the day-to-day operations of the medical office and provides general information that affects all employees

Theory Recall

True/False

Indicate whether the sentence or statement is true or false.

___ 1. A supply order should only be paid from a statement.

___ 2. A professional cleaning staff typically cleans the office every night and arranges the reception area.

___ 3. HIPAA provides federal regulations that require all public buildings be accessible to everyone.

___ 4. A dedicated telephone line permits faxes to be sent and received 24 hours a day.

___ 5. When leasing equipment, the office owns the equipment.

Multiple Choice

Identify the letter of the choice that best completes the statement or answers the question.

1. Tongue blades, syringes, and printer paper are all examples of _____ goods.
   a. disposable
   b. noncapital
   c. capital
   d. none of the above

2. _____ is the optimal quantity of a supply to be ordered at one time.
   a. reorder point
   b. safety stock
   c. order quantity
   d. lead time

3. When an order is received, a(n) _____ is included in the package.
   a. purchase order
   b. packing slip
   c. invoice
   d. statement

4. Which one of the following is the first step in organizing a meeting?
   a. Prepare an agenda.
   b. Select a location and a meeting room.
   c. Send reminder notices to all participants.
   d. Assemble materials needed for the meeting.

5. Which one of the following is NOT needed to make travel arrangements for the physician?
   a. Dates of travel
   b. Number of people traveling
   c. Hotel reservations
   d. Favorite food

6. _____ explains the day-to-day operations of the medical office.
   a. Policy manual
   b. Guidebook
   c. Procedure manual
   d. None of the above

7. When a medical office is closed and unavailable to handle incoming calls, which one of the following is the most efficient method routinely used?
   A. Answering service
   B. Answering machine
   C. Forwarding all calls to the physician's home phone
   D. Both A and B are equally efficient

8. Maintenance of a procedure manual requires that _____.
   A. the physician's attorneys approve it
   B. the physician sends a memo once a year to remind everyone there is a procedure manual.
   C. all employees are required to date and initial that they have read the manual.
   D. none of the above

9. Which one of the following is NOT considered a medical office marketing tool?
   A. Brochure
   B. Web page
   C. Press release
   D. All of the above are marketing tools

10. Leasing is essentially _____ equipment for the office.
    A. buying
    B. renting
    C. both A and B
    D. neither A and B

11. Inventory records are used in maintaining an adequate supply for use in the office for _____ purposes, and in case of fire or theft.
    A. depreciation
    B. capitation
    C. entrepreneurship
    D. none of the above

12. The first step in preparing a fax for transmission after gathering supplies and equipment is to _____.
    A. copy the patient's file
    B. check the file for a release of information
    C. prepare a coversheet
    D. photocopy the materials to be faxed on yellow paper for better transmission

13. _____ items are usually expensive and are expected to be permanent or at least last several years.
    A. Disposable
    B. Noncapital
    C. Capital
    D. None of the above

14. The *best* color of ink to use on a faxed document is _____.
    A. blue
    B. red
    C. black
    D. purple

15. If a fax is marked "for physician only," what should the medical assistant do?
    A. Do not accept the fax.
    B. Hand it directly to the physician.
    C. Give it to the office manager for his or her decision.
    D. Annotate it and then give to the physician.

16. en maintaining office equipment a file should be created for _____ or type of equipment.
   vendor
   medical assistant
   physician
   none of the above

17. meet the minimum standards of the ADA, a wheelchair ramp longer than _____ feet must have railings.

   0
   2

18. rnal restroom door widths must be _____ inches wide to be in compliance with the ADA.
   4
   2
   6
   2

19. ch one of the following is NOT a legal concern regarding fax machines and HIPAA regulations?
   onfidentiality–authorization signed
   mount of information being sent
   ocation of fax machine
   ll of the above are legal concerns

20. _____ is a document that includes the length of a meeting, topics to be covered, their order, and person responsible for each.
   inerary
   genda
   IPAA mandate
   one of the above

Se   e Completion

Co   each sentence or statement.

1. n ordering supplies, a(n) _____ is typically initiated to keep track of what was red and when.

2. _____ describes a trip and indicates what is scheduled to happen each day.

3. may want to create a(n) _____ to remind you that maintenance is routinely required our office equipment.

4. _____ is a violation of a patient's right to privacy.

5. ket-sized computer used for appointments, telephone numbers, etc., is called a(n) _____.

6. _____ is an automated stamp machine.

7. _____ is the time it takes to receive an order.

8. em that is _____ is temporarily out of stock and will be shipped at a later date.

9. _____ is the term used for maintaining the atmosphere and physical environment of an

10. A(n) is _____ a card that accompanies a purchased item that provides protection for the buyer against defective parts for 90 days.

Short Answers

1. Design a plan for a medical office reception area that reflects HIPAA and ADA regulations and incorporates the seven considerations for a reception area.

   _____

   _____

   _____

   _____

2. List six types of office equipment and explain how each is used in the medical office.

   _____

   _____

   _____

   _____

3. Explain why inventory records are kept.

   _____

   _____

   _____

   _____

4. List three factors to be considered when establishing an inventory control system.

   _____

   _____

   _____

   _____

Critical Thinking

The physician has requested a 10-mL syringe be available in exam room 3 for an I&D of a sebaceous cyst. When you went to the storage room to obtain the syringe, the box was empty. After searching the exam rooms, you were able to locate one 10-mL syringe, which you took into the doctor. After the procedure, you check the inventory supply reorder form for 10-mL syringes. No one has requested that 10-mL syringes be ordered. The office is completely out of 10-mL syringes; what would you now do?

Internet Research

Keywords: Health Insurance Portability and Accountability Act, Americans with Disabilities Act

Choose one of the following topics to research: patient confidentiality as it applies to HIPAA guidelines or the accommodations required of a medical facility under ADA guidelines. Write a two-paragraph report supporting your topic. Cite your source. Be prepared to give a 2-minute oral presentation should your instructor assign you to do so.

What Would You Do?

If you have accomplished the objectives in this chapter, you will be able to make better choices as a medical assistant. Take a look at this situation and decide what you would do.

Janine is a new member of the office staff. She has not had any training in the medical assisting field but has been working as a receptionist in a loan office. On her first day at work, Janine is assigned to work at the front desk with the receptionist. As the patients for the day come in, Janine asks many personal questions about each patient and then proceeds to tell the receptionist what she knows about the patient. When told to be sure the names of the patients have been obliterated from the sign-in sheet, she uses a yellow highlighter. As she answers the telephone, everyone in the office can hear her conversations. Janine immediately moves the large plants in the reception area around so one is partially blocking the door. A fax from a surgeon arrives for Dr. Lopez, and Janine lays it on the front counter next to the sign-in sheet until she has a chance to give it to Dr. Lopez. When asked to move the fax, Janine replies that it would definitely be easier if the fax was just placed next to the front window rather than in the back room so she would not have to walk so far. Also, Janine does not understand why this office needs a dedicated line for the fax machine. Why not just let the fax line be connected to the multiline telephone at the front desk?

Janine was asked to leave a week later after she refused to maintain the equipment. As the office personnel looked for the manuals for the new equipment that had been purchased, no manuals could be found when she was contacted, Janine admitted discarding them.

What should Janine be told about why she was asked to leave her job at the medical office?

1. In many ways, Janine has broken confidentiality in the medical office as required by HIPAA. Name ways that are obvious.

_____

_____

_____

_____

2. What is HIPAA, and how does it affect patient care?

_____

_____

_____

_____

3. Why is a multiline phone system important in a medical office?

_____

_____

_____

_____

4. What special features should be considered when deciding on a phone system for the medical office?

_____

_____

_____

_____

5. How is ADA important in the medical office? What are three of the design features that are important for patient safety?

_____

_____

_____

_____

6. How did Janine make Dr. Lopez's office dangerous for a person with a physical disability?

_____

_____

_____

_____

7. Why is it important to keep manuals that are sent with new equipment?

_____

_____

_____

_____

8.   l you want Janine to be a fellow employee in a medical office with you? Defend your answer.

_____

_____

_____

_____

Ch   Quiz

Mu   Choice

Ide   he letter of the choice that best completes the statement or answers the question.

1.   mandates patient rights by providing guidelines for health care providers and insurance carriers.
          IPAA
          DA
          MA
          ate government

2.   _____ is a piece of office equipment that scans a document, translates the information, and
          mits an exact copy of the original over telephone lines.
          mail
          ostage meter
          x machine
          ersonal digital assistant

3.   cument that includes the length of a meeting, topics to be covered, their order, and the person
          onsible for each is called a(n)_____.
          nerary
          genda
          inutes
          emo

4.   goods are durable and expensive and are expected to last a few years.
          xpendable
          oncapital
          apital
          one of the above

5.   _____ is(are) documentation of physical assets and information that includes item description,
          of purchase, and price.
          voice
          ventory records
          ckaging slip
          irchase order

6.   is the concept of maintaining the atmosphere of the physical environment of an office.
          ckordering
          fety stocking
          cilities management
          eventive maintenance

7. Which one of the following is the first step in organizing a meeting?
   A. Assemble materials needed for the meeting.
   B. Send reminder notices to all participants.
   C. Select a location and a meeting room.
   D. Prepare an agenda.

8. A(n) _____ contains specific instructions on how tasks are to be performed.
   A. policy manual
   B. procedure manual
   C. guidebook
   D. none of the above

9. Which one of the following is NOT needed to make travel arrangements for the physician?
   A. Dates of travel
   B. Mode of transportation
   C. Hotel reservations
   D. Allergies

10. _____ occurs when a sign-in sheet is used that requests the patient to identify the reason for their visit.
    A. Fraud
    B. Malfeasance
    C. Breach of contract
    D. Breach of confidentiality

11. Which one of the following is NOT a function of a medical office reception area?
    A. Provides a place to greet patients upon their arrival
    B. Provides an area for patients to wait for provider
    C. Allows intake of patient information
    D. All are functions

12. To provide a comfortable reception area for patients, the temperature should not be above _____° F.
    A. 64
    B. 68
    C. 70
    D. 73

13. Only artificial plants or flowers should be used in the patient waiting area.
    A. True
    B. False

14. A typical multiline telephone system has _____ buttons.
    A. 3
    B. 6
    C. 9
    D. none of the above

15. The _____ feature on the telephone calls the last number dialed.
    A. call forwarding
    B. conference calling
    C. privacy
    D. repeat call

16. _____ calling feature on a telephone system allows the physician to have a three-way conversation consulting physicians and patient's families.
    onference
    edicated
    all forwarding
    aller ID

17. _____ is a business entity that handles patient calls during hours the medical practice is closed.
    oice mail
    nswering service
    ager
    nswering machine

18. _ is the science of adjusting the work environment so that injuries will be prevented.
    steopathy
    hiropractics
    rgonomics
    one of the above

19. that has been metered in the office takes longer to reach its destination.
    rue
    alse

20. ed equipment cannot be sold because it is not owned by the practice.
    ue
    lse

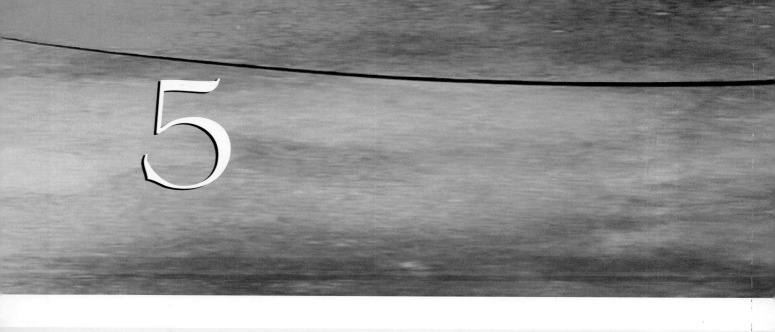

5

Objectives

COMPUTERS IN THE MEDICAL OFFICE

KEY TERMS

back Copying data from a computer's hard drive to
  a storage device, such as a floppy disk, CD, or "thumb
  d protect against losing all data if the system fails or
  "

bit llest unit of data and is an abbreviation for binary
  di

boot Term used to indicate that a computer system has
  be vated and is ready for use.

brow gram for "surfing" the Internet.

byte g of bits used to represent a character, digit, or
  sy

CD-R condary storage device for computer data; holds
  m a than a floppy disk.

centr essing unit (CPU) The "brain" of the computer.

cold tarting the computer when it has been in "off"
  m

curso ing line on the computer screen that indicates
  w e characters typed will appear.

datal inagement Productivity software that allows the
  co user to work with facts and figures.

defau ction or option automatically chosen by most
  co programs (when the user hits "enter") if not
  di y the user to do otherwise.

encou rm Superbill, charge ticket; office form attached
  to nt's record where the physician records the
  di and the procedures and services performed, for
  po narges.

flash A portable data storage device.

flopp Secondary storage device for computer data.

font er style (appearance) of typeface on a document.

guara erson who is responsible for paying the costs of a
  pa reatment.

hard Main device in the computer used to store and
  ret formation.

hardw echanical devices and physical components of a
  co system.

host Computer that is the main computer in a system of
  connected terminals.

initialized Formatted to hold data.

ink-jet printer Printer that produces characters and graphics
  by imprinting ink onto paper.

interface Connection between the user and the computer.

Internet service provider (ISP) Company that provides a
  "host" access to the Internet (e.g., Earthlink, AOL).

keyboard Input device that includes letter and number keys
  and computer task keys.

laser printer Printer that uses heat to fuse a fine dark powder
  (toner) onto paper to create graphics and text.

menus List of commands or options, typically found on the top
  of the computer screen, which can be selected by the user.

microprocessor Circuit found on the main board that controls
  and coordinates many functions of the computer (e.g., speed
  of processing).

modem Device that transfers data from one computer to
  another over telephone or cable lines.

monitor Display device that converts electrical signals from the
  computer into points of light that form an image.

motherboard Circuit board that contains memory chips, power
  supply, and vital components for processing data in the
  computer.

mouse Pointing device that directs activity on the computer
  screen.

network Computers interconnected to exchange information.

optical character recognition (OCR) Computer system that
  scans and reads typewritten characters and converts them to
  digitized files.

password Special set of characters known only to the user and
  the person who assigned the password; designed to secure
  and protect unauthorized entry to a computer.

patient Person who receives medical treatment, not necessarily
  the guarantor.

peripherals External components attached to the computer,
  such as the speakers.

KEY TERMS—cont'd

point Size of typeface; number of characters per inch.

practice management Sum total of managing all the facets (financial, personnel, patient) of running a medical practice.

printer Output device that reproduces information from a computer onto paper.

prompt Message displayed by the computer to request information or to help the user proceed.

random-access memory (RAM) Read and write memory that the CPU uses for storage.

read-only memory (ROM) Stored data that can be read but not changed (e.g., instructions to the CPU on how to set itself up).

scanner Device that converts texts or graphics on paper into an electrical format that a computer can display, print, and store.

search engine Specialized program designed to find specific information on the Internet.

software "Intelligence" of a computer; tells the computer what to do; computer program.

sound card Internal component for multimedia that functions for sound and animation.

spreadsheet Productivity software application that helps the user do calculations by entering numbers and formulas in a grid of rows and columns (e.g., Excel).

tape backup External storage unit.

toggle key Allows the user to switch back and forth from one function to another (e.g., Caps Lock—lower to upper case and back).

touch screen Monitor that displays options that can be selected by touching them on the screen.

trackball Pointing device that has a ball that is rolled to position the pointer on the screen; serves the same function as a mouse.

tutorial Self-guided, step-by-step learning process that teaches generic skills needed to use software.

URL Uniform (or universal) resource locator; Internet address.

user ID Combination of letters and numbers that serves to identify the person using the computer.

warm boot Term used when the computer system has been on and must be restarted because it "freezes up."

wizards Sequence of screens that direct the user through a multistep software task.

word processing Computer-based application used to produce text-based documents.

zip drive External disk storage device that holds large amounts of data.

...hat Would You Do?

...ntos has just hired Terrell, a medical assistant, to ...er demographic and insurance data from the cu... paper records to the computerized patient ac... ng system. Terrell's assignment is to ensure that all ...ormation on current patients is up to date in the co... r and that the latest updates and additions to the ...uter program are installed. As each new patient ar... t the office, Terrell has the duty of obtaining int... on for the data entry. He then must be sure that the appointment has been scheduled into the computer so that medical notes and insurance information will be available as needed. Kate, an established patient, comes to the office and sees the new computer system in operation. Terrell explains that the office is becoming more technologically advanced and that the computer will be used to schedule appointments, store transcription, and manage patient accounts in the future.

Would you be prepared to use the computer to perform data entry, scheduling, and other medical office tasks?

...ntion technology and most people think ...f computers. Every facet of our lives ...as some computerized component (e.g., appl... s, television, and car), and the medical offic... different. A computer in a medical office allo... medical assistant to prepare documents (e.g. ...rs and memos), schedule patient appoint- men... rocess patient's insurance claims, post chai... d payments to the patient's accounts, send ...il, and browse the Internet.

A ...edical assistant, you may become the prim... perator of a computer system in your med... ffice. In many medical offices, computers are ...eing used for practice management and man... ent of patient accounts. Computers are desi... o help you do your job more efficiently. Und... ding the computer equipment and differ- ent ... of software used is an important part of you... s. Computers are becoming more preva- lent ...edical offices today, and this trend will cont...

H... computer skills will give you an edge whe... ing for employment, and these skills will mak... a valuable resource in the office. The first step ...taining these skills is to understand the func... components, and use of computers, as well ...e tasks that can be done more efficiently by ...practice management software in the med... ffice.

...TIONS OF THE COMPUTER

A c... er is an electronic device that converts data ...nformation. Since the computer does not und... d spoken words it uses a series of 0s and 1s t...ibe data to represent information. A **bit** is th...llest unit of data and is an abbreviation for binary digit. A **byte** is a string of bits used to represent a character, digit, or symbol. It is usually 8 bits. Computers function to take in (input), process, generate (output), and store information, as follows:

1. *Input.* Any information that is entered into the computer is done by using an input device (add-on component; e.g., mouse, keyboard, microphone, scanner).
2. *Processing.* The computer takes the data entered and performs a variety of tasks according to the software program being used.
3. *Output.* When data leave the computer through the monitor, speakers, printer, modem, and so on, information is provided to the user.
4. *Storage.* Computers have the capacity to store data on a hard drive, CDs, disks, and other devices and media for future use.

In the medical practice, computers handle both administrative and clinical tasks, as follows:

- In an administrative function, computers aid in patient billing, appointment scheduling, maintaining patient accounts, processing insurance claims, and in database management (Fig. 5-1).
- In the hospital clinical setting, a patient's entire medical record can be stored and accessed by computer. Some physician offices generate and store a patient's medical transcription in the computer, as well as laboratory reports and reports for ancillary services. Typically, **practice management** software can generate in-house reports of a patient's entire clinical history, including

Fig. 5-1 A medical assistant uses the computer to enter patient information.

dates of services, diagnoses, procedures, and the name of the attending physician for each visit.

The technical advances of the computer affect everyone who works in health care. The type of computer chosen depends on the needs of the facility or the practice. Many computers are used in hospitals because a hospital requires that large amounts of data be processed very rapidly and that all departments be wired (connected) so they can access the data they need. In a small medical practice one computer may be sufficient to handle the needs of the practice. Laptops are gaining popularity over bulky desktop models.

PATIENT-CENTERED PROFESSIONALISM

- How would the medical assistant make effective use of the computer in a medical office setting?

COMPONENTS OF THE COMPUTER

A *component* is a part. The computer has several types of parts, or components. **Hardware** is the mechanical devices and physical components of a computer system. Internal hardware includes the CPU, hard drive, other internal disk drives, and memory. Hardware can also be outside of the computer; this type of hardware is called a *peripheral*. **Peripherals** are electronic devices that can be attached to the computer, other than the standard input-output devices such as the monitor, keyboard and mouse. These external components include speakers, microphones, printers, digital cameras, and modems. These devices often require special software packages called *drivers*. These are usually included with the software package at the time of purchase and other devices (external storage media, scanners, speakers, microphones). Fig. 5-2 shows some of the various components of a computer system.

Hardware is the basic computer equipment, and **software** (computer program) is the "intelligence" of a computer. The software program installed tells the computer what to do or how to interact with the user and how to process the user's data. A computer without software is like a CD player without a CD. Without software, the user can only turn the computer on and off.

The following sections describe eight basic hardware parts in a computer system.

Central Processing Unit

The **central processing unit (CPU)** is responsible for interpreting and executing software instructions. Within the framework of the CPU is the **microprocessor** (CPU chip found on the main board), which controls and coordinates many functions of the computer (e.g., speed of processing). The CPU is the "brain" of the computer and is responsible for basic processing operations. The CPU retrieves instructions and data from RAM (electronic circuit that holds data and programs), processes those instructions, and then places the results back into RAM so they can be displayed or stored. The CPU contains memory to process mathematical calculations and compare data and runs the software programs by processing the data. Software programs are loaded into RAM when the processor needs to run them. When trying to remember the multiple functions of the CPU use the acronym CALM.

- **C** for control
- **A** for arithmetic
- **L** for logic
- **M** for memory

Connected directly to the CPU there are several specific types of memory in a computer.

Random-Access Memory
Random-access memory (RAM) is the read and write memory that the CPU can use for temporary storage when the computer is working. The more RAM a computer has, the more programs it can handle.

Read-Only Memory
Read-only memory (ROM) is a permanent type of memory that contains instructions to the CPU on how to set itself up when the system is initially turned on, or **booted up.** The ROM contains infor-

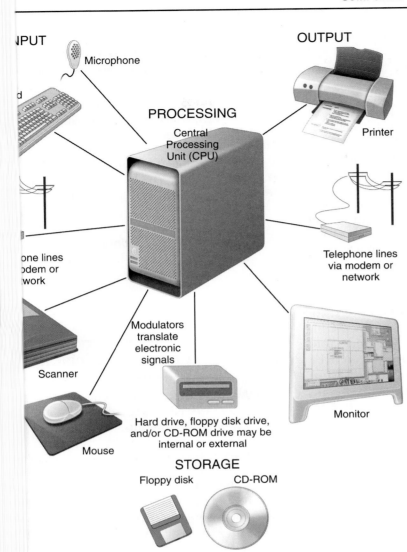

INPUT

Microphone

PROCESSING

Central
Processing
Unit (CPU)

OUTPUT

Printer

Telephone lines
via modem or
network

one lines
odem or
work

Modulators
translate
electronic
signals

Scanner

Hard drive, floppy disk drive,
and/or CD-ROM drive may be
internal or external

Mouse

Monitor

STORAGE

Floppy disk   CD-ROM

Fig. 5-2 Components of a computer system. (*Modified from Hunt SA: Saunders fundamentals of medical assisting*, *Philadelphia, 2002, Saunders.*)

mati... ...out the general configuration of the mach... ...at does not change. A **cold boot** occurs wher... ...power is first supplied to the computer. A **w... ...boot** occurs when the system has been activ... ...n "freezes up," and the operator must resta... ...computer. This can be done by pressing the "... ...button on the computer or with a combinat... ...f keystrokes (e.g., Ctrl, Alt, and Delete).

Stor... ...Devices

A sto... ...evice such as the hard drive and floppy disk... ...D-ROM (compact disc) allows for additiona... ...storage and provides a means for the CPU... ...cess more data. Storage capacity is measured... ...negabytes (MB) or *gigabytes* (GB) with 1000... ...qualing 1 GB.

Hard...

The **h... ...drive** is the main device a computer uses to sto... ...gram information and data for the long term.... ...hard drive is a fixed, rigid disk housed

inside the CPU that contains the operating system. It holds more data than a floppy and is more expensive. **Backing up** the hard drive means copying data from the hard drive to another form of storage device.

Floppy Disks Versus Flash Drives
Floppy disks are secondary storage devices that store information for or from your computer (Fig. 5-2). The original floppy disk was $5\frac{1}{4}$ inches square and was very flimsy and "floppy." Currently a floppy disk, or *diskette*, is about $3\frac{1}{2}$ inches square and is enclosed in a hard plastic shell. When diskettes are used for auxiliary storage, they must be formatted **(initialized)** to hold data. Many computers no longer come with floppy drives, which must be purchased separately.

 Flash drives (memory sticks, jump drives, travel drives, USB drives, thumb drives) are replacing floppy disks as an easy method for transferring data between systems. They plug into the **USB port** (Universal System Bus) port on a computer. These storage devices come in a variety of memory sizes (e.g., 64 MB to 16 GB) and are small enough to fit on a key chain.

CD-ROMs

A **CD-ROM** holds more data than a floppy disk or flash drive, but not as much as a hard drive (Fig. 5-2). CD-ROMS, DVDs, and recordable CDs have become the primary distribution medium for software. Most disks are "Read Only," meaning the computer can retrieve information from the disk, but cannot place information on it. Development in technology improved this to allow writing and rewriting data to a disk. CD-Rs can be recorded on, and CD-RWs (compact disc rewritable) can be recorded on, erased, and reused many times.

External Storage Devices

External storage devices such as **zip drives** or **tape backups** have high storage capacity (e.g., 600 GB). Hospitals and large practices generate and store huge volumes of data, some of which would be impossible to replace should a computer catastrophe occur. For this reason, practice managers are diligent about safeguarding their data by having backup done on a daily basis. Many practice management systems offer the possibility of backing up data "off site," with storage there as well.

Motherboard

The **motherboard** is the main circuit board that contains memory chips (programmed by people), the power supply, and vital components for processing. Components such as a CD-ROM drive, hard drive, video, and **sound cards** (internal components for multimedia functions such as sound and animation) are connected to the motherboard. If this important part of the system breaks, the system is said to have "crashed." The motherboard allows processing and storage to interact with each other.

Mouse

The **mouse** is a pointing device that can either be connected to the computer or be independent (wireless). Some computers use a **trackball** or *touch pad* that performs the same function as a mouse. The mouse functions to move a **cursor** (pointer) around the screen and allows the user to click on document parts, website links, and so on. The arrow keys also move the cursor around.

Keyboard

A **keyboard** is used to input data (by typing) and has various command keys on the keyboard that

---

BOX 5-1 Special Function Keys

- **Function keys (F1-F12):** Initiate commands or complete tasks in application programs
- **Alt, Ctrl, and Shift:** Used with function keys to extend number of possible functions; provides keyboard shortcuts to some commands
- **Esc:** Backs out of a program or menu
- **Print Screen:** Used alone or with Alt key to place the screen onto the clipboard
- **Arrow keys:** Move the cursor around on the screen in the direction of a key's arrow
- **Page Up/Down, Home, and End:** Move the cursor from one place to another quickly in a document or screen

---

BOX 5-2 Common Special Keys

- **Alphanumeric keys:** Used for data entry; resemble a typewriter keyboard layout
- **CAPS LOCK:** Used to switch between uppercase and lower case letters
- **Backspace:** Used to delete characters to the left of the cursor
- **Delete (Del):** Used to delete characters to the right of the cursor or removes character on which the cursor is on
- **Enter:** Used at the end of a paragraph or to enter commands
- **Insert:** Used to move between typeover and insert mode
- **Shift:** Used to produce uppercase letters or symbols
- **Tab:** Used to move the cursor for defined intervals, usually five spaces

---

direct the computer to perform a variety of different functions (e.g., Home; Delete; Page Up; up, down, and side arrows—see Box 5-1). The standard keyboard has the same alphabetical arrangement as a typewriter, with the addition of 12 function keys (F1 through F12) that can accomplish preset keystroking shortcuts. Box 5-2 lists common special function keys. Several of these special keys are considered to be **toggle keys.** These keys allow the user to switch from one mode of operation to another. For example pressing the insert key allows the user to switch between the insert function to the typeover mode; the CAPS LOCK allows the user to move from lower case letters to upper case ones.

Mo...

A **n...or** is similar to a television screen and prov... nstant visual feedback. It displays what has ... ntered into the computer; therefore, it is an o... device. When a patient asks about his or her ... t balance, the patient's name is entered, and ... PU retrieves the data and displays the info... n on the screen. Monitors are rated by the ... d number of dots, or *pixels*. The smaller and ... numerous the dots, the finer and more deta... e the images on the screen. When data are ... n the screen, the image presented is refer... as a soft copy.

Prin...

Prin... ...are output devices that reproduce infor-mati... to paper. A printed copy is referred to as a *har*... The type of printer required depends on the ... need for speed, print quality, and type of pape... The most popular types of printers for medi... fices tend to be ink-jet and laser printers. "Dot... x" printers were used frequently in the past ... ay still be used in some offices to process insu... claim forms.

- **In... printers** are quieter than earlier dot m... rinters. Ink-jet printers form characters on ... aper by imprinting ink in the shape of let... This type of printer can print text, color, an... hics.
- **La... rinters** produce high-quality copies at hi... eds (Fig. 5-3). Some laser printers can pri... or, and almost all laser printers can pri... phics and text.

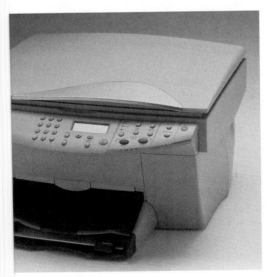

Fig. 5-3 Laser printer.

Modems

Modems allow computers to communicate with each other and with the Internet over phone lines, digital subscriber lines (DSL), or cable networks. These devices can be located within the computer or they can be a separate item. Modems have the capacity to transmit faxes and e-mail. All offices should have a dedicated line for the modem.

Other Auxiliary Input Devices

Optical Character Recognition

The **optical character recognition (OCR)** computer system scans and reads typewritten characters. The checkout at the grocery store uses this type of system. Third-party payers often use OCR to "read" CMS-1500 claim forms during processing.

Touch Screen

With a **touch screen,** a light pen or human touch is used to point to words, diagrams, or symbols. Many clinical settings are converting to the touch screen form of charting that is already used in a hospital setting.

Scanner

A **scanner** uses a light source similar to a photocopier to copy a picture or document placed on its bed (glass plate) and sends it through the modem or cable to a computer. The item scanned into data format is a reproduction of the original and can be viewed on the monitor, saved, printed, or used in other ways.

PDA

A **PDA,** the acronym for personal digital assistant, is an increasingly popular device. Initially PDAs were designed as personal organizers but they have evolved over the years to be much more. Consider them to be a small portable computer or microcomputer, but less powerful than a PC. There are two basic types of handheld devices that fit into the palm of the hand. One type has a miniature keyboard and touch screen and the other uses a *stylus* (point device shaped like a pen) to write on the screen to input data. PDAs are designed to complement PCs. A physician can use a PDA to access a patient's chart, pharmacy and medical information, financial data, and medical references.

PATIENT-CENTERED PROFESSIONALISM
• Why is it important for the medical assistant to understand the basic components of a computer system?

BASICS OF COMPUTER USE

To use a computer effectively a person must tell the computer what tasks to perform, but the information provided by the computer must be interpreted correctly. Sometimes the information comes from the user. A **prompt** message may ask the user to enter some type of data (e.g., "Enter patient name"). A sequence of prompts is used to develop an **interface** (connection) between the user and the computer. Many software packages use **wizards,** a sequence of screens that directs users through multiple steps to help them to add hardware or software.

Menus were developed to allow the novice to be able to use various options without having to remember specific commands. For example, when a menu tab is clicked (e.g., File), the menu appears on the screen, or "drops down," and gives a list of options. In almost every program, a Help button on the menu bar is available to instruct the user in various functions. A **tutorial,** on the other hand, is a step-by-step guide that self-teaches generic skills needed to use software.

When first learning to use a computer, many people find that "trial and error" is a good approach. Practice helps improve your skill with the mouse and understand how to use the various functions available to you. This section provides an overview of some essentials of computer use, including networks and security, Internet use, word processing, spreadsheet use, and database management.

Networks and Security

Computers interconnected to exchange information are referred to as a **network.** There are three basic types of networks, as follows:

- *Local area network (LAN):* A group of computers and other devices that are connected within the same building.
- *Wide area network (WAN):* A group of computers connected between buildings, cities, and even countries.
- *Intranet:* An organization's internal network, using either LAN or WAN. An intranet is not accessible to the public or those outside the organization. Typical information accessible within the intranet includes policy and procedure manuals, office forms, hospital information, and Internet links to various medical sites.

To gain access, networks require a **user ID** (combination of letters and numbers that serves to identify the user) and a **password** (a special set of characters known only to the user and the person who assigned the password) to protect and secure data. This limits those who have access to specific data.

In a medical setting, Health Insurance Portability and Accountability Act (HIPAA) regulations require strict adherence to maintaining the confidentiality of the patient's medical record. In its regulation, HIPAA provides a minimum standard by using a format that is global for anyone sending or receiving electronic information over computer lines via a modem. Each medical software program manufactured follows this HIPAA format. The HIPAA regulations regarding privacy of medical information were enacted to make certain that the privacy of patient information is secure (Box 5-3).

In addition to HIPAA regulations, three other safeguards for protecting patient privacy with regard to computers are as follows:

1. Pointing the computer screen away from the public.
2. Using *screen savers* to cover information if the computer is not used in a set period.
3. Placing printers and fax machines in a secure area away from the general public.

Internet Use

The largest WAN that exists is the Internet, a global network that connects computers together. The Internet is the largest electronic library. Physicians often retrieve articles from medical databases to keep current with medical advancements in their field of practice. Each computer connected to the Internet is a **host** and is independent of the others. An **Internet service provider (ISP)** is a company that provides a host access to the Internet (e.g., Earthlink, America Online). Each user is given an address specific to his or her computer.

Messages are transmitted over the Internet when a **URL** (address) is entered into the **browser.** Common browser programs include Netscape Navigator and Microsoft Internet Explorer. For example, when the URL http://www.cdc.gov is entered, the home page for the Centers for Disease Control and Prevention appears. Here is an explanation of each part of the address.

- *http* (Hypertext Transfer Protocol)—the protocol is the way computers exchange information on the Internet.
- *www (World Wide Web)*—A graphical interface for the Internet made up of Internet servers that provide access to documents, which in turn lead to other documents.

BOX 8 3 Computer and Network Security

As ... patient information is stored on computers, sh... computer networks that can often be accessed fro... ysician's home, and sent electronically to third-pa... rs, security and privacy have become national pri... Several legal and regulatory measures can im... ealth care organizations and the way they main-tai... ity of electronically recorded and stored patient inf... on.

... measures include federal regulations, as ... uidelines from professional organizations and ... g agencies such as The Joint Commission. The ... nprehensive regulation is provided by the ... surance Portability and Accountability Act of 19... PAA), which protects patient privacy by requir-ing ... creation of uniform standards for electronic tra... on of health information. The process of de... g and adopting standards has progressed m... vly than expected. Standards have been devel-op... everal areas. Once they are formally adopted, org... ons have 24 months to demonstrate compli-an... standards have been adopted, as follows:

... ctronic transmission of financial (claims-pro-sing) information

... of standard code sets

... of national provider identifiers (NPIs)

... of employer identification numbers (EINs)

... fidentiality and security protection measures ... establish and enforce security within an orga-nization, measures to maintain security of the physical parts of a computer system where data is stored, measures to control access to data, and measures to protect information and restrict access to electronically transmitted data

Health care providers must become aware of these standards and must ensure that their facilities conform to them.

In addition, within a medical office, each individual who uses the computer should have a unique *password,* which should be changed on a regular basis. The password is a set of alphanumerical characters that allows the user to *log on* (enter) the system or specific parts of the computer system. Individuals should not share their passwords with others.

Each individual should have access to only the types of information and applications that fall within his or her scope of work and responsibility. System security should be designed in such a way that each security level permits access to only the applications and databases each individual needs to perform his or her tasks. Each specific application should know which individuals are authorized to use it.

If a practice uses a service bureau to prepare documents, all documents, in paper or electronic form, should be returned to the practice at the end of the contractual period.

Modi... om Hunt SA: *Saunders fundamentals of medical assisting,* Philadelphia, 2002, Saunders.

• ... *v*—The *domain name* that indicates the ... of the system or location of the ... uter. "Cdc" is the name, and ".gov" ... domain in which the name is ... ered. Common domains are listed in ...-4.

Br... s and websites contain **search engines** that ... a user to enter a topic, word, or group of word... a text box. When this is done, the search engi... l search the Internet for matches. A list of m... will appear, and the user can click on each ... g to reference the information provided. Com... earch engines are Google.com, Dogpile. com, ... Webcrawler.com. There are even search engi... ecifically for medical and health-related searc... .g., Mayo Clinic, MedAlert).

B... provides more information about effec-tively... ucting a search on the Internet.

FOR YOUR INFORMATION

Primary method of Internet access in 2006
- **Dial-up:** 8.7 percent
- **Cable:** 50 percent
- **DSL:** 39.7 percent
- **Satellite Internet:** 1.6 percent

Word Processing

Medical offices use computers to produce written correspondence, reports, forms, and other documents. **Word processing** is a system of entering and editing text that requires interaction between a person and a computer. Word processing improves business communications by using automated equipment to produce letters, memos, and reports.

BOX 5-4   Common Internet Domains

.com	Commercial site; operated by VeriSign Global Registry Services.
.net	Network site; operated by VeriSign Global Registry Services.
.gov	Government site; reserved exclusively for the U.S. Government; operated by the U.S. General Services Administration.
.edu	Educational site; reserved for postsecondary institutions accredited by an agency on the U.S. Department of Education's list of Nationally Recognized Accrediting Agencies; registered only through Educause.
.org	Noncommercial site; .org is intended to serve the noncommercial community, but all are eligible to register; operated by Public Interest Registry.
.mil	Military site; reserved exclusively for the U.S. military; operated by the U.S. Department of Defense Network Information Center.

Word-processing software programs allow the user to merge individual paragraphs into one paragraph; insert an address, date, and salutation; and perform many other document preparation functions. When a person begins keying in the text of a document, typing errors are a minor concern. After completion the software allows the user the flexibility to improve the quality of the document by using the spell-check program, change the **font** and **point** (character style and size), and change the format (e.g., double or single spacing). Remember, however, that these useful features do not eliminate the need for careful review of the document. Another advantage of word processing is the capability of reusing documents. An example of reusing a document is the resume. It can be retrieved, updated periodically, printed, and stored until needed again.

Spreadsheets

Spreadsheet software aids in manipulating numerical data for financial management, as in setting up a budget. A grid of rows and columns is displayed on the screen. Numbers can be entered and a mathematical formula assigned. The computer automatically calculates the result. The advantage is medical practices can set up their own formulas or use the built-in formula functions. Spreadsheets can be used for many purposes in the medical office, especially financial applications and reports (e.g.,

accounts payable, profit and loss, payroll, budget management).

Database Management

Software for **database management** helps the user work with facts and figures comparable to those kept on file cards or in a Rolodex. The program stores, organizes, and locates the files when needed to review or update. If a patient moves, the software searches for his or her record from the database file and changes it according to the input entered. Patient records can be located easily and stored with little effort using a database. A medical office computer database also stores information about providers, insurance carriers, procedural and diagnostic codes, charges, and payment information. This information provides a link between related pieces of information and helps to process paperwork (e.g., insurance forms).

PATIENT-CENTERED PROFESSIONALISM

- Why must the medical assistant follow established security measures concerning the use of computers?

COMPUTER SYSTEMS IN MEDICAL PRACTICE MANAGEMENT

Many software packages are available for the medical practice. Medical software is not limited to administrative functions. For example, some software programs insert laboratory reports directly to the patient's Electronic Medical Record (EMR). Software has been developed to allow the physician to write prescriptions, thus minimizing medical errors by alerting the physician if the drug prescribed interacts with other medications and eliminating errors from poor handwriting. Mastering the tasks in any program takes practice and patience. The key to understanding the workings of a program is to begin by reviewing the operating manual, which discusses special features, prompts, menu selection, and keys that assist the user in navigating through the software. New users will have to be familiar with the latest version of *Windows* (or the current operating system being used on the computer system) and have a basic understanding of keyboarding and medical practice management. Experienced users can focus on the operating functions of the program. Understanding these features will help the user be more productive. Some software companies will provide in-house, on-site training for all staff members.

BOX 5   Effective Research on the Internet

Th[...] net is a valuable tool for locating information
if [...] nderstand how to use it effectively. Two key
me[...] of researching the Internet involve using director[...] search engines.

Us[...]

Directories (Browsing)

A [...] y is a group of categories (subjects). Using a
dir[...] you can select a topic of interest by clicking
on [...] cting a broad category will take you to a listing
of [...] egories. Selecting a subcategory will take you
to [...] topics in that subcategory. You can keep narrow[...] own until you have pinpointed the topic you
wa[...] research. As you narrow down, the topics
be[...] nore and more specific to your interest.

Ad[...]es
- [...] ries are created and maintained by a person,
  [...] ss, or organization in an attempt to provide
  [...] uality sites that will be most useful and to
  [...] out" the unhelpful sites.
- [...] lo not fully understand the organization of your
  [...] eneral directories are a good place to start.

Dis[...]tages
- [...] ries contain fewer sites than search engine
  [...] es because they have been organized manu-
  [...] d attempt to provide only high-quality sites.
  [...] er, some high-quality sites may not be
  [...] d.
- [...] ectory is only as good as the person, business,
  [...] nization that established and maintains it.

Us[...] Search Engines (Keyword Searching)

A s[...] engine allows the user to "key in" a word or
phr[...] interest. The search engine looks for matches
to t[...] vords in all the websites in its database. The
sea[...] ults are prioritized (usually by which words
are[...] t to what the user entered in order and form)
and[...] ayed as a list of "hits." Many people don't
real[...] wever, that search engines do not cover all
web[...] on the Internet. Therefore, it is a good idea
alw[...] use several different search engines. Different
sea[...] ines produce different results, and something
not[...] on one search engine may be found on
an[...] me search engines have "advanced" options
that[...] you to enter more specific criteria for the
sea[...] o, if you are unable to find what you are
loo[...] in the first 20 to 30 hits, vary your keywords
and[...] again.

Advantages
- Search engines are very helpful when looking for specific terminology, topics, or information.
- Search engines are also helpful when looking for specific websites or information on organizations or institutions.
- Other online sources (e.g., newspapers, journals, other web-based publications) can often be found easily using search engines.

Disadvantages
- Search engines allow you to enter keywords, not provide context. For example, entering "cold" would produce more results than necessary. Entering "cold medicine" or "common cold," however, would narrow the search by providing context.
- Search engines often produce many results. The user should not assume that the first result is the "best"; several searches may have to be performed using different keywords and different search engines.

Evaluating the Information

Directories and search engines are great places to start your research. However, your research is not complete until you have verified the credibility of the sources of information. Anyone can publish information on the Internet, and some people or groups may be motivated to publish information that is not true or that is distorted.

Ask yourself the following questions about the websites you use for research:

1. Who created the website? Is it part of a library, university, or government website? Was it created by an individual who wants to express his or her opinions or sell something? Why is this information being provided?
2. Could the information be biased?
3. Are sources of data and information given? (Does the website specify where it received its information?) If so, are these sources unbiased and credible?
4. Can the information presented on the site be found on other websites about this topic? Is the information comparable?

Always check to be certain you are using credible sources.

Choosing a Software Program

With so many types of practice management software on the market today, choosing a new computer system for the medical practice can be a daunting task. If this becomes your responsibility, first organize the facts, then proceed as follows:

1. Obtain input from the physicians and staff as to which functions and capabilities are needed by the system to handle office functions.
2. Determine the office budget; what is the practice willing to spend for the system?
3. Inquire among other practices what type of system they are using. Are they satisfied with it? Does it still fit their needs? Would they purchase it again? Why or why not?
4. If possible, visit other offices to see their systems in use. Ask the staff how complicated the system is to use. Ask what features they like and which ones they dislike.
5. Ask for competitive bids from any company whose product interests you.
6. Determine what type of training they offer: in-house, at their site, one-on-one?
7. Ask what other features are included in the contract: periodic updates (e.g., CPT and ICD-9-CM codes every year), service maintenance, and training.
8. Ask if the medical practice can lease or must buy the program. Can the practice lease with an option to buy?

After assembling the facts, discuss the options with the physicians and make a decision. Remember to save all the paperwork used in making the choice.

Program Installation and Setup

Before practice management software can be installed, certain *software requirements* must be met. The software usually is on a CD and accompanied by installation instructions. The installer must be certain the following features are available:

- Windows-compatible computer (if this is the operating system the software requires; most of these programs are Windows compatible)
- Minimum amount of RAM needed for the software
- Enough hard-drive space
- Updated operating system (e.g., Microsoft Windows, Mac OS, OS/2)

After the program is installed, the basic setup sequence might proceed as follows:

1. Enter practice information (e.g., address, tax ID number, practice type).
2. Enter provider information. This information, besides demographic information, must include the physician's license information, Social Security and DEA numbers, and the option box to indicate that the provider's signature is on file. This is used on the CMS-1500 insurance form, Box 31.
3. Enter insurance company data to include demographics and type (e.g., Blue Cross).
4. Enter patient data to include demographics, birth date, gender, Social Security number, and insurance information, including a guarantor. A **patient** is the person who receives medical treatment; a **guarantor** is the person who guarantees to pay for the treatment.
5. Enter the procedural codes (CPT) and diagnostic codes (ICD) most frequently used by the practice, and renew and update yearly. Optional information to add is code description and standard fee.
6. Enter billing information. This portion is the medical practice's greatest asset. This function manages transactions, general billing forms, and statements.
7. Enter other features if available, such as electronic claim processing, collection letters, and managed care referral generation.

The list above provides basic information, but vendors often have a tutorial for their programs, or they may provide on-the-job training.

Tasks

Many tasks can be performed with medical office management software. The tasks vary depending on the brand purchased. However, some common tasks of medical practice software are entering new patients, scheduling, insurance processing, and generating reports.

New Patient Entry

Entering new patients is done either when opening a new practice or when adding a patient to an existing practice. A common way to enter a new patient is as follows:

1. Select *new patient* from the file menu.
2. Enter all patient information in the appropriate fields.
3. Select *save* from the file menu.

At this point, the computer will assign an account number to this newly registered patient (Fig. 5-4).

Fig. establish becau insu

t is essential to enter information on new and patients accurately into the computer system, s will impact claims filed with the patient's ompany.

Fig.
for I
varyi
requi

ooking more than one 15-minute time slot ore's patients allows for appointments of gths. Longer appointments would probably our on the schedule.

Ty
winc
num
mati
num

information required in the patient e the patient's name, address, telephone surance information, employment information irth date, gender, and Social Security

Sche   g
An a
a pra
sche
daily
typic
date
proc
tiona
listin
uled

tment scheduler is usually included in management program (Fig. 5-5). Patient reports can be generated to include kly, and monthly reports. These reports nclude patient name, account number, ice, attending physician, diagnosis code, code, and charge, possibly with addi- rmation. The program usually allows for the type of appointment that is sched- ppointment date or a range of dates can

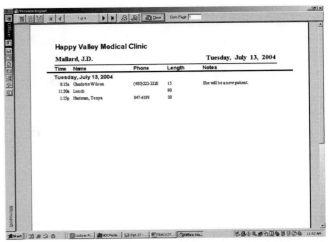

Fig. 5-6 Computers can generate a "clinic list" of all appointments scheduled for a particular day, for a range of dates, or by provider or office site.

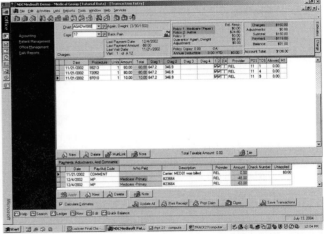

Fig. 5-7 Codes and charges from the encounter form are posted to the patient's account on the transaction entry screen. This screen also provides relevant information about the current status of the patient's account.

be used to generate a report for a particular provider (Fig. 5-6), a particular CPT code, or a diagnosis. This information can be used to manage appointment or surgery scheduling.

Insurance Processing
Most programs allow for easy accessibility to patient billing and insurance information. This allows the medical practice to post charges and payments at any time. Using the information on the **encounter form,** the diagnosis and procedures performed are entered into the patient's account; this posts the charges for the claim (Fig. 5-7). After this new information has been entered, pressing *enter* should **default** the claim to the primary insurance listed for the patient's account. This claim will then drop

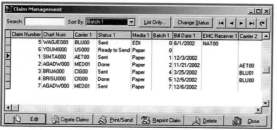

Fig. 5-8 The claim management screen provides an electronic history of each claim. It functions as an "insurance tracking log."

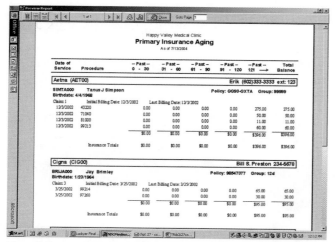

Fig. 5-9 "Primary Insurance Aging" reports help determine which accounts need personal attention and collection efforts.

Fig. 5-10 Daily backups prevent permanent loss of data should a system failure occur.

it for use if the system crashes. Some systems permit off-site data backup and storage.

To safeguard the data files of the practice, the files should be updated at the end of each workday. The backup files should be removed from the office at close of business or placed in a fireproof site in case of fire. If the hard drive were destroyed, without backup, all data would have to be reentered. Once the activities of the day have been backed up, the user can exit the program (Fig. 5-10).

PATIENT-CENTERED PROFESSIONALISM

- Why is it important for the medical assistant to understand how practice management software functions?

CONCLUSION

Computers continue to become smaller in size, larger in capacity, faster in processing, and lower in cost. Still, the newest computer software and hardware cannot solve all office problems. The computer is only as good as the person managing the system. A responsible individual who knows how to use the technology to perform office tasks will make the equipment perform in an efficient and effective manner. Remember that, although computers may improve the speed and accuracy with which office tasks can be performed, these systems do not reduce the need for good communication, organization, and time management skills. A computer makes the medical office run more smoothly, but only when it is operated by a capable, competent medical assistant whose focus is providing the best possible service and care to patients.

SUMMARY

Reinforce your understanding of the material in this chapter by reviewing the curriculum objectives and key content points below.

into the insurance queue, and the next time an insurance billing cycle is run, it will automatically be included (Fig. 5-8).

Report Generation

The "reports" feature of any practice management program allows the medical practice to manage its cash flow, budget, and staff. "Aging" reports, transaction reports, end-of-quarter and end-of-year reports, and "productivity by physician" reports all help track the finances of the practice and are useful for planning staff increases, budgets, equipment purchases, and hiring of new physicians (Fig. 5-9).

Backup and Exit

Protecting the data on the hard drive is a major priority because it contains so much data necessary to maintaining patient and practice records. A tape backup was once used by practices to prevent the overwhelming task of trying to reconstruct lost data. If the system crashed, the data from the backup tape could be copied to the hard drive. Currently, a CD is often used to read and write the data and save

1. ..., appropriately use, and spell all the Key
   ... for this chapter.
   ...ew the Key Terms if necessary.

2. ...our main functions of a computer
   ...
   ...puter systems function to input, process,
   ...erate, and store information.

3. ...ur uses of a computer system in the
   ...al practice.
   ...puter systems in medical practices aid
   ...atient billing, appointment scheduling,
   ...base management, and report generation
   ...fiscal practice management.

4. ...e eight main components of a computer
   ...
   ...t components of a computer system are
   ... CPU, motherboard, mouse, keyboard,
   ...itor, printers, modems, and other auxil-
   ...input and output devices.

5. ...e "network" and list three types of
   ...rks.
   ...etwork is a group of computers intercon-
   ...ted to exchange information.
   ...Ns (local area networks) are groups of com-
   ...ers within the same building.
   ...Ns (wide area networks) connect comput-
   ...between buildings, cities, and countries.
   ...anets are internal networks within orga-
   ...tions using either LAN or WAN.

6. ...in the importance of maintaining network
   ...ty, and list three safeguards for medical
   ...computer use.
   ...AA guidelines require certain standards to
   ...tect the security and privacy of patient
   ...ormation transmitted or accessed over
   ...works.
   ...eguards to protect electronic patient infor-
   ...tion include passwords so that patient
   ...ormation is available only on a "need to
   ...ow" basis; an audit trail so that access to
   ... information can be traced through pass-
   ...rds; and screen savers so that patient infor-
   ...tion does not remain open on an inactive
   ...een.

7. ...onstrate how to access a website on the
   ...net.
   ...tering an Internet address into a browser
   ...dow is one way to access a desired website
   ...ge.

8. ...rentiate between a "directory" and a
   ...ch engine" and explain the advantages
   ...lisadvantages of each.
   ...lirectory is a listing of categories that can
   ...used for browsing; a search engine is used
   ...locate websites based on keywords.
   ...ectories can be advantageous because they
   ...tain prescreened sites (so their listings

tend to be more useful), and they are a good
starting point to organize a search. Directories can be disadvantageous because some
useful sites may be missing since the sites are
prescreened. Also, a directory is only as good
as the organization that maintains it.

- Search engines can be advantageous because
  they are helpful when searching with specific
  terminology since searches are keyword generated, and they provide links to other useful
  online sources (e.g., journals). Search engines
  can be disadvantageous because they require
  a refined use of terms, and they often produce
  too many results.
- Always perform your Internet searches using
  more than one directory or search engine to
  ensure you are obtaining more varied
  results.
- Always check the credibility of the websites
  that you use for research.

9. List five ways a word-processing document can
   be changed.
   - Word processing allows users to move text
     and delete or add sections of text, perform
     spelling and grammar checks, merge individ-
     ual paragraphs into one paragraph, change
     the font and point of the type, and change
     the format and spacing of the document.

10. List three ways a spreadsheet can be used in the
    medical practice.
    - Spreadsheets can be used to generate payroll,
      estimate budgets, and generate other finan-
      cial reports (e.g., profit and loss statements,
      accounts receivable).

11. Explain the purpose of a database.
    - The purpose of a database is to store large
      amounts of related information. For example,
      each patient's pertinent information in the
      database can be added, stored, retrieved,
      updated, or deleted as needed.
    - Databases allow users to manipulate data for
      various purposes.

12. List three things to check before installing
    practice management software onto the office
    computer system.
    - Before installing software, it is important to
      be sure the office computer has the appropri-
      ate operating system, amount of RAM, and
      amount of hard-drive space.

13. List four important office tasks that can be com-
    pleted with practice management software.
    - New patient entry and patient record updat-
      ing, scheduling, insurance processing, and
      report generations are tasks that can be per-
      formed with practice management software.

14. Explain the importance of backing up medical
    office data regularly.

- It is critical to back up medical office data in case the data on the computer are lost because of fire or damage to the hard drive.

15. Analyze a realistic medical office situation and apply your understanding of computers in the medical office to determine the best course of action.
    - Medical assistants must be able to understand and operate medical office computer systems.
    - Medical assistants must keep up to date with the changes in technology.

16. Describe the impact on patient care when medical assistants understand the essentials of computers and their use in the medical practice.
    - Patient care is enhanced because of increased productivity within the office. All information about the patient is located in one place and, with authorization, can be shared with other health care providers.

FOR FURTHER EXPLORATION

Research medical software products using the Internet. As a worldwide computer network, the Internet provides access to a variety of resources. Finding additional information concerning the different types of software available for use in a medical office is a valuable tool for the student.

Keywords: Use the following keywords in your search: medical practice management software, Lytec, Medi-Soft, Medical Manager.

Ethics in Health Care

23. Explain the difference between ethics and law.
24. State the five parts of the American Association of Medical Assistants Code of Ethics.
25. Describe the legal and ethical importance of maintaining patient privacy and confidentiality.
26. Describe the expectations patients have for effective care.
27. List three bioethical situations and explain the considerations for each.

Patient-Centered Professionalism

28. Analyze a realistic medical office situation and apply law and ethics to determine the best course of action.
29. Describe the impact on patient care when medical assistants have a solid understanding of law and ethics.

KEY TERMS

abandonment Failure to make arrangements for a patient's medical coverage.

administrative law Branch of law that functions to regulate business practices.

age of majority Person who is considered by law to have acquired all the rights and responsibilities of an adult (age 18 in most states).

agent Representative of the facility (e.g., medical assistant acts as an agent for the physician).

assault Threat or perceived threat of doing bodily harm to another person.

battery Intentional act of touching another person in a socially unacceptable manner without the person's consent.

bioethics Ethical decisions and issues that deal with scientific situations.

breach of contract The breaking of an established contract.

Centers for Disease Control and Prevention (CDC) Federal agency established to protect the health and safety of people.

confidentiality Keeping something (e.g., information) private.

consideration Benefit or payment.

constitutional law Branch of public law concerned with relations between government and citizens.

contract Agreement between two or more persons resulting in a consideration.

criminal law Branch of public law that deals with the rights and responsibilities of the government to maintain public order.

damages Payment used to compensate for physical injury, damaged property, or loss of personal freedom or used as a punishment.

emancipated minor A minor who has legally been declared independent; held responsible for own debts.

endorsement Occurs when a state accepts the scores of a national examination.

ethics Moral principles.

euthanasia Intentional ending of the life of terminally ill persons.

examination Method by which a person is tested for knowledge; can be oral, written, or a combination of both.

expressed contract Written or oral contract agreeing to specific conditions.

felony Serious crime against the public (e.g., practicing medicine without a license).

fiduciary A position of trusted responsibility.

genomics The science of understanding the complete genetic inheritance of an organism.

Good Samaritan Act Legislation that provides protection from lawsuits for an individual who gives lifesaving or emergency treatment.

gross negligence Intentional omission or commission of an act.

Health Insurance Portability and Accountability Act (HIPAA) Legislation that regulates patients' rights; federal regulation that mandates the protection of privacy and holds information to be confidential.

implied contract Agreement that is created by a set of actions or behavior.

infraction Violation of a law resulting in a fine.

international law Laws that govern relations among nations.

laws General rules and standards to regulate conduct.

libel Written form of defamation.

license Legal document that allows persons to offer their skills and knowledge to the public for compensation.

malfeasance Performance of an unlawful act that causes harm.

malpractice Specific type of negligence; liability.

material safety data sheet (MSDS) Forms that identify chemical structure and safety measures to be used in case of an accidental spill.

Medical Practice Acts Laws that govern the practice of medicine.

misdemeanor Crime that is punishable in jail for a year or less.

misfeasance Improper performance of an act resulting in harm.

negligence Accidental omission or commission of an act that a prudent person would or would not do.

noncompliance Failure of a patient to comply with the physician's treatment plan; grounds for dismissal of a patient from a physician's medical care.

nonfeasance Failure to do what is expected.

Occupational Safety and Health Administration (OSHA) Federal agency that enforces safe working conditions for all employees.

Patient Care Partnership Document produced by the American Hospital Association concerning communication between patients and hospitals.

Patient's Bill of Rights Document formulated by the American Hospital Association to define the rights of patients.

private law Branch of law concerned with rights and duties of private individuals.

public law Branch of law that deals with offenses or crimes against the welfare or safety of the public.

quid pro quo Latin phrase meaning "something for something"; equal exchange, similar to give and take.

reciprocity Exchange that occurs when one state accepts another state's licensing requirements.

res ipsa loquitur Latin phrase meaning "the thing speaks for itself"; legal principle that applies when the situation itself shows negligence.

respondeat superior Latin phrase meaning "let the master answer"; legal doctrine that places responsibility on physicians for actions by their employees (vicarious liability).

risk management Proactive management of potential risks that could result in a lawsuit.

slander Spoken form of defamation.

statute of limitations Time limits to bring forth a lawsuit.

statutes Laws.

subpo [le]gal document that requires a person to appear in
    cou[rt or] be available for a deposition.

subpo[ena du]*ces tecum* Legal document that requires a person
    to a[ppear i]n court and bring the records.

tort Wrongful act that causes harm, committed by a person
    against another person or property.

vicarious liability Liability of an employer for the wrongdoing
    of an employee while on the job.

What Would You Do?

Read the following scenario and keep it in mind as you learn about law and ethics in this chapter.

Jill is a medical assistant with on-the-job training in a medical office setting. She always strives to be caring, courteous, and respectful of patients and co-workers. Because of her caring attitude, the patients with whom Jill works all appreciate her attitude and her work. One of Jill's favorite patients, Shandra, a 24-year-old mother of two young children, has been diagnosed with cancer and recently was told by the physician that her condition is terminal. Shandra is at the office for an appointment and, feeling very upset about her terminal illness, she pours out her heart and fears to Jill. Wanting to comfort Shandra, Jill tells her, "Don't worry. You'll be just fine. You know the doctor will make you better."

Shandra is comforted by Jill's words and tells her how much Jill means to her. In fact, she has so much faith in Jill that she believes that she *will* be fine and tells her family what Jill has said. Sadly, a few months later, Shandra dies. Believing she would be fine, Shandra had not made any plans for her children and family. Her family is upset with the physician and with Jill. The family thinks they have been betrayed because they believed that Shandra would be fine. The family is discussing what to say to the physician about this betrayal and whether to bring a lawsuit, because Shandra did not have a will.

How might this situation been avoided? What are the possible implications for Shandra's family, Jill, the physician, and the practice?

Law and ethics are two of the most important aspects of patient-centered professionalism. As reported in the news, the cost of health care is rising quickly. One reason is the growing number of lawsuits against physicians. Laws and ethical standards protect both the physician and the patient. A truly patient-centered health professional follows not only the law, but also the ethical principles of the profession.

≋ LAW AND LICENSURE IN MEDICAL PRACTICE

In the United States, **laws** protect the physical and social well-being of the citizens. Laws, or **statutes,** are general rules and standards to regulate conduct. They must be followed, or a punishment occurs. During the 20th century, a system for protecting the public from unsafe medical practitioners was mandated by law in all states. This system, spelled out in the **Medical Practice Acts,** is based on the ethical belief that practitioners should "do no harm." Medical assistants should understand this system, which involves licensure and credentialing.

Medical Practice Acts

Medical Practice Acts are statutes created by states to oversee the practice of medicine. The acts establish a medical board to review licensing requirements, guidelines for suspension and loss of licenses, and renewal requirements for physicians in the state. These acts allow the physician-employer to

hire and train unlicensed health care workers, and the acts are recognized in most states. If a physician allows unlicensed health care workers to perform diagnostic or treatment procedures, the physician's license can be revoked or suspended. All 50 states have laws that protect people from unqualified persons practicing medicine.

All physicians' offices must follow the laws and regulations set forth by the city and state where the practice is located. Medical assistants are required to report situations in which the law is being broken or that may lead to the harm of another person, including the patient. However, before taking action that could do irreparable harm to another person's character, verify the facts and follow the facility's chain of command.

Licensure

Many health professionals have some form of regulation of their profession to ensure competence. A **license,** the strongest form of professional regulation, is a legal document that allows a person to offer skills and knowledge to the public for pay. A license is required for persons practicing in certain professions, including doctors of medicine (MDs) and registered nurses (RNs). Rules for licensing are developed by Medical Practice Act statutes in each state. The following three ways are used to obtain a state license:

1. **Examination:** Oral and written exams for a particular state are taken and passed.
2. **Reciprocity:** A state accepts a current license from another state.

BOX | Requirements for Physician License

- M   dividual state requirements
- C   te education requirements through an
  a   d medical school
- C   te an approved residency program
- P   examinations required by the state board
  o   cal examiners
- B   od moral character
- A   e age of majority as defined by state
  st

3.   rsement: A state accepts the scores of
      nal examination.

Lice   nust be renewed, and proof of continuing ed   n must be current. A license that is not
renew   the deadline automatically becomes
inactiv   acticing medicine without an active
license   felony.

Pra   ng Without a License

Dr. N   vent to medical school but never took the
cred   g examinations. He moved to a different
locat   ened an office, and began to practice
fami   licine without a license. The community
cam   espect and trust him. He had a good
beds   anner and often referred patients to spe-
cialis   eighboring communities. Another physician   ched him about developing a partnership,
but   sed. His reluctance concerned the other
phys   vho did some research and found that
"Dr."   e was not truly an MD. The physician
repo   s to the state medical board. Dr. Moore
was   ally charged for practicing without a
licen

The P   ian and Licensure

Box 6-   the requirements physicians must meet
to earn   nse. Physicians are usually required to
renew   license biennially (every 2 years). To
renew,   are required to have 50 continuing
medica   ation hours (CMEs) each year, including 5 h   of **risk management.** The physician
must b   sed by the state to prescribe medications.   scribe scheduled medications, such as
narcoti   e physician must also obtain a license
from th   . Drug Enforcement Agency (DEA). A
physici   nnot prescribe medication to anyone,
includi   friend or acquaintance, without first

BOX 6-2 Reasons for Revocation or Suspension of a Physician's License

1. Conviction of a crime
   - Felony (e.g., practicing without a license, murder, rape, larceny, substance abuse)
   - Fraud (e.g., billing for more treatments than given; up coding)
2. Unprofessional conduct
   - Failure to adhere to ethical standards
   - Breach of confidence
   - Fee splitting
   - Addiction to drugs or alcohol
   - Advertising falsely
   - Incapacity to perform duties

examining the person as a patient and performing the necessary tests, making a diagnosis, and properly documenting the medical record.

A physician's license can be suspended or revoked in certain situations (Box 6-2).

In addition to maintaining a license to practice, the physician is responsible for hiring qualified employees. The doctrine of ***respondeat superior*** (RA-spon-dant su-per-e-or; Latin for "let the master answer") places the liability on the physician for an employee's actions. This means that a physician is held responsible for the actions of the employees under his or her supervision. Even though the medical assistant has a responsibility to the physician to perform all duties competently, the physician is held liable for the medical assistant's actions. This is called **vicarious liability.**

Vicarious Liability

Janet, a medical assistant, is driving from one office to another and stops at a bakery to pick up a cake for an office birthday party. After leaving the bakery, she speeds through a school zone, sideswiping a car and injuring three children walking home from school. Because the accident occurred while Janet was on "company business" (performing activities for her job), the physician-employer could well be named in a resulting lawsuit.

Credentialing

Credentialing is a voluntary process that health professionals can go through to earn certifications and other proof of their knowledge and skills. Credentials are earned by meeting a set of expectations. Steps in the process may include the following:

1. Graduating from an accredited program.
2. Selecting a test site.
3. Completing an application and returning it with the appropriate application fee.
4. Taking and passing the examination.
5. Renewing by completing the required continuing education units (CEUs) in a defined period.

Credentialing for physicians can also refer to the process of applying to a hospital for staff privileges. Physicians must present proof of their education and medical competency, along with peer recommendations, for approval by the hospital's board of directors.

The Medical Assistant and Credentialing

Some states have statutes that protect the medical assistant's right to practice. Other states may limit what a medical assistant can do. It is important to know the statutes of your state because you can only do what you have been trained to do and what the state law allows you to do (Procedures 6-1 and 6-2). Credentialing is not a requirement in all states. However, it is highly recommended because it helps ensure a competent level of knowledge and training.

Standard of Care

The standard of care as it pertains to a medial assistant must be distinguished from the medical assistant's scope of practice. From a legal perspective, each medical assistant is required to perform all duties in a manner that meets or exceeds that of a reasonably competent and knowledgeable medical assistant. Also, medical assistants cannot perform any duties for which they have not been trained. A medical assistant should treat every chart touched as if it will end up in a court of law. Remember, if it is not in the chart, there is no way to prove an event happened. The courts hold that a physician must do the following:

- Use reasonable care, attention, and diligence in the performance of professional services
- Follow his or her best judgment in treating patients
- Have and exercise reasonable skill and care that are commonly had and exercised by other reputable physicians in the same type of practice in the same or a similar locality

In the worst case, a physician or medical facility may be faced with wrongful death litigation. A wrongful death **allegation** is one in which the physician or medical facility is blamed for the death of a patient because of error or inappropriate treatment. A wrongful death suit usually is brought by the family of the **decedent** against the physician or others involved with the patient.

PATIENT-CENTERED PROFESSIONALISM

- In some states a medical assistant can work without being credentialed. What do you see as the value of being credentialed?
- How might obtaining credentials as a medical assistant affect patients' view of you as a professional?
- Why do you think a medical practice would want its medical assistants to be credentialed?

LAW AND LIABILITY

Medical assistants need a good understanding of what law is and how it applies to the medical practice. Learning about the categories of law and how liability (guilt) is determined is a good place to begin. Laws can be divided into two main categories: public law and private law (also referred to as *civil law*). Each branch has its own subcategories. Both public law and private law affect the medical practice (Figs. 6-1 and 6-2).

Public Law

Public law deals with offenses or crimes against the welfare or safety of the public. The main divisions are administrative, criminal, constitutional, and international law. The medical profession mainly deals with the administrative and criminal aspects of public law.

Administrative Law
Administrative law regulates business practices. These laws are enforced by government agencies such as the DEA and the Food and Drug Administration (FDA). This branch of public law creates the state board of medical examiners for physicians.

Criminal Law
Criminal law deals with the rights and responsibilities of the government to the people and the people to the government. Box 6-3 lists the offenses considered under criminal law. This branch of public law protects the welfare and safety of the public by establishing what is legal and illegal. It also provides guidelines on how those committing crimes will be punished.

Procedure 6-1 Demonstrate Knowledge of Federal and State Health Care Legislation and Regulations

L: To be aware of federal and state legislation and regulations that apply to the employer's facility.

PMENT AND SUPPLIES
- mputer
- cess to organizational websites that have established legislation and regulations that pertain to medical ilities
- ormation about changes to and new federal and state legislation and regulations

PRO   RAL STEPS

1.   tently review applicable legislation and
          ions that apply to the facility.
)SE: To ensure compliance with the law.

2.   er the federal and state ramifications of
          related to healthcare workers, such as:
          ulatory bodies
          cation and credentials
          be of practice
          qualifications
          requirements
          of credentials
)SE: To ensure full compliance in the
          l facility.

3.   and understand federal and state
          on and regulations related to:
          ericans and with Disabilities Act
          rolled Substance Schedules

- OSHA
- Centers for Disease Control
- Local Public Health Departments
- Materials Safety Data Sheets (MSDS)

PURPOSE: To ensure full compliance in the medical facility.

4. Review and understand accrediting agency requirements that affect the facility.
   PURPOSE: To ensure full compliance in the medical facility.

5. Stay aware of new state and federal legislation and regulations.
   PURPOSE: To ensure full compliance in the medical facility.

6. Always follow office policy when performing any action at the facility.
   PURPOSE: To ensure full compliance in the medical facility.

Procedure 6-2 Perform Within Legal Boundaries

To perform duties within legal boundaries in the state where employed as a medical assistant.

MENT AND SUPPLIES
- nputer
- ess to text of various laws and regulations affecting the practice

PRO   AL STEPS

1. B   e familiar with the laws that affect
   n   practices in your state.
   P   SE: To understand which laws apply to
   th   ployer's facility.

2. R   e laws and regulations thoroughly.
   P   SE: To understand the concept and
   in   the laws and regulations.

3. O   dditional training on compliance with
   th   and regulations, if necessary.
   P   SE: To make certain that all actions and
   p   res in the office are in compliance with
   a   e, current laws.

4. R   rnals and any information available
   ab   e laws.
   PU   E: To remain current in compliance
   ac

5. St   re of licensure issues that affect the
   ph   , including:

- Licensure
- Registration
- Certification
- Suspension
- Revocation

PURPOSE: To ensure that the physician is always practicing legally.

6. Know the scope of practice for a medical assistant.
   PURPOSE: To ensure that the medical assistant is always practicing legally.

7. Make certain that information is available on current laws and regulations at all times.

8. Perform all activities in accordance with applicable laws and regulations.
   PURPOSE: To insure compliance with applicable laws and regulations.

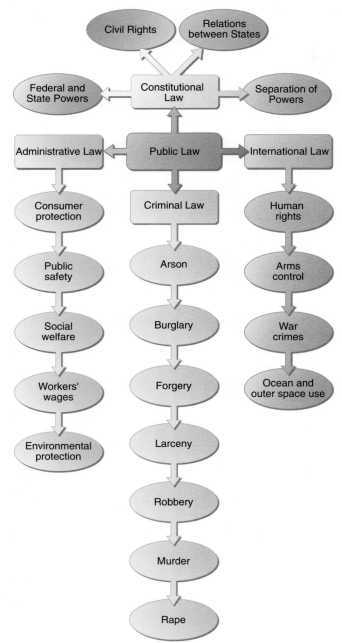

Fig. 6-1   Public law flowchart.

BOX 6-3   Offenses Considered under Criminal Law

- **Felony:** A serious crime that is punishable, as defined in the state statute, by death or incarceration. Crimes against the public that fall into this category are murder, rape, assault, and larceny (theft of a large amount of money).
- **Misdemeanor:** A crime that is punishable in jail for less than 1 year. It is considered less serious than a felony and includes disorderly conduct and petty theft.
- **Infraction:** A violation of a law or ordinance that usually results in a fine. This is the least serious of all offenses (e.g., jaywalking).

issues involving private individuals. Crimes considered under private law are solely against an individual person or property. The main divisions of private law are property law, family law, inheritance law, corporate law, contract law, and tort law. Contract and tort laws apply to everyday living and the medical practice more than the other divisions.

Contract Law
Contractual agreements occur every day, both in our professional and personal lives. Health professionals must understand several aspects of contract law.

A **contract** is an agreement between two or more people promising to work toward a specific goal for adequate **consideration** (payment or benefit). The physician-patient relationship is considered a contractual agreement. The two parties in this type of contract are the physician and the patient. As with any contract, a physician-patient contract must meet certain requirements to be valid and enforceable by law, as follows:

1. There must be an offer and acceptance among the parties.

Dr. Sanford is a licensed general practitioner who accepts new patients. Mr. Smith wants Dr. Sanford to become his physician. He calls Dr. Sanford's office to make an appointment. Dr. Sanford's office agrees to give Mr. Smith an appointment the next day.
OFFER → AGREEMENT → ACCEPTANCE

An offer must be specific and communicated in words or actions. Mr. Smith communicated his desire to become a patient by calling Dr. Sanford's office to make an appointment. Acceptance of this offer occurred when Dr. Sanford agreed to examine

Constitutional Law
Fundamental laws of a nation or state are defined in a constitution. **Constitutional law** interprets and defends a constitution. State constitutions are subordinate to the U.S. Constitution.

International Law
International law protects and asserts the rights and privileges of a sovereign nation.

Private Law or Civil Law
Private law is concerned with the enforcement of rights, the performance of duties, and other legal

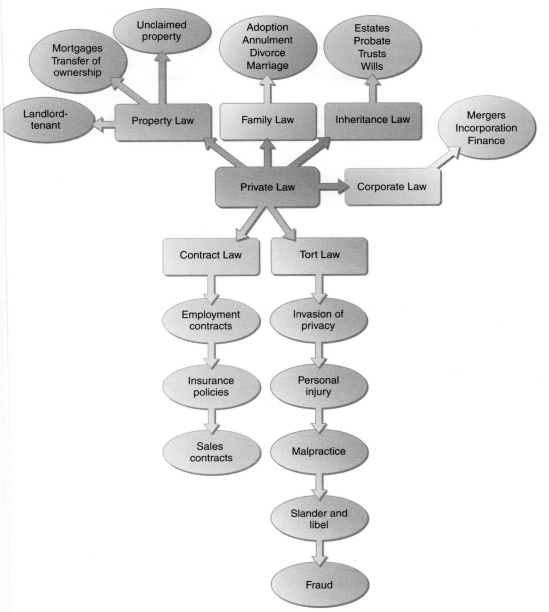

Fig. 6-2   Private law flowchart.

Mr. Sm... th the understanding that Dr. Sanford would ... d for his services.

2. The ... ust be a valid consideration (so... ng of value must be exchanged, such ... noney or services).

Dr. Sa... greed to examine Mr. Smith in exchange for pay ... Mr. Smith also agrees to follow Dr. Sanford's ... in exchange for being seen. The *consideration* ... s physician-patient contract between Dr. Sanfor ... Mr. Smith is the money Dr. Sanford receive ... he examination.

ACCEP ...   → CONSIDERATION

Both the patient and the physician have responsibilities in the physician-patient contract.

The physician is expected to do the following:

1. Diagnose and treat each patient to the best of his or her ability.
2. Be available to the patient for care.
3. Arrange for a substitute physician to take patient calls if unavailable (failure to do this is considered **abandonment**).

The patient is expected to do the following:

1. Truthfully impart past and present medical information.

2. Follow all treatments prescribed by the physician.
3. Take all medications.
4. Keep all scheduled appointments.
5. Be responsible with an appropriate (agreed-on) reimbursement plan.

3. The agreement must have a lawful purpose.

Receiving medical care from a licensed physician is not illegal. Had Dr. Sanford not been licensed, however, the contract would have been invalid because Dr. Sanford would have been practicing without a license, which is a felony.

If the service is illegal, there is no contract. State statutes govern all agreements.

4. All parties must be competent (have the legal capacity to make a contract).

Both Mr. Smith and Dr. Sanford are over age 18, are considered competent (able to make sound judgments), and understand what is being agreed to, so they were able to enter into the physician-patient contract. Had Mr. Smith been underage (under 18 in most states), a parent or legal guardian would have had to form the contract with Dr. Sanford.

A competent person is capable of making decisions for himself or herself. Anyone under the **age of majority** is considered by law to be a minor and cannot enter into a contract. An exception to this rule is the **emancipated minor,** an underage person who has legally separated from parents for various reasons (e.g., military service, marriage).

5. The agreement must be in the form required by law.

Mr. Smith and Dr. Sanford's contract was verbal. Contracts may also be written, as in consent forms. Each state has a required format to be considered valid.

When all requirements for a contract have been met, the contract is considered valid and is enforceable in a court of law. If one of the parties fails to meet the terms of the contract, this is considered **breach** (break) **of contract.**

Dr. Sanford and Mr. Smith could breach their physician-patient contract in the following ways:
• Mr. Smith could fail to follow Dr. Sanford's medical advice.

• Dr. Sanford or his staff could promise that Mr. Smith's illness would be cured through treatment, and this promise would be in danger of being broken because of unforeseen circumstances or conditions.
• Dr. Sanford could promise to provide Mr. Smith with the latest treatments and then not follow through.

Occasionally the physician may want to withdraw from the care of a patient because the patient is displaying **noncompliance** (failing to follow the treatments prescribed). To do so, the physician is required to withdraw from the physician-patient contract formally and must do the following:

1. Notify the patient in writing.
2. Indicate the reason(s) for the withdrawal.
3. Give a date when this withdrawal takes effect (minimum of 30 days).
4. Provide a list of physicians who may be willing to treat the patient.
5. Provide for transfer of the patient's medical record.
6. Send the letter by certified mail with return receipt requested, and retain a copy of the letter and the return receipt for legal protection.

If a patient withdraws from a physician's care, this must be fully documented in the patient's chart. When a patient requests that their records be sent to another physician for transfer of care, the signed and dated records release form must be filed in the patient's chart.

TYPES OF CONTRACTS

The two most common types of contracts used in a medical setting are expressed and implied contracts.

Expressed. An **expressed contract** is one that is specifically stated aloud or written and is understood by all parties.

When a third party (e.g., not the insurance company or patient, usually a relative) agrees to pay for any medical services not covered by insurance, the expressed contract must be in writing.

Mr. Smith's adult son calls Dr. Sanford's office and says, "Send me Dad's bills and I'll pay them." This is not enforceable unless the agreement is in writing. The statute of frauds in each state indicates which contracts must be written.

Oral contracts exist when both parties agree to a specified condition with proper consideration.

Duri... interview between Dr. Sanford and Ms. John... applicant for a medical assisting position in hi... e, an agreement is reached about the job dutie... cted. Dr. Sanford offers Ms. Johnson a speci- fied ... and she accepts. A valid oral contract has beer... e.

Im... . An **implied contract** is one that is sugge... or expected, but not clearly expressed. Most ... at occurs in a medical office is by implied agree... The physician-employer places staff, inclu... edical assistants, in a position to act as his or... **gent** (a person who is authorized to act for or... ice of another). Remember that a physi- cian ... ponsible for the actions of his or her emplo... while they are performing within their scope ... ining. As a medical assistant, you will encou... physician-patient contract situations. The p... will interpret your words and actions as a med... sistant to be speaking and acting for the physi... nd will see you in a position of trusted respo... ty **(fiduciary).**

Wher... Smith called Dr. Sanford's office for an appo... t, kept the appointment, and received treat- ment ... as expected to pay the bill under the terms of th... ed contract. Even though Dr. Sanford may not ... nade the appointment for Mr. Smith in perso... ause his staff was acting on his behalf, the physi... tient contract was still valid.

Tort L...
A **tor**... wrongful act committed by a person agains... ther person or property that causes harm. ... law concerns health professionals becau... eals with negligence and medical **mal- pract**... *medical professional liability,* and covers the ar... ere no contract exists. Malpractice is a specifi... of negligence in which a professional fails to... vith reasonable care. The person com- mittin... oractice is held liable for the **damages** if the a... sed harm (e.g., physical injury, damaged proper... loss of personal freedom). Remember, if the ... professional does no harm, there is no tort. T... an be classified as either intentional (willfu... ionintentional (accidental) (Fig. 6-3).

INTENTI... ORT
Violati... person's rights or property with the intent ... harm is an *intentional tort.* **Gross neg- ligenc**... itentional negligence, or a wrongful act done (... done) on purpose. Money is typically award... rictims of intentional torts. Intentional torts ... o result in the person being charged under ... al law. This type of tort can be broken down ... he following two categories:

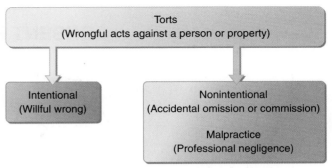

Fig. 6-3   Classification of torts.

Assault is the threat or the perceived threat of doing bodily harm by another person.
Battery is the act of touching or doing bodily harm without consent (permission).

Sandy Johnson, Dr. Sanford's new medical assistant, is asked to draw Mr. Smith's blood. Mr. Smith tells Sandy he doesn't want it done, but Sandy pulls Mr. Smith's arm down and draws the blood anyway. In this situa- tion, Sandy is actually guilty of battery because she did not have Mr. Smith's consent.

You must have the patient's consent to carry out any treatment or procedure.

To avoid being accused of battery, *informed consent* must be given by the patient before a treatment or procedure. For surgical procedures the physician must explain the following, using words the patient can understand:

1. What procedure is to be done and why.
2. What is going to happen.
3. Who will be doing the procedure.
4. Whether or not others will be involved (e.g., will there be another person assisting with the procedure).
5. What results are expected.
6. What risks are involved.
7. What the consequences are if the procedure is not done.
8. What alternative treatments are available and the risks.
9. Any other important information the patient needs to make a decision. It is best if this is in writing (see Fig. 6-4 for a sample of a Consent for Surgery form). Only the physi- cian can do the informing; a medical assistant can act as a witness.

However, what if the patient cannot give informed consent before treatment? Emergency situations in which a patient's life, health, or safety is in immedi- ate danger are exceptions to the informed consent rule. Under the **Good Samaritan Act,** implied consent applies if no one is available to consent for

CONSENT FOR SURGERY

DATE: _____   TIME: _____

I authorize the performance of the following procedure(s) _____

_____ on _____

To be performed by _____, MD.

The following have been explained to me by Dr. _____

     1. Nature of the procedure: _____

     2. Reason(s) for procedure: _____

     3. Possible risks: _____

     4. Possible complications: _____

I understand that no warranty or guarantee of the effectiveness of the surgery can be made.

I have been informed of possible alternative treatments including _____

_____

and of the likely consequences of receiving no treatment, and I freely consent to this procedure.

I hereby authorize the above named surgeon and his/her assistants to provide additional services including administering anesthesia and/or medications, performing needed diagnostic tests including but not limited to radiology, and any other additional serviced deemed necessary for my well-being. I consent to have removed tissue examined by a pathologist who may then dispose of the tissue as he/she sees fit.

Signed _____   Relationship to patient _____
          Patient / Parent / Guardian

Witness _____

Fig. 6-4 Consent for Surgery form.

the patient and if a "reasonable" person would consent under similar circumstances. For example, a medical assistant is in a restaurant and sees a man clutching his throat and unable to speak. She rushes to his side and performs abdominal thrusts until the food is dislodged. She therefore performed reasonable assistance to a person in need. The Good Samaritan Act may vary from state to state but basically provides that care given in good faith by a health professional or a non–health professional is protected from civil liability if the person provided care within their scope of training. The implied consent would end if the patient became able to answer on his or her own behalf. In this case the rescuers would let the person know what they were doing and would ask, "Is it okay to continue?"

O[...]

[...]xamples of intentional torts follow:

1. [...] [...]nation of character occurs when false [...]ments, written or spoken, are made public [...]t another person with the intent to [...]ge the person's reputation.
   [...]bel is defamation of character in [...]iting.
   [...]nder is defamation of character with [...]ech. To be considered in a court of [...], a third person must be present when [...]nder is taking place.

2. [...] *imprisonment* is the unlawful restraint [...] patient or employee. For example, you [...]t stop a patient from leaving the [...].

3. [...] refers to a deceitful practice. Examples [...]e not telling a patient about the risks of [...]edure, performing an experimental pro-[...]e on a patient without letting the patient [...] it is experimental, and charging the [...]nce company for procedures not done.

4. [...]*on of privacy* is an unlawful intrusion [...] the personal life of another person [...]ut cause or disclosure of public informa-[...] without the person's consent. This [...]les the public release of information [...] a person or the use of photographs of [...]on without the person's consent. This is [...]ch of confidentiality and privacy and [...] result in a lawsuit.

[...]TE: Liability insurance protects the [...]d from the risk of liabilities brought [...] by lawsuits from third party insurance [...]; (someone suffering a loss). Personal [...] insurance protects the insured's negli-[...]cts and or omissions that result from [...]slander, invasion of privacy, or false [...]onment.

NONIN[...]AL TORT

Ordin[...] **[...]gligence** is not doing (or doing) something [...] reasonable person would do (or not do).
Ordin[...] [...]egligence is not intentional. Forms of
ordina[...] [...]gligence are malfeasance, misfeasance,
and n[...] [...]sance. *Feasance* is the performance of
an act [...]

1. [...]**asance** is the performance of an unlaw-[...] improper act causing or resulting in [...]. An example of malfeasance is a medical [...]nt practicing beyond the scope of his or [...]ining. A medical assistant cannot imply [...]she is a nurse.

wrong thing completely

2. [...]**asance** is the improper performance of [...] that results in harm to the patient. Mis-[...]ce occurs, for example, when a patient [...]s a burn during ultrasound therapy.

doing it wrong

3. **Nonfeasance** is the failure to do what is expected, resulting in harm to the patient. For example, a patient comes in with an arm injury, the physician fails to order an x-ray film, and later it is found that the patient has a broken arm.

Lawsuits

More than 85% of medical lawsuits are for ordinary negligence (mistakes made in good faith). It is important for all health professionals to understand the actions that could lead to a lawsuit and the ways to avoid them (risk management). When such actions cannot be avoided, it is necessary to be familiar with the trial process so that you can be a credible witness.

Causes for Lawsuit

Four components, or "four Ds," must be present before an attorney will pursue a case for professional negligence, as follows:

1. *Duty* occurs when the physician-patient relationship is established.

   A new patient sees the physician and makes a follow-up appointment for an experimental procedure.

2. *Dereliction of duty* occurs when a health care professional fails to meet accepted standards of care. ***Res ipsa loquitur*** (ras ep-sa lo-kwi-tur; Latin for "the thing speaks for itself") is the principle that applies when the very existence of the situation shows negligence (e.g., surgical sponge left in the abdomen after surgery).

   At the follow-up appointment, the physician treats the patient with an experimental procedure, even though the physician knows he has not had adequate training to perform this procedure safely.

3. *Direct cause* or *proximate cause* must be shown between the patient's injury and the actions of the health care professional.

   The patient develops a new medical problem proven to be caused by the improper performance of the procedure.

4. *Damages* (money) awarded will compensate the victim for the permanent injury (Table 6-1).

   The patient is awarded money as compensation for the medical problem.

TABLE 6-1	Damages in Lawsuits		
Type of Damages		**Compensation**	**Awarded for**
General compensatory damages Payment for injuries or losses that have been demonstrated		Monetary award	Any of the following as a result from the injury: Pain Suffering Mental anguish Any physical disability
Special compensation Payment for costs incurred because of the negligent act		Monetary award	Any of the following as a result from the injury: Loss of earnings Medical bills Rehabilitation therapy
Punitive damages Payment for injury or loss caused by gross negligence		Monetary award as determined by state statute	Any conduct that is considered by the court to be intentional or malicious. Award is not to compensate the plaintiff, but to punish the defendant.

Each state has laws that limit the length of time a person has to take legal action. The **statute of limitations** (time limits to bring forth a lawsuit) for malpractice varies in length and by situation. Medical office professionals must be aware of the statute of limitations in their state because it will impact the way medical records are kept. The dates and information recorded in the medical record can be used in a lawsuit, so the medical records must be up to date, accurate, and complete. For example, a patient falls getting off the exam table but says she is okay and refuses help by the medical assistant and physician. Three years later the patient complains of a knee injury caused by her fall years earlier. How important is the prior documentation of the incident to the issue of the injury?

A patient's own negligence may impact damages awarded. In some states, if the patient has contributed to the injury, this is called *contributory negligence,* and no damages will be awarded. In some states, if the physician and the patient were both at fault, it is considered to be *comparative negligence,* and compensation will be less.

Avoiding Lawsuits or Risk Management

The best way to avoid a lawsuit for malpractice is to keep the lines of communication open between the medical staff and the patient. Establishing and maintaining a good relationship builds mutual trust and respect. Box 6-4 provides guidelines to avoid a lawsuit. Remember accurate documentation is the best form of risk management. When dealing with an angry patient, the use of positive body language (e.g., smile) and a kind word can do wonders to calm the patient.

Lawsuit Process

Even when the guidelines for avoiding a lawsuit are followed, it may not always be enough. If a patient's attorney decides that the "four Ds" of negligence exist, the attorney will file a complaint and the process begins. As a medical assistant you need to understand what happens in a lawsuit in case you are involved in preparing materials for one or testifying in court. Table 6-2 shows the different phases in the lawsuit process as well as what the medical assistant needs to know about each.

PATIENT-CENTERED PROFESSIONALISM

- What is the benefit to patients when the medical assistant understands the contract process (and the physician-patient contract)? What is the benefit to the medical assistant and the practice?
- How can the lawsuit process affect patients? Medical assistants? The medical practice?
- Why is it better to avoid a lawsuit rather than go to trial, even in situations in which the practice would "win" the lawsuit?
- What should you keep in mind about your appearance, your communication, and your professionalism when testifying in court? What does it matter whether the people in the courtroom think you look and sound credible as long as you are telling the truth?

communicable diseases. Other reportable situations are injuries caused by a lethal weapon (gun or knife), bad reactions to vaccines, certain diseases in newborns (e.g., congenital syphilis), and suspected abuse (Box 6-5). Medical assistants must report all suspected child abuse, elder abuse, spousal abuse, and drug abuse. Even if abuse is only suspected, it must be reported. The forms and reports required for each reportable incident will vary. Medical assistants must be familiar with what is required in their state.

Guidelines to Avoid a Lawsuit (Risk Management)

Ne

- [ ] e a specific outcome, such as a cure, as a [ ] f the procedure or treatment.
- [ ] riticism or negative comments about the [ ] n, patient, or other health care profession- [ ] p your opinions to yourself.
- [ ] e negative comments about the medical
- [ ] edical advice or diagnose, even when asked [ ] inion.
- [ ] o the plaintiff or their attorney without the [ ] l of the physician's attorney.
- [ ] medical record by using "white out" or cor- [ ] tape.

Al

- [ ] o the patient's concerns or complaints; [ ] e facts or write "the patient states."
- [ ] ent accurately what you did, what you [ ] d, and what the patient said.
- [ ] e physician or attorney review any patient's [ ] before copying them.
- [ ] within your scope of training.
- [ ] safe work habits.
- [ ] tient information confidential.
- [ ] issed appointments.
- [ ] nt phone calls.
- [ ] p with test results in a timely manner by [ ] g the patient a specific time frame in which [ ] t the results.
- [ ] when the patient has been notified of the [ ] lts and the action taken.
- [ ] patients equally and with respect.

CARE LEGISLATION

In add [ ] to contract law and tort law, the medical assista [ ] ds to be aware of other national, state, and l [ ] ws and regulations. These regulations invol [ ] rting requirements, living wills, donation c [ ] s body or organs, debt collection, and workp [ ] sues.

Repo [ ]   Requirements

Some [ ] affect the health, safety, and welfare of th [ ] eral public and must be reported despit [ ] identiality. All states require the report of vit [ ] tistics, including births, deaths, and

Patient Awareness and Protection

Some health care legislation protects patients and helps make them aware of their rights. As a medical assistant you need to understand these laws so that you will be able to follow them and explain them to patients when necessary. The Patient Self-Determination Act, the Uniform Anatomical Act, and the Fair Debt Collection Practices and Bankruptcy Acts all help protect patients' rights and wishes.

Patient Self-Determination Act

The *Patient Self-Determination Act* of 1990 requires health care institutions to give patients written

TABLE 6-2 Lawsuit Process

Phase	What Happens	What You Need to Know as a Medical Assistant
Summons	After receiving the complaint, the court issues a *summons,* and the complaint is delivered to the defendant (the physician). The defendant notifies his or her attorney and insurance carrier. A response to the summons must be filed with the court addressing the charges and making any applicable counterclaims.	You may be asked to make copies of medical records. Always check with the physician or the physician's attorney before copying them.
Collection of information	If no motions to dismiss or move the trial are approved, a period of discovery begins to uncover evidence to support charges. A *deposition* is a formal retrieval of information about the charges and is either written or given orally. An *interrogatory* is a written set of questions requiring written answers. A **subpoena** is a document requiring a person to appear in court or to be available for a deposition. A **subpoena duces tecum** is an order to appear in court with the original records; in this case, the patient's chart. *Testimony* is a statement given under oath about what a person knows. If the evidence is obvious (e.g., surgical instrument left inside a body cavity after surgery), testimony of an expert may not be needed. This doctrine is called *res ipsa loquitur* ("the thing speaks for itself").	You may be asked to supply information or records during this process.
Trial	A jury is selected. Each attorney makes opening statements. The plaintiff's (patient's) attorney calls witnesses and the defendant's (physician's) attorney cross-examines. The defendant's attorney calls witnesses and the plaintiff's attorney cross-examines. Both attorneys make closing arguments to explain why the jury should decide in their favor. The judge gives the jury instructions and asks them to reach a *verdict* based on the evidence. If the jury finds the defendant not guilty, the case is dismissed; if the jury finds the defendant guilty, a monetary settlement is awarded.	If called as a witness to testify, you need to be prepared. When you testify, your statements will be evaluated not only on what you have to say, but also on how credible you appear to be. You can increase your credibility in the following ways: *Appearance* • Dress appropriately (e.g., conservative hairstyle and makeup, simple jewelry). • Do not chew gum or bite nails. • Maintain good posture. *Behavior* • Remain calm. • Make eye contact with the attorneys, judge, and jury. • Have a professional manner at all times. *Communication* • Only give answers that you know as fact. • Only give answers to what is asked. • Answer questions clearly.
Appeal	Either attorney can file an *appeal* to a higher court to reconsider the decision.	Again, you may be asked to provide more oral or written information during this phase.
Arbitration	An alternative to going to trial, in some cases, is having the dispute go before an arbitrator. Both sides present their case, and the arbitrator decides the outcome. In binding *arbitration*, the decision is final.	You may be asked to provide oral or written information for this process.

BOX 5 Characteristics of Emotional Abuse, Neglect, Child Abuse, and Elder Abuse

Emotional abuse occurs when a parent, guardian, or spouse needlessly yells, calls a person derogatory names, or tells them they are useless. An example is a parent yelling at a child, "You're stupid! You can't do anything right! What good are you?"

Neglect occurs when a safe place is not provided to live in and grow up. The emotional scars from neglect do not show up like bruises and burns. Forms of neglect include

* Leaving a child alone
* Not locking up poisons (e.g., bleach, bug spray)
* Not feeding and bathing a child on a regular basis
* Not providing a child with adequate clothing for the weather
* Not providing a child with medical attention when needed

Child abuse can be physical or sexual in nature.

Signs of Physical Abuse
* Bruises on the face, lips, mouth, cheeks, buttocks, back, chest, abdomen, and inner thighs
* Bruises taking the shape of an object (e.g., belt, buckle, hanger, rope) on the same areas as described for bruises

* Burns and scalds of the hands, feet, back, or buttocks
* Fractures of the nose, skull, legs, or arms
* Bite marks on any part of the body

Signs of Sexual Abuse
* Bruises or bleeding of genitalia, mouth, or anus
* Stains or blood on undergarments
* Difficult or painful urination
* Vaginal discharge and genital odor
* Difficulty walking
* Pregnancy

Elder abuse signs may or may not be physical in nature and include:

* Living conditions that are unclean and unsafe
* Poor personal hygiene
* Weight loss resulting from poor nutrition and fluid intake
* Frequent or recurring injuries
* New and old bruises that can be seen
* Patient who is anxious and fearful, and a caregiver who is always present and does not let the patient answer questions
* Frequent trips to the emergency department
* Medications not taken or taken improperly

---

information about advance directives before life-sustaining measures become necessary. *Advance directives* are documents that state people's wishes in case they become incapable of making decisions. Two types of advance directives are the *living will* and *durable power of attorney for health care*. These documents provide written instructions and are legally binding documents.

LIVING WILL

A living will is a statement to the family, physician, or lawyer that conveys a person's decisions about medical treatment if the person becomes unable to make the decision. The living will does not go into effect until the person becomes terminally ill (Fig. 6-5).

A living will is characterized by the following:

* Must be witnessed by two persons, one of whom is neither a spouse nor a blood relative.
* Can be revoked or amended at any time by the individual who initiated it.

* Only pertains to health, *not* finances.
* Should be copied and given to the physician, family, attorney, and kept with the individual's legal papers.
* Requires a physician and the hospital staff to abide by the individual's wishes.

DURABLE POWER OF ATTORNEY FOR HEALTH CARE
The durable power of attorney for health care is a statement that gives a person's representative (including same-sex partner) clear authority and instructions about life-support decisions (Fig. 6-6). For example, Jeff's parents want to make decisions about his medical care following surgery but the medical durable power of attorney has been given to his same-sex partner Steve, therefore giving Steve the authority to make life-support decisions.

Uniform Anatomical Gift Act of 1968
Under the *Uniform Anatomical Gift Act,* competent individuals who have reached the age of consent in their state may donate their body or body parts after they die. The decision to donate can be stated

LIVING WILL

To my family, physician, and spiritual advisor;
To any medical facility that has been entrusted with my care;
To anyone who should have interest in my health, welfare, or affairs:

I willfully and voluntarily make this my definite expression of my desires:
If the situation arises in which I cannot participate in my own decision making regarding my health care decisions and the attending physician and another consulting physician determine I have:

☐ A Terminal Condition; meaning a condition caused by injury or illness from which there is no reasonable medical probability of recovery and which, without treatment, can be expected to cause death;

or

☐ An End-Stage Condition; meaning a condition that is caused by injury or illness which has resulted in severe and permanent deterioration, indicated by incapacity and complete physical dependency, and for which, to a reasonable degree of medical certainty, treatment of the irreversible condition would be medically ineffective;

or

☐ A Persistent Vegetative State; meaning a permanent and irreversible condition of unconsciousness in which there is (1) the absence of voluntary action or cognitive behavior of any kind and (2) an inability to communicate or interact purposefully with the environment.

Then, I request that I be allowed to die and that life-prolonging procedures not be either initiated or provided. I direct that I am not to be kept alive by ventilators, artificial means, or through "heroic measures" and that nutrition and hydration not be administered by artificial means through invasive medical procedures. I wish to be treated with dignity and do not wish to suffer the indignities of hopeless pain, loneliness, and isolation. I request that medication be administered to me to alleviate pain and suffering, acknowledging that this may hasten death but without the intention of taking my life.

Other Personal Instructions: _____

_____

I understand the full import of this declaration, and I am emotionally and mentally competent to make this declaration. These directions express my legal right to preserve my right to privacy and self-determination. Therefore, I direct my family, doctors, and all those concerned with my care to regard themselves as morally bound in accordance with my directions.

In witness whereof, I have signed this declaration this ____ Day of _____ , 20 ____

_____   _____
Signature   Print Name

I attest that the signature or mark of the principal was knowingly and voluntarily signed in my presence. (Witnesses must be adults who are not themselves surrogates. One witness shall not be either the principal's spouse nor blood relative.)

_____   _____
Witness Signature   Witness Signature

_____   _____
Witness Name, Address, Phone Number Witness Name, Address, Phone Number

Fig. 6-5 Example of a living will.

DURABLE POWER OF ATTORNEY
FOR HEALTH CARE

able Power of Attorney made this _____ day of _____ , 20 _____

_____ , (insert name and address of principal)

by appoint _____ , (insert name and
ess of agent) as my attorney in fact (my agent) to act for me and in my name in any
I could act in person to make any and all decisions for me concerning my personal care,
ical treatment, hospitalization, and health care and to require, withhold, or withdraw
type of medical treatment or procedure, even though my death may ensue. My agent
have the same access to all my medical records that I have, including the right to
ose the contents to others. My agent shall also have full power to make a disposition of
part or all of my body for medical purposes, authorize an autopsy of my body, and direct
lisposition of my remains.

ABOVE GRANT OF POWER IS INTENDED TO BE AS BROAD AS POSSIBLE SO THAT
R AGENT WILL HAVE AUTHORITY TO MAKE ANY DECISION YOU COULD MAKE TO
AIN OR TERMINATE ANY TYPE OF HEALTH CARE, INCLUDING WITHDRAWAL OF
RISHMENT AND FLUIDS AND OTHER LIFE-SUSTAINING OR DEATH-DELAYING
SURES, IF YOUR AGENT BELIEVES SUCH ACTION WOULD BE CONSISTENT WITH YOUR
NT AND DESIRES. IF YOU WISH TO LIMIT THE SCOPE OF YOUR AGENT'S POWERS OR
SCRIBE SPECIAL RULES TO LIMIT THE POWER TO MAKE AN ANATOMICAL GIFT,
HORIZE AUTOPSY, OR DISPOSE OF REMAINS, YOU MAY DO SO IN THE FOLLOWING
AGRAPHS.

he powers granted above shall not include the following powers or shall be subject to the
ving rules or limitations (here you may include any specific limitations you deem
opriate, such as your own definition of when life-sustaining or death-delaying measures
ld be withheld; a direction to continue nourishment and fluids or other life-sustaining or
n-delaying treatment in all events; or instructions to refuse any specific types of
ment that are inconsistent with your religious beliefs or unacceptable to you for any
n, such as blood transfusion, electroconvulsive therapy, or amputation):

_____

_____

_____

_____

_____

_____

_____

_____

_____

_____

Fig. 6-6 Example of durable power of attorney for health care.

in a will, in a written agreement, or by signing the back of the driver's license. Medical schools, research institutions, and tissue banks accept these organs, which are also used in transplant surgery.

Consumer Protection

Medical assistants should be aware of two consumer protection acts.

The *Fair Debt Collection Practices Act* provides guidelines for collecting money owed. When contacting people to collect money owed to the medical office, you may not harass them with threats or abusive language. Also, contact must only be made during reasonable hours (9 a.m. to 9 p.m.), and you can only call once a week.

The *Bankruptcy Act* protects people who have a considerable amount of debt and allows for fair payment to the people or businesses the person owes. Once a medical office has been notified of a patient's bankruptcy through the court system, no further bills or statements can be sent to the patient. The office can ask for payment for any future visits but cannot refuse to send a copy of the patient's medical record to another physician.

Miscellaneous Laws and Regulations

So far you have learned about many of the laws that protect patients' rights and wishes. Other laws protect health care professionals on the job. You need to be familiar with the laws on employment safety, work-related injuries, and disabilities. These laws exist to protect your rights as an employee.

Occupational Safety and Health

The *Occupational Safety and Health Act* protects employees from on-the-job exposure to chemicals, disease, and injury. Two major areas that have been addressed are the *Hazardous Chemical Standards* and the *Bloodborne Pathogens Standard*.

The Hazardous Chemical Standards focuses on exposure to chemicals. It requires that:

- All employees have a "right to know" within 30 days of their employment how to handle exposure to various chemicals.
- An exposure control plan must be written for the facility.
- Each chemical used on the job must have a **material safety data sheet (MSDS)** from the manufacturer on file.
- There must be a yearly inventory of all chemicals.

The Bloodborne Pathogen regulations concern exposure to blood and body fluids and tissues. Human immunodeficiency virus (HIV) and hepatitis B virus (HBV) are the two main concerns for health care workers. The Bloodborne Pathogen regulations provide the following:

BOX 6-6	**Hepatitis B Vaccination Schedule for a New Employee**

First dose: Must be offered within 30 days of employment at no charge to the employee.

Second dose: Given 30 days after the first injection.

Third dose: Given 2 months after the second dose and at least 4 months after the first dose.

- Promote the use of standard precautions established by the **Centers for Disease Control and Prevention (CDC)** to reduce the risk of cross-contamination. The CDC is a federal agency established to protect the health and safety of populations and people at home and abroad.
- Mandate that all employees at risk must be offered the hepatitis B vaccine within 30 days of employment at no cost to the employee. An employee can decline the vaccine by signing a *declination* (waiver). Box 6-6 lists the hepatitis B series time frame.
- Require training for employees concerning the control and exposure plan. OSHA standards provide that job training be provided during working hours.
- Require that the labeling and the disposing of biological waste be done according to procedure.

OSHA is a federal agency that enforces these regulations. OSHA can inspect a workplace at any time unannounced. The sole purpose of OSHA is to ensure a safe working environment for all employees. Violations of an OSHA regulation can result in fines of $10,000 per violation.

Workers' Compensation

Even though OSHA regulates standards for safety in the workplace, work-related injuries still occur. Employers having a certain number of employees (as determined by the state) must carry workers' compensation insurance. This insurance covers medical care and rehabilitation costs and offers temporary or permanent pay for the injured employee.

Title VII of the Civil Rights Act

Title VII of the Civil Rights Act of 1964 concerns hiring practices, treatment of employees, and the employment of those with disabilities. Three aspects

of th... that relate directly to medical assistants
are ... tion from sexual harassment, emergency
fami... l medical leave, and the hiring of disabled
peop... mplaints are filed with the Equal Employ-
men... ortunity Commission (EEOC).

SEXU... ...ASSMENT

The ... defines sexual harassment as follows:

Un... ome sexual advances, requests for sexual
fav... nd other verbal or physical conduct of a
se... ature constitute sexual harassment when
(1) ... nission to such conduct is made either
ex... y or implicitly a term or condition of an
in... al's employment; (2) submission to or
rej... of such conduct by an individual is used
as ... sis for employment decisions affecting
su... lividual; or (3) such conduct has the
pu... or effect of unreasonably interfering with
an... ividual's work performance or creating
an... nidating, hostile, or offensive working
en... nent.

Th... nition specifies what is not acceptable in
the ... ace. It protects the employee from "this
for t... r the "something for something" (**quid
pro** ... kwid pro kwo]) issues. It covers not only
the ... ance or rejection of unwanted sexual
cond... ut also the condition of the working
envi... nt. A hostile working environment might
inclu... l language, off-color jokes, inappropriate
pictu... other offensive actions or items that can
affec... her person's job performance.

FAMIL...

The ... and Medical Leave Act (FMLA) allows an
empl... o take up to 12 weeks of unpaid leave per
year ... ternity leave (male or female), adoptions,
and ... for sick family members. It also permits
exter... npaid leave for employees with serious
medi... nditions. To qualify, the employee must
have ... actively employed for 1 year. Only com-
panie... 50 or more employees are affected. This
law p... s the employee by requiring that employees b... led to return to their original job or one
with ... pay and benefits after the leave.

HIRIN... ...ISABLED PEOPLE

The A... ans with Disabilities Act (ADA) mandates
equal... rtunity for government services, public
facilit... ommercial accommodations, and trans-
porta... It also prevents hiring discrimination
again... ple with disabilities. If the most qualified
perso... the job is a person with a disability, a
reaso... effort must be made to accommodate
this p... in the workplace. For example, a ramp
or el... could be added to accommodate an
empl... a wheelchair.

FOR YOUR INFORMATION

Acceptable and Unacceptable Ways for Employers to Ask Interview Questions

Age

Acceptable: "Are you over the age of 18?"

Unacceptable: "How old are you?" "What is your date of birth?" "What year did you graduate from high school?"

Religion

Acceptable: "Can you work Saturdays and Sundays?"

Unacceptable: "What church do you belong to?" Any question that inquires into a job applicant's religious background is illegal.

Gender

Acceptable: No question regarding gender is acceptable.

Unacceptable: "Do you wish to be addressed as Mrs., Miss, or Ms.?" "Do you have children?" "Do you plan to have more children?" "What arrangements have you made for child care?"

Race

Acceptable: Stating that a photograph may be required after hiring is acceptable.

Unacceptable: Stating that a photograph will be required with the application and asking about a person's ethnic origin are unacceptable.

Salary

Acceptable: "What are your salary expectations?"

Unacceptable: "What is the lowest salary you will accept?"

Disability

Acceptable: "Is there any reason why you would not be able to perform the duties of this job?"

Unacceptable: "Do you have any disabilities?" "What prescription drugs are you taking?"

Residence

Acceptable: "What is your place of residence?"

Unacceptable: "Do you own or rent?"

Military Service

Acceptable: "Did you serve in the U.S. Armed Forces?"

Unacceptable: "Are you currently in the military reserves?"

PATIENT-CENTERED PROFESSIONALISM

- How can reporting births, deaths, certain diseases, and abuse benefit patients and society?
- Why is it important for patients to know about advance directives and living wills? If asked, could you explain these documents to a patient?
- How do the CDC and OSHA work together to protect employees? How is patient care improved when workplace safety is practiced?
- How does the Civil Rights Act impact you as a medical assistant? How might it impact the care that a patient receives from health professionals?

≋ ETHICS IN HEALTH CARE

FOR YOUR INFORMATION

Who Decides What is Ethical?

When we weigh the question of who decides what is ethical, the answer is evident: you do. Every day medical professionals face the task of making ethical decisions. As with any important choice, the short- and long-term effects and consequences must be considered. Although depending on groups and committees to guide ethical decisions is a completely acceptable practice, the responsibility for making these decisions ultimately rests with individual.

Organizations that study ethical dilemmas may decide that a concept such as abortion is an ethical medical practice. But if an individual does not find abortion to be an acceptable practice for religious or other reasons, abortion is not ethical for that individual. A great freedom that Americans often take for granted is that we can exercise free will in decisions related to individual conscience in this country, that we can choose from a variety of options; however, we must exercise this responsibility carefully.

Laws are rules established by governing entities (e.g., city, state, and federal governments) that must be followed. **Ethics** are moral guidelines developed over time and influenced by family, culture, and society. Something considered unethical may not be against the law.

While shopping, Calvin finds an envelope containing $100 in the aisle of the store. The envelope has no name or any means to identify the owner. It is not against the law for him to keep it, but is it ethical? Should he turn it in to the front office, or keep it under the doctrine of "finders keepers, losers weepers"?

Our personal and professional ethics influence the decisions we make and the actions we take. It is important for medical assistants to understand ethics and its importance, as well as special ethical situations that affect health care.

Ethical Standards

Your ethical standards as a health care professional are determined by many influences. Some of these influences are principles, personal integrity, professional responsibilities, confidentiality, and responsibilities to the patient.

Principles

Ethics refers to moral principles that govern a person's behavior and reflect the person's understanding of right and wrong. Throughout history there have been standards of behavior and professionalism. As times change, however, ethical standards and principles may change. Think about how standards of behavior have changed over the past several hundred years.

Personal Integrity

A person with *integrity* is seen as being honest and having high moral values. Personal integrity impacts the decisions you make. By asking yourself the following three questions, you can decide whether a solution to a problem is ethical:

1. *Is it legal?* If the solution to a problem is illegal, it is unethical.
2. *Is it well balanced?* The decision must treat everyone fairly. If one person benefits and another does not, the decision may not be ethical.
3. *Would most people agree?* Think about how you will be affected by this decision. If your decision were to be broadcast on the 6 p.m. news, would you still think it is the right thing to do?

If you can answer all three of these questions with a "yes," the decision is probably ethical. If not, you should think carefully and review the situation in more depth before making the decision.

If he were trying to decide whether it was ethical to keep the money he found, Calvin might answer these questions as follows:
1. *Is it legal?* Would it be a crime for Calvin to keep the money in the envelope? Keeping unidentified money found in a public place is not usually considered a crime.
2. *Is it well balanced?* Would keeping the envelope full of money treat everyone fairly? Calvin would benefit, but the person who lost the money would not.

3. I _most people agree?_ Would Calvin like it if
   ry were broadcast on the news? How would
   ople watching the news feel about Calvin's
   n to keep the money? Most people would
   y think Calvin should have turned the money
   the store manager or to the police.

Prof___   al Responsibilities

Heal___ _fessionals establish a relationship with the ___ t, the family of the patient, their co-work___ nd society in general. All have expectations ___ t how health care professionals should beha___ ometimes a person can become torn betw___ hical obligations and legal obligations.

A pa___ t your office is HIV positive. You find out that this ___ t is dating your best friend's daughter. What can ___ o? The conflict arises from the concern for the ___ f the public (best friend's daughter) and the brea___ confidentiality (patient's right to privacy).

Bo___ 7 and 6-8 illustrate expectations of the phys___ and the medical assistant according to their ___ essions. Professional, patient-centered medi___ istants follow their code of ethics.

Confi___   lity

All h___ are professionals have a legal obligation to m___ n the patient's privacy. A breach of **con-fiden___ ty** is not only against the law, but it is also ___ cal. The **Health Insurance Portability a___ countability Act (HIPAA)** is a federal regul___ that requires all health professionals to prote___ privacy and confidentiality of patients' healti ___ rmation. This includes oral communication, ___ corded on paper, and electronic records. Box ___ ts some of HIPAA's key requirements. Confi___ lity breaches occur most often as a result of ca___ ess in elevators or hallways and when eating ___ "over lunch"). Even though a breach of confi___ lity is not intended to be a violation of a pati___ ghts, it still is an invasion of the patient's priva___ member, HIPAA was enacted to prevent fraud ___ buse in health care.

Fo___   R INFORMATION

Cou___

The ___
deve ___
ciati___
anal ___
fron ___
also ___
late ___
ethi ___
mec ___

Ethical and Judicial Affairs

___ il on Ethical and Judicial Affairs (CEJA) ___ thics policy for the American Medical Asso-___ MA). The Council prepares reports that ___ d address timely ethical issues that con-___ cians and the medical profession. CEJA ___ dicial responsibilities, which include appel-___ tion over physician members' appeals of ___ ed decisions made by state and specialty ___ cieties.

Breach of Confidentiality

A jury ordered an emergency medical technician (EMT) and her employer to pay a fine as a result of an invasion of the privacy of an overdose patient. The EMT told the patient's co-worker about the overdose, who then told others at a local hospital where both the co-worker and the overdose patient were nurses. The EMT claimed she called the co-worker out of concern for the patient. The jury decided that, regardless of her intentions, the EMT had no right to disclose confidential medical information.

BOX 6-8   American Association of Medical Assistants (AAMA) Code of Ethics

The Code of Ethics of AAMA shall set forth principles of ethical and moral conduct as they relate to the medical profession and the particular practice of medical assisting.

Members of AAMA dedicated to the conscientious pursuit of their profession, and thus desiring to merit the high regard of the entire medical profession and the respect of the general public which they serve, do pledge themselves to strive always to:

A. render service with full respect for the dignity of humanity;

B. respect confidential information obtained through employment unless legally authorized or required by responsible performance of duty to divulge such information;

C. uphold the honor and high principles of the profession and accept its disciplines;

D. seek to continually improve the knowledge and skills of medical assistants for the benefit of patients and professional colleagues;

E. participate in additional service activities aimed toward improving the health and well-being of the community.

American Association of Medical Assistants Creed

I believe in the principles and purposes of the profession of medical assisting.

I endeavor to be more effective.

I aspire to render greater service.

I protect the confidence entrusted to me.

I am dedicated to the care and well-being of all people.

I am loyal to my employer.

I am true to the ethics of my profession.

I am strengthened by compassion, courage and faith.

Courtesy of American Association of Medical Assistants.

Respect for the privacy of patients in your care is the law, not an option. Information about a patient may not be given out without the permission of the patient or legal guardian. Fig. 6-7 provides an example of a patient consent form using HIPAA criteria. An exception to this does occur in situations where workers' compensation is an issue or instances where public safety is in question (Box 6-10).

Organizational Ethics

Organizational ethics, like personal and professional ethics, is a code of conduct. It states expected behavior of employees. This organizational code will also define the internal policies to be followed if a breach of ethics occurs.

Responsibilities to the Patient

Health professionals interact with people whose cultures and beliefs may not match their own. A judgmental attitude is not tolerated in health care. All health care professionals are responsible for respecting the following rights of patients:

Right to: **Consideration and respect**
- The patient is treated with kindness and a caring attitude.
- The patient's personal values and cultural beliefs and practices are considered when care is provided.

Right to: **Information**
- Information is provided in terms the patient can understand.
- The physician explains the diagnosis, treatment, alternatives, and prognosis.

Right to: **Refuse treatment**
- The patient does not have to accept treatment.
- The patient must be informed of the health risks involved in refusing treatment.

Right to: **Privacy**
- The patient's records and care and the information received from the patient are kept private.
- The right to privacy is protected even after death.

Right to: **Confidentiality**
- Information can only be shared after the patient gives written consent.
- No information is to be shared with another health care worker unless that person is directly involved in the patient's care.

Right to: **Competent care**
- The patient expects all care provided to be given by a qualified person.

The American Hospital Association (AHA) has created documents to help increase awareness of

Patient Protections in the Health Insurance Portability and Accountability Act (HIPAA)

Fol... are the patient protections listed in the Department ...Health and Human Services (DHHS) HIPAA Fac... t.

- **...s to medical records.** Patients generally ...be able to see and obtain copies of their ...l records and request corrections if they iden... ...rs and mistakes. Health plans, doctors, hospi... ...ics, nursing homes, and other covered entities ...lly should provide access to these records ...30 days and may charge patients for the cost ...ing and sending the records.

- **...of privacy practices.** Covered health plans, ..., and other health care providers must provide ...e to their patients how they may use personal ...l information and their rights under the new ...regulation. Doctors, hospitals, and other ...are providers generally will provide the notice ...patient's first visit following the April 14, 2003, ...nce date and upon request. Patients gener... ...be asked to sign, initial, or otherwise acknowl... ...at they received this notice. Patients also may ...ered entities to restrict the use or disclosure ...information beyond the practices included in ...ice, but the covered entities would not have ...e to the changes.

- **...on use of personal medical information.** ...vacy rule sets limits on how health plans and ...d providers may use individually identifiable ...nformation. To promote the best quality care ...ents, the rule does not restrict the ability of ..., nurses, and other providers to share informa... ...eded to treat their patients. In other situations, ...personal health information generally may ...used for purposes not related to health care, ...vered entities may use or share only the ...im amount of protected information needed ...articular purpose. In addition, patients would ...sign a specific authorization before a covered ...ould release their medical information to a life ...a bank, a marketing firm, or another outside ...s for purposes not related to their health

- **Prohibition on marketing.** The final privacy rule sets new restrictions and limits on the use of patient information for marketing purposes. Pharmacies, health plans, and other covered entities must first obtain an individual's specific authorization before disclosing their patient information for marketing. At the same time, the rule permits doctors and other covered entities to communicate freely with patients about treatment options and other health-related information, including disease-management programs.

- **Stronger state laws.** The new federal privacy standards do not affect state laws that provide additional privacy protections for patients. The confidentiality protections are cumulative; the privacy rule will set a national "floor" of privacy standards that protect all Americans, and any state law providing additional protections would continue to apply. When a state law requires a certain disclosure—such as reporting an infectious disease outbreak to the public health authorities—the federal privacy regulations would not preempt the state law.

- **Confidential communications.** Under the privacy rule, patients can request that their doctors, health plans, and other covered entities take reasonable steps to ensure that their communications with the patient are confidential. For example, a patient could ask a doctor to call his or her office rather than home, and the doctor's office should comply with that request if it can be reasonably accommodated.

- **Complaints.** Consumers may file a formal complaint regarding the privacy practices of a covered health plan or provider. Such complaints can be made directly to the covered provider or health plan or to HHS' Office for Civil Rights (OCR), which is charged with investigating complaints and enforcing the privacy regulation. Information about filing complaints should be included in each covered entity's notice of privacy practices. Consumers can find out more information about filing a complaint at http://www.hhs.gov/ocr/hipaa or by calling (866) 627-7748.

From ...epartment of Health and Human Services Fact Sheet: *Protecting the privacy of patients' health information*, April ...03.

patie... ...ghts. AHA established a **Patient's Bill of R...** in 1998 (Box 6-11), then created the **Patie... ...are Partnership** document in 2001. This ...ure is the AHA's new guide outlining expec... ...s of patients and hospitals. To enhance this ...rce document, the AHA created a

"Blueprint for Action" to assist with the implementation of this revised plan. This document is divided into the following two parts:

1. An organizational checklist to assist hospitals in assessing their strengths and weaknesses.

Patient Consent to the Use and Disclosure of Health Information for Treatment, Payment, or Health Care Operations

I understand that as part of my health care, the practice originates and maintains paper and/or electronic records describing my health history, symptoms, examination and test results, diagnoses, treatment, and any plans for future care or treatment. I understand that this information serves as:

- A basis for planning my care and treatment,
- A means of communication among professionals who contribute to my care,
- A source of information for applying my diagnosis and treatment information to my bill,
- A means by which a third-party payer can verify that services billed were actually provided,
- A tool for routine health care operations, such as assessing quality and reviewing the competence of staff.

I have been provided the opportunity to review the *"Notice of Patient Privacy Information Practices"* that provides a more complete description of information uses and disclosures. I understand that I have the following rights:

- The right to review the *"Notice"* prior to acknowledging this consent,
- The right to restrict or revoke the use or disclosure of my health information for other uses or purposes, and
- The right to request restrictions as to how my health information may be used or disclosed to carry out treatment, payment, or health care operations.

Restrictions:

I request the following restrictions to the use or disclosure of my health information:

_____

_____

May discuss treatment, payment, or health care operation with the following persons:

(Please check all that apply)   Spouse [   ]   Your Children [   ]   Relatives [   ]   Others [   ]   Parents [   ]

Please list the names and relationship, if you checked "Relatives" or "Others" above

_____

_____

Messages or Appointment Reminders: (Please check all that apply)

May we leave a message on your answering machine at home [   ] or at work [   ]. **Do not leave a message [   ]**

May we leave a message with someone at your **home** using the doctor's name or the practice name: Yes [   ]   No [   ]

May we leave a message with someone at your **work** using the doctor's name or the practice name: Yes [   ]   No [   ]

Messages will be of a nonsensitive nature, such as appointment reminders.

I understand that as part of treatment, payment, or health care operations, it may become necessary to disclose health information to another entity, i.e., referrals to other health care providers, labs, and/or other individuals or agencies as permitted or required by state or federal law.

I fully understand and accept the information provided by this consent.

_____   _____   _____
        Signature   Print name of person signing   Date

*If other than patient is signing, are you the parent, legal guardian, custodian, or have Power of Attorney for this patient for treatment, payment, or health care operations? Yes [   ]   No [   ]

_____

FOR OFFICE USE ONLY
[   ] Patient refused to sign the consent form.
[   ] Restrictions were added by the patient (see restrictions listed above)
[   ] "Consent form" received and reviewed by _____ on (date) _____
[   ] "Consent form" placed in the patient's medical record on (date) _____

Fig. 6-7   Example of HIPAA-compliant patient consent forms.

GENERAL MEDICAL HEALTH CARE

AUTHORIZATION FOR RELEASE OF MEDICAL INFORMATION

_____ ____/____/____ _____ hereby authorize
　　　Print Patient's Name　　　　　　　　Date of Birth　　　Social Security Number

General Medical Health Care 1234 Riverview Road, Anytown, FL 33333

ase medical, including HIV Antibody Testing, Psychiatric/Psychological, Alcohol and/or Drug Abuse
ation records to:

_____

s _____
　　　(Street)　　　　　　　　　　　　(City)　　　　　　(State)　　　　(Zip)

purpose of:　　1. Drs. appointment on: _____

　　　　　　　　2. Other: _____

　　　　　　　　_____
　　　　　　　　　　　　　Please Specify Reason for Disclosure

stand that if I consent to the release of any of my medical records, the results of any HIV
ly Testing, Psychiatric/Psychological, Alcohol and/or Drug Abuse information will be released.

stand this consent may be cancelled upon written notice to the hospital, except that action by the
l has been taken in reliance on this authorization, and that this authorization shall remain in force
-day period in order to effect the purpose for which it is given. Alcohol and drug abuse information,
nt, has been disclosed from records whose confidentiality is protected by Federal Law.
AL REGULATIONS (42CFR, part II) prohibit making any further disclosure of records without the
written authorization of the undersigned, or as otherwise permitted by such regulations.
fidentiality of HIV antibody test results is protected by Florida Law [Fla. Stat.ANN. 381.609 (2) (F)],
rohibits any further disclosure by a person to whom this information has been disclosed,
specific written consent of the undersigned or as otherwise permitted by state law.

_____　　From: _____　To: _____
(Date of Authorization)　　　　　　(Dates to be Released)

_____
　Patient's Signature

_____
, Legal Guardian, or Authorized
Representative Signature

_____
　Relationship to Patient

_____
　　Witness

Fig. 6-7, cont'd

BOX 6-10   Guidelines for Release of Information

- A release of information form does not need to be signed if:
  - Information is required by law (e.g., abuse)
  - Court ordered
- Provide a copy of the requested information
- Only release information related to the request
- Unless requested by the patient and or legal guardian, never release mental health conditions or treatments for drug/alcohol conditions unless required by law
- Information cannot be released over the telephone

- Never release the original medical record unless court ordered
- Patient can rescind the authorization from the health care facility:
  - Must be in writing
  - Signed by the patient or patient's representative
  - Delivered to health care facility
  - Takes effect when medical facility receives it, unless the facility or others (e.g., insurance company) have already relied on its use

BOX 6-11   Patient's Bill of Rights*

The American Hospital Association presents a Patient's Bill of Rights with the expectation that it will contribute to more effective patient care and be supported by the hospital on behalf of the institution, its medical staff, employees, and patients. The American Hospital Association encourages health care institutions to tailor this bill of rights to their community by translating and/or simplifying the language of this bill of rights as may be necessary to ensure that patients and their families understand their rights and responsibilities.

1. The patient has the right to considerate and respectful care.
2. The patient has the right to and is encouraged to obtain from physicians and other direct caregivers relevant, current, and understandable information concerning diagnosis, treatment, and prognosis.

   Except in emergencies when the patient lacks decision-making capacity and the need for treatment is urgent, the patient is entitled to the opportunity to discuss and request information related to the specific procedures and/or treatments, the risks involved, the possible length of recuperation, and the medically reasonable alternatives and their risks and benefits.

   Patients have the right to know the identity of physicians, nurses, and others involved in their care, as well as when those involved are students, residents, or other trainees. The patient also has the right to know the immediate and long-term financial implications of treatment choices insofar as they are known.
3. The patient has the right to make decisions about the plan of care prior to and during the course of treatment and to refuse a recommended treatment or plan of care to the extent of this action. In case

of such a refusal, the patient is entitled to other appropriate care and services that the hospital provides or transfer to another hospital. The hospital should notify patients of any policy that might affect patient choice within the institution.
4. The patient has the right to have an advance directive (such as a living will, health care proxy, or durable power of attorney for health care) concerning treatment or designating a surrogate decision maker with the expectation that the hospital will honor the intent of that directive to the extent permitted by law and hospital policy.

   Health care institutions must advise patients of their rights under state law and hospital policy to make informed medical choices, ask if the patient has an advance directive, and include that information in the patient records. The patient has a right to timely information about hospital policy that may limit its ability to implement fully a legally valid advance directive.
5. The patient has a right to every consideration of privacy. Case discussion, consultation, examination, and treatment should be conducted so as to protect each patient's privacy.
6. The patient has the right to expect that all communications and records pertaining to his or her care will be treated as confidential by the hospital, except in cases such as suspected abuse and public health hazards when reporting is permitted or required by law. The patient has the right to expect that the hospital will emphasize the confidentiality of this information when it releases it to other parties entitled to review information in these records.
7. The patient has the right to review records pertaining to his or her medical care and to have the

BO **1** Patient's Bill of Rights—cont'd

nation explained or interpreted as necessary,
>t when restricted by law.

8. >atient has the right to expect that, within its
   :ity and policies, a hospital will make reason-
   -esponse to the request of a patient for appro-
   : and medically indicated care and services.
   iospital must provide evaluation, service, and/
   ierral as indicated by the urgency of the case.
   n medically appropriate and legally permissible,
   ien a patient has so requested, a patient may
   ansferred to another facility. The institution to
   a the patient is transferred must first have
   >ted the patient for transfer. The patient must
   iave the benefit of complete information and
   nation concerning the need for, risks, benefits,
   ilternatives to such a transfer.

9. >atient has the right to ask and be informed
   e existence of business relationships among
   iospital, educational institution, other health
   >roviders, and payers that may influence the
   it's care and treatment.

10. itient has the right to consent or decline to
    ipate in proposed research studies or human

experimentation affecting care and treatment or
requiring direct patient involvement, and to have
those studies fully explained prior to consent. A
patient who declines to participate in research or
experimentation is entitled to the most effective
care that the hospital can otherwise provide.

11. The patient has the right to expect reasonable conti-
    nuity of care when appropriate and to be informed
    by physicians and other care givers of available and
    realistic patient care options when hospital care is
    no longer appropriate.

12. The patient has the right to be informed of hospital
    policies and practices that relate to patient care,
    treatment, and responsibilities. The patient has the
    right to be informed of available resources for
    resolving disputes, grievances, and conflicts such
    as ethics committees, patients' representatives, or
    other mechanisms available in the institution. The
    patient has the right to be informed of the hospital's
    charges for services and available payment
    methods.

From   can Hospital Association, 1992.
*Thes   s can be exercised on the patient's behalf by a designated surrogate or proxy decision maker if the patient
lacks   >n-making capacity, is legally incompetent, or is a minor.

2.   studies highlighting action taken by hos-
         ; to improve communication among the
         nts.

Spe   thical Considerations

Bioe   concerns the special ethical decisions
that   be made because of advancements in
medi   iearch. The federal government has tried
to an   :e and work with these advances through
laws   gulations. Some special ethical consideration   relate to health care include the "right
to di(tility, abortion, genetic engineering, and
resou   location.

"Righ   ie" Issues

Do p   have the "right to die" if they are suffering? I   k Kevorkian brought attention to **eutha-**
nasi;   iroviding the means and information to
termi   ill patients to allow them to commit
physi   issisted suicide. Although the courts
woul   convict Dr. Kevorkian initially, he was
foun(y of second-degree murder in 1999 and
sente   to prison. Upon his release, he said he

still feels that people have a right to decide when
they want to die. He will work to have it legalized,
but will not break any laws doing it. Some of the
arguments for and against this issue lie in religious
teachings, scientific findings, and quality-of-life
issues.

Beginning-of-life issues arise when an infant is
born with severe disabilities. The physicians' code
implies that treatment should begin, except for
those who would clearly not benefit. What if the
parents do not want treatment started? Should
quality-of-life issues be addressed?

End-of-life issues are more in the public eye now
than ever before. People today are living longer, but
is the quality of life what they expected? Do they
have a right to terminate their life or ask someone
to assist them in the termination? The law says
"no," but some believe that in certain circumstances
this is justifiable.

Some argue that we are kinder to animals with a
terminal illness than we are to humans. The use of
advance directives at least allows a patient some say
in the matter, but are they enough? What do you
think?

Fertility

Health professionals can use various ways to help women conceive or become pregnant. *In vitro fertilization* (e.g., test tube fertilization) and *artificial insemination* are two methods. Controversy exists over whether religious and ethical principles are being violated. Fertility treatments resulting in multiple fetuses may pose a threat to the mother and babies. Physicians may recommend "selective reduction" (aborting the weakest fetuses so the others might survive), which poses an ethical dilemma for the parents.

Such types of "assisted conception" also lead to legal questions about parentage (e.g., does a surrogate mother or a sperm donor have any parental responsibilities or rights?). Some states have laws dealing with these issues, but others do not. States without laws rely on the physician to act with reasonable care. Questions regarding legal protection and parentage should be addressed to an attorney when considering these procedures.

Abortion

Roe v. Wade in 1973 was the court case that established the rights of women to control their bodies. Basically, the decision mandates that the states have no authority to regulate abortions within the first 13 weeks of pregnancy. Some states responded by denying the use of federal funds for abortions. There are many religious and scientific theories about when life begins. Does life begin at conception, at birth, or somewhere in between? Often the issue is not whether women should be able to have an abortion, but whether women should have control over their own bodies.

Genetic Engineering

Amazing progress has been made in the fields of genetics and **genomics,** the science of understanding the complete genetic inheritance of an organism. The same gene-splicing technology that could eliminate genetic disease in children also could be used to change how they look, how they act, or how they think. Likewise, the same genetic test that helps a physician assess disease risks and recommend preventive measures could also be used by health insurance carriers to deny health care coverage or by employers to withhold promotions or terminate employment.

Another issue is the ability to *clone* (duplicate). It may be possible in the future to clone humans, but is it ethical? Currently there is no federal statute outlawing embryonic stem cell research in the United States. The barriers are largely due to restrictions placed on the use of federal research dollars.

Resource Allocation

A *resource* is something of value to the public, whether a heart or liver or an appointment, or anything that has limited access. Allocation is deciding who receives the resource. Some believe that the only fair way to allocate is to use the lottery system, or "luck of the draw." Others think that a list of criteria would help with the decision process. Questions could include the following:

- Who would benefit the most?
- What would the benefit do to the quality of life?
- How long would the benefit last?
- What is the urgency of need?
- How much of the resource is needed?

Allocation of resources poses moral dilemmas. Would it be ethical to refuse a liver transplant to an alcoholic patient who declines treatment for his alcoholism? Another issue relating to resource allocation is the treatment of patients who have HIV infection or acquired immunodeficiency syndrome (AIDS). Insurance companies create more ethical questions when they refuse insurance to individuals who have these diseases. Patients with an HIV infection or AIDS have the same rights as people with other life-threatening illnesses and should be treated with dignity and respect by health professionals.

PATIENT-CENTERED PROFESSIONALISM

- What are some ways your ethics could be challenged as a medical assistant in a medical office setting?
- How could releasing confidential patient information hinder a patient's chances for employment? For health or life insurance coverage? Relationships with friends and family?
- You will come into contact with patients who do not share your views on bioethical issues (e.g., "right to die," cloning, abortion). What can you do to maintain a healthy relationship with patients regardless of their ethical beliefs?
- Why is it important for medical assistants to stay current on the laws associated with bioethical issues, such as the "right to die," fertility, abortion, and genetic engineering?

☰ CONCLUSION

In order to perform your duties legally and ethically, it is necessary for you to know the legal and ethical boundaries associated with medical assisting.

Al   lth professionals have a responsibility
to b   legally and ethically. They respect the
right   their patients and provide competent,
effec   are. Medical assistants who strive to be
patie   itered professionals help their physician-
empl   meet patient expectations and avoid lawsuits. ys remember that one misplaced word or
inap   ate action could result in legal problems
not j   r you, but for the whole organization in
whic   work. Ignorance is no excuse; it is part
of yo   b as a patient-centered professional to
know iws and to follow them. While working
withi   law, follow the medical assistants' code
of et   help you make choices about the "right
thing   o.

SUM   Y

Reinf   our understanding of the material in this
chapt   reviewing the following curriculum
objec   ind key content points.

1. D   appropriately use, and spell all the Key
   T   or this chapter.
   •   w the Key Terms if necessary.

2. D   e the purpose of the Medical Practice
   A
   •   Medical Practice Acts were created to
        ct people from unqualified health care
        ssionals.

   •   Medical Practice Acts establish a medical
        l to review licensing requirements,
        lines for suspension and revocation of
        es, and renewal requirements for physi-
        in their state.

3. Li   three ways health professionals can
   b   licensed.
   •   hree ways to obtain a license are by
        ination, reciprocity, or endorsement.

4. Li   ie six licensure requirements for
   pl   ins.
   •   nse is a legal document that allows a
        n to work in a particular profession;
        state will develop rules for licensing.

   •   tain a license, physicians must (a) meet
        dual state requirements, (b) complete
        tion requirements through an approved
        al school, (c) complete an approved
        ncy program, (d) pass all examinations
        ed by the state board of medical exam-
        (e) be of good moral character, and (f)
        the age of majority as defined by state
        ɔ.

5. Ex   how a physician could have his or her
   lic evoked or suspended.

- A physician could have his or her license revoked or suspended because of conviction of a crime, unprofessional conduct, or incapacity to perform duties.
- A physician-employer is ultimately responsible for the actions of his or her staff; permitting unqualified staff to endanger patients jeopardizes the physician's right to practice.

6. Distinguish between public law and private law.
   - Public law is concerned with the welfare or safety of the public.
   - Private law deals with issues against private individuals.

7. Describe abandonment and give an example.
   - Abandonment occurs if a physician fails to provide physician coverage in his or her absence.
   - Refusal to treat in cases of noncompliance can also be considered abandonment if the patient is not formally notified and given the opportunity to transfer care to another physician.

8. List the six steps in formally withdrawing from the physician-patient contract.
   - The patient must be notified in writing.
   - Reasons for dismissal must be stated.
   - An effective date is given when treatment will cease.
   - A list of possible new physicians is provided.
   - A form is enclosed for transfer of the patient's records.
   - A letter is sent via certified mail, and return receipt is requested.

9. Define *express contract* and *implied contract* and give an example of each.
   - A contract requires that an offer be made by one person and accepted by another.
   - "Expressed" means spoken, stated, or written. Voluntary hospital admission requires the patient's signed forms agreeing to payment of the hospital bill.
   - "Implied" means suggested or expected. Treatment is rendered before any agreement on payment.

10. Explain how malpractice relates to liability.
    - Malpractice is a specific type of negligence in which a professional fails to act with reasonable care, and persons who commit malpractice are liable (held accountable for their actions).

11. Explain the difference between *intentional* negligence and *nonintentional* negligence.
    - Negligence is *not doing* something a reasonably prudent person *would do* in a similar

situation, or doing something a reasonably prudent person would not do in a similar situation.

- A tort is a wrongful act committed by one person against another.
- Intentional torts include assault and battery, defamation, invasion of privacy, false imprisonment, and medical abandonment.
- Nonintentional torts include negligence and *res ipsa loquitur*. The majority of U.S. malpractice suits are nonintentional torts.

12. Explain the importance of informed consent.
- Informed consent must be given by the patient before treatment or procedures.
- The physician, before treatment, must give sufficient information about the procedure (risks, alternatives) to enable the patient to make an informed decision.

13. Describe the purpose of the Good Samaritan Act.
- The Good Samaritan Act allows a person to assist an injured person without fear of a lawsuit as long as they stay within their scope of training.

14. List the three types of nonintentional negligence.
- Ordinary (nonintentional) negligence is the accidental commission or omission of an act.
- Types of negligence include malfeasance, misfeasance, and nonfeasance.

15. State the "four Ds" of negligence.
- The four Ds of negligence must be present before an attorney will pursue a case for professional negligence: *D*uty of care to the patient, breach of that *D*uty (Dereliction of Duty), *D*irect connection between breach of duty and patient injury, and *D*amage sustained by the patient.

16. Explain the importance of keeping accurate medical records.
- A patient's medical record follows them for life. Accurate records ensure continuity of care for any health care team treating the patient.
- The dates and information recorded in the medical record can be used in a lawsuit, so the medical records must be kept up to date, accurate, and complete.

17. List 10 guidelines of risk management to avoid a lawsuit.
- Refer to Box 6-4.

18. Describe the trial process.
- Refer to Table 6-2.

19. List five types of patient information that, by law, must be reported to state or local authorities.

- Reportable events include birth, death, communicable diseases, and injuries caused by weapons or suspected abuse.

20. Explain the purpose of a living will.
- A living will is a statement to the family, physician, or lawyer that conveys a person's decisions about medical treatment if the person becomes unable to make the decision.
- The Patient Self-Determination Act provides for advanced directives concerning life-support decisions.

21. Explain the purpose of the Uniform Anatomical Gift Act.
- The Uniform Anatomical Gift Act allows a person to donate his or her body or body parts after death for research or to preserve life.

22. List three laws that concern workplace issues and explain how they can protect medical assistants and other workers.
- OSHA's laws and regulations protect employees from hazardous work environments. Each state has a branch of OSHA enforcement.
- Workers' compensation laws assist employees with work-related injuries.
- Laws enacted under the Americans with Disabilities Act prevent hiring discrimination against disabled persons.

23. Explain the difference between ethics and law.
- *Ethics* is a moral, voluntary choice—right or wrong.
- *Law* is a mandated choice—right or wrong.
- Law you *must* do; ethics you *should* do.
- Something that is unethical may not be illegal.

24. State the five parts of the American Association of Medical Assistants Code of Ethics.
- Refer to Box 6-8.

25. Describe the legal and ethical importance of maintaining patient privacy and confidentiality.
- Patients expect and have a right to privacy and confidentiality by law.
- The AAMA's code of ethics encourages respectful treatment of patients' privacy and confidentiality.

26. Describe the expectations patients have for effective care.
- All health care workers have a responsibility to their patients to be respectful, competent, maintain a code of ethics, and to "do no harm."
- The American Hospital Association formulated the Patient Care Partnership.

27. List three bioethical situations and explain the considerations for each.

ht-to-die" issues, in vitro fertilization, resource allocation are all ethical iderations.

28. e a realistic medical office situation and law and ethics to determine the best of action.
- ys follow the law.
- tice the ethics established by your ssion.

29. Describe the impact on patient care when medical assistants have a solid understanding of law and ethics.
- Illegal and unethical practices can have a devastating, even lethal, impact on patients.
- The medical practice is affected by the legal and ethical behavior of its staff.

FURTHER EXPLORATION

1. rch the legal history of the Terry Schiavo This case focused attention on end-of-life al ethics and the need for some type of ed directives by individual.
ords: Use the following keyword in your Schiavo.

2. rch OSHA laws and regulations to learn about how they protect employees. OSHA erned with protecting employees from harm hey do their jobs. OSHA also checks to see ese laws and regulations are followed and es for punishment when they are not.

Keywords: Use the following keywords in your search: OSHA, Occupational Safety and Health Act.

3. Research your state's statutes that require practitioners to report certain diseases/conditions to their public health department. The Bureau of Epidemiology at the Department of Health uses data collected from each states' public health department to tract incidence of disease outbreaks across the country.

Keywords: Use the following keywords in your search: public health, public health reporting, reportable diseases.

Chapter Review

Vocabulary Review

Matching

Match each term with the correct definition.

A. age of majority

B. contract

C. damages

D. euthanasia

E. Good Samaritan Act

F. infraction

G. noncompliance

H. reciprocity

I. subpoena

J. vicarious liability

_____ 1. Liability of an employer for the wrongdoing of an employee while on the job

_____ 2. Legislation that provides protection from lawsuits for an individual providing lifesaving or emergency treatment

_____ 3. Occurs when one state accepts another state's licensing requirements

_____ 4. Failure of a patient to comply with the physician's treatment plan; grounds for dismissal of a patient from a practice

_____ 5. Person who is considered by law to have acquired all the rights and responsibilities of an adult (age 18 in most states)

_____ 6. Payment used to compensate for physical injury, damaged property, or a loss of personal freedom or used as a punishment

_____ 7. Violation of a law, resulting in a fine

_____ 8. Legal document that requires a person to appear in court or be available for a deposition

_____ 9. Intentional ending of life for the terminally ill

_____ 10. Agreement between two or more persons resulting in a consideration

The   ecall

True   e

Indic   ether the sentence or statement is true or false.

_____   ertification is the strongest form of professional regulation, as it is a legal document.

_____   nder the "Good Samaritan Act," implied consent applies if no one is available to consent for   e patient and if a "reasonable" person would consent under similar circumstances.

_____   nder the Uniform Anatomical Gift Act, incompetent individuals may donate their body or   dy parts after they die.

_____   onfidentiality breaches occur most often as a result of carelessness in elevators or hallways and   er lunches in medical facilities.

_____   is the medical assistant's responsibility to know the laws and to follow them to the letter.

Mul   Choice

Ident   letter of the choice that best completes the statement or answers the question.

1. T   lure to make arrangements for a patient's medical coverage is termed _____.
   A   tery
   B   ss negligence
   C   ndonment
   D   lied contract

2. ___   a written form of defamation.
   A   el
   B   ony
   C   der
   D   feasance

3. ___   the performance of an unlawful act causing harm.
   A   ndonment
   B   lfeasance
   C   feasance
   D   d pro quo

4. A   ch of law that deals with offenses or crimes against the welfare or safety of the public is _____.
   A   lic law
   B   inistrative law
   C   inal law
   D   rnational law

5. ___   the science of understanding the complete genetic inheritance of an organism.
   A   ciary
   B   uropathy
   C   rapathy
   D   omics

6. The document that was formulated by the American Hospital Association to define the rights of patients is the _____.
   A. Patient Care Partnership
   B. Patient Bill of Rights
   C. Private law
   D. Good Samaritan Act

7. Which one of the following is NOT a means of obtaining licensure?
   A. Examination
   B. On-the-job training
   C. Reciprocity
   D. Endorsement

8. Physicians are required to renew their license every _____ years.
   A. 2
   B. 3
   C. 4
   D. 5

9. The doctrine of _____ places the liability on the physician for his or her employee's actions.
   A. *quid pro quo*
   B. *res ipsa loquitur*
   C. *respondeat superior*
   D. subpoena *duces tecum*

10. _____ is a voluntary process that professionals can go through to earn certification and other proof of their knowledge and skills.
    A. Endorsement
    B. Reciprocity
    C. Continuing education
    D. Credentialing

11. _____ deals with the rights and responsibilities of the government to the people and the people to the government.
    A. Administrative law
    B. Public law
    C. Criminal law
    D. Civil law

12. A(n) _____ is one that is specifically stated aloud or written and is understood by all parties.
    A. implied contract
    B. illegal contract
    C. breach of contract
    D. expressed contract

13. A(n) _____ is a negligent, wrongful act committed by a person against another person or property that causes harm.
    A. tort
    B. implied contract
    C. slander
    D. fiduciary

14. A threat or the perceived threat of doing bodily harm by another person is _____.
    A. slander
    B. libel
    C. assault
    D. battery

15. ary _____ is not doing (or doing) something that a reasonable person would do (or would not

   gligence
   lfeasance
   sfeasance
   nfeasance

16. s the failure to do what is expected, thereby resulting in harm to the patient.
   gligence
   lfeasance
   sfeasance
   nfeasance

17. one of the following is NOT a component that must be present before an attorney will pursue
   for professional negligence?
   ty
   reliction of duty
   ect cause or proximate cause
   yment for services rendered

18. _____ of 1990 requires health care institutions to give patients written information about advance
   ves before life-sustaining measures become necessary.
   ient Bill of Rights
   ient Care Partnership
   ient Self-Determination Act
   iform Anatomical Act

19. _____ provides guidelines for collecting money owed.
   nkruptcy Act
   r Debt Collection Practices Act
   nsumer Debt Act
   cupational Safety and Health Act

20. efers to "this for that" or the "something for something" issues that may occur in the
   lace.
   id pro quo
   ipsa loquitur
   pondeat superior
   poena duces tecum

Sent Completion

Comp ich sentence or statement.

1. A(_____ is an agreement between two or more people promising to work toward a
   sp goal for adequate consideration.

2. A(_____ is an underage person who has legally separated from parents for various
   re and is legally capable of consent to treatment.

3. Al s require the reporting of _____, including births, deaths, and communicable
   di

4. Ea emical used on the job must have a(n) _____ from the manufacturer on file.

5. Employers, by law, must carry _____. This plan covers medical care and rehabilitation costs and offers temporary or permanent pay for the injured employee.

6. The Council on Ethical and Judicial Affairs (CEJA) develops ethics policies for the _____.

Short Answers

1. List three bioethical situations and briefly explain the considerations for each.

_____

_____

_____

_____

_____

_____

2. Compare the differences between law and ethics.

_____

_____

_____

_____

3. Create a scenario involving a breach of confidentiality that might occur in a medical office.

_____

_____

_____

_____

4. Describe your opinion of the legality and ethics of genetic engineering.

_____

_____

_____

_____

_____

Crit   Thinking

1.   ternship Terry overheard two employees of the medical clinic discussing the specifics of a
      t's case, in the clinic's break room. The comment that caught Terry's attention was that the
      t had been physically abused by her spouse. Terry knew this patient personally; the patient was
      d to Terry's cousin. Terry could not believe what she had overheard and was appalled that the
      al assistants would be making such claims.

      d the two employees in the medical clinic breach confidentiality?

      _____

      uld Terry say anything to the patient or to her cousin?

      _____

      gally and ethically, did the two employees violate any laws or regulations? If so, what are the
      lations?

      _____

      _____

      _____

      at would you do if you were in Terry's place?

      _____

      _____

Inte   Research

Keyv   Medical Practice Acts in your state

Rese   he medical practice acts for your state. Identify the section(s) that pertain to medical assistants
pract   their profession.

Wha   uld You Do?

If yo   ? accomplished the objectives in this chapter, you will be able to make better choices as a
medi   sistant. Take a look at this situation and decide what you would do.

Jill is   dical assistant with on-the-job training in a medical office setting. She always strives to be
carin   rteous, and respectful of patients and co-workers. Because of her caring attitude, the patients
with   n Jill works all appreciate her attitude and her work. One of Jill's favorite patients, Shandra, a
24-ye   mother of two young children, has been diagnosed with cancer and recently was told by the
physi   hat her condition is terminal. Shandra is at the office for an appointment and, feeling very
upset   t her terminal illness, she pours out her heart and fears to Jill. Wanting to comfort Shandra, Jill
tells l   Don't worry. You'll be just fine. You know the doctor will make you better."
    Sh   is comforted by Jill's words and tells her how much Jill means to her. In fact, she has so much
faith   that she believes that she will be fine and tells her family what Jill has said. Sadly, a few
mont   er, Shandra dies. Believing she would be fine, Shandra had not made any plans for her children
and f   Her family is upset with the physician and with Jill. The family thinks they have been
betra   cause they believed that Shandra would be fine. The family is discussing what to say to the
physi   bout this betrayal and whether to bring a lawsuit, because Shandra did not have a will.

How   this situation been avoided? What are the possible implications for Shandra's family, Jill, the
physi   nd the practice?

1. Jill has been trained on the job and is uncredentialed. What are the disadvantages to Jill of not having a formal medical assisting education? Would having credentialing and an education make a difference in what Jill said to Shandra?

_____

_____

_____

2. Would credentialing make a difference if Shandra's family decides to bring a lawsuit? If so, what are the benefits to the physician if the medical assistant is credentialed?

_____

_____

_____

3. Why was it important for Shandra to have an advance directive?

_____

_____

_____

4. What are the legal ramifications of Jill telling Shandra not to worry and that she would be fine? What ethical guidelines should be considered in this situation? Did Jill do something illegal, something unethical, neither, or both? Explain why or why not.

_____

_____

_____

Application of Skills

1. Contact your local Public Health Department and request a list of reportable diseases in your area and state. Conduct a Web search using the keywords "reportable diseases, notifiable diseases." Which diseases require mandatory written reporting? Which require mandatory reporting by telephone? Which diseases must also be reported to the CDC?
2. Clip one current newspaper, magazine, or Internet article pertaining to medical, legal, or ethical issues. Summarize the article by writing a paragraph describing your impression of the article and the impact it has on the medical community. Cite the specific legal or ethical implications.
3. Complete forms: Consent for Surgery and Patient Consent on yourself.

CONSENT FOR SURGERY

TE: _____   **TIME:** _____

uthorize the performance of the following procedure(s) _____

_____ on _____

be performed by _____, MD.

e following have been explained to me by Dr. _____

    1. Nature of the procedure: _____

    2. Reason(s) for procedure: _____

    3. Possible risks: _____

    4. Possible complications: _____

derstand that no warranty or guarantee of the effectiveness of the surgery can be made.

ve been informed of possible alternative treatments including _____

_____

of the likely consequences of receiving no treatment, and I freely consent to this procedure.

reby authorize the above named surgeon and his/her assistants to provide additional services
uding administering anesthesia and/or medications, performing needed diagnostic tests
uding but not limited to radiology, and any other additional serviced deemed necessary for
well-being. I consent to have removed tissue examined by a pathologist who may then
ose of the tissue as he/she sees fit.

ned _____   Relationship to patient _____
      Patient / Parent / Guardian

ness _____

Patient Consent to the Use and Disclosure of Health Information
for Treatment, Payment, or Health Care Operations

I understand that as part of my health care, the practice originates and maintains paper and/or electronic records describing my health history, symptoms, examination and test results, diagnoses, treatment, and any plans for future care or treatment. I understand that this information serves as:

- A basis for planning my care and treatment,
- A means of communication among professionals who contribute to my care,
- A source of information for applying my diagnosis and treatment information to my bill,
- A means by which a third-party payer can verify that services billed were actually provided,
- A tool for routine health care operations, such as assessing quality and reviewing the competence of staff.

I have been provided the opportunity to review the *"Notice of Patient Privacy Information Practices"* **that provides a more complete description of information uses and disclosures. I understand that I have the following rights:**

- The right to review the *"Notice"* prior to acknowledging this consent,
- The right to restrict or revoke the use or disclosure of my health information for other uses or purposes, and
- The right to request restrictions as to how my health information may be used or disclosed to carry out treatment, payment, or health care operations.

Restrictions:

I request the following restrictions to the use or disclosure of my health information:

_____

_____

May discuss treatment, payment, or health care operation with the following persons:

(Please check all that apply)   Spouse [   ]   Your Children [   ]   Relatives [   ]   Others [   ]   Parents [   ]

Please list the names and relationship, if you checked "Relatives" or "Others" above

_____

_____

Messages or Appointment Reminders: (Please check all that apply)

May we leave a message on your answering machine at home [   ] or at work [   ]. **Do not leave a message [   ]**
May we leave a message with someone at your **home** using the doctor's name or the practice name: Yes [   ]   No [   ]
May we leave a message with someone at your **work** using the doctor's name or the practice name: Yes [   ]   No [   ]
Messages will be of a nonsensitive nature, such as appointment reminders.

I understand that as part of treatment, payment, or health care operations, it may become necessary to disclose health information to another entity, i.e., referrals to other health care providers, labs, and/or other individuals or agencies as permitted or required by state or federal law.

I fully understand and accept the information provided by this consent.

_____   _____   _____
Signature   Print name of person signing   Date

*If other than patient is signing, are you the parent, legal guardian, custodian, or have Power of Attorney for this patient for treatment, payment, or health care operations?   Yes [   ]   No [   ]

_____

FOR OFFICE USE ONLY
[   ] Patient refused to sign the consent form.
[   ] Restrictions were added by the patient (see restrictions listed above)
[   ] "Consent form" received and reviewed by _____ on (date) _____
[   ] "Consent form" placed in the patient's medical record on (date) _____

Cha   Quiz

Mul   Choice

Iden   e letter of the choice that best completes the statement or answers the question.

1.   l document that requires a person to appear in court and bring the records is (a) _____.
       ppoena
       ipsa loquitur
       ppoena *duces tecum*
       ient Bill of Rights

2.   l document that allows a person to offer their skills and knowledge to the public for
       nsation is a(n) _____.
       tification
       nse
       DS
       loma

3.   tentional act of touching another person in a socially unacceptable manner without their
       t is called _____.
       el
       ach of duty
       tery
       ault

4.   s legislation that regulates patients' rights and federal regulation that mandates the protection
       acy and holds information to be confidential.
       alth Insurance Portability and Accountability Act
       ient Care Partnership Act
       ndard of Care Act
       od Samaritan Act

5.   n of trusted responsibility is a(n) _____.
       ancipated minor
       iciary
       endent
       todian

6.   or _____, are general rules and standards designed to regulate conduct.
       s
       dical practice acts
       ts
       utes

7.   egulates business practices.
       ate law
       nership law
       ninistrative law
       lic law

8.   king arrangements for a substitute physician to take patient calls if the physician is
       able could be grounds for a lawsuit and termed as _____.
       feasance
       ery
       ch of contract
       ndonment

9. For there to be a valid physician-patient contract, the patient must meet or perform all of the following EXCEPT _____.
   A. truthfully disclose past and present medical information
   B. having reached the age of 14 years old
   C. take all medications
   D. be responsible with an appropriate reimbursement plan

10. In order for a physician to withdraw from patient care, all of the following must be achieved EXCEPT _____.
    A. notify the patient in writing
    B. give a date when this is to take effect (minimum of 30 days)
    C. provide a personal telephone call from the physician
    D. provide for transfer of medical records

11. An _____ contract is one that is specifically stated aloud or written and is understood by all parties.
    A. expressed
    B. implied
    C. invalid
    D. assumed

12. A _____ is a negligent, wrongful act committed by a person against another person or property that causes harm.
    A. fiduciary
    B. tort
    C. liability
    D. fraud

13. _____ is intentional negligence, or a wrongful act done (or not done) on purpose.
    A. Malfeasance
    B. Minor negligence
    C. Gross negligence
    D. Nonfeasance

14. _____ is defamation of character in writing.
    A. Slander
    B. Battery
    C. Libel
    D. Assault

15. If a patient were to receive a burn during ultrasound therapy, the charge may be _____.
    A. misfeasance
    B. malfeasance
    C. nonfeasance
    D. none of the above

16. _____ occurs when a health care professional fails to meet accepted standards of care.
    A. Breach of contract
    B. Dereliction of duty
    C. Fraud
    D. All of the above

17. Each state has laws that limit the length of time a person has to take legal action. This is called the _____.
    A. duration of care
    B. expressed contractual agreement
    C. standard of care requirements
    D. statute of limitations

18.   est way to avoid a lawsuit is to _____.
        ep the lines of communication open
        ten to patient's concerns or complaints; chart the facts
        ep patient information confidential
         of the above

19.   roviding a child with clothing for the weather could be considered _____.
        andonment
        glect
        od parenting
        se imprisonment

20.   ployer must provide every employee with the opportunity to receive a hepatitis B vaccination.
        cond dose in the series of three should be given _____ after the first dose.
         days
         days
         days
        0 days

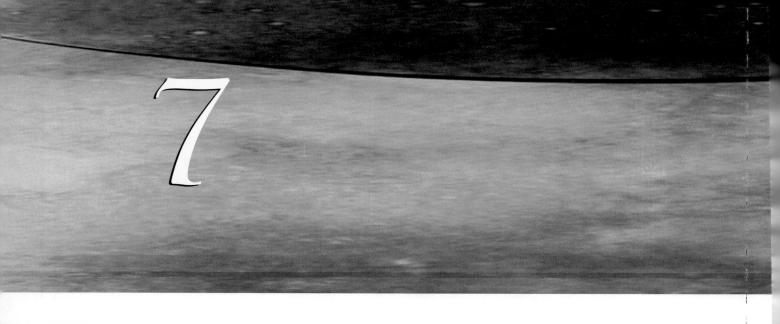

OBJECTIVES

1. Define, spell, and pronounce the terms listed in the vocabulary.
2. Explain the meaning of the word *professionalism*.
3. Discuss several characteristics of professionalism.
4. Explain why confidentiality is so important in the medical profession.
5. Discuss the role of the medical assistant's attitude in caring for patients.
6. List some examples of office politics.
7. Identify specific ways that teamwork can be promoted in the physician's office.
8. Discuss the meaning of insubordination and why it is grounds for dismissal.
9. Identify several categories of prioritizing tasks and their meaning.
10. Talk about goal setting and how this helps in achieving career success.

PROFESSIONAL BEHAVIOR IN THE WORKPLACE

KEY TERMS

chara **s** Distinguishing traits, qualities, or properties.

comm **te** (ku-men'su-rut) Corresponding in size, amount, ext degree; equal in measure.

compe aving adequate or requisite capabilities.

conno kah-nuh-ta'-shun) An implication; something sug by a word or thing.

credib e quality or power of inspiring belief.

demea -me'-nur) Behavior toward others; outward ma

detrim e-truh-men'-til) Obviously harmful or damaging.

discret -kre'-shun) The quality of being discrete; having or s good judgment or conduct, especially in speech.

dissem (di-se'-muh-na-ted) To disburse; to spread arou

initiativ ause or facilitate the beginning of; to initiate som nto happening.

insubor n (in-suh'-bor-din-a-shun) Disobedience to auth

morale (mo-ral') The mental and emotional condition, enthusiasm, loyalty, or confidence of an individual or group with regard to the function or tasks at hand.

optimistic Inclined to put the most favorable construction on actions and events or to anticipate the best possible outcome.

persona (pur-so'-nuh) An individual's social facade or front that reflects the role in life the individual is playing; the personality that a person projects in public.

procrastination (pruh-kras-tuh-na'-shun) Intentionally putting off doing something that should be done.

professionalism The conduct or qualities characterized by or conforming to the technical or ethical standards of a profession; exhibiting a courteous, conscientious, and generally businesslike manner in the workplace.

reproach An expression of rebuke or disapproval; a cause or occasion of blame, discredit, or disgrace.

What Would You Do?

Read the following scenario and keep it in mind as you learn about professional behavior in the workplace in this chapter.

Karen Yon has wanted to work in the medical field for most of her adult life. She studied very hard in high school and graduated with honors. She volunteered in a local hospital, then after working for 3 years in restaurants as a server, she enrolled in medical assistant classes. After her externship, she was asked to continue as a regular employee at a family practice in her area.

Karen strives to do all of her duties professionally and compassionately in the physician's office. She maintains a professional image to patients and co-workers. However, it was difficult to learn how to be professional at all times and show compassion to patients through only the classroom experience. These are important aspects of her job, and she was able to gain valuable experience in these areas on her externship. Because this is her first job in the medical field, she wants to make a good impression on her employer and be a team player.

Throughout most of Karen's training as a medical assistant, her grandmother was confined to a rehabilitation center after a stroke. Although she has progressed well with treatment, Karen is the only relative who lives close to the rehabilitation center, and her family depends on her to check on her grandmother from time to time. Karen enjoys spending time at the center reading to her grandmother, because they are close. Still, Karen realizes that the stroke has caused permanent damage, and her grandmother's health seems to be on the decline.

What is professional behavior? We tend to hold medical personnel to a higher standard of **professionalism** than those in most other career fields. The medical assistant who works to improve his or her professional approach in the workplace will be an asset to the employer and will be promoted to positions of more responsibility quickly within the health care industry.

THE MEANING OF PROFESSIONALISM

Professionalism is defined as exhibiting a courteous, conscientious, and generally businesslike manner in the workplace. It is characterized by or conforms to the technical or ethical standards of a certain profession. Conducting oneself in a professional manner is essential for successful medical assistants. The attitude of those in the medical profession is generally more conservative than in other career fields. Patients expect professional behavior and will base much of their trust and confidence in those who exhibit this type of **demeanor** in the physician's office (Fig. 7-1).

Fig. 7-1 The professional medical assistant is an asset to the physician's office.

[CHA]RACTERISTICS OF [PRO]FESSIONALISM

Ma[ny ch]aracteristics make up the professional pos[ture r]equired of medical assistants. Student med[ical a]ssistants should begin developing these cha[racteri]stics while in school; these qualities will not [typi]cally appear when the student begins wor[king w]ith actual patients. Although we might thin[k tha]t we would always behave appropriately duri[ng an] externship or in a job setting, the habits deve[loped] in school will carry over into these experien[ces. If] the behavior is unacceptable, it will be **det[rimen]tal** to the medical assistant's professional care[er. If] the medical assistant wishes to advance and [recei]ve wage increases, promotions, and the trust [of th]e employer, the following characteristics mus[t be] part of his or her **persona.**

> ### S[TOP A]ND THINK?
>
> • [How] can students practice professional behavior [while] still in the classroom situation?
> • [When] students are practicing clinical skills, how [can th]ey demonstrate proficiency in professional [behavi]or?

Loy[alty]

Loya[lty is] a faithfulness or allegiance to a cause, idea[l, cust]om, institution, or product. Loyalty to an emp[loyer] means that the employee is appreciative of the [opport]unity provided through the job and supports [the c]ompany by giving the best effort possible. Man[y indi]viduals today are interested only in what the e[mploy]er can provide them. However, this is an imm[ature] approach to take toward a job. When a pers[on is e]mployed by a company, use of skills is exch[anged] for different types of compensation. Each bene[fits th]e other. Often we forget that experience alon[e is a g]reat benefit from working. Loyalty to the empl[oyer is] important, and the employee should feel a sen[se of l]oyalty from the company as well.

> ### ST[OP A]ND THINK?
>
> • [How] can Karen demonstrate loyalty to her [employ]er?
> • [What a]re some ways that her employer can recip[rocate] Karen's loyalty?

Dep[enda]bility

One o[f the] most valuable traits of a successful medical assist[ant is] dependability. Be on time and make

Fig. 7-2 The physician will depend on the medical assistant to be at work on time and on each scheduled day. Absent or tardy employees cause scheduling difficulties and can greatly inconvenience the patients and remaining staff.

Fig. 7-3 Taking a few moments to explain forms and bills to a patient is a courteous way to avoid misunderstandings and promote goodwill.

every attempt to be at work every day. When staff members arrive late, the schedule for the entire day can be delayed (Fig. 7-2). A medical assistant must follow through when the physician or supervisor gives an order. That person will count on the medical assistant to remember and complete all assigned duties. Supervisors should be confident that once given a task to do, the medical assistant will carry it out accurately and in a timely manner.

Courtesy

Show courtesy to the patients and co-workers in the physician's office. Kind words and compassion go far in building trust between the medical assistant and patients (Fig. 7-3). All visitors and staff members in the office should be shown kindness and consideration. The fact that a medical assistant is having a bad day is no excuse for inflicting his or her anger or irritation on patients. Always demonstrate a good attitude and offer patients and visitors a sincere smile.

Initiative

Employee lack of **initiative** is one of the more common complaints from supervisors. Taking initiative means that the medical assistant looks for the opportunity to be of help, assisting others as the workload demands. Instead of waiting to be told to perform a task, the **competent** medical assistant looks for jobs that need to be completed; never remain idle. Some task can always be done in the medical office. Filing needs to be done on a continual basis. Inventories, supply ordering, or restocking can be performed when there is extra time. Cleaning countertops and straightening areas as work is done will help to keep the facility tidy. The medical assistant should also keep an eye on the reception area, since it may need attention several times during the day.

STOP AND THINK?

- How can Karen show her initiative on the job?
- What types of duties can she perform when she has finished her workload for the day and there is still time left before leaving the office?

Flexibility

A medical assistant must be able to adapt to a wide variety of situations. An emergency could occur in the office, and the staff must be flexible enough to adjust the schedule and care for all patients. Being flexible also means that staff members are willing to assist one another in the performance of their duties. No one in the physician's office should ever say, "That's not my job." The patients must come first, and every staff member must be willing to lend a hand where needed. Some medical assistants trade or rotate their duties. If one assistant does not particularly enjoy doing a certain task, perhaps another assistant would be willing to trade tasks. This way, both are more satisfied with their jobs. Being able to adapt quickly and cheerfully will make the medical assistant a valuable asset to the office.

Credibility

Credibility is the perceived competence or character of a person. It leads to the belief that a person can be trusted. Because trust is a vital component of the physician-patient relationship, the credibility of the physician and those who assist in the office should be strong. The information provided to patients must be accurate. Patients expect that the physician and medical assistant will instruct them in a manner that will enhance their health and provide positive results. One must take care in giving any advice to patients, because they view the medical assistant as an agent of the physician. Patients may not distinguish between the medical assistant's comments and the physician's orders. Remember that giving anything that could be construed as medical advice is outside the scope of the duties of the medical assistant. To avoid charges of practicing medicine without a license, a medical assistant must be sure to suggest only what the physician has authorized.

Confidentiality

The importance of confidentiality cannot be stressed enough in the medical environment. Patients are entitled to privacy where their health is concerned, and they should be confident that medical professionals use information only to care for them. Never reveal any information about any patient to anyone without specific permission to do so. Always verify that the person seeking information has the right to see it and that the patient has signed a consent form. Casual conversations in hallways, elevators, and break rooms between staff members can be overheard by a family member or friend of the patient. These are a few places in the facility where confidentiality is often breached.

The rules regarding confidentiality extend beyond the medical office. While at home, medical assistants should not discuss details about patients with their families and friends. Those outside the medical profession do not understand how vital it is to keep information confidential and may pass along damaging facts to others. Medical assistants must make it a rule never to discuss a patient with anyone unless information must be shared for patient care and treatment. The Health Insurance Portability and Accountability Act (HIPAA) was created in part to ensure patient confidentiality. HIPAA was discussed in Chapter 6.

Attitude

Possibly the most important asset a medical assistant brings to the office is a good attitude. A good attitude involves courtesy and kindness to others, refraining from jumping to conclusions, giving the other person the benefit of the doubt, and being **optimistic.** This trait alone can influence promotions, terminations, and the entire atmosphere of the office (Fig. 7-4). Individuals are able to control their attitudes with practice. It takes skill to react calmly to people who are very upset, rather than to respond in kind, especially if being harassed or accused. Speaking in an even tone and perhaps a little softer than normal will force the listener to lower his or her voice to hear. Offer to help resolve

Fig. 7- [g]ood attitude goes a long way in patient and staff re[lations]hips.

the pr[o] and attempt to move to a private room out of [h]earing range of other patients to talk. Always [displ]ay a good attitude with co-workers and be will[ing to] assist them with their duties, especially on hec[tic da]ys.

OB[STRU]CTIONS TO PROFESSIONALISM

[I]t is not [alway]s easy to be a professional. Sometimes [p]atients[, co-w]orkers, and supervisors try our patience, [a]nd it ca[n be h]ard to maintain a professional attitude [i]n these [times]. Some of the obstructions to profes[s]ional be[havio]r are discussed in this section.

[P]erson[al Pr]oblems and "Baggage"

[E]veryon[e has] a life outside of the workplace, and [so]metim[es we] face challenges and difficult times [th]at are [hard to] put aside. During working hours our [th]oughts [shou]ld be on the job at hand, especially [w]hen we [are d]ealing with patients. However, there [m]ay be s[ituatio]ns in our lives that are so critical or [di]stractin[g that] we find ourselves thinking of them [co]nstantl[y. Thi]s personal baggage can interfere with [ou]r abilit[y to pr]operly perform job duties.

[W]hen [a situa]tion intrudes on thoughts at work, it [o]ften be[st to t]ake the time to talk with a supervisor. [I]t is not [alway]s necessary to share the intimate [det]ails, bu[t a qui]ck explanation that some difficulties [are] occurr[ing ou]tside of work will help the supervisor [und]ers[tand] any changes in habit or attitude.

Fig. 7-5   Gossip and rumors have no place in the medical profession. Avoid employees who participate in this type of activity.

However, some supervisors are uncaring and are concerned only with satisfactory job performance. The medical assistant will have to use some **discretion** when discussing private affairs with the supervisor.

Never transfer personal problems and baggage to the patient. A professional medical assistant does not share personal information or problems with anyone at the medical facility, especially patients. The workday should be centered around patient care, so never allow personal business to impinge on time that should be spent assisting patients and the physician.

> #### STOP AND THINK?
>
> It is often hard to keep from thinking about a problem while you are working. How can Karen do this if she is concerned about a grandmother who is critically ill?

Rumors and the "Grapevine"

A rumor by definition is talk or widely **disseminated** opinion with no discernible source, or a statement that is not known to be true. The definition alone suggests that spreading rumors should be avoided. Most people enjoy working in an environment in which employees cooperate and get along with each other, but rumors can cause problems with employee **morale** and are often great exaggerations or manipulations of the truth. By promoting the grapevine, rumors are passed along and become more and more outrageous with each retelling. A medical assistant should refuse to participate in the office rumor mill and should attempt to be cordial and friendly to everyone at work (Fig. 7-5). Supervisors regard those who spread or discuss rumors as unprofessional and untrustworthy. Avoid passing along work-related rumors to patients, family, and friends.

Personal Phone Calls and Business

It is wise to avoid receiving unnecessary phone calls to the office from friends and family. The office phone should be considered a business line and must be used as such, except in emergencies. Using personal cell phones during working hours is not acceptable. Use breaks and lunch hours to take care of business on the phone. Never take a personal call or respond to text messages on a cell phone while working with a patient. If a phone must be carried, place it on the vibrator setting, and always step into a hall or break area if a call absolutely must be taken. This should only happen in rare cases. Visitors should not frequent the office, especially not in the area where the medical assistant is working. If someone must come to the office, always offer the reception area as a waiting room. Visitors should never be allowed to enter patient areas.

Checking personal email should also be avoided in the workplace. Any type of personal business, such as studying, looking up information on the Internet for personal use, or balancing a personal checkbook, should be done at home and not in the office setting. All of these actions distract the medical assistant from the job at hand; the focus should be on serving the patients in the office at all times.

STOP AND THINK?

- Karen has a friend who works in a video store close to her office. Her friend has begun the habit of stopping in daily during her lunch hour to chat with Karen. How can Karen politely discourage her friend from doing this?
- Karen feels the need to check on her grandmother's condition as often as possible during the days she is ill. How might she accomplish this in a professional way?

Office Politics

Most people associate office politics with some underhanded scheme or plans to move upward in the company in whatever way possible, whether the methods used are ethical or not. The tendency is to give the word politics a negative **connotation.** *Politics* can be defined as the art or science of influencing and guiding government or some other orga-

nization. The same can be applied to medical office politics. When an individual wishes to move upward in an organization, he or she may use a positive strategy. Many people develop a specific plan regarding how they will advance and in what time period they will accomplish their goals. Medical assistants who wish to advance should be productive workers, accept responsibility, be dependable, and always conduct themselves in a professional manner. Using underhanded techniques and instigating trouble is not an effective method of career advancement.

Procrastination

Procrastination is often a symptom of the fear of failure. Some people procrastinate because this gives them an excuse for failure. Others procrastinate because they are perfectionists and feel that only they can complete a project the right way. Procrastination is the surest way to see that goals remain unfulfilled. The best way to stop this habit is to *do* something. Divide projects into small steps, and complete one at a time. When a project is divided into small segments, it is much less overwhelming. The stronger the motivation, the easier it is to fight the urge to procrastinate.

≋ PROFESSIONAL ATTRIBUTES

Teamwork

If managers were asked what the most important attributes would be for medical professionals, teamwork would be high on the list (Fig. 7-6). Staff members must work together for the good of the patients. They must be willing to perform duties outside the formal job description if they are needed in other areas of the office. Many supervisors frown

Fig. 7-6 Teamwork is a vital part of the medical profession. All staff members must work together to care for the patient and perform required duties in the physician's office.

on oyees who state, "That's not in my job des on." Any order that is given by a supervisor bec mandatory, and an individual who refuses to p such a task can have his or her employ-me ninated for **insubordination.** A medical assi should perform the duty and later discuss with supervisor any valid reasons that it should hav assigned to someone else.

A gh we would all enjoy working in an office in w everyone gets along and likes every other emp , this does not always happen. Personal feeli ust be set aside at work, and all employees mus perate with others to get the job done effic . If a medical assistant has an issue with anot mployee, the first move would be to discu privately with the other person. Then, if the s on does not improve, perhaps a supervi-sor s be involved for further discussions.

Time nagement

We h ften heard the expression "work smart." This s that we are to use our time efficiently and c trate on the duties that are most impor-tant To do this we must first prioritize our duties arrange our schedules to ensure that these s can be performed. The first way to impro ne management is to plan the tasks that need done that day. Taking 10 minutes to write the tasks for the day will help to ensure that t e done. Then it is important to stay on sched roughout the day, unless emergencies disrup schedule. Even then, when office days re we ned, allowances can be made for emer-gencie n if they happen often, and the major-ty of sks can still be completed. The key to manag me is prioritizing.

Priori

rioriti s simply deciding which tasks are most nport Many people make a "to do" list for the ay's a es, but the secret to success is prioritiz- g tho ivities into categories that give order to e tas

Most can be prioritized into three general tegor ose that must be done that day, those at *sh* e done that day, and those that could done ne permits. Once you have a general t of ta eview the list and further prioritize it, ing a such as M for must, S for should, and for cc or this might be further simplified by ing th ers A, B, and C). Once the tasks are ided these categories, they can be further ssified in each section. For instance, if there six gory duties, meaning they must be ne th , these six can be numbered in the

order they should be performed. The same process is completed with the B and C categories, and then as the tasks are completed, they are checked off for that day. Other categories can be added to custom-ize the list. For example, an H category can be used for duties to perform at home, P could represent phone calls that need to be made, and E could rep-resent errands to run. Customizing the categories will make the list more user-friendly.

Setting Goals

Those who succeed in life are planners and goal-setters. The first step in becoming a proficient goal-setter is to take the time to really think about what is to be accomplished throughout one's lifetime. These goals must be written down and reviewed often. Goals should be set for all areas in a person's life, including personal growth, career, home life, family, spiritual needs, and any others that apply to the individual. The goals should not be unreason-able. They should be measurable and specific, with written steps detailing how they will be reached. Determination and persistence in reaching the goals will help to make them happen, along with a healthy dose of hard work. The goals should be reviewed often and progress evaluated; then goals can be reset as necessary.

Remember to celebrate accomplishments and move past any goals that are missed, evaluating and restating the goals if necessary. Charles Kettering, an inventor who is most well known for his inven-tion of the automobile self-starter, once said, "The only time you can't afford to fail is the last time you try." Never quit trying to improve and experience personal growth.

STOP AND THINK?

- What are some goals that Karen might set related to her behavior on the job?
- List several goals for the new medical assistant to work toward during his or her first year in the field.

KNOWING THE FACILITY AND ITS EMPLOYEES

A much-circulated story tells of a college professor who used to end a critical test with the question, "What is the name of the woman who cleans our wing of the building?" This would perplex most students, but the question makes a good point. A professional medical assistant should attempt to get to know the people who work in the facility and

Fig. 7-7 Knowing which employee to call when help is needed promotes goodwill among employees and often gets a task done more efficiently.

should have a good idea of who handles which duties (Fig. 7-7). When patients have specific problems with which they need help, they can be referred to the person who knows the most about that particular issue. It is wise to express appreciation to others whenever possible. Say "thank you" often or "I appreciate your help" when working with others. This will make co-workers more likely to assist at other times when their help is needed.

DOCUMENTATION

From the standpoint of professional behavior, documentation skills are vital to medical assistants. Charting accurately with legible, neat handwriting can make a difference in the perception of professionalism in the medical office. Be complete in any narrative regarding patients. Be sure to state facts, not opinions, and never use sarcastic remarks when charting. Phone messages must be documented carefully as well, and handled in a professional manner. Never use sarcasm when reporting messages to the physician or anyone else in the office. Use conservative speech and proper wording in all situations in the medical facility.

Note Taking

Whenever office meetings or seminars are held, be prepared by having a pad and pencil ready for note taking. A medical assistant should never be without paper and pen so that accurate information from the meeting can be jotted down for future reference.

It is wise to keep a notebook or file on office meetings to refer to in case clarification of an order or a point is needed. Another good idea is to keep a small spiral notebook in a pocket with a pen, so that if an order is given in passing by the physician, the medical assistant will have a place to jot it down until he or she has access to the patient's chart. This avoids giving incorrect dosages of medication or forgetting to order a laboratory test, as well as many other errors that could be made by relying on memory.

WORK ETHICS

Work ethics can involve a whole range of activities, from individual acts to the philosophy of the entire facility. A person who has good work ethics is one who arrives on time, who is rarely absent, whose work output is **commensurate** with the pay received, and who uses his or her best abilities. Work ethics also involves other situations. If another employee is seen taking drugs from the supply cabinet or money from the cash box, the act should certainly be reported. However, if the guilty employee is also a close friend of the person who witnesses the act, an ethical dilemma is present. Ways to solve ethical problems were discussed in Chapter 6. A medical assistant must always act in such a way that his or her actions are above **reproach.**

INTERPERSONAL SKILLS

Interpersonal skills are paramount in working with patients and other health professionals. A medical assistant should work hard to perfect his or her communication techniques. Often the success of a business is directly related to the ability of its employees to communicate effectively.

When speaking to patients and providing them with information, remember that most do not have any medical background and do not understand many of the phrases used by the medical community. A medical assistant must be patient and explain in a courteous manner any aspect of the instructions or details that the patient does not understand. When educating the patient, the medical assistant should have a professional attitude of concern and helpfulness. Assure the patient that medical assistants and the rest of the staff in the facility are bound by rules of patient confidentiality if the patient seems concerned about revealing pertinent information.

CONCLUSION

Pati[ ] expect and deserve professional behavior fro[ ] [ ]se who work in medical facilities. Always sho[ ] [ ]npassion, caring, and consideration for a pers[ ] [ ]ho comes to the office, whether a patient, visit[ ] co-worker. By displaying these traits, the med[ ] [ ]ssistant will earn the respect of co-workers and [ ] [ ]ome indispensable to the physician-emp[ ] Behaving in a professional manner in the med[ ] [ ]ffice will help to gain the patient's trust. Trus[ ] [ ]e of the most important factors in avoiding [ ] [ ]f medical professional liability. Treating patie[ ] [ ]ith care and not subjecting them to poor attitu[ ] [ ]nd unnecessary information will keep the patie[ ] [ ]ysician relationship a strong one, conducive [ ] [ ] health and recovery of the patient.

SUM[ ]RY

1. D[ ] spell, and pronounce the terms listed in
   th[ ] [ ]abulary.
   - [ ]ing and pronouncing medical terms correctly adds credibility to the medical assistant. Knowing the definition of these terms promotes confidence in communication with patients and co-workers.

2. Ex[ ] the meaning of the word *profession.*
   - [ ]sionalism is the characteristic of being conforming to the technical or ethical standards of a profession. It involves exhibiting courtesy, being conscientious, and conducting oneself in a businesslike manner at the workplace. Professionalism is vitally important in the medical profession.

3. Dis[ ] several characteristics of professionalism.
   - Some of the characteristics of professionalism include loyalty, dependability, courtesy, initiative, flexibility, credibility, confidentiality, and good attitude.

4. Exp[ ] why confidentiality is so important in the [ ]al profession.
   - Confidentiality is vitally important in the medical profession. Patients depend on medical personnel to keep their health information confidential and private. Breach of patient confidentiality is one reason that an employee could be immediately terminated from his or her position and can result in litigation between the patient and the physician-employer.

5. Discuss the role of the medical assistant's attitude in caring for patients.

- Because most patients are not at their best when visiting the physician's office, the attitude of the staff plays an important role in patients' attitudes while in the office. Medical assistants need patience when working with those who are ill. A smile or a reassuring pat on the back will go a long way and be encouraging.

6. List some examples of office politics.
   - Office politics can be negative or positive. A person who uses others to be promoted in the company or takes credit for a team effort may be using office politics in a negative way; a person who strategically plans advancement through outstanding performance, dependability, and teamwork uses office politics in a positive manner. Knowing when to speak and when to listen will help the medical assistant to play the game of politics well in the medical facility.

7. Identify specific ways that teamwork can be promoted in the physician's office.
   - Teamwork makes any job easier to complete. By helping those who may be overwhelmed with duties, the medical assistant may find willing co-workers who will help when the situation is reversed in the future. If two assistants both have duties they dislike, they might trade the duties and both be satisfied. Everyone must work together for the good of the facility and the patients it serves.

8. Discuss the meaning of insubordination and why it is grounds for dismissal.
   - Insubordination can be used as grounds for immediate dismissal. Insubordination is being disobedient to any type of authority figure, usually the supervisor. When given a task to complete, the medical assistant should carry out the order unless it is unlawful or unethical. If the medical assistant does not carry out an order, the patient's life may be at risk. If the medical assistant feels that the duty should have been performed by someone else or there was some reason it should not have been performed, the supervisor should be consulted. Discuss the issue and attempt to reach an agreement about the appropriateness of performing the task in the future.

9. Identify several categories of prioritizing tasks and their meaning.
   - Prioritizing tasks can help the medical assistant to accomplish more tasks. Prioritizing can be used for work, home, and extracurricular activities. Tasks can be identified as those that must, should, or could be done that day. Then within each of these categories the tasks

can be numbered in the order in which they should be completed.

10. Talk about goal setting and how this helps in achieving career success.
    - Goals should be written down and reviewed often to check progress. Taking small steps toward goals will help ensure that they are eventually reached. Individuals should set goals in each area of their lives, breaking the tasks down into manageable parts. Goals should not be unreasonable or unattainable but should provide the opportunity for small successes along the way to reaching the ultimate goal.

Chapter Review

Vocabulary Review

Fill   blanks with the correct vocabulary terms from this chapter.

1.   abinski struggles with _procrastination_, often putting off doing tasks that should be completed.

2.   has worked as a medical assistant for almost 30 years, and her professionalism and compassion

    ove _competent_.

3.   Bessler is a CMA who has supervised externships for almost 10 years; she expects students to

    y _professionalism_ when performing their duties at her clinic.

4.   _persona_ is one of the most important attributes that medical assistants should display as

    o about their duties.

5. J   has learned that he must use _discretion_ when dealing with the patients in the clinic,
    b   careful not to reveal any confidential information to an unauthorized third party.

6. R   _desseminated_ the notes from the last staff meeting to all employees.

7. A   of the _characteristics_ that the professional medical assistant should employ include loyalty,
    ir   e, and courtesy.

8. Be   Julia has been dishonest about her reasons for missing work, her _morale_ has been
    ca   nto question.

9. Kr   has a pleasant _persona_ when working with patients.

0. M   assistants receive pay that is usually _conmensapate_ with their experience and training.

1. Jes   olds drawings for small gifts at her staff meetings, which helps to raise employee

    initative.

2. Ge   okes a professional _demeanor_ when talking with patients that encourages them to
    pla   ir trust in him.

3. Me   assistants must take _initiative_ when they are performing both externship and job
    dut

.   _insubordination_ is a cause for immediate dismissal from employment.

.   The   se "office politics" has a negative _connalation_.

Skills and Concepts

Part I: Short Answer Questions

Briefly answer the following questions.

16. List the eight characteristics of the professional medical assistant.

loyalty, dependability, initiative,
flexibility, credibility, confidentiality,
attitude

17. List five obstructions to professionalism.

Baggage, personal problems, rumors and
personal phone calls, business office
politics, procrastination

18. Define teamwork in your own words.

Teamwork is the ability to work with
people and work together with opinions
and ideas

Pa   Practicing Professional Behavior

Ans   he following questions.

19.   has developed a friendship with Angela, who has a wonderful personality but does not always
        share in the family practice clinic where they work together. Dr. Rabinowitz shares with Karen
        Angela is going to be terminated on Friday, and has asked Karen to take over some of Angela's
        until a replacement is found. How can Karen demonstrate loyalty to her employer in this
        ion? To her friend, Angela?

        he can show loyalty to her employer

20.   Smith is a patient who always disrupts the clinic. He constantly complains about everything
        he moment he enters until the moment he leaves. Karen is at the desk when he arrives to
        ut and pay his bill. When she tells him that he has a previous balance from a claim that his
        ce did not pay, he argues that Karen filed the claim incorrectly. Karen is not in charge of filing
        ce claims and did not handle any part of the claim in question. How can she be courteous to
        tient?

        she should explain how she doesn't
        andle billing, but encourage him to make
        he situation better.

1. Ka   orks in the office laboratory. She is often asked questions about insurance and billing that she
    m   er to other personnel. How should Karen efficiently request information or assistance for the
    pa   from other office personnel?

        e would need to call the patient for
        ore information

22. Karen and her fiancé ended their relationship last week. How can she deal with personal stressors while she is in the workplace?

_____

_____

_____

_____

23. A patient needs to be scheduled for an outpatient endoscopic examination. When Karen gives the instruction sheet to the patient, she suspects from his reaction that the patient is unable to read. How can Karen professionally handle this situation without causing embarrassment to the patient?

_____

_____

_____

_____

24. Which of the characteristics of professionalism is your greatest strength? Explain why.

_____

_____

_____

_____

25. Which of the five obstructions to professionalism will be most difficult for you to overcome? Explain why.

_____

_____

_____

_____

Case Study

Read the case study and answer the questions that follow.

Aaron is a new medical assistant in Dr. Roye's family practice. He was an exceptional student and consistently performed well on his externship, receiving commendations from the externship office manager as well as a written recommendation from the physician. One month after he started his job, Bethany asked him to make a bank deposit for her, usually a duty that she performed daily. Bethany told him that she was leaving the bank deposit in Aaron's bottom left drawer at his desk. When Aaron looked for the deposit at the end of the day, it was not anywhere in his desk—he looked in every drawer, and even took the drawers out to make certain that it had not fallen behind them. All of the employees looked for the deposit, which was not found. No one was able to reach Bethany on the phone. The next morning when Aaron opened his left bottom desk drawer, the deposit bag was there, but it was empty. Bethany had already reported to the physician that the deposit had not been made. The physician calls Aaron to his office to discuss the situation.

What do you think happened?

How can you deal with employees who are determined to cause problems for others in the clinic?

How can situations such as this be proven effectively when one is unsure about exactly what happened?

Workplace Application

Professionalism is a word used often with regard to medical personnel. What does professionalism mean? Write a report on the meaning of professionalism, and highlight a person whom you believe is the epitome of professionalism in the medical field. This person could be an instructor, a physician, or some other health care worker you have come to know. Be specific about the ways that professionalism is apparent in his or her actions and speech.

Internet Activities

1. Find four articles on medical professionalism. What seem to be the primary issues when attempting to maintain professionalism in medical facilities?
2. What are some ways that medical professionalism is taught in medical schools? Do these methods apply to medical assistants?

What Would You Do?

Karen Yon has wanted to work in the medical field for most of her adult life. She studied very hard in high school and graduated with honors. She volunteered in a local hospital, then after working for 3 years in restaurants as a server, she enrolled in medical assistant classes. After her externship, she was asked to continue as a regular employee at a family practice in her area.

Karen strives to do all of her duties professionally and compassionately in the physician's office. She maintains a professional image to patients and co-workers. However, it was difficult to learn how to be professional at all times and show compassion to patients through only the classroom experience. These are important aspects of her job, and she was able to gain valuable experience in these areas on her externship. Because this is her first job in the medical field, she wants to make a good impression on her employer and be a team player.

Throughout most of Karen's training as a medical assistant, her grandmother was confined to a rehabilitation center after a stroke. Although she has progressed well with treatment, Karen is the only relative who lives close to the rehabilitation center, and her family depends on her to check on her grandmother from time to time. Karen enjoys spending time at the center reading to her grandmother, because they are close. Still, Karen realizes that the stroke has caused permanent damage, and her grandmother's health seems to be on the decline.

1. How do professional medical assistants put aside personal issues and devote themselves to the patients in the office?

_____

_____

_____

2. How can Karen meet her familial and work obligations equally well?

_____

_____

_____

3. W   steps should Karen take to ensure that both her family and her supervisors understand her
o   ions to the other?

_____

_____

_____

4. H   n Karen exhibit professional behavior and compassion for patients on a daily basis at the
pl   an's office?

_____

_____

_____

Chap   Quiz

1. W   of the following words is misspelled?
   a.   cteristic
   b.   itence
   c.   nensurate

2. Of   litics are always negative.
   a.
   b.

3. To   ionally put off something that should
   be   is called:
   a. i   ive
   b. j   stination
   c. j   sionalism
   d. c   ion

4. Insu   nation can be grounds for
   term   on.
   a. T
   b. F

5. A _____, by definition, is talk or
   widely disseminated opinion with no
   discernible source or a statement that is not
   known to be true.

6. The process of working well with others to
   achieve mutual goals is called

   _____.

7. Insubordination might be justified if you are
   asked to perform an illegal act.
   a. True
   b. False

8. Which of the following words is misspelled?
   a. Demeanor
   b. Discretion
   c. Disemminated
   d. Detrimental

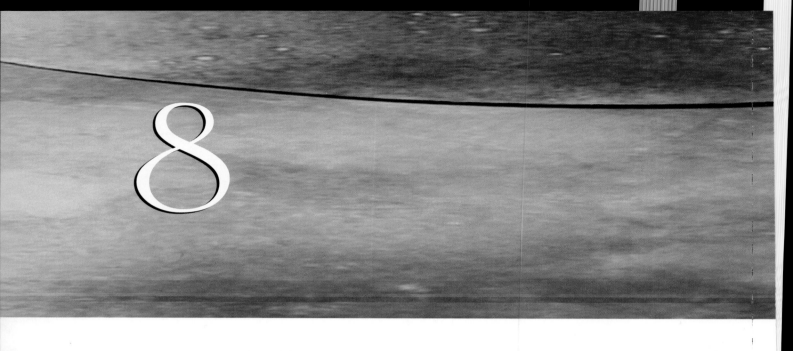

8

"Health . . . is not a static condition, but rather is manifested in dynamic responses to the stresses and challenges of life. The more complete the human freedom, the greater the likelihood that new stresses will appear—organic and psychic—because man himself continuously changes his environment through technology, and because endlessly he moves into new conditions during his restless search for adventure."
—René Jules Dubos

OBJECTIVES

1. Understand the role of DSM-IV TR and definitions of mental and behavioral health.
2. Recognize and use terms related to the pathology of mental and behavioral health.
3. Recognize and use terms related to the diagnostic procedures for mental and behavioral health.
4. Recognize and use terms related to the therapeutic interventions for mental and behavioral health.

CHAPTER AT A GLANCE

WORD PARTS

PREFIXES	SUFFIXES	COMBINING FORMS
an-	-mania	acr/o
bi-	-phobia	agor/a
dys-		anthrop/o
eu-		claustr/o
para-		hedon/o
		iatr/o
		klept/o
		nymph/o
		orex/o
		ped/o
		phil/o
		phor/o
		pol/o
		psych/o
		pyr/o
		somat/o
		somn/o
		thym/o

KEY TERMS

Alzheimer disease	bipolar disorder (BP)	generalized anxiety disorder (GAD)	paraphilia
amnesia	borderline personality disorder	hallucination	parasomnia
anhedonia	bulimia nervosa	kleptomania	posttraumatic stress disorder (PTSD)
anorexia nervosa	cyclothymia	libido	psychotic disorders
attention deficit/hyperactivity disorder (ADHD)	dementia	obsessive-compulsive disorder	schizophrenic disorders
autism	depressive disorder	panic disorder (pd)	somatoform disorder
	dysphoria		

OCD

≋ INTRODUCTION TO MENTAL AND BEHAVIORAL HEALTH

Recent national statistics reveal the following:

- One out of every five American adults and children has a mental disorder.
- More than 25% of the 100 top-selling medications are for psychiatric disorders.
- The eighth most common diagnostic category for inpatient admissions is substance-related mental disorders.
- Approximately 19 million Americans are diagnosed with anxiety.
- An estimated 44% of inpatient admissions for mental disorders are for alcohol- and substance-related disorders.
- Approximately 2 to 2.5 million Americans are mentally retarded.*

Given these statistics, behavioral health is a content area that cannot be ignored.

The term *behavioral health* reflects an integration of the outdated concept of the separate nature of the body (physical health/illness) and the mind (mental health/illness). Advances in research continually acknowledge the roles of culture, environment, and spirituality in influencing physical and behavioral health. The use of the term *behavior* refers to observable, measurable activities that may be used to evaluate the progress of treatment.

This chapter examines disorders that result when an individual has a maladaptive response to his or her environment (internal or external). However, even though some mental illnesses have organic causes in which neurotransmitters and other known brain functions play a role, there is no mental "anatomy" per se. Instead, behavioral health is a complex interaction among an individual's emotional, physical, mental, and behavioral processes in an environment that includes cultural and spiritual influences.

Mental health may be defined as a relative state of mind in which a person who is healthy is able to cope with and adjust to the recurrent stresses of everyday living in a culturally acceptable way. Thus mental illness may be generally defined as a functional impairment that substantially interferes with or limits one or more major life activities for a significant duration.

The American Psychiatric Association (APA) publishes the official listing of diagnosable mental disorders: the *Diagnostic and Statistical Manual of Mental Disorders* (DSM). The codes that are used within the DSM are coordinated with the International Classification of Diseases (ICD), which provides acceptable billing codes in the United States. Major revisions to the DSM occur at approximately 10-year intervals, with minor updates about every 5 years.

COMBINING FORMS FOR MENTAL AND BEHAVIORAL HEALTH

MEANING	COMBINING FORM
mind	psych/o, thym/o
study	log/o
treatment	iatr/o

---

*It should be noted that mental retardation is not an illness; it is a condition characterized by developmental delays and difficulty with learning and social situations.

cise 8-1: INTRODUCTION TO MENTAL AND BEHAVIORAL HEALTH

Circl   correct answer.

1. W   ablishes the official listing of mental disorders for the United States? *(American Medical
   A   ion, American Psychiatric Association)*
2. W   the abbreviation of the name for this listing? *(DSM, ICD)*
3. M   evisions for the official listing of mental disorders for the United States are accomplished
   ap   mately every *(5, 10)* years.
4. Cu   thinking acknowledges the influence of *(spirituality, climate)* on behavioral health.
5. Th   n *(behavioral, mental)* refers to observable, measurable activities that may be used to evaluate
   tre   nt.

P   OLOGY

Ter   lated to General Symptoms

TERM		WORD ORIGIN	DEFINITION
Akath ack ul zsa		*a-* lack of **kathis/o** sitting *-ia* condition	Inability to remain calm, still, and free of anxiety.
Amne am Nl			Inability to remember either isolated parts of the past or one's entire past; may be caused by brain damage or severe emotional trauma. memory loss
Anhe an hee nee ah		*an-* without **hedon/o** pleasure *-ia* condition	Absence of the ability to experience either pleasure or joy, even in the face of causative events.
Catat kat tah nee ah		*cata-* down **ton/o** tension *-ia* condition	Paralysis or immobility from psychological or emotional rather than physical causes.
Confa on kon fa LAY shun			Effort to conceal a gap in memory by fabricating detailed, often believable stories.
Defen chanism			Unconscious mechanism for psychological coping, adjustment, or self-preservation in the face of stress or a threat. Examples include **denial** (lack of acknowledgment) of an unpleasant situation or condition and **projection** (placing blame) of intolerable aspects onto another individual.
Deliriu dih LEE um			Condition of confused, unfocused, irrational agitation. In mental disorders, agitation and confusion may also be accompanied by a more intense disorientation, incoherence, or fear, and illusions, hallucinations, and delusions.
Delusio dih LOC			Persistent belief in a demonstrable untruth or a provable inaccurate perception despite clear evidence to the contrary.

Continued

Terms Related to General Symptoms—cont'd

TERM	WORD ORIGIN	DEFINITION
Dementia dih MEN shah		Mental disorder in which the individual experiences a progressive loss of memory, personality alterations, confusion, loss of touch with reality, and **stupor** (seeming unawareness of, and disconnection with, one's surroundings).
Echolalia eh koh LAYL yuh	*echo-* reverberation *-lalia* condition of babbling	Repetition of words or phrases spoken by others.
Hallucination hah loo sih NAY shun		Any unreal sensory perception that occurs with no external cause.
Illusion ill LOO zhun		Inaccurate sensory perception based on a real stimulus; examples include mirages or interpreting music or wind as voices.
Libido lih BEE doh		Normal psychological impulse drive associated with sensuality, expressions of desire, or creativity. Abnormality occurs only when such drives are excessively heightened or depressed.
Psychosis sye KOH sis	*psych/o* mind *-osis* abnormal condition	Disassociation with or impaired perception of reality; may be accompanied by hallucinations, delusions, incoherence, akathisia, and/or disorganized behavior.
Somnambulism som NAM byoo liz um	*somn/o* sleep *ambul/o* walking *-ism* condition	Sleepwalking.

⊠ BE CAREFUL!

The suffix *-thymia* means a condition of the mind, but *thym/o* refers to the thymus gland and to the mind.

Affects

Affects are observable demonstrations of emotion that can be described in terms of quality, range, and appropriateness. The following list defines the most significant affects encountered in behavioral health:

Blunted: Moderately reduced range of affect.
Flat: The diminishment or loss of emotional expression sometimes observed in schizophrenia, mental retardation, and some depressive disorders.
Labile: Multiple, abrupt changes in affect seen in certain types of schizophrenia and bipolar disorder.
Full/wide range of affect: Generally appropriate emotional response.

depress, bipolar

Terms Related to Moods

TERM	WORD ORIGIN	DEFINITION
Anger		As a symptom, anger is pathological in nature if it is inappropriate for the situation, caused by feeling of lack of control.
Anxiety		Feeling of apprehension. Accompanied by restlessness, tension, tachycardia, and breathing difficulty not associated with an apparent stimulus.

Terms Related to Moods—cont'd

TERM	WORD ORIGIN	DEFINITION
Dys... dis F... ah	*dys-* abnormal *phor/o* to carry, to bear *-ia* condition	Generalized negative mood characterized by depression.
Euph... you F... e ah	*eu-* good, well *phor/o* to carry, to bear *-ia* condition	Exaggerated sense of physical and emotional well-being not based on reality, disproportionate to the cause, or inappropriate to the situation.
Euthy... yoo T... nee ah	*eu-* good, well *-thymia* condition of the mind	Normal range of moods and emotions.

❖ E... se 8-2: SYMPTOMS, AFFECTS, AND MOODS OF MENTAL ILLNESS

Matchi...

_____ hedonia	A. sleepwalking
_____ usion	B. paralysis from psychological causes
_____ lucination	C. normal range of moods and emotions
_____ nentia	D. lack of memory
_____ phoria	E. restlessness, inability to sit still
_____ hymia	F. normal drive of sensuality, creativity, desire
_____ esia	G. mental condition characterized by confusion and agitation
_____ 8 hisia	H. inaccurate sensory perception based on a real stimulus
_____ 9 abulation	I. belief in a falsehood
_____ 10 ium	J. lack of ability to experience pleasure
_____ 11 onia	K. negative mood characterized by dissociation
_____ 12. on	L. condition characterized by dissociation with reality
_____ 13. nosis	M. making up stories to conceal lack of memory
_____ 14. ambulism	N. unreal sensory perception
_____ 15. ...	O. condition characterized by loss of memory, personality changes, confusion, and loss of touch with reality

Circle the ... answer.

16. Anger... ...ety, and dysphoria are examples of a patient's *(affect, mood)*.
17. Indivi... ...whose emotions change rapidly are said to have a *(labile, blunted)* affect.
18. Patien... ...o subconsciously blame another person for their own problems are using a defense mecha... ...called *(denial, projection)*.

Terms Related to Disorders Usually First Diagnosed in Childhood

TERM	WORD ORIGIN	DEFINITION
Asperger disorder		Disorder characterized by impairment of social interaction and repetitive patterns of inappropriate behavior.
Attention-deficit/hyperactivity disorder (ADHD)		Series of syndromes that includes impulsiveness, inability to concentrate, and short attention span.
Autism AH tiz um		Condition of abnormal development of social interaction, impaired communication, and repetitive behaviors.
Conduct disorder		Any of a number of disorders characterized by patterns of persistent aggressive and defiant behaviors. **Oppositional defiant disorder (ODD),** an example of a conduct disorder, is characterized by hostile, disobedient behavior.
Mental retardation		Condition of subaverage intellectual ability, with impairments in social and educational functioning. The "intelligence quotient" (IQ) is a measure of an individual's intellectual functioning compared with the general population. **Mild mental retardation:** IQ range of 50-69; learning difficulties result. **Moderate mental retardation:** IQ range of 35-49; support needed to function in society. **Severe mental retardation:** IQ of 20-34; continuous need of support to live in society. **Profound mental retardation:** IQ <20; severe self-care limitations.
Rett disorder		Condition characterized by initial normal functioning followed by loss of social and intellectual functioning.
Tourette syndrome Too RETT		Group of involuntary behaviors that includes the vocalization of words or sounds (sometimes obscene) and repetitive movements; vocal and multiple tic disorder.

◆ **Exercise 8-3: DISORDERS USUALLY FIRST DIAGNOSED IN CHILDHOOD**

Choose the correct answer from the following list.

attention-deficit/hyperactivity disorder, mild mental retardation, severe mental retardation, autism, Rett disorder, Asperger disorder, conduct disorder, oppositional defiant disorder, moderate mental retardation, Tourette syndrome

1. Type of mental retardation in which the IQ range is 20 to 34. _____

2. Disorder characterized by impairment of social interaction caused by repetitive patterns of behavior.

   _____

3. Group of involuntary behaviors that include tics, vocalizations, and repetitive movements.

   _____

4. Group of disorders characterized by persistent aggressive and defiant behaviors. _____

5. I   ge of 50 to 69. Most prevalent form of mental retardation, which manifests itself in learning

   d   ties. _____

6. I   ge of 35 to 49. Adults will need support to live in society. _____

7. A   of syndromes that include impulsiveness, inability to concentrate, and a short attention span.

   ___ _____

8. C   on of pathological social withdrawal, impairment of communication, and repetitive behaviors.

   ___ _____

9. Pe   t negative behavior characterized by hostile, disobedient behavior. _____

10. Cc   on characterized by initial normal functioning followed by loss of social and intellectual

    fu   ing. _____

Subst   Related Disorders

The mc   idly increasing group of disorders are substance-related disorders. These i   e abuse of a number of substances, including alcohol, opioids, cannabino   datives or hypnotics, cocaine, stimulants (including caffeine), hallucin   s, tobacco, and volatile solvents (inhalants). Classifications for substan   use include psychotic, amnesiac, and late-onset disorders. It is importa   be aware that addiction is not a character flaw. Rather, addiction has a n   gical basis; the effects of specific drugs are localized to equally specific   of the brain.

An in   ual is considered an "abuser" if he or she uses substances in ways that thr   health or impair social or economic functioning. Levels of abuse vary.

Terms ed to Substance Abuse		
TERM	**WORD ORIGIN**	**DEFINITION**
Acute in tion		Episode of behavioral disturbance following ingestion of alcohol or psychotropic drugs.
Delirium ens (DTs) deh LEER TREM un	See **Did You Know?** box.	Acute and sometimes fatal delirium induced by the cessation of ingesting excessive amounts of alcohol over a long period of time.
Depende ndrome		Difficulty in controlling use of a drug.
Harmful		Pattern of drug use that causes damage to health.
Tolerance		State in which the body becomes accustomed to the substances ingested; hence the user requires greater amounts to create the desired effect.
Withdraw te		Group of symptoms that occurs during the cessation of the use of a regularly taken drug.

Schizophrenic, Schizotypal, and Delusional Disorders

These disorders are not always easy to classify but carry with them some common characteristics. Roughly, these disorders can be grouped as follows:

Acute and transient psychotic disorders: Heterogeneous group of disorders characterized by the acute onset of psychotic symptoms, such as delusions, hallucinations, and perceptual disturbances, and by the severe disruption of ordinary behavior. *Acute onset* is defined as a crescendo from a normal perceptual state to a clearly abnormal clinical picture in about 2 weeks or less. For these disorders, there is no evidence of organic causation. Perplexity and puzzlement are often present, but disorientation to time, place, and person is not persistent or severe enough to justify a diagnosis of organically caused delirium. The disorder may or may not be associated with acute stress (usually defined as stressful events preceding the onset by 1 or 2 weeks).

Persistent delusional disorders: Variety of disorders in which long-standing delusions constitute the only, or the most conspicuous, clinical characteristic and cannot be classified as organic, schizophrenic, or affective.

Schizophrenic disorders: Disorders characterized by fundamental distortions of thinking and perception, coupled with affects that are inappropriate or blunted. The patient exhibits characteristic inability to recognize an appropriate perception of reality (Fig. 8-1). The patient's intellectual capacity is usually intact. Symptoms may include hallucinations, delusions, and thought disorder.

- **Catatonic schizophrenia** (kat tah TAH nick skit zoh FREH nee uh) is dominated by prominent psychomotor disturbances that may alternate between extremes, such as hyperkinesis and stupor, and may be accompanied by a dreamlike (oneiric) state and hallucinations.

⊠ BE CAREFUL!

The combining form *phren/o* can mean mind or diaphragm.

A

B

Fig. 8-1   **A,** This drawing by a patient with schizophrenia demonstrates thought disorder. **B,** Drawing by a delusional patient with schizophrenia. *(Part B from Stuart GW, Larnia MT:* Principles and practice of psychiatric nursing, *St Louis, 2001, Mosby.)*

- **ganized schizophrenia** is characterized by prominent affective ...es, fleeting and fragmentary delusions and hallucinations, and i...nsible and unpredictable behavior. Shallow, inappropriate mood, f... thoughts, social isolation, and incoherent speech are also present.
- **oid schizophrenia** is dominated by relatively stable, persistent ...ns, usually accompanied by auditory hallucinations and ...ual disturbances in affect, volition (will), and speech.
- **S...typal** (skiz zoh TIE pull) **disorder,** although sometimes d...ed as borderline schizophrenia, has none of the characteristic s...hrenic anomalies. Patients may exhibit anhedonia, eccentric b...or, cold affect, and social isolation.

◆ **E...se 8-4:   SUBSTANCE ABUSE AND SCHIZOPHRENIC DISORDERS**

Fill in ...nks with the following terms.

schizo...nia, hallucinations, persistent delusional, disorganized, delusions, alcohol, inhala...dream, controlling substance use

1. A pa... with the DTs is showing withdrawal symptoms from _____.

2. Vola...lvents are included under the category of _____.

3. Dep...ce syndrome is a condition in which the patient has difficulty _____.

4. Audi...allucinations, delusions, and thought disturbances are characteristic of _____.

5. A pa...ith oneiric symptoms acts as if he or she is in a _____ like state.

6. The ...nce between schizophrenic and schizotypal disorders is that the schizotypal patient does not

   have ...ned _____ or _____.

7. The ...r most conspicuous, clinical characteristic of patients with _____ disorders is
   the p...e of long-standing aberrant beliefs or perceptions.

8. Shall...appropriate mood, flighty thought, social isolation, and incoherent speech are all symptoms

   of wh...pe of schizophrenia? _____

Mood D...lers

Patients ...nood disorders, also called *affective disorders,* show a disturbance of affect ...g from depression (with or without associated anxiety) to elation. The moo...nge is usually accompanied by a change in the overall level of activity; ...of the other symptoms are either secondary to, or easily under- stood in ...ntext of, the change in mood and activity. Most of these disorders tend to b...rrent, and the onset of individual episodes can often be related to stressf...ts or situations.

Terms Related to Mood Disorders

TERM	WORD ORIGIN	DEFINITION
Bipolar disorder (BP) bye POH lur	*bi-* two *pol/o* pole *-ar* pertaining to	Disorder characterized by swings between an elevation of mood, increased energy and activity (hypomania and mania), and a lowering of mood and decreased energy and activity (depression).
Cyclothymia sye kloh THIGH mee ah	*cycl/o* cycling *-thymia* condition of the mind	Disorder characterized by recurring episodes of mild elation and depression that are not severe enough to warrant a diagnosis of bipolar disorder.
Depressive disorder		Depression typically characterized by hopelessness. Its degree (minimal, moderate, severe) or number of occurrences (single or recurrent, persistent) further define the illness. Patient exhibits dysphoria, reduction of energy, and decrease in activity. Symptoms include anhedonia, lack of ability to concentrate, and fatigue. Patient may experience **parasomnias** (abnormal sleep patterns), diminished appetite, and loss of self-esteem.
Dysthymia dis THIGH mee ah	*dys-* difficult *-thymia* condition of the mind	Mild, chronic depression of mood that lasts for years but is not severe enough to justify a diagnosis of depression.
Hypomania hye poh MAY nee ah	*hypo-* decreased *-mania* excessive preoccupation	Disorder characterized by an inappropriate elevation of mood that may include positive and negative aspects. Patient may report increased feelings of well-being, energy, and activity, but may also report irritability and conceit.
Persistent mood disorders		Group of long-term, cyclic mood disorders in which the majority of the individual episodes are not sufficiently severe to warrant being described as hypomanic or mild depressive episodes.
Seasonal affective disorder (SAD)		Weather-induced depression resulting from decreased exposure to sunlight in autumn and winter.

Terms Related to Anxiety Disorders

TERM	WORD ORIGIN	DEFINITION
Acrophobia ack roh FOH bee ah	*acr/o* heights, extremes *-phobia* fear	Irrational fear of heights.
Agoraphobia ah gore uh FOH bee ah	*agor/a* marketplace *-phobia* fear	Irrational fear of leaving home and entering crowded places.
Anthropophobia an throh poh FOH bee ah	*anthrop/o* man *-phobia* fear	Irrational fear of scrutiny by other people; also called **social phobia.**
Claustrophobia klos troh FOH bee ah	*claustr/o* a closing *-phobia* fear	Irrational fear of enclosed spaces.
Generalized anxiety disorder (GAD)		One of the most common diagnoses assigned, but not specific to any particular situation or circumstance. Fear and apprehension with symptoms that may include persistent nervousness, trembling, muscular tensions, sweating, lightheadedness, palpitations, dizziness, and epigastric discomfort.

Term...[rel]ated to Anxiety Disorders—cont'd

TERM	WORD ORIGIN	DEFINITION
Obse[ssive]-com[pulsiv]e diso[rder (]OCD)		Characterized by recurrent, distressing, and unavoidable preoccupations or irresistible drives to perform specific rituals (e.g., constantly checking locks or excessive hand washing) that the patient feels will prevent some harmful event.
Panic [disord]er (PD)		Recurrent, unpredictable attacks of severe anxiety (panic) that are not restricted to any particular situation. Symptoms may include vertigo, chest pain, and heart palpitations.
Posttra[umat]ic stress diso[rder (]PTSD)		Extended emotional response to a traumatic event. Symptoms may include flashbacks, recurring nightmares, anhedonia, insomnia, hypervigilance, anxiety, depression, suicidal thoughts, and emotional blunting.

Terms [Rela]ted to Adjustment Disorder, Dissociative Identity Disorder, and S[omat]oform Disorder

TERM	WORD ORIGIN	DEFINITION
Adjustm[ent] disord[er]		Disorder that tends to manifest during periods of stressful life changes (e.g., divorce, death, relocation, job loss). Symptoms include anxiety, impaired coping mechanisms, social dysfunction, and a reduced ability to perform normal daily activities.
Dissoci[ative] identi[ty] disord[er]		Maladaptive coping with severe stress by developing one or more separate personalities. A less severe form, **dissociative disorder** or **dissociative reaction,** results in identity confusion accompanied by amnesia, a dreamlike state, and somnambulism.
Somato[form] disord[er] soh MAT[oh] form	*somat/o* body	Any disorder in which the patient expresses unfounded physical complaints, despite medical assurance that no physiological problem exists. One type of somatoform disorder is **hypochondriacal disorder,** which is the preoccupation with the possibility of having one or more serious and progressive physical disorders.

Terms R[elate]d to Eating Disorders

TERM	WORD ORIGIN	DEFINITION
Anorexia [nervo]sa an oh REC[...] e ah nur VOH s[ah]	*an-* without *orex/o* appetite *-ia* condition	Prolonged refusal to eat adequate amounts of food and an altered perception of what constitutes a normal minimum body weight caused by an intense fear of becoming obese. Primarily affects adolescent females; emaciation and amenorrhea result (Fig. 8-2).
Bulimia n[ervos]a boo LIM e[ah] nur VOH s[ah]		Eating disorder in which the individual eats large quantities of food and then purges the body through self-induced vomiting or inappropriate use of laxatives.

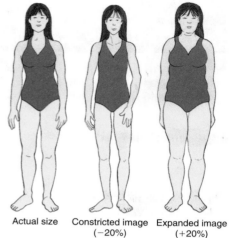

Actual size   Constricted image (−20%)   Expanded image (+20%)

Fig. 8-2 The perception of body shape and size can be evaluated with the use of special computer drawing programs that allow a subject to distort (increase or decrease) the width of an actual picture of a person's body by as much as 20%. Subjects with anorexia consistently adjusted their own body picture to a size 20% larger than its true form, which suggests that they have a major problem with the perception of self-image.

Sleep Disorders

Sleep disorders are called **dyssomnias** (dih SOM nee ahs), or difficulties with the sleep-wake cycle, and **parasomnias** (pair ah SOM nee ahs), or abnormal activation of physiological functions during the sleep cycle. **Nightmare disorder** and **sleep terrors** are examples of parasomnias, and insomnia and hypersomnia are examples of dyssomnias. They may take a variety of forms.

Terms Related to Sleep Disorders

TERM	WORD ORIGIN	DEFINITION
Dyssomnia	*dys-* bad *somn/o* sleep *-ia* condition	Difficulty with the sleep-wake cycle. Examples include **insomnia,** the chronic struggle either to fall asleep or stay asleep, and **hypersomnia,** abnormally deep or lengthy periods of sleep.
Parasomnia	*para-* abnormal *somn/o* sleep *-ia* condition	Abnormal activation of physiological functions during the sleep cycle. Examples include **sleep terrors,** in which repeated episodes of sudden awakening are accompanied by intense anxiety, agitation, and amnesia.

Terms Related to Sexual Dysfunction

TERM	WORD ORIGIN	DEFINITION
Hypoactive sexual disorder		Indifference or unresponsiveness to sexual stimuli; inability to achieve orgasm during intercourse. Formerly called **frigidity.**
Nymphomania nim foh MAY nee ah	*nymph/o-* woman *-mania* excessive preoccupation	Relentless drive to achieve sexual orgasm in the female. In the male the condition is called **satyriasis** (sat tih RYE ah sis).
Premature ejaculation		Involuntary, anxiety-induced ejaculation of semen during sexual activity.
Sexual anhedonia an hee DOH nee ah	*an-* without *hedon/o* pleasure *-ia* condition	Inability to enjoy sexual pleasure.

Personality Disorders

Personality disorders have several common characteristics, including long-standing, inflexible, dysfunctional behavior patterns and personality traits that result in inability to function successfully in society. These characteristics are not caused by stress, and affected patients have very little to no insight into their disorder.

Terms Related to Personality Disorders

TERM	WORD ORIGIN	DEFINITION
Borderline personality disorder		Disorder characterized by impulsive, unpredictable mood and self-image, resulting in unstable interpersonal relationships and a tendency to see and respond to others as unwaveringly good or evil.
Dissocial personality disorder		Disorder in which the patient shows a complete lack of interest in social obligations, to the extreme of showing antipathy for other individuals. Patients frustrate easily, are quick to display aggression, show a tendency to blame others, and do not change their behavior even after punishment.
Paranoid personality disorder		State in which the individual exhibits inappropriately suspicious thinking, self-importance, a lack of ability to forgive perceived insults, and an extreme sense of personal rights.
Schizoid personality disorder		Condition in which the patient withdraws into a fantasy world, with little need for social interaction. Most patients have a limited capacity to experience pleasure or to express their feelings.

Terms Related to Habit and Impulse Disorders

TERM	WORD ORIGIN	DEFINITION
Kleptomania klep toh MAY nee ah	klept/o steal -mania excessive preoccupation	Uncontrollable impulse to steal.
Pyromania pye roh MAY nee ah	pyr/o fire -mania excessive preoccupation	Uncontrollable impulse to set fires.
Trichotillomania trick oh till oh MAY nee ah		Uncontrollable impulse to pull one's hair out by the roots.

Terms Related to Paraphilias (Sexual Perversion) or Disorders of Sexual Preference

TERM	WORD ORIGIN	DEFINITION
Exhibitionism eck sih BISH un iz um		Condition in which the patient derives sexual arousal from the exposure of his or her genitals to strangers.
Fetishism FET ish iz m		Reliance on an object as a stimulus for sexual arousal and pleasure.

Continued

Terms Related to Paraphilias (Sexual Perversion) or Disorders of Sexual Preference—cont'd

TERM	WORD ORIGIN	DEFINITION
Pedophilia ped oh FILL ee ah	*ped/o* child *phil/o* attraction *-ia* condition	Sexual preference, either in fantasy or actuality, for children as a means of achieving sexual excitement and gratification.
Sadomasochism say doh MASS oh kiz um		Preference for sexual activity that involves inflicting or receiving pain and/or humiliation.
Voyeurism VOY yur iz um		Condition in which an individual derives sexual pleasure and gratification from surreptitiously looking at individuals engaged in intimate behavior.

◆ **Exercise 8-5: MISCELLANEOUS BEHAVIORAL DISORDERS**

Fill in the blanks with the following terms.

kleptomania, posttraumatic stress disorder, anorexia nervosa, hypomania, satyriasis, somnambulism, sadomasochism, dysthymia, bipolar disorder, obsessive-compulsive disorder, social phobia, cyclothymia, hypersomnia, paranoid personality disorder, premature ejaculation, pyromania, depressive disorder, hypochondriacal disorder, dissociative identity disorder, generalized anxiety disorder, claustrophobia

1. An alternative name for anthropophobia is _____.

2. Fear of enclosed spaces is called _____.

3. Patients who experience symptoms of persistent nervousness, trembling, muscular tension, sweating, lightheadedness, palpitations, dizziness, and epigastric discomfort may be diagnosed with

   _____.

4. Patients who are compelled to have repetitive thoughts or repeat specific rituals may have a diagnosis

   of _____.

5. Extreme trauma that may result in flashbacks, nightmares, hypervigilance, or reliving the trauma is

   called _____.

6. Patients who develop separate personalities as a result of a severely stressful situation are diagnosed

   with what disorder? _____

7. Patients who continually express physical complaints that have no real basis have a type of

   _____.

8. Episodes of mood changes from depression to mania are called _____.

9. P⎯⎯s who have a loss of energy, of pleasure, and of interest in life may be experiencing

⎯⎯ ⎯⎯⎯⎯⎯.

10. A⎯⎯ppropriate, persistent elevation of mood that may include irritability is called ⎯⎯⎯⎯⎯⎯.

11. P⎯⎯ with chronic, extremely mild depression that varies to mild elation may suffer from

⎯⎯ ⎯⎯⎯⎯⎯.

12. A⎯⎯ic depression that lasts for years but does not warrant a diagnosis of depression may be

te⎯⎯ ⎯⎯⎯⎯⎯.

13. W⎯⎯ the health care term for walking in one's sleep? ⎯⎯⎯⎯⎯⎯

14. W⎯⎯ the term for an insatiable sexual desire in men? ⎯⎯⎯⎯⎯⎯

15. M⎯⎯ients who experience uncontrollable ejaculation caused by anxiety may be diagnosed with

⎯⎯ ⎯⎯⎯⎯⎯.

16. W⎯⎯ the health care term for sleep that is excessive in depth or duration? ⎯⎯⎯⎯⎯⎯

17. W⎯⎯ the disorder in which patients refuse to maintain a body weight that is a minimum weight

for⎯⎯t? ⎯⎯⎯⎯⎯⎯

18. WI⎯⎯ he health care term for the pathological impulse to set fires? ⎯⎯⎯⎯⎯⎯

19. WI⎯⎯ he health care term for a severe, enduring personality disorder with paranoid tendencies?

⎯⎯ ⎯⎯⎯⎯⎯

20. A p⎯⎯nce for sexual activity that involves pain and humiliation is called ⎯⎯⎯⎯⎯⎯.

21. Un⎯⎯llable stealing is called ⎯⎯⎯⎯⎯⎯.

Age Matters

Pedia

Aside from the disorders first diagnosed in childhood—Asperger, ADHD, autism, conduct disorders, mental retardation, and Rett disorder—children are being diagnosed in increasing numbers for depressive disorders, substance abuse, and eating disorders.

Geria

Seniors are seen with disorders associated with depression and anxiety, along with those caused by dementia.

DIAGNOSTIC PROCEDURES

Behavioral diagnoses must take into account underlying health care abnormalities that may cause or influence a patient's mental health. Some of the common laboratory and imaging procedures are mentioned here, along with procedures that are traditionally considered to be psychological.

Diagnostic Criteria

DSM-IV-TR multiaxial assessment diagnosis: Diagnostic tool measuring mental health of the individual across five axes. The first three (if present) are stated as diagnostic codes, whereas Axis IV is a statement of factors influencing the patient's mental health (e.g., lack of social supports, unemployment), and Axis V is a numerical score that summarizes a patient's overall functioning.
1. Axis I: Clinical Disorders
2. Axis II: Personality Disorders and/or Mental Retardation
3. Axis III: General Medical Conditions
4. Axis IV: Psychosocial and Environmental Problems
5. Axis V: Global Assessment of Functioning Scale (GAF)

Mental status examination: A diagnostic procedure to determine a patient's current mental state. It includes assessment of the patient's appearance, affect, thought processes, cognitive function, insight, and judgment.

Laboratory Tests

Patients may have blood counts (complete blood cell count [CBC] with differential), blood chemistry, thyroid function panels, screening tests for syphilis (rapid plasma reagin [RPR] or microhemagglutination assay-*Treponema pallidum* [MHA-TP]), urinalyses with drug screen, urine pregnancy checks for females with childbearing potential, blood alcohol levels, serum levels of medications, and human immunodeficiency virus (HIV) tests in high-risk patients.

Imaging

Imaging is most helpful in ruling out neurological disorders and in research; it is less helpful in diagnosing or treating psychiatric problems. Computed tomography (CT) scans and magnetic resonance imaging (MRI) can be used to screen for brain lesions. Positron emission tomography (PET) scans can be used to examine and map the metabolic activity of the brain (Fig. 8-3).

Psychological Testing

Bender Gestalt Test: A test of visuomotor and spatial abilities; useful for children and adults.

Draw-a-Person (DAP) Test: Analysis of patient's drawings of male and female individuals. Used to assess personality.

Minnesota Multiphasic Personality Inventory (MMPI): Assessment of personality characteristics through a battery of forced-choice questions.

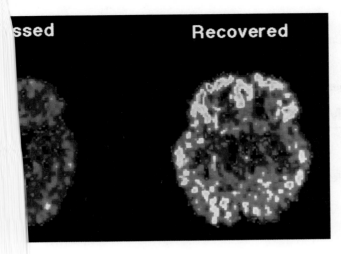

Fig. 8-3 PET scans of the same depressed individual's brain when depressed *(left)* and after recovery through treatment with medication *(right)*. Several brain areas, particularly the prefrontal cortex *(at top)*, show diminished activity *(darker colors)* during depression. *(From Fortinash KM: Psychiatric mental health nursing, ed 3, St Louis, 2005, Mosby.)*

Rorschach projective test using inkblots to determine the patient's ability to integ... tellectual and emotional factors in his or her perception of the env... ent.

Thematic ...erception Test (TAT): Test in which patients are asked to make up ...es about the pictures they are shown. This test may provide informa... bout a patient's interpersonal relationships, fantasies, needs, conflicts ... defenses.

Wechsler ...t Intelligence Scale (WAIS): Measure of verbal IQ, performa... Q, and full-scale IQ.

◇ Exerc... -6:   DIAGNOSTIC PROCEDURES

Matching.

_____ 1. W...

_____ 2. TA...

_____ 3. PE...

_____ 4. MM...

_____ 5. Rorschach

_____ 6. GAF

_____ 7. Bender Gestalt

A. numerical measure of overall mental health

B. provides information about needs, fantasies, interpersonal relationships

C. measures personality characteristics

D. IQ test

E. test of visuomotor and spatial skills

F. imaging of metabolic activity (in brain)

G. examines integration of emotional and intellectual factors

Castlewood Health Care System
14037 Marion St.
Reno, NV 89512

MENTAL STATUS EXAMINATION

Patient: Rosita Wellor

Evaluation Date: 3/29/20xx

Medical Record Number: 123456

Report Date: 3/30/200x

Patient was a pleasant, alert, well-groomed woman who showed no evidence of distractibility. Orientation was intact for person, time, and place. Eye contact was appropriate. There were no abnormalities of gait, posture, or demeanor. Vocabulary and grammar skills were suggestive of intellectual functioning within the high-average range.

The patient's attitude was warm, open, and cooperative. Her mood was euthymic. Affect was appropriate to verbal content and showed broad range. Memory functions were grossly intact with respect to immediate and remote recall of events and factual information. Her thought processes were intact, goal oriented, and well organized. Thought content revealed no evidence of delusions, paranoia, or suicidal/homicidal ideation. There was no evidence of perceptual disorder. Her level of personal insight appeared to be very good, as evidenced by her ability to state her current diagnosis of PTSD and to identify events that contributed to its exacerbations. Social judgment appeared good, as evidenced by appropriate interactions with other patients in the waiting room.

◆ **Exercise 8-7: MENTAL STATUS REPORT**

Using the mental status report above, answer the following questions.

1. What term indicates that the patient exhibited a normal range of emotions? _____.

2. What term indicates that the patient exhibited a variety of moods that were appropriate to the

   conversation? _____.

3. How do you know that the patient did not exhibit any persistent beliefs in things that are untrue?

   _____.

4. What is her current diagnosis? _____.

THERAPEUTIC INTERVENTIONS

Terms Related to Psychotherapy

TERM	WORD ORIGIN	DEFINITION
Behavioral Therapy		Therapeutic attempt to alter an undesired behavior by substituting a new response or set of responses to a given stimulus.
Cognitive Therapy		Wide variety of treatment techniques that attempt to help the individual alter inaccurate or unhealthy perceptions and patterns of thinking.
Psychoanalysis sye koh . ih sis		Behavioral treatment developed initially by Sigmund Freud to analyze and treat any dysfunctional effects of unconscious factors on a patient's mental state. This therapy uses techniques that include analysis of defense mechanisms and dream interpretation.

Terms Related to Other Therapeutic Methods

TERM	WORD ORIGIN	DEFINITION
Detoxification		Removal of a chemical substance (drug or alcohol) as an initial step in treatment of a chemically dependent individual.
Electroconvulsive therapy		Method of inducing convulsions to treat affective disorders in patients who have been resistant or unresponsive to drug therapy.
Light therapy		Exposure of the body to light waves to treat patients with depression due to seasonal fluctuations (Fig. 8-4).

Fig. 8-4 Broad-spectrum, fluorescent lamps, such as this one, are used in daily therapy sessions from autumn into spring for people with SAD. Patients report feeling less depressed within 3 to 7 days. *(Courtesy Apollo Light Systems.)*

◆ Exercise 8-8: THERAPEUTIC INTERVENTIONS

Fill in the blanks with the following terms.

cognitive therapy, ECT, behavioral, light therapy, psychoanalysis

1. Patients are treated with _____ therapy when an attempt is made to replace maladjusted patterns with a new response to a given stimulus.

2. What type of therapy uses exposure of the body to light waves to treat patients with depression caused by seasonal fluctuations? _____

3. What is a method of inducing convulsions to treat affective disorders in patients who have been resistant or unresponsive to drug therapy?

_____

4. What therapy is used to analyze and treat any dysfunctional effects of unconscious factors or a patient's mental state? _____

5. What are any of the various methods of treating mental and emotional disorders that help a person change attitudes, perceptions, and patterns of thinking? _____

PHARMACOLOGY

A major part of treatment for behavioral disorders is the use of drug therapy. For example, patients may be prescribed a type of selective serotonin reuptake inhibitor (SSRI) for major depression or depression in bipolar disorder. Serotonin is one type of neurotransmitter in many synapses in the brain. In depressed patients, there is not enough serotonin available at the postsynaptic neuron. SSRIs prevent the presynaptic neuron from taking the serotonin back up, thereby increasing the amount of serotonin available in the synapse. The psychiatric medications described appear in the top 100 prescribed medications in the United States. Medications are continually being developed and reevaluated and are closely regulated by the Food and Drug Administration. Examples include the following:

Antialcoholics: Drugs intended to discourage use of alcohol. Naltrexone (ReVia) can be used for alcohol and narcotic withdrawal. Disulfiram (Antabuse) is used to deter alcohol consumption.

Antidepressants: Medications intended to relieve symptoms of depressed mood. Many classes are available, including SSRIs, tricyclics (TCAs), monoamine oxidase inhibitors (MAOIs) and some newer unclassified agents. Examples include fluoxetine (Prozac), sertraline (Zoloft), mirtazapine (Remeron), tranylcypromine (Parnate), bupropion (Wellbutrin), and venlafaxine (Effexor).

Antipsychotics or neuroleptics: Medications intended to control psychotic symptoms such as hallucinations and delusions. Haloperidol (Haldol) and chlorpromazine (Thorazine) are examples of the typical antipsychotics while olanzapine (Zyprexa) and risperidone (Risperdal) are examples of the newer atypical antipsychotics.

Anxiolytics: Drugs whose effect is to relieve symptoms of anxiety. These drugs are often used as sedatives or sedative-hypnotics as well. Examples are lorazepam (Ativan), buspirone (BuSpar), and alprazolam (Xanax).

Cholinesterase inhibitors: These drugs combat the cognitive deterioration seen in disorders characterized by dementia, such as Alzheimer disease. Examples are donepezil (Aricept) and galantamine (Reminyl, Razadyne).

Hypnotics: These drugs promote sleep. Hypnotics, sedatives, sedative-hypnotics, and anxiolytics are often similar in effect and may be used interchangeably. Zolpidem (Ambien), zaleplon (Sonata), and flurazepam (Dalmane) are examples of hypnotics.

Mood stabilizers: Drugs that balance neurotransmitters in the brain to reduce or prevent acute mood swings (mania or depression). Lithium (Lithobid) is the most well-known mood stabilizer. Some anticonvulsants such as valproic acid (Depakote) and lamotrigine (Lamictal) are also considered mood stabilizers.

NMD... eptor antagonists: Agents used to preserve cognitive function in pat... uffering from progressive memory loss. The only approved agent is n... tine (Namenda).

Sedat... nd sedative-hypnotics: Overlapping classes of central nervous syst... pressant drugs that exert a calming effect with or without ind... sleep. The most commonly used agents are benzodiazepines and bar... es.

Stimu...: Generally intended to increase synaptic activity of targeted neu... hese drugs are amphetamine-like in nature and may be used to trea... lepsy and ADHD. An example is methylphenidate (Ritalin, Con...

E... se 8-9: PHARMACOLOGY

Match ... g class with the drug name.

_____ 1... d stabilizer   _____ 5. anxiolytic

_____ 2... depressant   _____ 6. stimulant

_____ 3... inesterase   _____ 7. antialcoholic
        bitor
                              _____ 8. hypnotic
_____ 4... ive

A. Anatabuse
B. Ritalin
C. fluoxetine
D. barbiturate
E. donepezil, galantamine
F. Ambien
G. lithium
H. alprazolam

Castlewood Clinic
14037 Marion St.
Reno, NV 89512

PROGRESS NOTE

Date: 04/06/XX	Vital Signs:	T	R
Chief Complaint: "Stressed"		P	BP

04/06/XX — 54-year-old female has stress, she just can't handle any more.

Issues circle around behavior of adopted son age 17 and excessive workload at her job. Past history includes molestation and house robberies. Last several nights been unable to sleep. Is having nightmares of being robbed. She just can't take it anymore and would like a sleeping pill.

IMPRESSION: Insomnia associated with nightmares/anxiety disorder

PLAN: Issued trazodone 25 mg to take 1-2 hours before bed for the next several nights. She is to schedule visit with a psychologist to begin to resolve these issues on a more prolonged basis.

William Obert, MD

Patient Name: Sherry Prichet
DOB: 3/18/19XX
MR/Chart #: 52311

◇ Exercise 8-10: PROGRESS NOTE

Using the progress note on p. 229, answer the following questions.

1. The impression notes that the patient has "insomnia." What is the meaning of the term?

   _____

2. What health care professional is she scheduled to visit? _____

3. What class of drug do you expect trazodone to be in? _____

4. She is diagnosed with a disorder in which the mood may be described as an "anticipation of impending danger and dread accompanied by restlessness, tension, tachycardia, and breathing

   difficulty not associated with the general stimulus." What is it? _____

Abbreviations

Abbreviation	Definition	Abbreviation	Definition
ADHD	Attention-deficit/hyperactivity disorder	O × 3	Oriented to time, place, and person
BD	Bipolar disorder	O × 4	Oriented to time, place, person, and objects
DT	Delirium tremens	OCD	Obsessive-compulsive disorder
GAD	Generalized anxiety disorder	ODD	Oppositional defiant disorder
ECT	Electroconvulsive therapy	PTSD	Posttraumatic stress disorder
GAF	Global Assessment of Functioning	SAD	Seasonal affective disorder
IQ	Intelligence quotient	SSRI	Selective serotonin reuptake inhibitor
MR	Mental retardation	Sx	Symptoms
O × 1	Oriented to time	WAIS	Wechsler Adult Intelligence Scale
O × 2	Oriented to time and place		

◇ Exercise 8-11: ABBREVIATIONS

Write out the abbreviations in the following sentences.

1. Michele was being treated with light therapy for her SAD. _____

2. John was diagnosed with GAD after exhibiting Sx of difficulty concentrating, excessive worry, and

   disturbed sleep over the last year. _____

3. The patient had a diagnosis of mild MR, with an IQ of 55, as determined by the WAIS.

   _____

4. Roger was referred to the school psychologist by his teacher to be evaluated for the possibility of an

   ADHD diagnosis after many behavioral problems at school and at home. _____

5. The patient was diagnosed with PTSD after she was assaulted. _____

Careers

Social Worker

Although many professions are involved in working with psychiatric and substance abuse patients, the career predicted to grow faster than average in the next few years in this area is that of social worker. Although a bachelor's degree is the minimum requirement, most positions require a master's degree that is a master's of social work (MSW). Individuals who choose social work as a profession tend to have a strong desire to help their clients overcome difficulties and solve personal or family problems. Because this is an extremely broad profession, most social workers specialize. Those who work with patients with mental or emotional problems may provide such services as crisis intervention, individual or group therapy, social rehabilitation, or training in everyday living skills. Substance abuse social workers assist drug and alcohol abusers in recovery from their dependencies. A common adjunct to this treatment is employment counseling. For more information on the field of social work, please visit the National Association of Social Workers website at http://www.nasw.org.

Psychologist

Psychologists are also professionals who work with patients, investigating and treating emotional and behavioral disorders. Most psychologists have a doctoral degree (PhD or PsyD) and are self-employed. Like social workers, they may specialize in a variety of areas including geropsychology (treatment of the elderly), clinical psychologists (working with mentally and emotionally disturbed patients), school psychologists (working with behavioral and learning issues that affect students), and industrialorganizational psychologists (applying their knowledge to the workplace setting). For more information on careers, visit the American Psychological Association website at http://www.apa.org.

Psychiatrist

Psychiatrists are medical doctors who specialize in the treatment of patients with psychological disorders. The range of disorders may range from mood disorders to substance abuse to sexual and gender identity disorders.

Unlike social workers or psychologists, psychiatrists are able to order diagnostic tests and to prescribe medications. Treatments may include psychotherapy, psychoanalysis, and hospitalization and medication. To become a psychiatrist, an individual normally has a bachelor's degree, a medical degree, and a residency in psychiatry. For more information on this career, you can visit the American Psychiatric Association's website at http://www.psych.org.

Art and Music Therapists

Two areas that students might want to consider when thinking of mental and behavioral health career options are art and music therapy.

Art therapists use a variety of media to help patients reflect on their abilities, interests, concerns, and conflicts, which cannot be easily accessed with normal talk therapy. Aside from working directly with patients admitted for psychiatric diagnoses, these therapists may work with HIV-positive patients, burn victims, and cancer patients to help them express their feelings. Art therapists must earn a master's degree, and these programs are generally at least 2 years in length. The association that credentials them is the Art Therapy Credentials Board, Inc. For more information about this career, visit http://www.arttherapy.org.

Music therapy is another profession in which individuals can use their creativity to help others. Music therapists use music in the same way as art therapists use their art to help patients, using music to improve the quality of their lives. After assessing a patient's needs, the therapist may assist the patient to create, sing, move to, or listen to music. Music therapy requires an undergraduate degree, including 127 semester hours of required courses and a 1040-hour supervised clinical internship. A master's degree of 30 semester hours is available. On successful completion of the baccalaureate degree, a student may sit for a certification exam administered by the Certification Board of Music Therapists. For more information, visit the American Music Therapy Association at http://www.musictherapy.org.

Chapter Review

A. Introduction

1. Who publishes the official listing of diagnosable mental disorders for the United States, and what is this listing called?

   _____

2. Describe behavioral health.

   _____

   _____

B. Pathology

3. The therapist records the symptoms of a patient who reports seeing lizards in her bathroom that are trying to attack her. She is having visual _____.

4. Since the death of her brother, Kate has been crying constantly and experiencing a great deal of difficulty eating, sleeping, and working. Her diagnosis is _____.

5. The counselor interviewed a client who expressed the belief that she is the current queen of England. Her symptom is considered a(n) _____.

6. John reported that the sound of the wind coming down his chimney was actually a voice. He was experiencing a(n) _____.

7. What is the term for a progressive, organic mental disorder characterized by disorientation, stupor, and loss of cognitive abilities? _____

8. What is the term for an appropriate range of emotion? _____

9. What is the health care term that describes restlessness and an inability to sit still? _____

10. Someone with a blunt affect has a(n) _____ range of emotions.

11. What is a "labile affect"? _____

12. What is the term for a person's normal psychological impulse drive? _____

13. A state of psychologically induced immobility is called _____.

14. Denial and projection are examples of _____.

15. A real sensory perception that does not result from an external stimulus and occurs in the waking state is a(n) _____.

16. What is a condition of confused, unfocused, and irrational agitation? _____

17. A dysphoric mood is characterized by _____.

18. What is the difference between euphoria and euthymia?

_____

_____

19. A misinterpretation of an external sensory stimulus is a(n) _____.

20. What is the term for difficulty in controlling use of a drug? _____

21. In which disorder does a patient have fundamental distortions of thinking and perception but with intact intellectual capacity? _____

22. An older term for borderline schizophrenia is _____.

23. When a patient experiences an acute onset of symptoms, such as delusions, hallucinations, perceptual disturbances, and a severe disruption of ordinary behavior, he or she has an acute, transient _____ disorder.

24. Mood disorders are also referred to as _____ disorders.

25. Bipolar affective disorder is characterized by two extremes of behavior: _____ and

_____.

26. Give an example of a dyssomnia: _____

27. Give an example of a parasomnia: _____

28. Dysthymia is _____.

29. Give an example of a health care term for a "fear" disorder and explain what it is.

_____

30. Patients who have recurrent, involuntary patterns of thought and meaningless activity may be diagnosed with _____

31. Patients who have an extended emotional response to a traumatic event may experience

_____.

32. Patients who develop multiple personalities as a result of severe stress are diagnosed with

_____.

33. An eating disorder characterized by an insatiable craving for food, followed by purging through vomiting or use of laxatives, is called _____

34. A group of disorders that have characteristics of long-standing, inflexible, dysfunctional behavior patterns and personality traits is what type of disorder? _____

35. An IQ range of 50 to 69 is considered what type of retardation? _____

36. Patterns of persistent aggressive and defiant behaviors may result in a diagnosis of _____.

37. A group of involuntary behaviors that include vocalizations and repetitive movements is called

_____.

Decode the medical term by writing the meaning of the word part in the space provided, then using the parts to form a definition.

Ex. anthropophobia

(anthrop/o *man, people* + -phobia *fear*)

fear of people

38. **acrophobia**

(acr/o _____ + -phobia _____)

_____

39. **pedophilia**

(ped/o _____ + phil/o _____ + -ia _____)

_____

40. **euthymia**

(eu- _____ + -thym/ia _____)

_____

41. **anhedonia**

(an- _____ + -hedon/o _____ + -ia _____)

_____

42. **echolalia**

(ech/o _____ + -lalia _____)

_____

43. **a____isia**

  (a _____ + -kathis/o _____ + -ia _____)

_____

44. **p____ania**

  (p _____ + -mania _____)

_____

Choose ____ppropriate word roots, combining vowels, prefixes, and suffixes to build terms that take the place of the ph____ bold. First, write the appropriate word parts in the space provided next to their type, then assemble the ter____ the line after the parentheses.

Ex: Du____ n episode of a **condition of walking during sleep**, Mattie awoke in the kitchen after trip____ over a stool.

  (so____ ord root/ *ambul* word root/ *ism* suffix)

  so____ bulism

45. Rog____ **ondition of excessive sleep** was causing him to miss work.

  (_____ prefix/ _____ word root/ _____ suffix)

_____

46. Ann____ ____ade an appointment to discuss her experience of several recurring episodes of elation and dep____ n. Her therapist diagnosed her with **a condition of a cycling mind.**

  (_____ word root/ _____ combining vowel/ _____ suffix)

_____

47. The ____t was treated for his **condition of being attracted (sexually) to children.**

  (_____ word root/ _____ combining vowel/ _____ word root/

  _____ suffix)

_____

48. Nath____ ____voided taking elevators because of his **fear of enclosed spaces.**

  (_____ word root/ _____ combining vowel/ _____ suffix)

_____

49. A pers____ th **a madness to set fires** was the cause of a recent rash of fires in the small town.

  (_____ word root/ _____ combining vowel/ _____ suffix)

_____

C. Diagnostic Procedures

50. What form of imaging uses a computerized nuclear medicine technique to examine the metabolic activity of the brain? _____

51. What are the five axes of the DSM-IV-TR multiaxial evaluation?

_____

52. Personality characteristics are assessed through which test? _____

53. Which test has the patient tell a story to go with a picture that is presented? _____

54. The WAIS measures _____.

D. Therapeutic Interventions

55. ECT is _____ and is used to treat _____.

56. A type of treatment that is used to help people change attitudes, perceptions, and patterns of thinking is _____ therapy.

57. An attempt at substituting a new response to a given stimulus occurs in what type of therapy?

_____

58. Detoxification is an initial step in treating _____.

59. Light therapy is used to treat which disorder? _____

E. Pharmacology

Fill in the blank next to the generic term with the type of medication.

NMDA receptor antagonists, stimulant, anxiolytic, antidepressant, sedative-hypnotic, antipsychotic

60. lorazepam _____

61. sertraline _____

62. memantine _____

63. chlorpromazine _____

64. methylphenidate _____

65. benzodiazepine _____

66. What agency controls the medications that are distributed in this country? _____

F. Abbreviations

67. If a patient is described as being O × 3, you know that _____.

68. If the abbreviation MR appears on a health care report, you know that it stands for _____, but do not know to what degree.

69. Patients who exhibit OCD have which disorder? _____

70. DTs is used to abbreviate a finding that occurs in patients undergoing withdrawal from which type of substance abuse? Identify the abbreviation and the substance. _____

71. Patients who exhibit GAD have which disorder? _____

G. Translations

Write the following in your own words.

72. The patient had <u>blunted affect</u>, <u>dysthymic mood</u>, and complained of <u>insomnia</u>.

_____

73. The year-old patient was admitted with a diagnosis of <u>anorexia nervosa</u>.

_____

74. Arielle explained that it would be difficult to go to school because she was <u>agoraphobic</u>.

_____

75. The patient was referred to a sleep therapist for <u>somnambulism</u>.

_____

76. The patient was diagnosed with <u>pyromania</u> after detectives had arrested him in connection with three intentionally set fires in his community.

_____

H. Be Careful

Provide meanings for each of the following word parts.

77. phren- _____ or _____

78. thym- _____ or _____

79. -thymia _____

Case Study with *Accompanying Medical Report*

Nadine White's husband of 39 years died last spring, and she has been unable to adjust to life without him. According to her daughter, Nadine did not put in a garden this year, stopped volunteering at the local hospital, and has no appetite. Today she is meeting with a psychiatric social worker, Andrew Dawson, to whom she was referred by her family physician, Dr. McGuire. Andrew has read Dr. McGuire's notes on Mrs. White and is prepared to begin his grief counseling with her.

Andrew gently questions Mrs. White about how her life is different now after her husband's death. In a voice barely above a whisper and devoid of emotion, she states that she is unable to be happy anymore. "I used to be so pleased to work in my garden, or read, or volunteer at the hospital. I didn't need to have my husband with me every minute; it wasn't like that. It's just—" she hesitates—"it's just that I knew I could always come home to him. We were best friends."

Andrew notes that Nadine's generally flattened affect is punctuated by bouts of tearfulness and anxiety. She says, "I know I'm unhappy—how else should I be? I'm tired, but I can't sit still. I go to sleep and then I wake up in the middle of the night. I try to read to take my mind off how bad I feel, yet I just can't concentrate. I know Arthur's not coming back. It just worries me that I'm never going to feel any better than I feel now. I don't know what to do!"

Andrew recognizes that Mrs. White is exhibiting classic signs of depression: fatigue, anhedonia, insomnia, and inability to concentrate. He empathizes with her about how hard it is to accept the death of a loved one, especially a life partner. "I want you to know, Mrs. White," he says, "that your symptoms are not unusual or untreatable. I think I can help you get back on track and enjoy life again. The bad news is, although you say you don't want to talk about

(From Potter PA, Perry AG: Fundamentals of nursing, *ed 6, St Louis, 2006, Mosby.)*

it, talking may be the best way to get through this. Let's try that first."

At the end of the scheduled session, Andrew suggests that Mrs. White participate in a bereavement group for women and men who have lost their partners. "I think you'd find it useful to hear how other people are coping with their losses. That group meets here one evening a week. I'd also like you to come back and see me once a week, so that we can continue to get to know each other and work on a new start for you. How do you feel about that?"

Mrs. White offers a glimmer of a smile as she clutches a well-used tissue and says, "I must admit that I was angry with my daughter when she first brought me to Dr. McGuire, but now that we've talked, I think I'd like to give counseling a try. When do we meet again?"

The problem-oriented medical record (POMR) was proposed by Lawrence Weed, MD, in the *New England Journal of Medicine* in the late 1960s. The record is composed of a problem list of health concerns organized by SOAP notes:

S subjective (the patient's complaints)
O objective (the physician's findings)
A assessment (interpretation by the physician)
P plan (action plan for what can be done for that particular problem)

This method is still being used, and applications have been extended to all disciplines, including veterinary medicine.

Castlewood Clinic
14037 Marion St.
Reno, NV 89512

Patie... dine White
DOE... /34
MR#... 5-69
Date... /02

S: ...58-year-old white female was brought here today by her daughter. She has a history of ...tension, GERD, and constipation. Her daughter states, "Mom has been sleeping a lot, ... very poorly, and seems uninterested in life" since the death of her husband. The ...t says that she has come only because her daughter insisted and admits that she has ...een eating or sleeping well. She has been using Correctol for her constipation, but ...hat it causes runny stools.

O: ...al: The patient is an older white female who appears to be fatigued and somewhat ...d tearful. HEENT: Tympanic membranes were clear bilaterally. Nose had some pale ...a, otherwise clear. Throat was clear. Neck was supple. Lungs: Clear to auscultation. ...vascular: Regular rate and rhythm without murmur. Abdomen: Soft and diffusely ...to a mild degree. Bowel sounds were active.

A: ...pression. (2) Hypertension. (3) GERD. (4) Constipation.

P: ...e will be referred to a psychiatric social worker for cognitive therapy. If she does not ...mproved within the month, a prescription for Zoloft or Prozac will be considered. ...r hypertension has been controlled through diet and is within normal limits today. ...r GERD is being treated with Tagamet. (4) For her constipation, I recommended ...or some similar type of fiber, increasing her fluid intake, and closely monitoring her ...additional roughage.

Patrick McGuire, MD

I. Health... e Report

80. If the ...iaxial format had been used, which diagnosis would have been included in Axis I?

   _____

81. Would ...patient have had a diagnosis appropriate for Axis II (with the information you have been

   given)... _____

82. What ... meaning of GERD? _____

83. Zoloft ...rozac are what types of medications? _____

84. What ...f therapy has been suggested for Mrs. White? _____

Reference _____

Dubos RJ: T... e faces of medicine, *Bull Am Coll Phys* 2:162-166, 1961.

OBJECTIVES

You will be able to do the following after completing this chapter:

Key Terms
1. Define, appropriately use, and spell all the Key Terms for this chapter.

Psychology and Personality
2. List and briefly define the three parts that make up a person's personality according to Freud.
3. List three factors that influence personality development.

Human Needs
4. List the five types of human needs.

Mental and Physical Health
5. Explain the importance of having good self-esteem.
6. List the four types of factors that can influence perception.
7. Differentiate between experiencing fear and having a phobia.
8. List five health problems caused by anxiety or stress.
9. Explain how fear, phobia, anxiety, and stress affect a person's mental and physical health.

Coping
10. List and describe six defense mechanisms.
11. List the five stages of grief and briefly describe each in the first person.

Patient-Centered Professionalism
12. Analyze a realistic medical office situation and apply your understanding of human behavior to determine the best course of action.
13. Describe the impact on patient care when medical assistants understand human behavior.

U DERSTANDING HUMAN B HAVIOR

KEY   MS

accept   oming to terms with an issue (e.g., impending
dea   ss).

anger   n caused by the feeling of loss of control.

anxiet   ng of apprehension, unease, or uncertainty.

bargai   rocess of making deals.

compe   Defense mechanism in which a strength is
emp   d to cover up a weakness in another area.

defens   anism Coping tactic used by the unconscious
min   oid unpleasant situations.

denial   scious behavior that does not acknowledge
unp   aspects of life.

depres   verall feeling of hopelessness.

displa   Defense mechanism in which aggressive
beh   placed onto something or someone else other
thar   urce of frustration.

ego Tl   of the personality that is alert to reality and
con   ces of behavior.

empat   lerstanding how someone else feels by placing
one   he person's place.

fantas   /dream.

fear A   ate reaction to genuine danger.

fight, 1   r fright Body's response to threat.

homec   The body in balance.

hospic   lle of services and team of people helping a family
dur   end stage of a patient's terminal illness.

id The   scious part of the brain associated with biological
driv   rgy source, and needs gratification.

labels Identifying names placed on an individual by others.

overcompensation Defense mechanism in which exaggerated
and inappropriate behavior is used to cover up an area of
inadequacy.

perception An individual's view of a situation based on the
environment.

phobias Irrational fears of objects, activities, or situations.

physiological Relating to the body's responses to its internal
and external environment.

projection Defense mechanism in which there is an
unconscious rejection of an unacceptable thought, desire, or
impulse, placing blame on something or someone else.

psychiatry Medical specialty that deals with the treatment and
prevention of mental illness.

psychology Scientific study of the mind and the behavioral
patterns of humans and animals.

psychosomatic Physical illness brought about by psychological
problems.

rationalization Inventing acceptable reasons for one's
behavior.

self-esteem Feelings of self-worth.

stress Body's response to any demand put on it, whether
positive or negative.

subconscious The part of the conscious that is not fully aware.

superego The part of the personality that includes the values
and standards designed to promote proper behavior.

sympathy Having concern for another person's situation.

What Would You Do?

Read the following scenario and keep it in mind as you learn about human behavior in this chapter.

Sara Ann is a 22-year-old single mother and a medical assistant. She has no assistance at home with child care or with any of the chores necessary to keep up a household. Sara Ann works as many hours as she can to support herself and her two children in the best way possible. On top of all of this, going to school has added major financial problems for Sara Ann.

On many days, Sara Ann is tired and frustrated, and wonders just how she will get through the day. Because of her lack of self-esteem and the lack of help, anxiety and stress are affecting the way Sara Ann deals with co-workers. Sara Ann's anxiety level often leads her to label

patients. In addition, Sara Ann has difficulty adapting to any variation in the daily schedule.

Because Sara Ann feels close to some patients with whom she has spent time in the medical office, she will often discuss her personal problems with these patients. Also, Sara Ann must handle some of her personal business (banking, errands) while at work because she does not leave work early enough to do these things when the businesses are open.

Sara Ann is experiencing a lot of stress, which is having an impact on her performance at work. If you were in Sara Ann's situation, what would you do to reduce stress?

The study of human behavior helps us understand how people learn, feel emotions, and establish relationships. This knowledge can help us adjust to the instant demands of an ever-changing world. As a medical assistant, you will be required to perform a wide variety of tasks each day. Although a few of these tasks may not involve interacting with people, most of your work will depend on your ability to relate to both patients and co-workers. To relate well to others, medical assistants need to develop "USA": *understanding, sensitivity,* and *accommodation* (adjusting) to patient needs. Human relations is the key to providing professional, high-quality care to patients. Skill in human relations develops over time and, as with other skills, must be practiced, fine-tuned, and nurtured every day.

PSYCHOLOGY AND PERSONALITY

Psychology is the scientific study of the mind and the behavioral patterns of humans and animals. **Psychiatry** is a medical specialty that deals with the treatment and prevention of mental illness. Sigmund Freud, an Austrian physician, was interested in understanding the development of the mind in order to treat psychological problems that his patients were experiencing. He was one of the first theorists to recognize that **subconscious** memory can affect a person's health. Further studies have shown that the mind and emotions have a powerful effect on an individual's ability to stay

healthy. Freud's theories attempted to explain the structure of personality and how it develops over time.

Basic Structure of Personality

Freud used a three-part organizational model to explain the structure of personality: the id, ego, and superego.

Id: The part of the brain associated with basic unconscious biological drives. The id is the main source of energy and desire and needs gratification (the satisfying of the body's needs).

An infant cries when hungry, when the diaper is wet or soiled, and when the infant wants to be held. Gratification is received when the infant receives food, when the diaper is changed, and the infant is held.

Ego: The part of the personality that is aware of reality and the consequences of different behaviors. Interacting with others develops the ego.

Toddlers learn that each time they use the toilet, praise is given, and when they soil their pants, praise is withheld. As they interact with their peers who are "potty-trained," toddlers want to be accepted, and praise from others (e.g., adults) is less important.

Superego: The part of the personality that acts as a conscience, or moral guide; the internalization of values and standards designed to promote proper social behavior.

It is a ___ble for an infant to cry to receive gratification. A___ nfant grows and becomes a toddler, crying
becor___ nacceptable behavior and often results in
negati___ nsequences. As the superego develops,
toddle___ gin to behave in an acceptable way that
allows ___ to be gratified.

Onc___ superego is developed, the ego acts as
the gat___ er and holds off the demands of the id
until p___ gratification is chosen that is acceptable to ___ uperego. As we develop, we learn to
control ___ mpulses.

What ___ is when a 10-year-old boy sees a candy
bar on ___ re counter but has no money?
• The ___ ts to grab the candy bar and run out of
  the s___
• The ___ nts to satisfy the id but knows there will
  be a ___ ment for stealing.
• The s___ 7o knows it is morally wrong to steal.
Freud b___ that the child's ego will repress the urges
of the i___ use of a fear of punishment, but as the
child de___ , the reality of right and wrong will take
over. E___ ugh the superego uses guilt to enforce
the rule___ rson who does what is acceptable to the
supereg___ pride and self-satisfaction.

As a ___ l assistant, when you confront difficult deci___ listen to your superego and make the
right ch___

Person___ Development

As a mec___ ssistant you will interact with people
who hav___ ypes of personalities. It is important
to under___ the factors that can influence the way
a person'___ onality develops. The study of behavior indic___ at the development of personality is
influence___ the following factors:

• Even___ at take place in a person's early
  dev___ ental years
• Biol___ (genetic) factors, such as whether a
  pers___ male or female
• Psyc___ ical (environmental) factors, such
  as p___ or wealth and a person's
  upb___ g

With al___ actors that impact the development
of person___ t is no wonder that no two people
are alike. ___ this in mind when working with
patients of___ rsonality types.

Other t___ s have expanded on the ideas of
Freud. Son___ e examined the way people gain
knowledge___ he way they think about things to
help expla___ onality development.

HUMAN NEEDS

Abraham Maslow, like Freud, studied human behavior. Maslow, an American psychologist, was interested in what motivates people to do what they do.
He recognized that a person's development and
behavior are affected by both physical and emotional needs. He believed that all humans have
needs that must be met. He placed these needs in a
hierarchy (rank order) to show which needs take
priority over others. He emphasized that all lower
needs must be met before the higher needs can be
satisfied.

Maslow's Hierarchy of Needs

Maslow's hierarchy of needs model has these five
categories (Fig. 9-1):

1. *Physical needs.* First level; foundation of a
   person's motivational drive.
   • Basic needs, including air, food, water, and
     shelter
   • Necessary for survival
   • When achieved, physical needs bring about
     homeostasis (balance) to the body
   • When *not* achieved, the person may
     experience illness, pain, and irritation
2. *Safety and security needs.* Second level; a person's
   physical needs are already met.
   • Psychological needs, including feeling
     safe from harm and feeling secure about
     safety
   • When achieved, safety and security
     needs bring a sense of stability and
     consistency
   • When *not* achieved, safety is not ensured and
     the person must be "on guard"
3. *Social needs.* Third level; a person's physical and
   safety needs are already met.
   • The need to feel loved and appreciated; the
     need to feel a sense of belonging

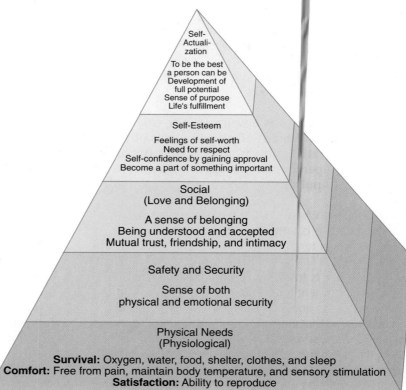

Fig. 9-1 Maslow's Hierarchy of Needs pyramid.

- When achieved, social needs bring friendship and companionship
- When *not* achieved, disappointment and loneliness may result

4. *Self-esteem.* Fourth level; physical, safety, and social needs are already met.
- The need to feel worthwhile and good about oneself
- Affected by attention and recognition from others
- When achieved, self-esteem creates a sense of being in control
- When *not* achieved, there may be a lack of appreciation for others or oneself

5. *Self-actualization.* Fifth level; physical, safety, social, and self-esteem needs are already met.
- The need of persons to "be all they can be" (to do their best and accomplish their goals)
- As the most advanced level, self-actualization may never be reached because it deals with becoming the absolute best a person can be

Box 9-1 lists Maslow's characteristics of a self-actualized person. Maslow's theories are widely used in the study of employee behavior, helping us understand what motivates people to perform well on the job. People are only motivated to reach

---

BOX 9-1   Maslow's Characteristics of a Self-Actualized Person

Effective perception of reality
Self-acceptance and acceptance of others
Having a need for privacy and solitude at times
Being problem centered rather than ego centered
Having a deep appreciation of the basic experiences of life
Having the ability for a deep interpersonal relationship
Having a good sense of humor
Having democratic attitudes
Being creative

---

for what they do not have, or their "unsatisfied needs." Satisfying needs is healthy, and the desire for gratification has a major influence on our actions.

Which level of Maslow's hierarchy is currently motivating you as a person? As an employee? How can you satisfy these needs and move to the next level?

UNDERSTANDING HUMAN BEHAVIOR 247

PATIENT-CENTERED PROFESSIONALISM

- P[a]... [y]our job as a medical assistant is to monitor pa... compliance with the physician's treatm... [pla]n. With this in mind, how can understandin... [whe]re patients are on Maslow's hierarchy of ne... [h]elp you encourage them to follow their tre[atmen]t plans?
- Ho[w] ... you use your understanding of a patient's ne... [w]hen communicating with patients?
- Ho[w] ... understanding your own needs and the ne... your co-workers help you provide better ca[re to p]atients?

MENTAL AND PHYSICAL HEALTH

Freud, M[aslo]w, and many others who study human behavio[r agre]e that mental health can affect physical hea[lth. P]eople who have a good opinion of themsel[ves an]d their abilities (e.g., high self-esteem) tend to [be he]althier than those who think negatively ab[out t]hemselves. In addition, when people go throu[gh str]essful situations in life, it wears down their res[istanc]e to disease. Stressful situations cause people t[o exp]erience fear and anxiety, which can impact t[heir h]ealth over time.

As a [medic]al assistant, you need to understand the imp[ortanc]e of a healthy self-esteem and good self-perc[eption], as well as the effect that fear and anxiety [can ha]ve on health.

Self-Esteem

How peo[ple fe]el about themselves at any given time is referre[d to as] their **self-esteem.** Self-esteem is the fourth le[vel in] Maslow's hierarchy. Positive or high self-estee[m is h]aving feelings of self-worth and emotional we[llbei]ng. It is an "I like myself" state of mind. In[dividu]als with negative or low self-esteem focus on [mistak]es and dwell on what they have not done ver[y well t]hat they have accomplished. Self-esteem is [influe]nced by labels, perceptions, and the way peo[ple ada]pt to change.

Labels

Labels (e[.g., g]enius, jock, stupid, nerd) placed on individua[ls by p]arents, family, and others influence how peop[le se]e themselves. Research shows that labels of a[ny ty]pe place limitations on people.

- Childre[n desc]ribed as being "shy" may never try to s[ociali]ze because they are expected to be shy.

- Children labeled "special ed" students may never reach their full potential because society (the school system) has placed a label on them that says they cannot learn. Just because a student is labeled as "special ed" does not mean the student cannot learn; it only means the student learns at a different pace or by different methods. However, a child labeled as "special ed" may come to believe that he or she cannot learn at all.
- Parents brag about their child getting all "A"s and refer to the child as a "genius." If the child receives a "B" on her next report card, she may think she has lost her "genius" status.

Labels can place too much pressure on a person, especially a child. Never "label" patients or co-workers.

Self-esteem fluctuates throughout the day based on the many challenges people face. Positive self-worth is not about accomplishments but rather is an acceptance of "self" no matter what setbacks have occurred. Always remember that you must be appreciative of the "good things in life" and use your mistakes as learning experiences to improve. Take negative beliefs and change them to positive ones. As a medical assistant it is important for you to have a healthy self-esteem. With a healthy self-esteem, you will be more confident in your ability to care for patients and more positive when interacting with both patients and co-workers.

No one can make you feel inferior without your consent.

—*Eleanor Roosevelt*

Perception

Perception is the process of interpreting information gathered from our surroundings. How we view an event, another person, and even ourselves is influenced by our life experiences. Our first impression is often inaccurate because our subconscious mind usually focuses on existing information, and we are slow to change our original impression, even if it is wrong. It takes effort to move beyond these "old habits" or past beliefs. Many factors influence how an individual will perceive any given situation, including psychological, **physiological,** and cultural influences and social roles.

PSYCHOLOGICAL INFLUENCES

The words we use influence how we perform.

- *Past experiences.* We recall past experiences when we perform similar tasks. "I've never been very good at it," versus "With some help, I am ready to tackle this."

- *Assumptions.* We make judgments about how things will go based on how things have gone so far. If the day begins with problems, "It's going to be a bad day," versus "Up to this point, it has not been a good day, and it can only get better."
- *Expectations.* We use reports of others to form our expectations. "I heard that the test was hard so I probably won't pass it," versus "I heard the test was hard so I will give it my best shot."
- *Knowledge.* The facts we have will influence our approach to a problem because facts provide a place to begin. "I only know part of what I need to know to do this," versus "I know some of the facts, and I can ask for help or research the rest."
- *Personal moods.* Our mood influences our perception. When you do not want to do something, "I am not the person for this task, and I know I won't do a good job," versus "I will do a better job after I have a chance to figure out what really needs to be done."

PHYSIOLOGICAL INFLUENCES

What we sense and feel influences how we perform.

- *Senses.* It is difficult to perform if we are not comfortable. Sights, sounds, smells, things we touch or feel, and tastes can affect us. One person may feel cold in a room, whereas another may feel comfortable.
- *Age.* People of different age groups may think and use words differently. An 80-year-old and a 23-year-old will have a different meaning for the words "grass," "coke," and "pot."
- *Number of experiences.* The amount of experience we have affects our perception. A recent graduate will approach a project differently than someone who has been in the field several years.
- *Health.* Not being healthy may take away the ability to focus. If you have a bad headache, you might not be able to type as quickly as usual.
- *Fatigue.* Proper rest is vital for peak performance. If you are tired, you could make a mistake you normally would not have made.
- *Hunger.* Satisfaction of hunger is one of the primary levels in Maslow's hierarchy. If your stomach is growling your mind may not be on your work.
- *Biological cycles.* Different people are best at different times of the day. Some people are fresh in the morning, whereas others do not start until noon.

CULTURAL INFLUENCES

Our culture influences how we believe and what we believe.

- Different cultural backgrounds can lead to misunderstanding. A person's cultural background will determine what the person regards as caring behavior.
- Do not make assumptions regarding a patient's understanding of health maintenance, causes of disease, treatment, and prevention.
- Many cultures believe in alternative medicine, faith healers, and other approaches to health and perceive Western medicine as ineffective or wrong. Do not discount their belief system.

SOCIAL ROLES

People have different beliefs about social roles.

- Different people have different beliefs about the roles of men and women. Some may think that women should stay home with children and that men are the heads of the household and should make all decisions. Others may think that men and women are equal partners in decision making.
- Patients who have certain beliefs about social roles may be uncomfortable, for example, with male or female physicians. Be considerate and understanding.

A person's perception of any given situation is influenced not only by physiological and psychological factors but also by personal needs and interests at the time. Medical assistants must be aware of their own perceptions versus those of patients and co-workers. Differing perceptions can cause fear and stress.

Adapting to Change

Change, whether considered to be positive or negative, can cause stress (Table 9-1). How we adapt or adjust to change has a major impact on both our physical and mental health. Adjusting or modifying our behavior depends on how we perceive the change will affect our usual routine. In early childhood, for example, infants develop feelings of security and emotional attachment by doing things the same way each time. Once these routines are established, the child will acquire new behavior or will slightly modify behavior when introduced to new situations. This is the process of adapting behavior to fit new situations. If change is introduced slowly, with full understanding and encouragement, it may be smooth and even welcomed. However, sudden changes are difficult for people to handle.

TABL		**Changes Affecting Behavior**	
Nega		**Positive**	
Fired f	p	Opportunity to go back to school Learn a new career	
Death	ly	Look at life differently Appreciate others and self	
Getting	rce	Opportunity to make new goals Go back to school	
Serious	nt	Learn to live with disability Become a counselor	

As pa   he life process, change occurs daily. Sometim   se changes are perceived as hassles or irritating   s; these do not require a major adjustment in   n's routine. Others are seen as *minor* changes,   as moving to a middle school from   school. Some changes, such as a death of   ed one, are perceived as being a *major* cha   Major changes challenge our ability to cope w   e situation. Common situations that require a   ustment in behavior include the following

- School   ildren face changes daily in their studies   other children, and with their teache
- Adoles   ace issues such as appearance, feeling   lf-worth, others' opinions, and their fu
- Young   are moving from the "I" to the "we" c   concerning education, job, home, and far
- Middle   a change for many people because their ch   are independent, often leaving home,   void is created.
- Old age   bring about the death of friends, loss of i   ndence, and decrease in income.

As a me   assistant it is important for you to consider tl   act of a positive self-esteem, differing percep   and people's ability to adapt to change. Be   nsitive and understanding will help you provic   er care to your patients.

Fear, Anx   and Stress

You have   d how certain factors establish a person's se   m and how labels, differing perceptions, a   e changes can impact a person's mental and   cal health. Fear, anxiety, and stress also affect r   and physical health. As a medical assistant yo   l to understand the effects of fear, anxiety, and stress so that you can be more helpful to patients in the medical office.

Fear

Fear is a *normal* reaction to a *genuine* danger. It is an emotional response that alerts the body to take appropriate action to protect itself from the danger. The emotional response causes the body to either stand up to the danger ("fight"), run away from the danger ("flight"), or freeze, "like a deer in the headlights" ("fright"). This is called the **fight, flight, or fright** response. This response is actually caused by physiological changes in the body that occur when a threat is sensed.

Examples of physiological responses to fear are sudden and can include increased heart rate, rapid breathing, and sweaty palms. Patients who are ill or injured may be experiencing fear and may display these physiological responses.

PHOBIAS

Phobias are *irrational* (unreasonable) fears of objects, activities, or situations. Phobias interfere with a person's ability to function in everyday life. A person with a phobia feels powerless to do anything about the situation. When a fear is constantly on a person's mind, causing lost sleep and an inability to focus when awake, this fear is classified as a phobia. Persons with a phobia avoid situations where they might encounter the object of their fear. This is called *avoidance behavior*. In addition, the degree of physiological responses helps professionals identify phobias. People who have phobias often experience the fight, flight, or fright response when merely thinking about the fearful object or situation.

> It is not abnormal to have a *fear* of poisonous snakes because of the real danger of being bitten. It is considered to be a *phobia* if a person not only fears all snakes but also avoids any situation where snakes could be present (e.g., will not go outdoors because there may be snakes).

Phobias can be classified into one of three categories: simple, social, or agoraphobia (Box 9-2).

Research has shown that phobias focus on objects and situations that people cannot predict or control, such as lightning (Table 9-2). Fears tend to be very *objective* because they are very *obvious* and almost everyone would share the fear. Phobias are fears that remain even when the person is not in any danger from the object or situation. You may encounter patients with phobias (e.g., hemophobia, the fear of blood). Always be considerate and understanding and seek help with these patients when necessary.

BOX 9-2   Types of Phobias

Simple
A persistent, irrational fear of a specific object or situation when in its presence.

Fears
- Objects (e.g., animals and reptiles, such as dogs, cats, or snakes)
- Transportation (e.g., flying, riding in a train or car)
- Closed spaces (e.g., elevators, rooms with the doors closed)
- Heights (e.g., going up a ladder or an elevator with glass sides)

Signs and Symptoms
- Avoiding these objects or situations.
- Withdrawing from these objects or situations.

Social: Anthropophobia
An irrational fear of being in certain social or performing situations.

Fears
- Looking ridiculous when speaking in public.
- Interacting with authority figures.
- Being ridiculed or thought of as "strange."
- Being suspicious of or fearing harm from other people (irrationally).

Signs and Symptoms
- Avoiding or refusing to eat in public.
- Refusing invitations from others.
- Having a reclusive lifestyle.
- Trembling hands, dry throat, or lump in the throat.
- Preoccupation with some aspect of appearance (e.g., refusing to wear bathing suits in front of others, having several cosmetic surgeries to look better).

Agoraphobia
An exaggerated fear of being in places where there is no escape or where embarrassment could occur.

Fears
- Being ridiculed or thought of as "strange" in public places.
- Being suspicious of others or fearing harm from other people (irrationally) in public places.

Signs and Symptoms
- Avoiding or refusing to go out (secluding oneself at home).
- Only going to stores or being in crowds if accompanied.

Anxiety
Anxiety is the feeling of apprehension, uneasiness, or uncertainty about a situation. These feelings are normal as long as the person is able to move on and function normally. We all have had periods of anxiety and worry when faced with new situations (e.g., on the first day at a new job, your heart may pound and your mouth may be dry). What makes anxiety different from a fear or phobia is that an anxiety is very *subjective*. A person may worry excessively over "bad things" that have not happened and may never happen. A person experiencing anxiety may display the following characteristics:

1. *Perception of future events is always negative.* The person may be uneasy, even for no real reason.
2. *The person almost always exhibits self-doubt.* The person may give up on something because of a lack of confidence in his or her ability.
3. *Crippling symptoms appear.* The person may be unable to sleep, may have difficulty breathing, or may have periods in which the person describes a feeling that "a tight band is around my head."

4. *Behavior and posture are different.* The person's facial expression may be tense and the voice may quiver. No eye contact is made, and the person may blush and begin to sweat and may also "fidget" and "wring" the hands.

When the biological and physical changes resulting from anxiety are long term, the body can experience physical problems and illness. These problems occur because of the added stress put on the body (e.g., ulcers, increased blood pressure). Box 9-3 lists medical conditions attributable to anxiety.

Stress
Stress is the body's response to any demand put on the body. Stress is an unavoidable fact of life. Some stress is good because it keeps a person alert and aware of what is happening (e.g., a runner may feel stress while waiting for the signal to begin the race). How well people adapt to stressful events in life is often the difference between a healthy mind and body and a life with many illnesses.

TABLE ... Common Phobias

Source	Phobia
Numb...	Triskaidekaphobia
Being...	Monophobia
Bees	Apiphobia
Birds	Ornithophobia
Blood	Hemophobia
Confin... ces	Claustrophobia
Going ... doctor	Iatrophobia
Eating ... llowing	Phagophobia
Germs	Verminophobia
Homo... y	Homophobia
Injecti...	Trypanophobia
Insects	Acarophobia
Laught...	Geliophobia
Light	Photophobia*
Lightnin... under	Brontophobia
Riding i...	Amaxophobia
Going t... ol	Didaskaleinophobia
Speakin... blic	Glossophobia
Spiders	Arachnophobia
Sunlight	Phengophobia
Water	Hydrophobia

*Although ... sually refers to a sensitivity to light.

Pressures ...	Raising a family	Earning a living
Conflicts	Choosing a spouse	Choosing a career
Frustrations	Renting and not owning a home	Not getting the promotion

REACTIONS ... ESS

During p... of stress, our natural body defense systems w..., fatigue takes over, and we become more susc... e to disease. Does stress always cause disease? N... ays, but these factors influence the likelihood ... ness:

1. Is the s... evere? Severe stress includes the death ... ouse or friend, a divorce, or a financi... s (vs. a hangnail or broken inexpe... lish).
2. Is the s... hronic (occurring every day)?
3. Does th... on perceive the event as stressful?

If the a... to these questions are "yes," the probability ... tress-related illness is greater. Consider what ... e may do in response to stressful situations ... smoke, drink, overeat, not eat). These unh... behaviors increase the chance of illness. Som... s our bodies force us to take it easy when our ... and minds refuse. Research has proved that ... **psychosomatic** disorders (phys-

BOX 9-3   Medical Conditions Associated with Anxiety*

Cardiac
Chest pain
Heart palpitations
Hypertension

Respiratory
Bronchial asthma
Hyperventilation

Digestive
Duodenal ulcer
Ulcerative colitis

Sensory
Deafness
Tinnitus
Nystagmus
Visual blurring

Endocrine
Hypoglycemia
Hyperthyroidism

*Appropriate tests can help physicians determine if these anxiety-related conditions have an organic cause.

ical illness caused by psychological problems) are caused by the effects of stress. Our health and susceptibility to disease also depend on other factors, such as genetic makeup, environmental factors, psychological factors, and the way we cope with problems.

At the first sign of stress, our body responds. Table 9-3 shows the phases and common symptoms of stress.

SHORT-TERM AND LONG-TERM STRESS

How you are able to cope with life's everyday challenges has both short-term and long-term effects on your body. If you allow a stressful situation to control you over a long period, it can have a great impact on your mental and physical health.

When a person does not cope with short-term stress and it becomes long-term stress, the following occurs:

Short Term	**Long Term**
Muscle tension	Headache, backache
Increased blood pressure	Hypertension
Heart palpitations	Heart disease
"Butterflies in stomach"	Ulcers

TABLE 9-3 Phases and Symptoms of Stress

Type	Symptoms
Awareness Stage	
Physical	Increase in blood pressure
	Heart palpitations
	Chills or heavy sweating
	Headaches
Behavioral	Constant irritability
	Inability to sleep
	Grinding the teeth (bruxism)
Psychological	Increased anxiety
	Forgetfulness
	Inability to concentrate
Energy–Conservation	
Physical	Decreased sexual desires
	Constant tiredness
Behavioral	Constant lateness to work or school
	Missing deadlines
	Increased consumption of caffeine or alcohol
Psychological	Putting things off
	Withdrawing from friends
	Negative attitude
	Argumentative
Exhaustion	
Physical	Chronic stomach upsets
	Constant tiredness
	Chronic headaches
Behavioral	Withdrawal from family
Psychological	Depression (sense of hopelessness)
	Mental fatigue

Fig. 9-2 Laughter increases blood circulation, lowering blood pressure. Laughing not only helps you feel good about yourself but also increases the activity of your body's T cells (natural killer cells) and antibodies. Research shows that a baby begins laughing at 2 to 3 months, a 6-year-old child laughs an average of 300 times a day, and an adult only chuckles between 15 and 100 times a day. How many times have you laughed today?

BOX 9-4 Healthy Habits to Reduce Stress

1. Exercise
2. Take deep breaths and stretch several times a day
3. Get adequate sleep
4. Take time for self and family
5. Receive proper nutrition and hydrate with water
6. Laugh (Fig. 9-2)

When a person takes steps to control the short-term stress and to prevent the effects of long-term stress, the following occurs:

Short Term

Exercise: increased circulation
Nutrition and relaxation techniques

Long Term

Good cardiac function
Improves the body's ability to resist disease

Table 9-4 lists disorders associated with long-term stress.

MANAGING STRESS

Knowing how to manage stress in the short term provides long-term rewards. When you are able to control the stress in your everyday life, you achieve

TABLE 9-4 Disorders Associated with Long-Term Stress

System	Disorders
Respiratory	Bronchial asthma
Digestive	Colitis
	Gastritis
	Ulcers (peptic or duodenal)
Circulatory	Hypertension
	Heart attack
	Raynaud disease
Nervous	Migraine headaches
	Cluster headaches
	Twitching
Reproductive	Sexual dysfunction
Integumentary	Eczema

an ov... ...eeling of satisfaction. Your life may becom... ...tic at times because of stressful situations a... ...ie and on the job. You need to be able to mar... ...our stress to stay healthy and provide good ... ...t care. Follow these steps to manage stress i... ...r life:

1. **Rec... ...ze the signs of stress.** Is it physical (e.g... ...ue, illness)? Behavioral (e.g., bad habi... ...motional or mental (e.g., negative thou... ...worries)?

2. **Ide... the cause of the stress.** Is it sickr... ...t injury? Problems at school or work? An a... ...ent with a friend or family member?

3. **Det... ...e the importance of the stress fact...** ...ow important is the cause of the stres... ...worth getting sick or upset over? Wha... ...e worst that could happen?

4. **Wor... ...reduce the impact of the stress fact...** ...e there workable alternatives? Can deleg... ...some of the responsibility help the situa... ...Can prioritizing the duties reduce the s... ...Will simple life changes and better healt... ...ts, such as those in Box 9-4, reduce your ... ...levels?

COP...

You now ... ...stand the importance of managing stress in ... ...veryday life. You also know some ways to r... ...the effects of stress. You can take action wh... ...1 are aware of the problem and how it can be ... ...1, but what about other types of problems? People may have subconscious problems (problems they do not realize they have). Terminal illness is another situation that cannot be "solved" but still must be confronted. People cope with their problems and conflicts in ways that are healthy and in other ways that are not healthy. As a medical assistant you need to know how to work with patients who are coping with conflicts or difficult situations.

Defense Mechanisms

Sometimes we have deep-seated problems that we are not aware of or that we choose to ignore. Our bodies and minds have a way of coping with these types of problems. Freud's unconscious awareness theory implies that we unconsciously avoid situations (conflicts) that could cause us feelings of anxiety (dread, uneasiness). If we cannot recognize the real problem or situation or choose not to confront it directly, we may use a **defense mechanism** to cope with the problem. Defense mechanisms are coping tools that help us deal with conflict. These behavioral responses keep our minds off of the conflict, thus preventing or decreasing anxiety and allowing us to maintain our self-image. We have all used defense mechanisms at one time or another. The key to good mental health is not using defense mechanisms too often instead of facing our real conflicts or problems.

Table 9-5 lists several types of defense mechanisms (the first seven are the most common). You may encounter patients using one or more of these defense mechanisms. Keep in mind that patients can hide a variety of thoughts or feelings (e.g., anger, fear, sadness, depression, helplessness) by using defense mechanisms. It is important that you listen not only to what patients say but also to *how* they say it so that you can "read between the lines" and address the deeper issues.

Death and Dying

One of the most difficult situations that people face is death and dying. Whether they face their own death or that of a loved one, they must learn to cope with the situation. As a medical assistant you may be involved with a terminal (dying) patient. Understanding the stages of the dying process can prepare you to help patients going through this process while maintaining a good relationship with them.

Stages of Grief

Elisabeth Kübler-Ross is known for her research and theories on the dying process, which are based on many studies of terminally ill patients and their families. She believes that dying people, and often

TABLE 9-5 Defense Mechanisms

Term	Definition	Examples
Compensation	When personal strengths in one area are emphasized to cover up a weakness in another area; can be a good thing unless the person gives up too soon on worthwhile tasks or lowers self-expectations when "the going gets tough."	A new medical assistant might brag about how well she did in school to cover up her discomfort at starting a new career. An insecure co-worker may compensate by acting tough and "bullish." A parent may give a child many material things to compensate for not being able to spend much time with the child.
Denial	Refusing to acknowledge or face the unpleasant facts of life. By denying a problem exists, the importance of the unpleasant information or situation is temporarily relieved.	A person who experiences chest pain decides that it is indigestion and buys antacids instead of going to the emergency room. A wife whose husband leaves her tells friends that they have agreed to a trial separation.
Displacement	Behaving aggressively toward someone who cannot fight back as a substitute for anger toward the source of frustration. The bottled-up feeling is taken out on something or someone less threatening (a scapegoat) than what actually caused the negative feelings.	A co-worker who is angry with the physician may take out his anger on another co-worker instead of the physician. A patient tells the physical therapist, "I hate you!" when the physical therapist is trying to help the patient recover from a painful injury.
Fantasy	Daydreaming inappropriately. People using fantasy as a way to cope try to satisfy their desires by imagining achievements.	A trainee in a medical office daydreams about a higher position instead of working on a solution to make it happen. A student who is teased by other students imagines herself taking revenge inappropriately.
Overcompensation	Exaggerated and inappropriate behavior of a person in one area to handle inadequacy in some other area.	A co-worker who feels shy may talk too much or too loudly in an attempt to not be seen as shy. A parent who does not spend enough time with the family works overtime to provide extra money.
Projection	Projecting one's own unacceptable qualities or thoughts onto others or blaming others for these unacceptable qualities or thoughts in oneself.	A medical receptionist who cannot get promoted to office manager because of poor skills projects his failure onto another co-worker by believing the co-worker makes him look bad. A wife who has cheated on her husband may feel guilty and accuse her husband of being unfaithful.
Rationalization	Inventing excuses or reasons for one's behavior.	A medical assistant who talks about a patient's condition with a co-worker rationalizes it with the excuse that the co-worker knows the patient's family so they "need to know" about the patient's condition. A person who has paid too much for an item says, "It's a good investment and the resale value is high."
Aggression	Attacking the real or imaginary source of frustration.	A patient is upset about her medical bill and screams at the medical receptionist.
Conversion reaction	Emotional conflict causes a physical symptom.	A person loses the use of his legs after a car accident that was his fault. There is no neurological cause for the paralysis.

Defense Mechanisms—cont'd

Term	Definition	Examples
Intelle...tion	Making emotional conflict bearable by analyzing it in a logical way.	A person diagnosed with a terminal illness dismisses it by saying, "We all have to die sometime."
Repres...	Blocking out ideas, memories, and feelings that cause conflict. Repression tends to lower self-esteem.	A victim of abuse cannot remember how she got her bruises.
Regres...	Behaving in an immature way when frustrated.	An older child soils his pants in reaction to the birth of a sibling.
Sublim...	Transforming an unconscious conflict into a more socially acceptable form.	An aggressive child works hard to become a star athlete instead of a bully.
Withdr...	Physically or emotionally pulling away from people or conflict.	An office manager's reaction to office conflict is to avoid becoming involved by acting as if the conflict does not exist.

their fam... go through five stages of grief when coming t... ...s with their impending death. These stages on... ...blish guidelines; a person could skip a stage o... ...return to a stage during the dying process. ... ...ast or slow a person moves through a stage v... ...pend on his or her beliefs, values, inner stre... ...spiritual growth, and support system (family a... ...iends). Kübler-Ross's five stages of grief are ... ...ows:

1. **De...** ... a defense mechanism that allows the ... ...t time to deal with the shock. It is usu... ...temporary phase. Reactions may incl... ...y of the following:
   - "... not happening."
   - "... t be true."
   - "... nade a mistake at the lab."
   - C... ...ng physicians.
   - C... ...ing on as if nothing is wrong.
   - R... ...g to talk about the problem.
   - R... ...g treatment.

   As part ... ...e health care team, it is important that you ... ...to patients and not argue. Allow them to ... ...heir frustration and remain calm. Sometime... ...at is needed is for someone to listen without i... ...tion.

2. **Ang...** ... a normal reaction caused by the feeli... ...osing control. Emotions run high at th... ...t, and the anger may turn to rage and ... ...ment directed at anyone in the way. ... ...ons vary but usually include the follo...
   - Te... ...antrums.
   - "W... ...?"

- Feeling of envy toward healthy people.
- Periods of yelling and withdrawal.

Again, listening and allowing the person to vent help the patient deal with this phase.

3. **Bargaining** is making deals with anyone in sight, including the physician, a higher power, and the family. This phase is very goal directed and important; otherwise a person could lapse into despair. The patient may become agreeable and cooperative in an effort to buy more time. Reactions to this phase include the following:
   - "Give me just enough time to see the birth of my grandchild (*or* attend my child's wedding or graduation)."
   - "If I can get a second chance, I will. . . ."

4. **Depression** can be described as an overall feeling of hopelessness. In this stage health is usually declining, pain may be increasing, symptoms are worsening, and relationships may have been severed. Reactions to depression are as follows:
   - Negative body language (e.g., no eye contact, stooped shoulders, excessive sleeping).
   - Not caring about personal appearance.
   - Relief is sought through crying.

Listening and giving reassurance that it is normal to have these feelings benefit the dying patient more than saying the person should not feel this way. *Touch* is reported to help during this time; it is the unspoken word that often meets the need of the patient.

5. **Acceptance** is coming to terms with dying or the loss of a loved one. The patient or family can use this time together to make plans, such as finalizing a will, completing advance directives, and preparing for the funeral. If this phase is reached, the reward is the peace of mind that is achieved. Reactions to this phase are as follows:
   - Planning a trip to a place where the person has always wanted to go.
   - Giving away personal items.
   - Emptying closets of clothes.

Arriving at this stage is the most beneficial of the stages for the patient and the family. **Hospice** is a bundle of services and a team of people helping patients and their families during the end stage of a terminal illness. The hospice team (e.g., physician, nurse, social worker) works on the concept of listening to the needs of the patient and family, whether physical, psychological, or spiritual. The purpose of the team is to preserve the dignity of the dying patient. Hospice is concerned with quality of life, pain management, and offering comfort.

How to Help

Health care workers can best help during the dying process by showing more **empathy** than **sympathy.** Empathy is putting yourself in another person's situation. It means not being judgmental when anger is displayed or when the other person is vocal about the situation. Sympathy is showing concern for a person's situation. People who are dying need someone to understand their emotional state and allow them to express themselves freely. Part of this process is coming to realize that their plans for the future have changed.

Research has shown that dying patients need a good relationship with their health care team (Fig. 9-3). The patient wants to be recognized as a unique

Fig. 9-3 When dealing with terminal patients, show empathy rather than sympathy. Sometimes the best thing you can do is listen.

and whole individual, not just a disease. The family also needs to be recognized as individual people, not just the family of a terminal patient. Studies have shown that if the family's psychological and spiritual needs are met in addition to the treatment of the patient's disease, the dying process is less distressing for all those involved.

PATIENT-CENTERED PROFESSIONALISM

- Why do medical assistants need to understand and to be able to recognize the defense mechanisms used by patients? By co-workers? By themselves?
- As a medical assistant, how can understanding the stages of grief help you work with patients who are dying?
- How can understanding these stages benefit terminal patients' families?
- How does the medical practice benefit when terminal patients and their families are treated with courtesy and respect?

CONCLUSION

As a medical assistant, you will be working with people. You will see many types of behaviors, some positive and some negative. Understanding what causes people to behave the way they do will help you to provide better care to the patients with whom you work. It will also help you to be a more effective member of the health care team. Much research and knowledge exist about human behavior. Patient-centered professionalism means studying this knowledge and applying it in your day-to-day medical assisting duties.

SUMMARY

Reinforce your understanding of the material in this chapter by reviewing the curriculum objectives and key content points below.

1. Define, appropriately use, and spell all the Key Terms for this chapter.
   - Review the Key Terms if necessary.
2. List and briefly define the three parts that make up a person's personality according to Freud.
   - The *id* is concerned with basic unconscious biological drives (e.g., food, sleep).
   - The *ego* is aware of reality and the consequences of behavior.
   - The *superego* (conscience) demands that decisions be made morally and ethically.

3. List three factors that influence personality development.
   - Begins early in life
   - Physical factors
   - Psychological factors

4. List five types of human needs.
   - Abraham Maslow developed the Hierarchy of Needs, which deals with the stages in personal fulfillment: physical needs, safety and security needs, social needs, self-esteem, and self-actualization.

5. Explain the importance of having good self-esteem.
   - Self-esteem deals with feelings of self-worth. Good self esteem permits people to fulfill their potential.

6. List four types of factors that can influence perception.
   Perception is the process of interpreting information gathered from surroundings.
   - Psychological influences include past experiences, assumptions, expectations, knowledge, and emotional moods.
   - Physiological influences include senses, age, nutrition, of experiences, health, fatigue, hunger, and biological cycles.
   - Culture influences what we believe and how we behave; alternative medicine may be a choice.
   - Beliefs about male and female roles (social roles) influence perception.

7. Differentiate between experiencing fear and having a phobia.
   - Fear is an appropriate reaction, whereas a phobia is an irrational fear causing avoidance behavior.

8. List five health problems caused by anxiety or stress.
   - Many health problems can be caused by anxiety or stress, including ulcers, hypertension, heart disease, headache, and backache.

9. Explain how fear, phobia, anxiety, and stress affect a person's mental and physical health.
   - Fears and phobias are mentally crippling and encourage avoidance behavior. Anxiety and stress are part of everyday living. Not learning to deal with these reactions exacts a physical and mental toll on the body.

10. List and describe six defense mechanisms.
    Defense mechanisms are used by the unconscious mind to block out awareness of unpleasant events and help individuals deal with conflict. The most common defense mechanisms are the following:
    - Compensation emphasizes a strength to cover up a weakness.
    - Denial is refusing to acknowledge that a problem exists.
    - Displacement is finding a scapegoat.
    - Fantasy is daydreaming inappropriately.
    - Overcompensation is exaggerated behavior in one area to compensate for inadequacy in another area.
    - Projection is projecting one's unacceptable qualities onto another person or blaming that person for one's shortcomings.

11. List the five stages of grief and briefly describe each in the first person.
    - Denial: "This can't be happening to me."
    - Anger: "I'm a good person; why is this happening to me?"
    - Bargaining: "Just let me live until the baby is born."
    - Depression: "I really am going to die, and there is nothing I can do about it."
    - Acceptance: "I have made my peace, and I am ready to go."

12. Analyze a realistic medical office situation and apply your understanding of human behavior to determine the best course of action.
    - Understanding why patients behave the way they do helps medical assistants interact more positively with them.

13. Describe the impact on patient care when medical assistants understand human behavior.
    - When patients think that the office staff understands and wants to help them, they are more likely to follow their prescribed treatment plan and be satisfied with their care.

FOR FURTHER EXPLORATION

1. **Research other theories about the development of personality.** Understanding the development of personality helps medical assistants provide more effective care to patients. Many theories exist that help people understand how personality develops. Learn about the personality theories of Erik Erikson, Jean Piaget, and Lawrence Kohlberg.
   Keywords: Use the following keywords in your search: Erik Erikson, Jean Piaget, Lawrence Kohlberg, personality development.

2. **Research stress and its effects on humans.** Medical assistants need to understand what stress is, what causes it, how it affects people, and how it can be managed.
   Keywords: Use the following keywords in your search: stress relief, stress, effects of stress, stress-related illness.

Chapter Review

Vocabulary Review

Matching

Match each term with the correct definition.

A. anger

B. compensation

C. defense mechanism

D. depression

E. empathy

F. homeostasis

G. perception

H. phobias

I. physiological

J. psychiatry

K. psychology

L. self-esteem

M. stress

N. subconscious

O. sympathy

_____ 1. Having to do with the body's responses to its internal and external environment

_____ 2. Filtering tactic used by the unconscious to avoid unpleasant situations

_____ 3. Understanding how someone else feels by placing yourself in his or her place

_____ 4. Body in balance

_____ 5. Reaction due to the feeling of loss of control

_____ 6. Feeling of self-worth

_____ 7. Body's response to any demand put on it, whether it be positive or negative

_____ 8. Individual's view of a situation based on the environment

_____ 9. Having concern for a patient's situation

_____ 10. Overall feeling of hopelessness

_____ 11. Irrational fears of objects, activities, or situations

_____ 12. Scientific study of the mind and the behavioral patterns of humans and animals

_____ 13. Defense mechanism in which a strength is emphasized to cover up a weakness in another area

_____ 14. Part of the conscious that is not fully aware

_____ 15. Medical specialty that deals with the treatment and prevention of mental illness

The___ ___ecall

True ___ ___

Indic___ ___ether the sentence or statement is true or false.

_____ ___e study of human behavior helps us understand how people learn, feel emotions, and ___tablish relationships.

_____ ___e id is the part of the personality that is aware of reality and of the consequences of different ___haviors.

_____ ___mund Freud, a German psychologist, was interested in the understanding of dreams.

_____ ___e superego is concerned with the internalization of values and standards designed to promote ___per social balance.

_____ ___owing how to manage stress in the short term provides long-term rewards.

Multip___ ___oice

Identify ___ ___tter of the choice that best completes the statement or answers the question.

1. Of ___ ___llowing statements, which response BEST describes factors that influence the development of per___ ___ty?
   A. ___ s in early development form all of a person's personality.
   B. ___ ___logical factors such as poverty or wealth do not contribute to an individual's personality.
   C. ___ ___c factors are the only true markers of personality.
   D. ___ of the above statements are correct.

2. In ___ ___v's Hierarchy of Needs, _____ needs are being met when we feel loved and appreciated.
   A. ___
   B. ___ ___al
   C. ___
   D. ___ ___ualization

3. Wh___ ___s level of Maslow's hierarchy is achieved, an individual has a sense of being in control.
   A. ___ ___il
   B. S___ ___eem
   C. S___
   D. S___ ___ualization

4. _____ ___e process of interpreting information gathered from our surroundings.
   A. E___ ___tions
   B. P___ ___ons
   C. S___ ___em
   D. C___ ___sus

5. _____ ___e of the primary levels of Maslow's hierarchy.
   A. H___
   B. Fa___
   C. Pa___ ___eriences
   D. Ag___

6. _____ are (is) a psychological influence on how we perform.
   A. Senses
   B. Number of experiences
   C. Expectations
   D. Health

7. Young adults are moving from the _____ concept concerning education, job, home, and family.
   A. us to them
   B. I to we
   C. you to them
   D. them to them

8. Fear is a(n) _____ reaction to _____ danger.
   A. abnormal, perceived
   B. normal, perceived
   C. abnormal, genuine
   D. normal, genuine

9. An emotional response that alerts the body to take appropriate action to protect itself from danger is _____.
   A. fight or flight
   B. fright or freeze
   C. flee or be
   D. none of the above

10. Of the following which is NOT a phobia category?
    A. Interference
    B. Simple
    C. Social
    D. Agoraphobia

11. _____ is the feeling of apprehension, uneasiness, or uncertainty about a situation.
    A. Fear
    B. Anxiety
    C. Phobia
    D. Stress

12. Symptoms of anxiety include all of the following EXCEPT _____.
    A. inability to sleep
    B. self-doubt
    C. difficulty breathing
    D. direct eye contact

13. During periods of _____, our natural body defense systems weaken, fatigue takes over, and we become more susceptible to disease.
    A. fear
    B. stress
    C. anxiety
    D. elation

14. Resear ___ proved that many _____ disorders are caused by the effects of stress.
    A. psy ___ natic
    B. phy ___ ical
    C. psy ___ c
    D. ter ___

15. Long-___ ress can cause any or all of the following disorders EXCEPT _____.
    A. hea ___
    B. ulc ___
    C. mu ___ nsion
    D. hy ___ ion

16. If a p___ annot recognize a real problem or situation, or chooses not to face it head-on, a _____ may ___ to cope with it.
    A. psy ___ matic disorder
    B. de ___ echanism
    C. ph ___
    D. ter ___ illness

17. _____ ___ fense mechanism that allows a patient to deal with the shock of death.
    A. De ___
    B. An ___
    C. Ba ___ g
    D. All ___ above

18. _____ ___ process of making deals with anyone in sight, including the physician, a higher power, and/o ___ ly members when dealing with grief.
    A. De ___
    B. An ___
    C. Ba ___ g
    D. All ___ above

19. _____ ___ ing to terms with dying or the loss of a loved one
    A. De ___
    B. Ac ___ ce
    C. De ___ n
    D. An ___

20. Puttin ___ rself in another person's situation is called (a) _____.
    A. de ___ echanism
    B. em ___
    C. syr ___
    D. soc ___

21. _____ ___ sidered daydreaming inappropriately.
    A. Dis ___ nent
    B. Pro ___ n
    C. Fan ___
    D. Co ___ ation

22. Inventing excuses or reasons for one's behavior is called _____.
    A. compensation
    B. rationalization
    C. repression
    D. sublimation

23. A co-worker who feels shy may talk too much or too loudly in an attempt to not be seen as shy. This is called _____.
    A. rationalization
    B. aggression
    C. displacement
    D. overcompensation

24. Physically or emotionally pulling away from people and/or conflict is called _____.
    A. conversion reaction
    B. sublimation
    C. withdrawal
    D. repression

25. An example of a simple phobia might include _____.
    A. fear of being ridiculed
    B. fear of snakes
    C. fear of public speaking
    D. fear of crowds

Sentence Completion

Complete each sentence or statement.

1. _____ is a package of services and a team of people helping patients and their families during the last months of a terminal illness.

2. Studies have shown that if a family's psychological and _____ needs are met in addition to the treatment of the patient's disease, the dying process is less distressing for all concerned.

3. _____ is a change for many people because their children are independent, often leaving home, and a void is created.

4. We recall _____ when we perform similar tasks: "I've never been very good at it" versus "With some help, I am ready to tackle this."

5. Physical needs are met when the body is in _____.

Short Answers

1. List in order of importance for survival Maslow's Hierarchy of Needs.

_____

_____

_____

_____

2. Explain why it is important to YOU to have a good self-esteem.

_____

_____

_____

_____

_____

3. Contrast the differences among fear, phobia, anxiety, and stress.

_____

_____

_____

_____

_____

_____

4. List and describe six defense mechanisms.

_____

_____

_____

_____

_____

_____

_____

Critical Thinking

Tanya was hired by Dr. Ortega, an oncologist, 2 months ago. Many of Dr. Ortega's patients are terminally ill, and four patients have passed away this week. Tanya is not sure that she can cope personally with so many terminally ill patients. Tanya's mother died of breast cancer last year, which was one of the reasons that Tanya originally wanted to work for an oncologist. After a particularly upsetting day, Dr. Ortega asked Tanya to meet with her in her office, after the last appointment of the day. Dr. Ortega asked Tanya how she is handling the loss of the patients. "It has been very difficult. I am not sure that I am working through it. We talked about death and dying in school, but other than my mother passing away from cancer last year, I have never been around anyone else who has died." Dr. Ortega and Tanya talked for quite a while about ways for Tanya to work through the loss of her mother and come to terms with her overall feelings of death and then how she can best be supportive of the clinic's patients and families. Dr. Ortega gave Tanya a list of books on death and dying to read on her own and a homework assignment to write her own obituary if she were to die tomorrow and a second one if she were to die of old age at 93. Tanya thanked Dr. Ortega for being so understanding and promised to read the books, and even though she was extremely uncomfortable with writing her own obituary, she agreed to try.

A. Write your own obituary as if you were to die tomorrow.

B. Write your own obituary as if you were to die of old age at 93.

Internet Research

Keyword: Medical phobias

Research three websites and list five medical phobias. Cite the source of your information.

What Would You Do?

If you have accomplished the objectives in this chapter, you will be able to make better choices as a medical assistant. Take a look at this situation and decide what you would do.

Sara Ann is a 22-year-old single mother and a medical assistant. She has no assistance at home with child care or with any of the chores necessary to keep up a household. Sara Ann works as many hours as she can to support herself and her two children in the best way possible. On top of all of this, going to school has added major financial problems for Sara Ann.

On many days, Sara Ann is tired and frustrated, and wonders just how she will get through the day. Because of her lack of self-esteem and the lack of help, anxiety and stress are affecting the way Sara Ann deals with co-workers. Sara Ann's anxiety level often leads her to label patients. In addition, Sara Ann has difficulty adapting to any variation in the daily schedule.

Because Sara Ann feels close to some patients with whom she has spent time in the medical office, she often discusses her personal problems with these patients. Also, Sara Ann must handle some of her personal business (banking, errands) while at work because she does not leave work early enough to do these things when the businesses are open.

Sara Ann is experiencing a lot of stress, which is having an impact on her performance at work. If you were in Sara Ann's situation, what would you do to reduce stress?

1. How are Sara Ann's reactions to her work understandable under the circumstances? What reactions are related to the anxiety and loss of self-esteem?

_____

_____

_____

_____

_____

2. How are Sara Ann's reactions typical for someone who is not coping with personal or professional world?

_____

_____

_____

3. What are some of the reactions that you would expect from Sara Ann's fellow employees about her behavior?

_____

_____

_____

4. Where in Maslow's Hierarchy of Needs would you place Sara Ann? Why did you place her at that level?

_____

_____

_____

_____

5. Because Sara Ann has no one at home for emotional or financial support, how would you, as a patient, feel if she told you about her problems? Are her actions of involving patients ethical? Why?

_____

_____

_____

_____

Application of Skills

1. Select one defense mechanism from Table 9-5 and create a situational example of how a patient may exhibit the behaviors associated with the mechanism regarding an illness (two-paragraph minimum, single spaced).

2. Conduct research on the Internet or local library for methods of stress reduction. Select one method that appeals to you. Over the next 2 days, practice the method of stress reduction you selected at least once. Describe the method and your experience. Was it beneficial? Would you use it again?

3. Based on Maslow's Hierarchy of Needs, describe how to best respond to the following situations addressing physical and emotional needs.

   A. Angry patient: self-esteem

   _____

   _____

   _____

   B. Newly diagnosed terminal illness: safety

   _____

   _____

   _____

   C. Positive pregnancy test: survival and self-actualization

   _____

   _____

   _____

Chapter Quiz

Multiple Choice

Identify the letter of the choice that best completes the statement or answers the question.

1. Coming to terms with an issue (e.g., impending death or loss) is _____.
   A. depression
   B. anxiety
   C. acceptance
   D. compensation

2. The ___'s response to threat is called _____.
   A. ___ or flight
   B. l___ ___ing
   C. ___ ___alization
   D. ___ ___mpensation

3. The ___ of the personality that includes values and standards designed to promote proper behavior is called ___e) _____.
   A. i___
   B. e___
   C. s___ ___go
   D. s___ ___eem

4. _____ ___ defense mechanism in which there is an unconscious rejection of an unacceptable thought, desi___ ___pulse, and placing blame on someone else.
   A. R___ ___lization
   B. D___
   C. S___ ___scious
   D. P___ ___on

5. The ___ ___s the part of the brain associated with basic unconscious biological drives.
   A. id
   B. eg___
   C. su___ ___
   D. se___ ___em

6. _____ ___n Austrian physician who was interested in the development of the mind in order to treat psych___ ___cal problems.
   A. M___
   B. Ju___
   C. Hi___ ___ates
   D. Fr___

7. _____ ___edical specialty that deals with the treatment and prevention of mental illness.
   A. Psy___ ___gy
   B. Psy___ ___ry
   C. Ph___ ___gy
   D. Or___ ___y

8. The fi___ ___el of Maslow's hierarchy and the foundation of a person's motivational drive is _____.
   A. sec___ ___needs
   B. soc___ ___eds
   C. phy___ ___needs
   D. self___ ___m

9. The n___ ___ be all that you can be is called _____.
   A. soc___
   B. self ___m
   C. self ___ting
   D. self ___lization

10. Self-esteem can fluctuate throughout the day based on the challenges a person faces.
    A. True
    B. False

11. _____ is (are) the process of interpreting information gathered from our surroundings.
    A. Subconscious
    B. Perception
    C. Assumptions
    D. Past experiences

12. Physiological influences of what we sense and feel and how we perform include all of the following EXCEPT _____.
    A. fatigue
    B. age
    C. gender
    D. senses

13. _____ are irrational fears of objects, activities, or situations.
    A. Phobias
    B. Defense mechanisms
    C. Rationalizations
    D. Psychiatric responses

14. _____ is the fear of blood.
    A. Agoraphobia
    B. Hemophobia
    C. Claustrophobia
    D. Arachnophobia

15. _____ is the fear of water.
    A. Apiphobia
    B. Hydrophobia
    C. Agoraphobia
    D. Phagophobia

16. Glossophobia is the fear of speaking in public.
    A. True
    B. False

17. Physical symptoms of stress include all of the following EXCEPT _____.
    A. forgetfulness
    B. chronic upset stomach
    C. headaches
    D. chills or heavy sweating

18. Dep___ ___ is a psychological symptom of stress.
    A. T___
    B. F___

19. Beh___ ___ aggressively toward someone who cannot fight back as a substitute for anger toward the sour___ ___ frustration is called _____.
    A. c___ ___sation
    B. d___ ___ement
    C. fa___
    D. p___ ___on

20. Exag___ ___d and inappropriate behavior of a person in one area to handle inadequacy in some other area___ ___ed _____.
    A. a___ ___on
    B. in___ ___tualization
    C. su___ ___ation
    D. o___ ___mpensation

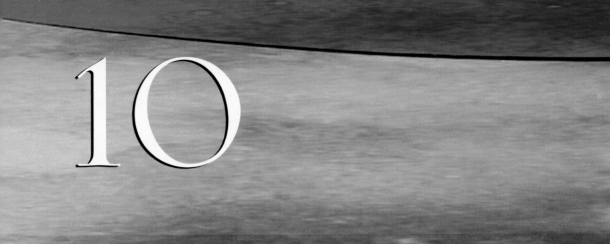

10

OBJECTIVES

You will be able to do the following after completing this chapter:

Key Terms
1. Define, appropriately use, and spell all the Key Terms for this chapter.

Development
2. List and describe the three areas of change during growth and development in a lifetime.
3. For each age level, list two age-appropriate ways that medical assistants can enhance interaction with patients.
4. Describe the basic developmental milestones for each developmental stage.
5. Explain why the medical assistant must understand the various body system changes involved in the aging process.

Cultural Diversity
6. List eight areas in which cultural differences exist.
7. Explain the importance of being knowledgeable about the cultural background of a patient.

Response to Illness
8. List four types of responses that patients commonly have toward illness.
9. List five things you can do when a patient becomes angry.

Patient-Centered Professionalism
10. Analyze a realistic medical office situation and apply your understanding of the patient's background and behavior to determine the best course of action.
11. Describe the impact on patient care when medical assistants understand how people react to illness and medical care and how they change at various stages of development.

Understanding Patient Behavior

KEY TE[RMS]

adulthood [Part of] the human life span concerned with an
  individu[al during] early, middle, and later years in life.

childhood [Part of] the human life span dealing with toddlers,
  presch[oolers,] school-age children, and adolescents.

cultural di[versity] A mix of ethnicity, race, and religion in a
  given p[opulatio]n.

developme[nt] [Pro]gressive increase of body function throughout
  one's lif[e.]

infancy Part of the human life span including birth through the
  first year.

mental growth An individual's cognitive development.

physical growth An individual's growth and development in
  physical size and in motor and sensory skills.

psychosocial growth An individual's emotional and social
  development.

What Would You Do?

Read the following scenario and keep it in mind as you learn about the importance of understanding patient behavior in this chapter.

Juan, 40 years old, has moved to the United States. His family is still in Mexico, but he hopes to find a good job soon and pay for them to come to the United States. Because Juan does not speak English very well, he has had difficulty finding employment and a place to live. Lately, he has been staying at a shelter for homeless people. His educational background is limited, and his broken English makes communicating difficult. Few Hispanic people live in the area where he has settled. Juan has lost 10 pounds, his vision is declining, and he has noticed that he is not hearing as well as he used to. Because of his constant weight loss and the vision problems, Juan decided to visit the local medical office. He has heard the office provides services to those who cannot pay.

When Juan arrives at the office his clothing is worn and torn. The new medical assistant tells Juan that he cannot be seen at the office unless he can pay for his visit before he is seen. She doesn't explain her statement, and because of his broken English, Juan doesn't ask further questions. He thinks that the physician will not see him and leaves the office very upset. He decides to start taking herbal medications and try home remedies. He now believes that seeing a physician in America just is not worth the trouble and embarrassment. Several weeks later, Juan is hospitalized with dehydration, starvation, and severe reactions to the herbal drugs.

This situation did not have to result in Juan's being hospitalized. If you were the new medical assistant, what would you have done differently?

In Chapter 9 you learned how personality, perception, motivation, self-esteem, and factors such as stress and anxiety affect human behavior. These elements, among others, also influence the way a person will *behave* as a patient in a medical setting. A patient's age not only influences the patient's behavior but also determines how the medical assistant should interact with the patient. Cultural differences can also influence patient behavior. Patients may have certain cultural beliefs that conflict with recommended treatment. There is the potential for communication problems with patients who do not speak English well. Finally, any patient can become irritated while waiting for the physician, or simply because the patient is not feeling well. This may bring on complaints or anger. Medical assistants need to understand how to work effectively with patients of all ages and stages of development as well as patients of all cultures.

DEVELOPMENT

Growth and change occur throughout our entire lives. Our bodies and body systems change, and so does the way we think, behave, and react. We have different needs at each stage in our lives. To provide effective care for patients from all age groups, medical assistants must understand the basic changes that people go through during their lifetime. Understanding these changes allows medical assistants to meet the needs of all patients in the health care setting.

There are basically three areas or categories of change during growth and **development** that occur in the human life span, as follows:

1. **Physical growth** (physical size, motor and sensory skills)
2. **Mental growth** (cognitive development, thinking, and understanding)
3. **Psychosocial growth** (emotional and social development)

As people approach each life stage, both heredity (genetics) and the environment influence their development. Basic principles of growth and development include the following:

- Each person is unique from the time of conception. Standards of development are only guidelines.
- Growth is continuous; it does not occur at the same rate for everyone.
- As physical size increases, skills will increase proportionately.
- Development depends on the balance among physical, mental, and psychosocial changes.
- If basic needs are not met, an individual's growth pattern is usually altered.

The human life span can be divided into the following three major phases:

1. Infancy: infants from birth to 1 year.
2. Childhood: toddlers, preschoolers, school-age children, and adolescents.

3. Ad...od: adults in the early, middle, late,
an... stages of life.

As a ...al assistant, you need to understand
the phys... ...ental, and psychosocial changes that
occur in ... phase so that you can interact posi-
tively wi... ...ients and their families while attending to pa... ...' age-related needs.

Infancy ...h to 1 Year)

Develop... ...through the **infancy** stage relies on
some far... ...ructure. The family's main role is to
foster se... ...allowing for growth and development of ... ...ersonality, body, and intellect of the
infant. P... ...l growth occurs in spurts.

Resear... ...roves that normal development
requires ... ...tinuous close relationship with nur-
turing ir... ...uals (mother, father, grandparents,
guardian... ...iver).

Birth   Months
Physica   *ory and Motor)*
Front fo...   (soft spot) will close
Fist to n...
Opens a...   ...ses hand
Raises h...   ...d chest (Fig. 10-1)

Mental   *tive)*
Reacts t...   ...d, motion, and light
Reacts t...   ...iver's voice
Hands a...   ...s coordinate
Imitates...   ...sounds

Psychos...   *Emotional and Social)*
Coos wh...   ...ppy
Smiles a...   ...eks
Cries wh...   ...d and uncomfortable

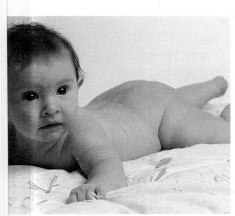

Fig. 10-1 ...onth-old child is able to raise the head
and chest. ...*Sorrentino SA:* Mosby's assisting with
patient car... ...*uis, 1999, Mosby.)*

Medical Assistants Should:
- Make eye contact when speaking
- Involve parents or guardians; when demonstrating procedures for home care, have them practice
- Encourage repeating of cooing and happy sounds made by the infant
- Share developmental status with caregivers and encourage bright-colored toys
- Focus on parents' concerns

4 to 7 Months
Physical
Nose-breathes   Permanent eye color
Respirations of 60 breaths   Doubles birth weight
  per minute   Rolls over and sits up
Teeth erupt   Grasps objects
Eye coordination good   (Fig. 10-2)
Relies on vision to
  explore environment

Mental
Explores by banging, dropping, and throwing
Reaches

Psychosocial
Imitates inflections of voices
Shows anger or tantrums
Self-entertaining (plays with hands and feet)

Medical Assistants Should:
- Make eye contact when speaking
- Involve parents or guardians; when demonstrating procedures for home care, have them practice
- Encourage grasping toys and toys with sound
- Follow up on prior health concerns
- Share developmental status with caregivers
- Review immunization records with caregivers
- Focus on eating and sleeping habits

The infant responds to touch and smiling. Parental involvement increases cooperativeness. *(From Chester GA:* Modern medical assisting, *Philadelphia, 1998, Saunders.)*

Fig. 10-2   A 6-month-old child is able to sit and grasp objects. *(From Sorrentino SA:* Mosby's assisting with patient care, *St Louis, 1999, Mosby.)*

Fig. 10-3   A 9-month-old child can enjoy his image in a mirror. *(From Christensen BL, Kockrow EO:* Foundations of nursing, *ed 4, St Louis, 2003, Mosby.)*

8 to 12 Months

Physical
Crawls
Stands upright
Increased interest in exploration
Able to grasp with thumb and forefinger

Mental
Shakes head "no"
Waves "bye-bye"
Begins to equate sound with action (running water to bathe)

Psychosocial
Smiles at self in mirror (Fig. 10-3)
Does not like confinement
Buries head in caregiver's shoulder (acts shy)

Medical Assistants Should:
- Make eye contact when speaking
- Involve parents or guardians; when demonstrating procedures for home care, have them practice
- Encourage playing with large blocks for stacking
- Be aware of family stresses that could interfere with the child's health

Childhood

Many changes occur during **childhood.** As a toddler becomes a preschooler, expectations about physical, mental, and psychosocial characteristics and abilities are raised. As a child becomes an adolescent, important body changes occur, and psychosocial issues are important.

Toddler (13 Months to 3 Years)

The toddler grows slowly, gaining only 5 to 10 pounds and growing 3 inches. Overall development speeds along as toddlers learn to walk, speak their first words, and refine their dexterity skills. They develop a unique personality, and if the environment is positive they will explore and learn.

13 to 18 Months

Physical
Coordination improves   Stacks objects
Feeds self (Fig. 10-4)   Points with index finger
Walks without support

Mental
Knows names and can point to body parts
Recognizes picture book upside down

Psychosocial
Has not grasped warnings,   Has separation
  but knows praise   anxiety
Tantrums more frequent   Self-loving

Medical Assistants Should:
- Make eye contact when speaking
- Involve parents or guardians; when demonstrating procedures for home care, have them practice

Fig. 10-4 ...ddler is able to use a spoon as coordina-tion impr... *From Sorrentino SA:* Mosby's assisting with patient c... *Louis, 1999, Mosby.)*

- Revi... ...munization records with current recom-men... ...hedule
- Revi... ...elopmental status with caregivers and provi... ...ormation on expectations
- Enco... ...space for movement
- Obse... ...havior and interaction with peers
- Enco... ...n identifying body parts (e.g., "Where's your...")

Establis... ...ust is important in gaining a toddler's coopera... *From Chester GA:* Modern medical assistin... ...delphia, 1998, Saunders.)

19 to ...onths

Physic...
Runs a... ...lbs
Can kic... ...l
Bladde... ...owel control
Drinks ... ...cup (Fig. 10-5)
Draws ...

Menta...
"So big... ...'all gone"
Voices ... ...ion

Psycho...
Sharing... ...a concept; "mine"
Feeling... ...pparent
Gives h... ...d kisses

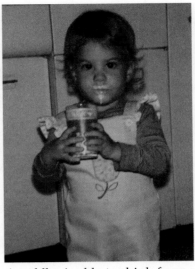

Fig. 10-5 A toddler is able to drink from a cup. *(From Christensen BL, Kockrow EO:* Foundations of nursing, *ed 4, St Louis, 2003, Mosby.)*

Medical Assistants Should:
- Make eye contact when speaking
- Involve parents and guardians; when demonstrat-ing procedures for home care, have them practice
- Review schedule of immunization
- Review developmental status with caregivers and provide information on expectations
- Encourage action toys (e.g., pushcart, telephone)
- Focus on eating, sleeping, and elimination
- Provide large crayons for drawing

24 to 36 Months

Physical
Can hop
Toilet training concluded

Mental
Sentences and vocabulary improve
Grasps categories of animals such as cats and dogs

Psychosocial
Likes to help
Can play alone (Fig. 10-6)
Says "no" more often

Medical Assistants Should:
- Make eye contact when speaking
- Develop rapport by explaining procedures to the child first and using words the child understands

Continued

Fig. 10-6 A toddler can self-entertain. *(From Christensen BL, Kockrow EO:* Foundations of nursing, *ed 4, St Louis, 2003, Mosby.)*

Fig. 10-7 Three-year-old children enjoy drawing, coloring, and cut-and-paste activities. *(From Sorrentino SA:* Mosby's assisting with patient care, *St Louis, 1999, Mosby.)*

- Demonstrate procedures on a toy and let the child do the procedure on the toy
- Praise expected behavior
- Provide parents with information on accident prevention and respiratory infections because these are the main health problems of toddlers
- Provide books or toys, blow bubbles, or pretend-play to build rapport or distract when necessary
- Involve parents and guardians; when demonstrating procedures for home care, have them practice

Preschool (3 to 5 Years)

By the time they reach the early preschool stage, children have developed attitudes, beliefs, and expectations about life. Unfavorable experiences during this phase can lead to mistrust and may hamper attempts at trying new things. Reassuring children during this phase is important.

36 to 48 Months

Physical
Can dress and undress self
Pedals and steers a tricycle
Can hold a pencil, draw, and color (Fig. 10-7)
Assembles simple puzzles
Can use small scissors and small musical instruments

Mental
Knows the difference between same and different
Can hear and tell a story
Wants to know "why"
Can organize experiences into concepts

Psychosocial
Increased social awareness
Sensitive to feelings
Needs rules
Separation anxiety
Makes decisions between two possibilities

Medical Assistants Should:
- Make eye contact when speaking
- Keep the caregiver in sight
- Build rapport by letting the child help (e.g., undressing)
- Use toys, hand puppets, or nurse or doctor kits to build rapport and distract when necessary
- Involve parents and guardians; when demonstrating procedures for home care, have them practice

Hands-on play or puppet play helps to alleviate the preschooler's fears. *(From Chester GA:* Modern medical assisting, *Philadelphia, 1998, Saunders.)*

Fig. 10-8 year-old children enjoy helping a parent. *(From Sorr SA:* Mosby's assisting with patient care, *St Louis, 1 osby.)*

Fig. 10-9 Belonging to a peer group is important to 6-year-old children. *(From Sorrentino SA:* Mosby's assisting with patient care, *St Louis, 1999, Mosby.)*

School Age (6 to 11 Years)
If a child has progressed through other experiences with little difficulty, the school-age years will be a time for physical and emotional growth.

4 to 5 s
Physical
Grows 2 ½ inches each year
Jumps r
Can lear int first name
Has exce energy

Mental
Can cou
Can lear ess and telephone number
Has a sh ention span
Develop oncept and body image

Psychos
Is asserti l independent
Relates t ortant people, caregivers, and siblings
(Fig. 1
Can follc s, but will stretch them
Behavior ied by reward and punishment
Can lear ers
Makes complex decisions among three
possib

Medical nts Should:
• Make ntact when speaking
• Provic rds for good behavior (e.g., sticker)
• Involv hild; demonstrate the procedure and
let th d be involved in treatments (e.g.,
nebul
• Let th express feelings
• Provic tive activities and puzzles
• Involv ts and guardians; when demonstrat-
ing p ures for home care, have them
practic

Physical
Loses baby teeth
Growth is slow and steady
Can assume responsibility (e.g., pet care)
Likes organized sports

Mental
Can use logic	Acquires knowledge
Will listen to other opinions	and new skills
Learns to compromise	quickly

Psychosocial
Peers gain importance (Fig. 10-9)
Family group not first
Will seek praise (Fig. 10-10)
Written rules acceptable

Medical Assistants Should:
• Make eye contact when speaking
• Explain procedures in correct but age-appropriate terminology
• Respect privacy; knock before entering
• Allow independence to make health choices
• Tell jokes or riddles; ask if the child has any to tell
• Praise good behavior
• Involve parents and guardians; when demonstrating procedures for home care, have them practice

Continued

Fig. 10-10 Being recognized as the big brother is gratifying for the school-age child. *(From Jarvis C:* Physical examination and health assessment, *ed 4, Philadelphia, 2004, Saunders.)*

The child in early elementary school responds well to praise and recognition. *(From Chester GA:* Modern medical assisting, *Philadelphia, 1998, Saunders.)*

Adolescent (12 to 18 Years)

Adolescence is the developmental stage between childhood and early adulthood. It can be the most confusing time for the adolescent and the caregiver. Peer pressure becomes an issue, and the adolescent is concerned with conforming to peers in dress, language, and goals. The caregiver does remain influential over values and long-term goals.

Physical
Rapid growth
Some awkward movements
Increased hormones
Increased appetite
Easily fatigued
Fine motor skills improve (Fig. 10-11)

Mental
Abstract and logical thinking
Cause and effect

Fig. 10-11 Movements are more coordinated and graceful in late childhood. *(From Sorrentino SA:* Mosby's assisting with patient care, *St Louis, 1999, Mosby.)*

Self-esteem development
Identity issues
Sets goals

Psychosocial
Confusion over growth changes
Appearance important
Self-esteem issues arise
Wants to be independent, but wants some dependence
Develops relationship with the opposite gender
Peers are primary influence (Fig. 10-12)

Medical Assistants Should:
* Make eye contact when speaking
* Be aware that illness is a threat to self-esteem and body image
* Allow adolescents to ask questions, and respect their opinions
* Avoid judgments concerning appearance
* Recognize that illness causes anxiety because the fear of always being dependent is strong
* Let adolescents help plan care
* Respect privacy issues
* Be aware of possible body image problems
* Ask about hobbies or organized physical sports
* If appropriate, demonstrate procedures for home care and have them practice

Fig. 10-1[   ]rs are the primary influence for the adolescent. (F[   ]rvis C: Physical examination and health assessmen[   ] Philadelphia, 2004, Saunders.)

Fig. 10-13   Young adults begin to develop a strong sense of responsibility. *(From Jarvis C:* Physical examination and health assessment, *ed 4, Philadelphia, 2004, Saunders.)*

The add[   ]t must be treated with respect and given au[   ]y. *(From Chester GA:* Modern medical [   ]ng, *Philadelphia, 1998, Saunders.)*

Adultho[   ]

Progressio[   ]o **adulthood** is often defined by changing [   ]l roles and family expectations. This phase be[   ]n the late teens (about age 19) and continue[   ]l the individual dies. As the body ages, cha[   ]ccur in each body system.

Early Adu[   ]d (19 to 45 Years)

Physica[   ]
Growth [   ]ge 30
Muscle e[   ]cy peaks in late 20s
Skin ton[   ]with decreased moisture
Some vi[   ]ianges
Decrease[   ]ring in high tones

Mental
Learning easier in early years
Takes longer to focus on new things

Psychosocial
Ages 20 to 30: evaluates future
Looks for place in society
Ages 30 to 45: reevaluates work, family, and social issues
Plans for economic security
Sense of responsibility (Fig. 10-13)
Some health care concerns

Medical Assistants Should:
- Make eye contact when speaking
- Provide education for lifestyle changes
- Explain options and offer choices
- Understand that illness at this time may cause self-image and self-esteem issues
- Recognize that medical treatment may be seen as a threat
- Be aware that illness during this stage can bring on anxiety responses or depression; the patient may revert to the defense mechanism of *denial*, which can prevent timely recovery and treatment
- Provide education for home health care if necessary (e.g., insulin testing)

Fig. 10-14 Middle-age adults often have more time for activities they enjoy. *(From Sorrentino SA:* Mosby's assisting with patient care, *St Louis, 1999, Mosby.)*

The medical assistant should use brochures to help teach patients.

Middle Age (45 to 59 Years)

Physical

Bone mass decreases	Hair decreases
Muscle mass declines	Slower reflexes
Wrinkles appear	Glasses may be required for reading

Mental
Short-term memory decreases
Looks back over life experiences
Stress response prolonged

Psychosocial
Begins to settle in on future goals
Concerns about health
May have to care for parents and family
May experience "empty nest" syndrome
Pursues hobbies and areas of interest (Fig. 10-14)
Measures accomplishments against goals

Medical Assistants Should:
- Make eye contact when speaking
- Give patients options and alternatives
- Provide literature on optimal health
- Provide education for home health care if necessary

Mature Adult (60 to 69 Years)

Physical

Heat and cold tolerance decreases	Hearing loss continues
Circulation to extremities decreases	Sense of smell and taste decreases
Skin thins and loses elasticity	Less saliva
Hair thins	Dexterity decreases
Loss of height	

Mental
Life-sharing memories

Psychosocial

Ages 60 to 70: comfort and acceptance (Fig. 10-15)	Examines feelings of self-worth
Mellowing	Retirement
Privacy important	Changes in relationships because of death, illness, and birth of grandchildren
Friends important	
Values high for truth and sincerity	
	Comes to terms with own death

Medical Assistants Should:
- Make eye contact when speaking
- Know the patient's support system
- Know how the patient receives nutrition
- Provide education for home health care if necessary

Later Maturity (70+ Years)

Physical
Gastrointestinal system slows down
Less absorption of nutrients
Drugs processed more slowly
Fat lost, so bones protrude
Bones more porous
Skin pigment changes (Fig. 10-16)
Skin sensitive and tears easily

Fig. 10-15 e and companionship are important to the matur . *(From Sorrentino SA: Mosby's assisting with patie St Louis, 1999, Mosby.)*

Cardiac output slows
Hardening of blood vessels
Urinary system problems (loss of bladder muscle tone)
Balance is decreased
Sleeps less

Mental
Learning is possible, but slower
Short-term memory declines further

Psychosocial
Relationships decrease because of death
Reflective
Living arrangements may need to be adjusted (Fig. 10-17)

Medical Assistants Should:
- Make eye contact when speaking
- Understand how the effects of aging decrease resilience and alter lifestyle
- Continue to assess the support system
- Be aware that nutrition and fluid intake needs increase
- Repeat directions as needed; mature adults may be slower to interpret sensory input
- Provide education for home health care if necessary

Medical assistants can help mature patients and their families accept and adjust to age-related changes.

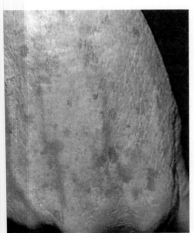

Fig. 10-16 pigment changes occur in later maturity. *(From L ill DP, Marks JG: Principles of dermatology, ed 2, P hia, 1993, Saunders.)*

Fig. 10-17 As a person reaches later maturity, living arrangements may need to be altered. *(From Sorrentino SA: Mosby's assisting with patient care, St Louis, 1999, Mosby.)*

PATIENT-CENTERED PROFESSIONALISM

- An infant's physical growth occurs in spurts. Why is it important for medical assistants to know what to expect concerning an infant's cognitive and social growth at 2-month through 12-month visits? How does the infant and the family benefit from a medical assistant who understands infant physical growth?
- As a child progresses from a toddler to an adolescent, many psychosocial changes occur that have an impact on self-esteem. How can medical assistants use their knowledge of expected changes during this time to provide better care to an adolescent patient?
- As a young adult moves through the life span, what changes in physical aspects and mental focus are expected? Does a feeling of self-worth have any impact on how a person approaches these life span changes? How can medical assistants use their understanding of these changes to provide better care to adult patients?

BOX 10-1 Different Cultures, Different Beliefs

- In the United States, the color black is a sign of mourning; to certain Asian cultures, the color white means mourning.
- Iranians (and other groups) may believe that all things are predetermined.
- Some cultures believe good health is a reward from a higher power, whereas other cultures may not believe in a higher power at all.
- Some cultures believe demons and evil spirits are the cause of illness, whereas other cultures believe illness is caused only by disease or injury.
- Many Americans believe in outward demonstrations of affection and engage in more casual touching than other cultures (e.g., slaps on the back, kissing pecks on the cheek, handshakes). Other cultures may be more reserved about their "persona."

CULTURAL DIVERSITY

We live in a culturally diverse society. **Cultural diversity** means there is a rich mix of ethnicity, race, and religion. Within each ethnic, race, or religious group, there are a variety of individual characteristics, such as gender, ability, socioeconomic status, family structure, and language spoken. Because our society is culturally diverse, our medical settings are also culturally diverse. As a medical assistant you will interact with health professionals and patients of many different cultures, beliefs, and individual characteristics. You must be aware of the cultural differences of your patients. If you are not knowledgeable about different cultures, you may have unrealistic expectations about patient behavior. This will prevent effective communication between you and culturally diverse patients.

Patient behavior can vary depending on religious, racial, ethical, economic, and social upbringing. Different cultures have different beliefs about what is acceptable and "correct" behavior in various situations. A behavior that is acceptable to someone in one culture in a certain situation may be totally unacceptable or even offensive to someone from a different culture because of differing beliefs (Box 10-1). For instance, in some cultures males are raised to be achievers while the females are expected to conform. Although this attitude is not part of most Western culture, it still is a part of other cultures and must be respected.

To understand how cultural diversity impacts medical assistants, you need to understand the importance of accepting diversity and must be knowledgeable about the cultural differences of patients.

Embracing Diversity

Medical assistants interact with people of different backgrounds daily. It is important to embrace each difference with an open mind. Do not make negative judgments concerning behavior because it differs from your own; the behavior may be the result of beliefs from a culture that has been passed down from one generation to the next.

All medical assistants have a responsibility to their profession and to patients to accept and respect the cultural beliefs of others even if they differ from their own. The goal is to be knowledgeable and sensitive to cultural attitudes and behaviors. This enables effective communication and mutual respect between the patient (and family) and the health professionals and will help establish a good relationship. To prepare yourself to work with people of many cultures and beliefs, you should research the cultural background and beliefs of the people in your community. If a classmate's ethnic background is different from your own, learn about the classmate's culture. Begin by explaining what you know or think you know about your classmate's belief system, and then ask questions about what you do not know. Gather fact-based information from reading material and compare it to your per-

ception (
share yo
10-1 sho
different

Underst   ng Cultural Differences

Knowled
ethnic t
behavior
valuable
care bec
standing:
pendenc
because
A patien
uncoope
being ill.
through
appropria
Planni
care requ
possible i
a patient'
als can b
into the
tural diff

- *Eye con
  contac
  even h
  people
  be con
- *Herbal
  Native
  and Ca
  an imp
  may be
  if the v
  recogn
  prescri
- *Gesture
  misunc
  commu
  believe
  insultir
  the poi
  How w
  and sai
  were a
  toward
  sweepir
  of your
  gesture
  made b
  togethe
  obscen

culture. In turn, you may be able to
ural beliefs with the classmate. Table
ne of the health and illness beliefs of
res.

patients' cultural background and
is necessary to understand their
knowledge and understanding are
assessing patients and providing
both can help prevent misunder-
example, if a culture stresses inde-
ss may be considered unacceptable
kes a person dependent on others.
these beliefs may be resistant or
and may not want to be seen as
rstanding this belief helps you work
atient's resistance and provide the
e.
lturally appropriate and acceptable
edical assistants to understand the
of a patient's cultural beliefs. Once
fs are understood, health profession-
to integrate the cultural influences
t's care. Common areas where cul-
s exist include the following:

n some Asian cultures, direct eye
nsidered to be disrespectful and
In Western culture, however,
do not maintain eye contact may
d rude, defiant, or inattentive.
ne. Many Americans, including
cans, as well as Asian immigrants
n Islanders, believe that herbs are
part of healing (Fig. 10-18). They
to the idea of Western medicine
of their alternative form is also
d taken into account when
edications.
tures can cause more
idings than any other form of
on. An Asian immigrant may
ing a finger at someone is
some Asian (and other) countries,
gesture is used to call animals.
ou feel if someone pointed at you
re, boy" or "Here, girl" as if you
t is more appropriate to gesture
atient with your palm down,
r hand toward them with the back
facing down. Another common
estern culture is the "okay" sign
hing the forefinger and thumb
ome cultures, this is seen as an
re. Shaking your head from side

to side means "no" in Western culture, but to a Bulgarian or someone from Taiwan, this gesture means "yes." A simple smile seems to be universally accepted and works well when all else fails.

- *Time.* Some Latin cultures are not sensitive to time. A 1 o'clock appointment may mean "sometime around one" to them. In Western culture being late is sometimes considered disrespectful. Be aware that the expression of time means different things to people of different cultures, and do not automatically assume the patient does not respect the medical office's time.
- *Foods.* Many Asians believe certain foods can heal or bring the body into balance, especially when an illness occurs. They believe alternating the use of hot and cold foods will achieve balance in their lives. Some cultures use hot foods for relieving a cold and use cold foods for relieving a fever.
- *Reactions.* Crying or showing any type of emotion in some cultures is seen as feminine or as a sign of weakness. Other cultures believe that saying "no" is being disrespectful; therefore a patient may say "yes" and really mean "no." Only the head of the family may make decisions and speak for the patient in some cultures. Some immigrants may not want the details of their illness to be included in the treatment plan.
- *Clothing.* Some cultures will not allow females to disrobe in the medical office unless another female member of the family is present. Religious beliefs may forbid the removal of certain garments, and the physician and medical assistant need to be sensitive to this and work around the situation.
- *Physical space.* Some cultures want to be very close during a conversation, whereas others require more personal space. Chinese people may not want to be touched by people they do not know. Some cultures will not let a female caregiver touch a male patient. Touching the head of a child is offensive to some cultures because the head is seen as sacred and can only be touched by a parent or the elder of the family.

Understanding cultural differences is important if there is to be a complete trust in the health care team. The patient interprets the workings of the medical office, the staff, and treatments from their own cultural perspective. Not everyone sees things the way you do. It will take patience and understanding to adjust to other ways of thinking, but it is worth the effort.

TABLE 10-1   Cross-Cultural Examples of Cultural Phenomena Affecting Health Care

Nations of Origin	Communication	Space	Time Orientation	Social Organization	Environmental Control	Biological Variations

Asian
China
Hawaii
Philippines
Korea
Japan
Southeast
  Asia (Laos,
  Cambodia,
  Vietnam)
	National language
	  preference
	Dialects, written
	  characters
	Use of silence
	Nonverbal and
	  contextual cuing
		Noncontact
		people
			Present	Family; hierarchical
				  structure
				Devotion to
				  tradition
				Many religions,
				  including
				  Taoism,
				  Buddhism,
				  Islam,
				  Christianity
					Traditional health
					  and illness
					  beliefs
					Use of traditional
					  medicines
					Traditional
					  practitioners,
					  Chinese
					  doctors, and
					  herbalists
						Liver cancer
						Stomach cancer
						Coccidioidomycosis
						Hypertension
						Lactose intolerance

African
West Coast
  (as slaves)
Many African
  countries
West Indian
  Islands
Dominican
  Republic
Haiti
Jamaica
	National languages
	Dialect, pidgin,
	  Creole, Spanish,
	  French
		Close personal
		space
			Present over
			future
				Family, many
				  female single
				  parents
				Large, extended
				  family networks
				Strong church
				  affiliation within
				  community
				Community social
				  organization
					Traditional health
					  and illness
					  beliefs
					Folk medicine
					  tradition
					Traditional healer:
					  rootworker
						Sickle cell anemia
						  Hypertension
						Cancer of the
						  esophagus
						Stomach cancer
						Coccidioidomycosis
						Lactose intolerance

European
Germany
England
Italy
Ireland
Spain
Other
  European
  countries
	National languages
	Many learn English
	  immediately
		Noncontact
		people
		Aloof
		Distant
		Southern
		  countries:
		  closer
		  contact and
		  touch
			Future over
			present
				Nuclear families
				Extended families
				Judeo-Christian
				  religions
				Community social
				  organizations
					Primary reliance
					  on modern
					  health care
					  system
					Traditional health
					  and illness
					  beliefs
					Some remaining
					  folk traditions
						Breast cancer
						Heart disease
						Diabetes mellitus
						Thalassemia

Native American
500 Native
  American
  tribes
Aleuts
Eskimos
	Tribal languages
	Use of silence and
	  body language
		Space very
		important
		and has no
		boundaries
			Present	Extremely family
				  oriented
				Biological and
				  extended
				  families
				Children taught to
				  respect
				  traditions
				Community social
				  organizations
					Traditional health
					  and illness
					  beliefs
					Folk medicine
					  tradition
					Traditional healer:
					  medicine man
						Accidents
						Heart disease
						Cirrhosis of the
						  liver
						Diabetes mellitus

Hispanic Countries
Cuba
Mexico
Central and
  South
  America
	Spanish or
	  Portuguese
	  primary language
		Tactile
		  relationships
		Touch
		Handshakes
		Embracing
		Value physical
		  presence
			Present	Nuclear family
				Extended families
				Compadrazzo:
				  godparents
				Community social
				  organization
					Traditional health
					  and illness
					  beliefs
					Folk medicine
					  tradition
					Traditional healers:
					  *curandero,
					  espiritista,
					  partera, señora*
						Diabetes mellitus
						Parasites
						Coccidioidomycosis
						Lactose intolerance

Compiled by Rachel Spector, RN, PhD.
(Modified from Potter PA, Perry AG: *Basic nursing*, ed 5, St Louis, Mosby, 2003.)

Fig. 10-1
tural grou
*Boston Co
nut Hill, i
nursing, e*

...ariety of remedies are used by many cul-
...the United States. *(Photo by Lucy Rozier,
...udio Visual Services, Boston College, Chest-
...n Potter PA, Perry AG:* Fundamentals of
...Louis, 1997, Mosby.)*

Althou
the belief
sary to u
patient b
detachme
patients i
team and
patients'
beliefs w
treatmen

...is impossible to be familiar with all
...practices of every culture, it is neces-
...tand the role that culture plays in
...or. Patient apathy, passiveness, or
...ncerning illness may be cultural;
...lace all their faith in the health care
...r spiritual being. Do not dismiss
...al beliefs. Instead, recognize their
...encouraging compliance with the
...nmended by the physician.

taking the patient's developmental stage and cultural differences into consideration. Besides developmental stages and cultural differences, another factor that influences a patient's behavior is the patient's *response* to being ill. Some patients may exhibit behavior that is challenging or difficult to handle when they are ill. This is understandable considering people are not at their best when feeling unwell. Coping mechanisms and emotional responses can cause patients to react in a way they normally would not.

Each patient must be evaluated on his or her own merits and accepted as an individual. Illnesses and disabilities have various psychological effects on individuals. A patient who is terminally ill, for example, may react with calmness and demonstrate a strong will to get better, whereas a person with a minor illness may react as though he or she is dying. Anxiety can result if a patient sees illness as a threat to self-image. The anxiety causes the patient to react. The type of reaction depends on the person's ability to cope and the defense mechanism used. Remember: defense mechanisms allow the patient to feel in control. The health care team must assess whether the defenses used are helpful or dangerous to the eventual recovery of the patient. Reactions vary from patient to patient. However, four common patient reactions to illness are fear, talkativeness, withdrawal, and anger.

Fear

The unknown can cause fear in the patient and regression in the patient's behavior. Fear of pain and death are two very strong emotions for most people. Fear may cause one person to seek medical attention, whereas another person may avoid seeking the necessary medical help or may not follow the prescribed treatment (Fig. 10-19). Fear is a natural reaction when a person is faced with a threatening situation. However, anxiety can be produced when patients worry about the "what if." This form of self-talk is pointless and destructive. To help the patient minimize the worry, you must involve the patient in the treatment plan and be a good listener. Treat patients' fears with kindness and reassurance. Answer their questions honestly to provide them with information. Turning the "unknown" into the "known" by providing more information will help reduce their fears. Once fearful patients see that treatment can help them feel better, their fears are likely to decrease.

Talkativeness

The talkative patient may just be anxious, nervous, or fearful. Listen to what the patient is saying. In

---

PATIEN   ENTERED **PROFESSIONALISM**

• Althou   ere are many commonalities among
  cultur   y is it important to understand each
  cultur   ues and its beliefs about health care?
  How   this understanding impact a medical
  assist   elationship with patients and their
  famili

• How   person's cultural value system as it
  relate   fesaving measures (e.g., transplants,
  feedir   s) affect the person's treatment? What
  is the   nt-centered, professional way for a
  medic   stant to work with a patient (or family)
  who   es with a prescribed medical treatment   se of cultural values or beliefs?

 RESP   E TO ILLNESS

Health ca   n members have expectations about
how patie   have. These expectations are based
on prior e   nce, assumptions, knowledge, and
even their   t moods. As you learned, a patient's
behavior   e understood to some degree by

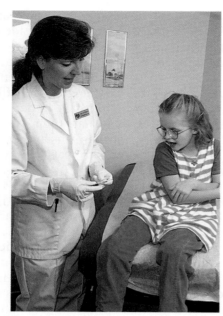

Fig. 10-19 Fear and anxiety are strong emotions that need to be acknowledged in order to achieve patient cooperation, especially in children. *(From Chester GA: Modern medical assisting, Philadelphia, 1998, Saunders.)*

your own words, reflect on the feelings and ideas expressed by the patient. Make your response goal directed (e.g., "What can I do to help?"). Communication is the key with talkative patients. Try to find the core concern that is causing their talkativeness, and address this concern.

Withdrawal

Withdrawn or depressed patients do not put out the energy and involvement required to get better. They may seem very apathetic about their recovery. They lose interest in their surroundings and have a feeling of hopelessness. Their appetite is decreased, and they may have various complaints unrelated to their illness. The longer the depression continues, the less chance there will be for recovery. A withdrawn patient requires great amounts of encouragement to be motivated to cooperate with the treatment plan. Do not give advice; this should be done by trained professionals such as physicians, psychologists, and psychiatrists. Instead, use questions such as, "What has happened to upset you?" Focus on where you need the patient to be in the treatment plan. This type of patient will need compassion, empathy, and understanding. Encourage patients to vent without placing undue pressure on them.

Anger

The angry patient must be addressed constructively. To be effective, try to put yourself in the patient's

place. You might say, "You sound upset," and "How can I help you?" Watch the patient's body language and expressions, and focus on what the patient is saying instead of worrying about what response to give. Try to find the underlying cause of the patient's anger. Helpful hints to deal with the angry patient are as follows:

1. Let the patient vent. Do not try and defend yourself or the office. Policies can be explained later, when the patient is calm and more apt to listen.
2. Make eye contact with the angry patient. Show interest in what is being said.
3. Be a good listener. Take a posture of attention (face the patient, make eye contact), and ignore putdowns. Do not allow yourself to become angry and lose control of the situation. Take notes on the patient's complaints.
4. Find some truth in the complaint; this often disarms the patient. ("You're right; we did make an error; here's what I will do to correct it" *or* "You're right; we could have handled it better; let's start over: What is it that you need?" *or* "What would you like us to do?")
5. Never make judgmental statements. Do not become hostile or defensive. Putting patients on the defensive will cause them to lose focus, and they will shut you out.
6. Clarify what has been said (e.g., "Okay, let me see if I have all the facts").
7. The best response may be silence. With this approach there is no argument, only the patient venting. Sometimes patients just want to be heard.
8. Avoid distractions so that the patient sees that he or she has your full attention. Take the patient out of the reception area and into a quiet place away from other patients.
9. Do not react to the patient with anger. Remain professional and courteous.

When a patient is fearful, talkative, withdrawn, or angry, always focus on objective facts and solutions. Talk about what really caused the problem and how it can be solved. Working effectively with these behaviors is not a test of power, but an opportunity to find out what a patient really needs. Avoid "why" questions because they tend to increase defensiveness. Success can only be achieved when an atmosphere of trust and cooperation is established. Use "I" statements such as "I hear what you are saying" or "I understand," and give solutions (e.g., "Let me give you some of your options"). Never give advice; this is not within a medical assistant's scope of practice. Always maintain the integrity of the other person, and never lose your own integrity.

BOX

Tips for Interacting with Patients Responding Negatively to Illness

1. Offe␣ ␣uragement that is consistent with the
   patie␣ ␣lefenses, self-image, and personality
   neec

2. Be ␣ ␣of other problems that the patient may
   have ␣ ␣as financial or employment problems
   and ␣ ␣instability. If a patient cannot work
   beca␣ ␣ an illness, the patient may be con-
   cern␣ ␣ut family welfare and paying the bills.
   This ␣ ␣eighten anxiety and may make the
   patie␣ ␣sponsive to health issues.

3. Try t␣ ␣patients through minor sources of irritation. ␣ ␣ight give them the energy to focus on
   the r␣ ␣blem.

Box 1C␣ ␣vides additional tips for dealing with
patients ␣ ␣eact negatively to illness.

PATIE␣ ␣ENTERED PROFESSIONALISM

- How ␣ ␣nderstanding the overall development
  (e.g., ␣ ␣al, mental, psychosocial) of people
  help ␣ ␣al assistants respond to a patient diag-
  nose␣ ␣a terminal illness?

- As a ␣ ␣al assistant, how would you interact
  with ␣ ␣lt patient diagnosed with cancer? What
  if this ␣ ␣t is always rude when he comes into
  the c

- What ␣ ␣benefit to terminal patients and their
  famili␣ ␣n a medical assistant understands the
  stage␣ ␣ing?

CON␣ ␣ION

As a medi␣ ␣sistant you have no way of knowing
exactly h␣ ␣patient is feeling as a result of an
illness, i␣ ␣ or medical procedure. You can,
however, ␣ ␣stand some of the basic characteristics or ty␣ ␣eactions of people in different developmental ␣ ␣es. You can also research the
backgrou␣ ␣d beliefs of people of different cultures in y␣ ␣ommunity so that you will have a
better un␣ ␣ding of reactions caused by cultural
difference␣ ␣ally, you can be empathetic with
patients ␣ ␣are experiencing fear, exhibiting
talkativen␣ ␣howing signs of withdrawal, or
displayin␣ ␣r. Being a patient-centered health
profession␣ ␣ans being courteous and caring to

all patients. It also means being knowledgeable about the different behaviors that patients exhibit and what causes these behaviors. Understanding patient behavior will help you provide effective care to patients of all ages, genders, cultures, personalities, and states of mind.

SUMMARY

Reinforce your understanding of the material in this chapter by reviewing the curriculum objectives and key content points below.

1. Define, appropriately use, and spell all the Key Terms for this chapter.
   - Review the Key Terms if necessary.

2. List and describe the three areas of change during growth and development in a lifetime.
   - Physical growth includes an increase in physical size and the development of motor and sensory skills.
   - Mental growth includes cognitive development and increased thinking and understanding.
   - Psychosocial growth includes emotional and social development.

3. For each age level, list two age-appropriate ways that medical assistants can enhance interaction with patients.
   - For infants, try to involve parents or guardians in care; follow up on previous health concerns.
   - For children, explain or demonstrate procedures first, and keep the caregiver in sight.
   - For adolescents, be sure to respect their privacy; offer choices when possible.
   - For adults, provide as much patient education and information as possible; know your patient's support system.

4. Describe the basic developmental milestones for each developmental stage.
   - Infants develop as they discover their surroundings.
   - Toddlers discover independence and develop quickly if the environment is positive.
   - Preschoolers have perceptions about life's expectations based on their experiences.
   - School-age children experience extensive physical and emotional development.
   - Adolescents undergo physical changes and are constantly challenged by peer group pressures.
   - Adults experience role definition and body changes throughout their life span.

5. Explain why the medical assistant must understand the various body system changes involved in the aging process.

- Body systems change and weaken as people age from early to late adulthood.
- Medical assistants can help patients accept and adapt to these changes.

6. List eight areas in which cultural differences exist.
   - Cultural differences can be expressed in various ways, including eye contact, nontraditional medicines, gestures, concept of time, food, emotions, social roles, and physical space.

7. Explain the importance of being knowledgeable about the cultural background of a patient.
   - Understanding the cultural background of a patient can help you communicate more effectively with the patient and address the patient's core concerns.

8. List four types of responses that patients commonly have toward illness.
   - Patients may be fearful, talkative, withdrawn, or angry because of illness, injury, discomfort, or pain.

9. List five things you can do when a patient becomes angry.
   - Never return a patient's anger; always remain calm and professional.
   - Just listen; some patients need to vent first.
   - Agree with them; sometimes the staff *is* at fault.
   - Make eye contact; give patients your full attention.
   - Clarify what has been said so that you are sure you have received the message correctly.

10. Analyze a realistic medical office situation and apply your understanding of the patient's background and behavior to determine the best course of action.
    - Cultural behaviors, when misunderstood, can create barriers to effective communication between patients and the medical assistant.

11. Describe the impact on patient care when medical assistants understand how people react to illness and medical care and how they change at various stages of development.
    - Understanding how people react to illness and how they change at various stages of their development allows medical assistants to modify their approach when interacting with patients. Age-appropriate responses to the patient by the medical assistant will facilitate care.

FOR FURTHER EXPLORATION

1. **Research additional life span changes from infancy through later maturity.** Medical assistants can provide effective care to their patients if they are aware of the many changes that occur during the life span.
   Keywords: Use the following keywords in your search: growth and development, life span changes, infancy, childhood, adolescence, developmental stages.

2. **Research alternative medicine.** Patients of different cultural or belief systems may seek alternative medical treatments. To provide effective patient care, it is necessary for medical assistants to understand these various alternative medical practice techniques.
   Keywords: Use the following keywords in your search: alternative medicine, folk medicine, culture in medicine, ethnicity in medicine.

3. **Research various cultural beliefs about response to illness.** Every person will respond differently to illness. It is important for the medical assistant to be aware of responses based on cultural beliefs, especially if these beliefs differ from the assistant's own beliefs, in order to provide meaningful patient care.
   Keywords: Use the following keywords in your search: cross-cultural health care, cultural response to illness, cultural response to death and dying.

Chapter Review

Vocabulary Review

Matching

Match each term with the correct definition.

A. adult

B. child

C. cultural diversity

D. infant

E. mental growth

F. physical growth

G. psychosocial growth

H. development

_____ 1. Part of the human life span including birth through the first year

_____ 2. Individual's emotional and social development

_____ 3. Individual's cognitive development

_____ 4. Part of the human life span concerned with an individual during early, middle, and later years in life

_____ 5. Mix of ethnicity, race, and religion in a given population

_____ 6. Individual's growth and development in physical size and motor and sensory skills

_____ 7. Part of human life span dealing with toddlers, preschoolers, school-age children, and adolescents

_____ 8. Progressive increases in the function of the body throughout a lifetime

Theory Recall

True/False

Indicate whether the sentence or statement is true or false.

_____ 1. Growth and change occur only during a human's adolescent years.

_____ 2. Medical assistants have a responsibility to their profession and to their patients to accept and respect the cultural beliefs of others even if they differ from their own.

_____ 3. Fear of pain and death are two very strong emotions for most people.

_____ 4. When a patient is fearful, talkative, withdrawn, or angry, the medical assistant should get the physician immediately to take care of the problem.

_____ 5. As a patient ages, the gastrointestinal tract slows down, learning is possible but slower, and drugs are processed more slowly.

Multiple Choice

Identify the letter of the choice that best completes the statement or answers the question.

1. There is a potential for ineffective communication when all of the following occur EXCEPT when

   _____.
   A. English is a second language
   B. the patient is angry, frightened, or in pain
   C. there are cultural differences
   D. direct eye contact is made

2. Which one of the following is NOT a category of change during growth and development of the human life span?
   A. Physical
   B. Socioeconomic
   C. Mental
   D. Psychosocial

3. Cognitive development occurs during _____ growth.
   A. physical
   B. socioeconomic
   C. mental
   D. psychosocial

4. During infancy, a baby who coos when happy or smiles at age 6 weeks is demonstrating _____ growth.
   A. physical
   B. socioeconomic
   C. mental
   D. psychosocial

5. Wh ring for an infant (birth to 3 months), in the office or clinic, the medical assistant should

   A.   eye contact when speaking to the infant
   B.   on eating and sleeping habits
   C.   rage grasping toys and toys with sounds
   D.   rage playing with large blocks for stacking

6. A t (13 months to 3 years) typically grows slowly, gaining only ＿＿＿ pounds and growing only 3 in

   A. 1
   B.
   C. 5
   D. 1 5

7. An   aged 8 to 12 months is capable of which of the following task(s)?
   A. S g head "no"
   B. V "bye-bye"
   C. B   and B
   D. N   A nor B

8. A 19 3-month-old is capable of which of the following task(s)?
   A. K   a ball
   B. H   g
   C. C   g within the lines
   D. N   f the above

9. The   al assistant should engage a child aged 24 to 36 months by ＿＿＿.
   A. e   ging cooing and happy sounds
   B. e   ging grasping toys and toys with sound
   C. e   ging play with large blocks for stacking
   D. n   the above

10. Wrin ypically first appear on patients in the age range of ＿＿＿ years.
   A. 19
   B. 45
   C. 70
   D. 80 older

11. In so ＿＿＿ cultures, direct eye contact is considered to be disrespectful.
   A. As
   B. La
   C. Af American
   D. Eu n

12. ＿＿＿ ause more misunderstandings than any other form of communication.
   A. Fo
   B. Cl   g
   C. Ge
   D. Ph   space

13. A(n) ＿＿＿ is a universal gesture accepted by every culture.
   A. wa
   B. Ol
   C. cry
   D. sm

14. Which one of the following is NOT an area of cultural difference?
    A. Eye contact
    B. Emotions
    C. Nontraditional/traditional health care
    D. All of the above

15. _____ is NOT a common response patients have toward illness, injury, or pain?
    A. Joy
    B. Anger
    C. Talkativeness
    D. Withdrawing

16. When dealing with an angry patient, it would NOT be productive to _____.
    A. remain calm and professional
    B. mimic the patient's level of anger
    C. listen, because some patients just need to vent
    D. agree with the patient; after all, you may be wrong

17. In the United States, the color black is a sign of mourning; in certain Asian cultures, the color _____ indicates mourning.
    A. yellow
    B. blue
    C. white
    D. purple

18. Bone mass begins to decrease in which age group?
    A. 20 to 25 years
    B. 30 to 35 years
    C. 40 to 45 years
    D. 45 to 59 years

19. Muscle efficiency peaks in the late _____.
    A. teens
    B. 20s
    C. 30s
    D. 40s

20. Minor motor skills greatly improve in which age group?
    A. Birth to 8 months
    B. 8 to 12 months
    C. 13 to 18 months
    D. 19 to 23 months

Sentence Completion

Complete each sentence or statement.

1. As a toddler becomes a(n) _____, expectations about physical, mental, and psychosocial characteristics and abilities are raised.

2. A(n) _____ development in infancy is a reaction to sound, motion, and light.

3. Involve _____ when demonstrating procedures for home care and have them practice the procedures.

4. A ch _____ to _____ months old will smile at himself or herself in the mirr

5. A ch _____ to _____ years old can learn to print his or her name.

Short _____ ers

1. List a _____ escribe the three areas of change during growth and development that occur in a lifetime.

_____

_____

_____

_____

2. Expla _____ y the medical assistant must understand the various body system changes involved in the aging _____ ss.

_____

_____

_____

_____

3. List fi _____ ngs a medical assistant can do when a patient becomes angry.

_____

_____

_____

_____

4. Explai _____ importance of being knowledgeable about the cultural background of a patient.

_____

_____

_____

_____

Critical Thinking

Simon lives in a large city and works as a medical assistant for a free health clinic with 15 physicians, 6 physician assistants, and 3 nurse practitioners on staff. Simon loves the fast pace of the practice. He enjoys working with the patients and their families and knows in his heart at the end of the day that he has given back to the community in which he grew up. The patient population is very diverse. Patients are from numerous ethnicities, with different religious beliefs, medical traditions, educational backgrounds, and age groups. The patients are very poor, and many are homeless. The practice's philosophy states that any person in the need of medical attention who comes through the door will receive treatment to the best of the facility's abilities. Some of the patients are on state-assisted programs or Medicare; many more of them pay on a sliding fee scale or do not pay at all. Simon speaks fluent Spanish and has learned several medical phrases in five languages, like "Where does it hurt?" "How long have you felt this way?" "What have you taken to help?" and "Did it help?" He cannot always understand the answers, but by watching the patient's nonverbal communication, he is able to form a basic understanding of what is going on. Simon has been able to learn the basics of many of the different cultures of his patients, and the patients respect Simon for his dedication.

A. Learn two medical phrases in Spanish and two medical phrases in another language of your choice that is not your primary language. Write them down and be able to repeat them verbally in class.

B. How do you think Simon learned about his patients' cultures?

C. List five nonverbal communication techniques for understanding "I am in pain here."

Internet Research

Keyword: Growth and development in infancy

Research three websites and list one physical, one mental, and one psychosocial development that occurs during infancy that is not listed in your textbook. Cite the source of your information.

What Would You Do?

If you have accomplished the objectives in this chapter, you will be able to make better choices as a medical assistant. Take a look at this situation and decide what you would do.

Juan, 40 years old, has moved to the United States. His family is still in Mexico, but he hopes to find a good job soon and pay for them to come to the United States. Because Juan does not speak English very well, he has had difficulty finding employment and a place to live. Lately, he has been staying at a shelter for homeless people. His educational background is limited, and his broken English makes communicating difficult. Few Hispanic people live in the area where he has settled. Juan has lost 10 pounds, his vision is declining, and he has noticed that he is not hearing as well as he used to. Because of his constant weight loss and the vision problems, he decided to visit the local medical office. He has heard the office provides services to those who cannot pay.

When Juan arrives at the office, his clothing is worn and torn. The new medical assistant tells Juan that he cannot be seen at the office unless he can pay for his visit before he is seen. She does not explain her statement, and because of his broken English, Juan does not ask further questions. He thinks that the physician will not see him and leaves the office very upset. He decides to start taking herbal medications and to try home remedies. He now believes that seeing a physician in America just is not worth the trouble and embarrassment. Several weeks later, Juan is hospitalized with dehydration, starvation, and severe reactions to the herbal drugs.

This situation did not have to result in Juan's being hospitalized. If you were the new medical assistant, what would you have done differently?

1. Wha   does age play in the symptoms that Juan is experiencing? Could the symptoms be related to
   the i   es as well? Explain.

   _____

   _____

   _____

   _____

2. What   ence did differing cultural backgrounds have in this situation?

   _____

   _____

   _____

   _____

3. How   the situation have turned out if the new medical assistant had studied cultural differences?
   What   ties would help the medical assistant in understanding diversity?

   _____

   _____

   _____

   _____

   _____

4. What   s led to Juan's withdrawal from medical care until he was hospitalized?

   _____

   _____

   _____

   _____

5. As the   cal assistant, how would you approach Juan differently?

   _____

   _____

   _____

   _____

Applicat   f Skills

1. Select   e group of growth and development. Interview two individuals (parents or guardians,
   depend   n the age group selected) that fall within the age group you selected. Using the

development charts in the textbook, ask or assess each individual (parent or guardian) if they have met or accomplished each guideline listed in all three categories: physical, mental, and psychosocial.

2. Research on the Internet or local library a culture other than your own. (You may ask an individual of that culture to provide you with information.) Write two or three sentences addressing the following areas. Cite your source(s) of information.

   A. History

   B. Food

   C. Music

   D. Medical traditions

   E. Clothing

   F. One holiday celebration unique to their culture

Chapter Quiz

Multiple Choice

Identify the letter of the choice that best completes the statement or answers the question.

1. _____ is the part of the human life span concerned with an individual during early, middle, and later years in life.
   A. Physical growth
   B. Adulthood
   C. Infancy
   D. Mental growth

2. An individual's emotional and social development is called _____.
   A. cultural diversity
   B. physical growth
   C. psychosocial growth
   D. mental growth

3. _____ is the mix of ethnicity, race, and religion in a given population.
   A. Social standards
   B. Cultural diversity
   C. Socioeconomic status
   D. Self-esteem

4. _____ is NOT a common patient response to illness.
   A. Anger
   B. Talkative
   C. Withdrawn
   D. Calmness

5. Dexterity decreases in patients aged _____.
   A. 10 to 12 months
   B. 15 to 20 years
   C. 40 to 49 years
   D. 60 to 69 years

6. Toilning should be completed by the age of _____ months.
   A. 6
   B. 18
   C. 24
   D. 236

7. An aged _____ months explores by banging, dropping, and throwing.
   A. 0
   B. 4
   C. 12
   D. 26

8. At wge should the medical assistant start to observe a child's behavior and interaction with peer
   A. 18 months
   B. 13 months
   C. 25 months
   D. Age is this appropriate

9. At we should a child be able to drink from a cup?
   A. 12 months
   B. 13 months
   C. 13 months
   D. 245 months

10. Duriiat age is a child most susceptible to unfavorable experiences that can lead to mistrust and hampempts to trying new things?
    A. 1ears
    B. 3ears
    C. 6ears
    D. 10years

11. Duriryears of _____, peer pressure becomes a major issue in the child's life.
    A. chod
    B. adnce
    C. ealthood
    D. ge

12. Wrinlpically first appear during the ages of _____ years.
    A. 20
    B. 30
    C. 45
    D. 64

13. The psocial occurrence of retirement typically occurs during what age group?
    A. 35years
    B. 40years
    C. 50years
    D. 60years

14. Does ng of self-worth have any impact on how a person approaches life span changes?
    A. Yes
    B. No

15. Religion, race, ethics, economics, and social upbringing have little, if any, impact on a patient's behavior.
    A. True
    B. False

16. In some cultures, it is believed that poor health is a punishment from a higher power.
    A. True
    B. False

17. Typically, financial and employment concerns do NOT contribute to the overall wellness of an individual.
    A. True
    B. False

18. Medical assistants must become very proficient in stereotyping their patients as quickly as possible to ensure they receive the best health care.
    A. True
    B. False

19. In the United States, the color _____ is a sign of mourning; whereas in certain cultures, the color white means mourning.
    A. black
    B. yellow
    C. white
    D. purple

20. Cognitive development occurs during _____ growth.
    A. physical
    B. socioeconomic
    C. mental
    D. psychosocial

Student _Samanta Martinez_   Date _8-12-13_

CHECK   : MEASURE BODY TEMPERATURE USING A DISPOSABLE ORAL THERMOMETER

TASK: A   ely measure and record a patient's oral temperature using a disposable thermometer.

CONDIT   Given the proper equipment and supplies, the student will be required to perform the proper method for meas   an oral temperature using a disposable oral thermometer.

EQUIPM   AND SUPPLIES   _Jasmine Toliver_
* Dispo   thermometer   _97.4°f_
* Dispo   gloves
* Bioha   s waste container
* Pen
* Patien   dical record

STANDA   Complete the procedure within _____ minutes and achieve a minimum score of _____%.

Time beg   _____   Time ended _____

Steps		Possible Points	First Attempt	Second Attempt
1. As e all supplies and equipment.		5		
2. Sa ands.		5		
3. Gr d identify the patient.		5		
4. Exp e procedure to the patient.		5		
5. De e if the patient has recently had a hot or cold beverage to r has smoked.		5		
6. Put sposable gloves.		5		
7. Op thermometer packaging.		5		
8. Pla thermometer under the patient's tongue and wait 60 sec		5		
9. Rer he thermometer and read the results by looking at the col ots.		5		
10. Dis e thermometer and gloves in a biohazardous waste cor		5		
11. Sar ands.		5		
12. Do t results in the patient's medical record.		10		
Total P Possible		65		

Comment   Points Earned _____   Instructor's Signature _____

Student N _____   Date _____

CHECK⌐ MEASURE BODY TEMPERATURE USING A TYMPANIC THERMOMETER

TASK: Ac⌐ y measure and record a patient's temperature using a tympanic thermometer.

CONDITI⌐ Given the proper equipment and supplies, the student will be required to role-play with another student th⌐ ⌐er method for measuring the tympanic temperature using a tympanic thermometer.

EQUIPM⌐ ND SUPPLIES
- Tympa⌐ ⌐rmometer
- Dispos⌐ ⌐obe cover
- Pen
- Patient ⌐ical record
- Biohaz⌐ ⌐waste container

STANDAR⌐ ⌐omplete the procedure within _____ minutes and achieve a minimum score of _____%.

Time beg⌐ ____   Time ended _____

Steps		Possible Points	First Attempt	Second Attempt
1. Ass⌐	all supplies and equipment.	5		
2. San⌐	⌐nds.	5		
3. Gre⌐	identify the patient.	5		
4. Exp⌐	procedure to the patient.	5		
5. Ren⌐	⌐e thermometer from the charger.	5		
6. Che⌐ set	⌐e sure the mode for interpretation of temperature is ⌐" mode.	10		
7. Che⌐	⌐ens probe to be sure it is clean and not scratched.	5		
8. Turn	⌐ thermometer.	5		
9. Inse⌐	⌐robe firmly into a disposable plastic probe cover.	5		
10. Wait	⌐igital "READY" display.	5		
11. With⌐ ear ⌐ the ⌐	⌐nd that is not holding the probe, pull adult patient's ⌐back to straighten the ear canal. For a small child, pull ⌐s ear down and back to straighten the ear canal.	10		
12. Inser⌐ cana⌐	⌐robe into the patient's ear and tightly seal the ear ⌐ng.	10		
13. Posit⌐	⌐ probe.	5		
14. Depr⌐	⌐ activation button.	5		
15. Relea⌐	⌐ activation button and wait 2 seconds.	5		
16. Rem⌐	⌐ probe from the ear and read the temperature.	5		

Steps	Possible Points	First Attempt	Second Attempt
17. Note the reading, making sure that the screen displays "oral" as the mode of interpretation.	5		
18. Discard the probe cover in a biohazardous waste container.	5		
19. Replace the thermometer on the charger base.	5		
20. Sanitize hands.	5		
21. Document results in the patient's medical record using ① to indicate a tympanic temperature was obtained.	10		
Total Points Possible	125		

Comments: Total Points Earned _____   Instructor's Signature _____

Student Na _____   Date _____

CHECKLI   DMINISTER AN INTRAMUSCULAR INJECTION USING
THE Z-TF   TECHNIQUE

TASK: Dem   e the correct technique to administer an intramuscular injection using the Z-track technique.

CONDITIOI   'en the proper equipment and supplies, the student will prepare and administer an intramuscular injection usi   Z-track technique.

EQUIPMEN   ) SUPPLIES
- Nonsteril   sable gloves
- Medicatic   r by physician
- Appropria   1ge for ordered dose
- Appropria   dle with safety device
- 2 × 2-inc   e gauze
- 70% isop   lcohol wipes
- Biohazarc   iste container
- Patient's r   l record

STANDARD: 1plete the procedure within _____ minutes and achieve a minimum score of _____%.

Time begar _____   Time ended _____

Steps		Possible Points	First Attempt	Second Attempt
1. Sani nds.		5		
2. Veri' rder, and assemble equipment and supplies.		5		
3. Foll("seven rights" of medication administration.		10		
4. Che medication against the physician's order three times bef ninistration.		10		
5. Che patient's medical record for drug allergies or conditions tha contraindicate the injection.		10		
6. Che iration date of the medication.		10		
7. Ca the correct dose to be given.		20		
8. Fol correct procedure for drawing the medication into syr		10		
9. Gre identify the patient, and explain the procedure to the pa		15		
10. Sel appropriate injection site and properly position the pa		5		
11. Ap posable gloves.		5		
12. Pr he injection site.		5		
13. W e prepared site is drying, remove the cover from the ne		5		

Steps	Possible Points	First Attempt	Second Attempt
14. Secure the skin at the injection site by pushing the skin away from the injection site.	10		
15. Puncture the skin quickly and smoothly, making sure the needle is kept at a 90-degree angle.	10		
16. Continue to hold the tissue in place while aspirating and injecting the medication.	15		
17. Inject the medication.	10		
18. Withdraw the needle.	10		
19. Release the traction on the skin to seal the track as the needle is being removed. Activate safety shield over needle.	10		
20. Discard the syringe and needle into a rigid biohazardous container.	5		
21. Remove gloves and discard in a biohazardous waste container.	5		
22. Sanitize the hands.	5		
23. Check on the patient.	5		
24. Document the procedure.	5		
25. Clean the equipment and examination room.	10		
Total Points Possible	215		

Comments: Total Points Earned _____   Instructor's Signature _____

Student _____   Date _____

CHECK   PERFORM VENIPUNCTURE USING THE EVACUATED-TUBE METHOD
(COLLE   N OF MULTIPLE TUBES)

TASK: Ol   venous blood specimen acceptable for testing using the evacuated-tube system.

CONDITI   Given the proper equipment and supplies, the student will be required to perform a venipuncture
using the   ated-tube system method of collection.

EQUIPM   ND SUPPLIES
- Nonste   osable gloves
- Person   ctive equipment (PPE) as required
- Tourniq   ex-free)
- Evacuat   e holder
- Evacuate   e multidraw needle (21 or 22 gauge, 1 or 1½ inch) with safety guards
- Evacuate   od tubes for requested tests with labels (correct nonadditive or additive required for ordered test)
- Alcohol \
- Sterile 2   ch gauze pads
- Bandage   -free) or nonallergenic tape
- Sharps c   er
- Biohazar   vaste container
- Laborato   uisition form
- Patient's   al record

STANDARD   mplete the procedure within _____ minutes and achieve a minimum score of _____%.

Time began _____   Time ended _____

Steps	Possible Points	First Attempt	Second Attempt
1. Saniti ids.	5		
2. Verify der, and assemble equipment and supplies.	5		
3. Greet atient, identify yourself, and confirm the patient's identit ort the patient to the proper room. Ask the patient to sit in otomy chair.	5		
4. Confir t the patient has followed the needed preparation (e.g.,).	10		
5. Explair procedure to the patient.	5		
6. Prepar evacuated tube system.	5		
7. Open erile gauze packet and place the gauze pad on the inside wrapper, or obtain sterile gauze pads from a bulk packag	10		
8. Positio remaining needed supplies for ease of reaching with nondo t hand. Place tube loosely in holder with label facing downv	10		
9. Positio examine the arm to be used in the venipuncture.	10		
10. Apply t urniquet.	10		
11. Apply g and PPE.	5		

Steps	Possible Points	First Attempt	Second Attempt
12. Thoroughly palpate the selected vein.	5		
13. Release the tourniquet.	5		
14. Prepare the puncture site using alcohol swabs.	10		
15. Reapply the tourniquet.	10		
16. Position the holder while keeping the needle covered, being certain to have control of holder. Uncover the needle.	10		
17. Position the needle so that it follows the line of the vein.	5		
18. Perform the venipuncture.	5		
19. Secure the holder. Push the bottom of the tube with the thumb of your nondominant hand so that the needle inside the holder pierces the rubber stopper of the tube. Follow the direction of the vein.	10		
20. Change tubes (minimum of two tubes) as required by test orders.	10		
21. Gently invert tubes that contain additives to be mixed with the specimen.	10		
22. While the blood is filling the last tube, release the tourniquet and withdraw the needle. Cover the needle with the safety shield.	10		
23. Apply direct pressure on the venipuncture site, and instruct the patient to raise the arm straight above the head and maintain pressure on the site for 1 to 2 minutes.	10		
24. Discard the contaminated needle and holder into the sharps container.	10		
25. Label the tubes as appropriate for lab.	10		
26. Place the tube into the biohazard transport bag.	5		
27. Check for bleeding at puncture site and apply a pressure dressing.	5		
28. Remove and discard the alcohol wipe and gloves.	5		
29. Sanitize the hands.	5		
30. Record the collection date and time on the laboratory requisition form, and place the requisition in the proper place in the biohazard transport bag.	10		
31. Ask and observe how the patient feels.	5		
32. Clean the work area using Standard Precautions.	5		
33. Document the procedure, indicating tests for which blood was drawn and the labs to which blood will be sent.	10		
Total Points Possible	250		

Comments: Total Points Earned _____   Instructor's Signature _____

Student Na _____   Date _____

CHECKLIS PERFORM VENIPUNCTURE USING THE SYRINGE METHOD

TASK: Obta   venous blood specimen acceptable for testing using the syringe method.

CONDITION   Given the proper equipment and supplies, the student will be required to perform a venipuncture using the sy   method of collection.

EQUIPMEN   ND SUPPLIES
- Nonsterile   posable gloves
- Personal   ctive equipment (PPE) as required
- Tournique   tex-free)
- Test tube
- 10-cc (10   ) syringe with 21- or 22-gauge needle and safety guards
- Proper eva   ted blood tubes for tests ordered
- Alcohol wi
- Sterile 2 ×   nch gauze pads
- Bandage (-free) or nonallergenic tape
- Sharps cor   ier
- Biohazardc   waste container
- Laboratory   uisition form
- Patient's m   cal record

STANDARDS mplete the procedure within _____ minutes and achieve a minimum score of _____%.

Time began _ ___   Time ended _____

Steps	Possible Points	First Attempt	Second Attempt
1. Sanitize nds.	5		
2. Verify th rder. Assemble equipment and supplies.	5		
3. Greet th atient, identify yourself, and confirm the patient's identity. ort the patient to the room for the blood draw. Position e patient in phlebotomy chair or on examination table.	5		
4. Confirm y necessary preparation has been accomplished (e.g., fas g). Explain the procedure to the patient.	5		
5. Prepare needle and syringe, maintaining syringe sterility. Break the seal the syringe by moving the plunger back and forth several ti es. Loosen the cap on the needle and check to make sure that e hub is screwed tightly onto the syringe.	15		
6. Place the vacuated tubes to be filled in a test tube rack on a work surf e in order of fill.	15		
7. Open the terile gauze packet and place the gauze pad on the inside of wrapper, or obtain sterile gauze pads from a bulk package.	5		
8. Position ar examine the arm to be used in the venipuncture.	10		
9. Apply glove and PPE.	5		

Steps	Possible Points	First Attempt	Second Attempt
10. Thoroughly palpate the selected vein.	10		
11. Release the tourniquet.	10		
12. Prepare the puncture site and reapply tourniquet.	10		
13. If drawing from the hand, ask the patient to make a fist or bend the fingers downward. Pull the skin taut with your thumb over the top of the patient's knuckles.	15		
14. Position the syringe and grasp the syringe firmly between the thumb and the underlying fingers.	10		
15. Follow the direction of the vein and insert the needle in one quick motion at about a 45-degree angle.	10		
16. If drawing from AC vein, with your nondominant hand pull the skin taut beneath the intended puncture site to anchor the vein. Thumb should be 1 to 2 inches below and to the side of the vein.	15		
17. Position the syringe and grasp the syringe firmly between the thumb and the underlying fingers.	10		
18. Follow the direction of the vein and insert the needle in one quick motion at about a 15-degree angle.	10		
19. Perform the venipuncture. If flash does not occur, gently pull back on the plunger. Do not move the needle. If blood still does not enter the syringe, slowly withdraw the needle, secure new supplies, and retry the draw.	10		
20. Anchor the syringe, and gently continue pulling back on the plunger until the required amount of blood is in the syringe.	10		
21. Release the tourniquet.	5		
22. Remove the needle and cover the needle with safety shield without locking.	10		
23. Apply direct pressure on the venipuncture site, and instruct the patient to raise the arm straight above the head. Instruct the patient to maintain pressure on the site for 1 to 2 minutes.	5		
24. Transfer the blood to the evacuated tubes as soon as possible.	10		
25. Properly dispose of the syringe and needle.	10		
26. Label the tubes and place into biohazard transport bag.	10		
27. Check for bleeding at venipuncture site and place a pressure dressing.	10		
28. Remove and discard the alcohol wipe and gloves.	5		
29. Sanitize the hands.	5		
30. Record the collection date and time on the laboratory requisition form, and place the requisition in the biohazard transport bag.	10		

Steps	Possible Points	First Attempt	Second Attempt
31. Ask and observe how the patient feels.	5		
32. Clean the work area using Standard Precautions.	5		
33. Document the procedure.	10		
Total Points Possible NOTE: Award points for Steps 13-14-15 OR 16-17-18, not both	255		

Comments: Total Points Earned _____   Instructor's Signature _____

Student N _____   Date _____

**CHECK
MULTIF**

PERFORM VENIPUNCTURE USING THE BUTTERFLY METHOD (COLLECTION OF VACUATED TUBES)

TASK: Ob venous blood specimen acceptable for testing using the butterfly method.

**CONDITI Given the proper equipment and supplies, the student will perform a venipuncture using the butterfly method o ction.

EQUIPMI ND SUPPLIES
- Nonste posable gloves
- Persona ective equipment (PPE) as required
- Tourniq tex-free)
- Test tub
- Winged on set with Luer adapter and safety guard
- Multidra edle (22 to 25 gauge) and tube holder, or 10-cc (10-mL) syringe
- Evacuat od tubes for requested tests with labels (correct nonadditive or additive required for ordered tests)
- Alcohol
- Sterile 2 nch gauze pads
- Bandag x-free) or nonallergenic tape
- Sharps ier
- Biohaza waste container
- Laborat uisition form
- Patient's cal record

**STANDARI omplete the procedure within _____ minutes and achieve a minimum score of _____%.

Time begar _____   Time ended _____

Steps	Possible Points	First Attempt	Second Attempt
1. Sanit nds.	5		
2. Verify rder. Assemble equipment and supplies.	5		
3. Gree patient, identify yourself, and confirm the patient's ident cort the patient to the proper room for venipuncture.	5		
4. Ask th ient to have a seat in the phlebotomy chair or on the exam n table.	5		
5. Confi y necessary preparation has been followed (e.g., fastin plain the procedure to the patient.	10		
6. Prepa winged infusion set. Attach the winged infusion set to either inge or an evacuated tube holder.	15		
7. Open terile gauze packet and place the gauze pad on the inside wrapper, or obtain sterile gauze pads from a bulk packa	5		
8. Positic d examine the arm to be used in the venipuncture.	10		
9. Apply urniquet.	10		
10. Apply s and PPE.	5		
11. Thorot palpate the selected vein.	10		

Steps	Possible Points	First Attempt	Second Attempt
12. Release the tourniquet.	10		
13. Prepare the puncture site and reapply the tourniquet.	5		
14. If drawing from the hand, ask the patient to make a fist or bend the fingers downward. Pull the skin taut with your thumb over the top of the patient's knuckles.	10		
15. Remove the protective shield from the needle of the infusion set, being sure the bevel is facing up. Position needle over vein to be punctured.	10		
16. Perform the venipuncture. With your nondominant hand, pull the skin taut beneath the intended puncture site to anchor the vein. Thumb should be 1 to 2 inches below and to the side of the vein. Follow the direction of the vein and insert the needle in one quick motion at about a 15-degree angle.	20		
17. After penetrating the vein, decrease the angle of the needle to 5 degrees until a "flash" of blood appears in the tubing.	5		
18. Secure the needle for blood collection.	10		
19. Insert the evacuated tube into the tube holder or gently pull back on the plunger of the syringe. Change tubes as required by the test ordered.	10		
20. Release the tourniquet and remove the needle.	10		
21. Apply direct pressure on the venipuncture site, and instruct the patient to raise the arm straight above the head. Maintain pressure on the site for 1 to 2 minutes, with the arm raised straight above the head.	10		
22. If a syringe was used, transfer the blood to the evacuated tubes as soon as possible.	10		
23. Dispose of the winged infusion set.	5		
24. Label the tubes and place the tube into the biohazard transport bag.	5		
25. Check for bleeding and place a bandage over the gauze to create a pressure dressing.	5		
26. Remove and discard the alcohol wipe and gloves.	5		
27. Sanitize the hands.	5		
28. Record the collection date and time on the laboratory requisition form, and place the requisition in the biohazard transport bag.	10		
29. Ask and observe how the patient feels.	5		
30. Clean the work area using Standard Precautions.	5		
31. Document the procedure.	10		
Total Points Possible	250		

Comments: Total Points Earned _____   Instructor's Signature _____

Student N _____   Date _____

CHECKL   PERFORM RANGE-OF-MOTION EXERCISES

TASK: Util   correct technique for performing range-of-motion exercises.

**CONDITIC   ven procedure, proper equipment and supplies the student will be required to perform various range-of-m   xercises.

EQUIPME   D SUPPLIES

• Patient
• Patient's   al record

**STANDARI   mplete the procedure within _____ minutes and achieve a minimum score of _____ %.

Time begar ____   Time ended _____

Steps		Possible Points	First Attempt	Second Attempt
1. Sani ds.		5		
2. Verif rder and assemble all supplies and equipment.		5		
3. Obta patient's medical record.		5		
4. Gree atient, introduce yourself, and confirm the patient's iden		5		
5. Expl procedure to the patient.		10		
6. Asse l joint function.		5		
7. Obse inflammation.		5		
8. Perfc M exercises: **a.** Fl nd extension of fingers **b.** Fl nd extension of wrist **c.** Sl r flexion **d.** Sl r abduction and adduction **e.** H ction and adduction **f.** K d hip flexion and extension		60 (each exercise worth 10 pts)		
9. Sanit ds.		5		
10. Provid nt with verbal and written instructions.		5		
11. Docun e results in the patient's medical record.		5		
12. Clean uipment and examination room.		5		
Total Poi ssible		120		

Comments: oints Earned _____   Instructor's Signature _____

Page numb... ...lowed by f indicate figures; t, tables; b, boxes.